The Search for Enlightenment:

The Working Class and Adult Education in the Twentieth Century

edited by Brian Simon

National Institute of Adult Continuing Education

National Institute of Adult Continuing Education
19B De Montfort Street
Leicester
LE1 7GE

First published by Lawrence and Wishart, 1990

First paperback edition by NIACE 1992
Selection and editorial matter © Brian Simon, 1990
Each essay © the author, 1990

BRITISH LIBRARY CATALOGUING IN PUBLICATION DATA
*A catalogue record for this book is available from
the British Library*
ISBN 0 872941 21 4

Photoset in North Wales by
Derek Doyle and Associates, Mold, Clwyd.
Printed and bound in Great Britain by
Billing & Sons Ltd, Worcester.

Contents

PART II 1945–1988

Foreword

The search for enlightenment has characterised the advance of the working population over the years. Despite the considerable limitations imposed by apathy, illiteracy and ignorance in our midst, many working men and women fashioned ideas and built movements which transformed the living and working conditions of their fellows.

In the rough, harsh circumstances of industrial Britain in the 1920s and 1930s adult education, in various forms, grew alongside and often within the unions. The striving for clarity of thought and determination in action to advance working-class interests was bound to emphasise independence from the orthodox 'education' offered by the ruling class which wanted a cheap and servile labour force.

Independent working-class education, especially that associated with the labour colleges, helped to build confidence amongst workers in the power of combination. Like many others in the trade unions my mind was stretched by participation in the classes and the correspondence courses. The trade unions gained numerous activists as a result of these educational developments. But the process was not always welcomed by complacent and compliant leaders, as I'm afraid my own experiences proved.

Nevertheless the trade union movement of today owes a great debt to the pioneers of independent working-class education whose efforts are studied in this book. Undoubtedly the collective approach to the solution of problems was given considerable impetus as a result of that early activity. It would indeed be fair to say that some part of the base was laid then for the later spread of shop stewards' education and training and the current work of such institutions as the Northern College.

Educational 'teach-ins' played quite a part in my own involvement in the organisation of the motor car and aircraft industries. Ideas picked up from my labour college days were put to good use in shop stewards' (and potential shop stewards') discussions and classes.

7

'Learning by doing' – workers teaching each other; participation in debate; grasping the essentials of negotiating and organising through such means strengthened our collective endeavours no end.

Perhaps, in retrospect, we could be criticised for over-concentration on the practical problems of analysing company balance sheets; studying labour law including the Factory Acts; working out negotiating tactics and the rest – but our efforts were really worthwhile. Trade union organisation and democratic participation was immensely strengthened thereby.

If the wider socialist analysis of capitalist society was somewhat missing in our considerations that criticism surely could not be applied to the early exponents of independent working-class education and that alone justifies the publication of this volume. I do most certainly welcome it and hope it will be read widely. Today's active trade unionists especially, both members and leaders, should gain from the knowledge of past experiences and, I hope, draw conclusions which will assist in strengthening contemporary working-class educational schemes and projects including those of the TUC itself.

Trade unionism, despite its critics, is certainly not dead. It survived periods more difficult than the present. But lack of understanding due to inadequate study can be an acute weakness and if this book helps to sound the alarm bells on the point it will do a service to the labour movement.

Jack Jones

Introduction

Working-class involvement in adult education has a history as long as that of the working class itself. From the late eighteenth century workers, caught up in the turmoil of industrial development, sought to understand the reasons for their consequent suffering. Thus the group of mechanics who formed the Sheffield Corresponding Society in the early 1790s, asked at a trial to explain the object of their meetings, replied:

> To enlighten the people, to show the people the reason, the ground of all their complaints and sufferings; when a man works hard for thirteen and fourteen hours a day, the week through, and is not able to maintain his family; that is what I understand of it; to show the people the ground of this; why they were not able.

'Instruction is the want of all', declared a publication of the London Corresponding Society at the same time (1794), and 'the Society ought to favour with all its powers the progress of human reason, and to place instruction within the reach of every citizen'.[1]

This book is devoted to illuminating aspects of this long-standing struggle for education during the present century. The field is a complex one, since several different groupings and organisations, each having different objectives, have been involved over the period, while at the same time the composition and character of the working class has itself undergone considerable change. In addition, the political context has changed radically over time. Unravelling the threads, therefore, is not easy; our intention, however, is to cast new light on areas which have, till now, been little studied.[2]

As outlined briefly at the start of the first essay, working-class adult education emerged at the turn of the century in two main forms. On the one hand there was the self-help tradition, originally developing from the work of the Corresponding Societies, which came to be known as independent working-class education. On the other, the

tradition of the provision of education *for* the working class – a
movement which (in its modern form) originated at Cambridge
University (and later Oxford) in the form of Extension lectures, and
was later institutionalised in the Workers' Educational Association.
These two traditions were, to some extent, opposed in their
objectives, and indeed it is that opposition which provided much of
the dynamic of development in the early years of the century.

Until recently, historians of adult education have focused on the
second of these two traditions, giving very short shrift to the former.
The result has been a one-sided interpretation. One major object of
this book is to correct this approach by examining, in Part I at least,
the relatively unknown but very deeply rooted history of the
independent tradition in the earlier part of the century. A more
rounded interpretation of this development is now becoming
possible, due partly to publications by those most closely involved –
W.W. Craik's *Central Labour College* (1964) and J.P.M. Millar's *The
Labour College Movement* (1979). Bill Craik was Principal of the
Central Labour College during most of its existence, while Jim Millar
was General Secretary of the National Council of Labour Colleges
(NCLC) for almost the whole of its 43 years' existence.

In these two volumes, each has presented his side of the story. The
picture is, therefore, now being filled out, and the essays by Edmund
and Ruth Frow and by Margaret Cohen in this volume break new
ground as case studies of the Labour College movement in a specific
area of the country – South-East Lancashire (including both
Liverpool and Manchester). Important and valuable studies have also
been made of the work on the Labour College movement in both
Scotland and Wales, arguably the two areas of its greatest strength,
and it is to be hoped that these, now in the form of university
theses, may also soon see the light of day as publications.[3] In
addition, Stuart Macintyre's *A Proletarian Science* (1980) and, in its
own way, Jonathon Rée's *Proletarian Philosophers* (1984) have both
made important new interpretations of this movement and its
contribution, though both focus specifically on an analysis and
critique of the development of an indigenous 'British' Marxism within
the movement. In any case, as a result of these (and related) studies,
the material is now becoming available for a more general historical
evaluation of this movement, to which the first three chapters in this
volume may be seen as a contribution.[4]

The first part of this book takes the analysis up to the Second
World War. It includes a second essay by Margaret Cohen which
concentrates on another independent educative initiative – the

establishment in 1931 of the Marx Memorial Library and Workers School (at Marx House in Clerkenwell), an organisation that is still functioning; her chapter covers also the story of the two Marx Houses in Manchester, operating in the 1930s. Part I concludes with an essay by Roger Fieldhouse on the political controversies affecting the Workers' Educational Association in the inter-war period.

Part II focuses on the period since World War Two. First, John McIlroy, in the sixth and seventh essays, working on a broad canvas, analyses new features in this period, in particular the developments within trade union education, the universities and the WEA. 1964 is taken as the final date for this analysis since it was this year that saw the demise of the National Council of Labour Colleges as a result of the long-planned 'takeover' by the Trade Union Congress. In an important sense, then, this year saw the end of Independent Working Class Education (IWCE) in its traditional, historic form, a development the effects of which are acutely analysed by the author. In the eighth essay John McIlroy contributes a sharply critical historical evaluation of the outcomes of these events, and especially of the move from the ideal of liberal education to that of technical training which he sees as dominant within TUC controlled initiatives in the latter period.

The final chapter, by Bob Fryer, makes a positive evaluation of the current situation within adult education and looks to the future. Accepting that there have been important changes in the structure of the working class, Fryer looks at the implications of this 'recomposition' for contemporary working class adult education from a variety of angles. His message is essentially an optimistic one, and concludes with a comprehensive agenda by which adult education, as a broadly based popular initiative, can become the means to foster intellectual vitality to master knowledge and use it. If we seize our opportunities, he argues, there is considerable scope for further development. This must involve the creation of new forms and the definition of new objectives.

This conclusion is in line with the optimistic thrust of the workers' education movement throughout its history, and it is as well that it should be restated as a conclusion of this book. No one working in the field, however, underrates the sharpness of the struggle which lies ahead. All forms of liberal adult education are now under attack; fundings being reduced – enhanced central control is leading to the imposition of a new instrumentalism and a continuing insistence on value to industry.[5] The threat to exterminate socialism as a political possibility has direct reference to adult working-class education. In these circumstances, the struggle to maintain and to extend the standards and traditions of the past is becoming increasingly an issue requiring clear thinking and united action. Our hope is that this book will contribute to this movement.

As editor I have to thank all the contributors, without exception extremely busy people, for their co-operation in this initiative. I have long valued my own connections with the movement. It is now over twenty years since Bill Craik (an original Ruskin College striker) first contacted me when writing his *Central Labour College*. Then already nearly 80, but still full of vitality and fire, we had many discussions and, since I was then working on the Ruskin strike and later developments, swapped chapters of our respective books in our mutual endeavour. Jim Millar addressed a meeting of the History of Education Society at Leicester some twelve years ago; since then my wife and I have visited him annually at his house overlooking the Dartmouth estuary. Here also we have had many discussions, again on the movement he was responsible for. This book may help, perhaps, to repay these debts. Whatever criticisms may be made, these two were the historical embodiment of the movement for Independent Working Class Education in this century. Their work did not go in vain.

Finally, we have to thank Jim Fyrth, deeply experienced in the field, who read the manuscript and proferred much wise advice; the editor and authors are, of course, finally responsible for the product. Especial thanks are also due to Jack Jones for his Foreword. A leading trade unionist (for many years General Secretary of the Transport and General Workers Union), Jack Jones has put on record his own involvement as a student in the Labour College movement (and the WEA) in Liverpool when a young man in a fascinating oral interview published in *History Workshop Journal*.[6] There is no one better qualified to introduce this book.

Brian Simon
January 1989

Notes

[1] Quoted in Brian Simon, *Studies in the History of Education, 1780–1870* (London, 1960), 180.
[2] No attempt has been made to cover the entire field of working-class adult education – rather, to focus on the more evidently decisive areas. The educational activities of the Co-operative movement, particularly important among women, was clearly of significance especially during the first half of

the century. This is certainly an area which requires further study; see, for example, John Attfield, *With Light of Knowledge: a hundred years of education in the Royal Arsenal Co-operative Society, 1877–1977* (London, 1981).

[3] On Wales, Richard Lewis, 'Leaders and Teachers: the Origins and Development of the Workers' Education Movement in South Wales, 1906–1940', unpublished Ph.D. dissertation, University of Wales (Swansea University College), 1979. On Scotland, J.H. Roberts, 'The National Council of Labour Colleges; an Experiment in Workers' Education: a study of the growth of the Labour Colleges with particular reference to independent working class education in Scotland', unpublished M.Sc. dissertation, University of Edinburgh, 1970. The first of these is a very thorough, two volume study. Both contain a mass of fascinating material on the IWCE movement in the two areas studied. See also Ian W. Hamilton, 'Education for Revolution: the Plebs League and the Labour College Movement, 1908–21', unpublished M.A. thesis, University of Warwick, 1972.

[4] Chapter 7 of Clive Griggs, *The TUC and the Struggle for Education, 1868–1925* (Brighton, 1983) covers the early TUC discussions on its role in adult education.

[5] See, for example, R. Taylor, K. Rockhill and R. Fieldhouse, *University Adult Education in England and the USA: A Reappraisal of the Liberal Tradition* (London, 1985).

[6] Jack Jones, 'A Liverpool Socialist Education', *History Workshop Journal*, No. 18, Autumn 1984. See also Jack Jones, 'Learning the hard way', *Times Educational Supplement*, 4 January 1974.

Part I, 1909–1945

Brian Simon
The Struggle for Hegemony, 1920–1926

1 Conflicts within Working Class Education

This essay focuses specifically on the conflicts that developed within the field of working-class education in the period immediately following the First World War, when a great extension of labour movement organisation took place. This expressed itself primarily in the massive growth in the membership of the trade union movement, and in a rapidly increasing electoral support for the newly reconstituted Labour Party. Trade union membership rose from just under 2,500,000 in 1910 to a peak of 8,300,000 in 1921, while Labour votes at General Elections rose from 500,000 in 1910 to nearly 4,500,000 in 1923. This was a period also when syndicalist ideas, relating specifically to workers' control of industry – or, perhaps better, 'industrial democracy' – gained considerable influence, and when a consciousness of the need for an education that would prepare workers to exercise such control reached a new level. Through the turbulent politics of these early post-war years, the provision of education, whether for or by the workers, took on a new urgency. A close study of this short period, climaxed by the General Strike of May 1926, allows an analysis of the different pressures and interests bearing specifically on educational initiatives. The issues which then came to the fore were to retain their significance for another half century – and indeed are still with us.

But it is impossible to break suddenly into the 1920s. The form and nature of the struggles of that, and succeeding periods, were already to some extent shaped by what went before. A rich, sometimes heroic, history of independent striving, on the part of the working class, for forms of education under its own control stretches from well over a century earlier – the 1790s. An understanding of the conflicts of the 1920s requires at least some reference to the historical context in which they were situated.

The crucial issue is that, from the first emergence of capitalist forms of production on a large scale in the mid-late eighteenth century – and so, of the emergence of a working class in its modern form – two tendencies, opposite in character, can be discerned. The first, in the strictly chronological sense, was that of *independent* educational activities carried on by and for the working class, and under its own control. The line of continuity can be traced from the activity of the early Corresponding Societies in the 1790s (involving intensive and highly organised reading and discussion within specific groups), through the widespread activities of the Hampden Clubs, the Political Protestants, and similar organisations which flourished particularly in Lancashire and Cheshire after the Napoleonic wars, to a climax in the late 1830s and 1840s within both the Owenite Socialist movement and the Chartist movement. Both of these movements, each national in scope, developed educational and recreative activities closely related to their respective social and political objectives. At Manchester, for instance, the Owenite Hall of Science and the Chartists' Carpenters Hall, the two largest social buildings in the city, were the centres of such activities.[1]

Following a period of relative quiescence after the decline of the Chartist movement, this tendency, or tradition, broke out afresh with extraordinary vitality with the re-emergence of socialism in the 1880s. This was related, of course, to the formation of socialist or labour political parties – the Social Democratic Federation (1884), the Socialist League (1885) and the Independent Labour Party (1893). This period also saw the organisation of mass trade unions for unskilled workers (dockers, gasworkers, etc.), the strengthening of the Trades Union Congress (founded in 1868) and of the Co-operative Union (also 1868). And in line with the new emergence of a mass labour movement, there developed a very wide variety of informally organised educational activities, now beginning to be influenced, to some extent, by Marxist perspectives.[2] It was this tradition that lay behind the crucial confrontation at Ruskin College,

Oxford, in 1909; a confrontation which gave a new impetus to independent working class education, and forms the immediate background to the events discussed in this essay.

This independent activity, on the part of the emerging working class, which of course changed its character during the century of its main development, represents the first of the two tendencies referred to earlier. The second tendency, or tradition, took root originally as a deliberate response to this initiative, the lead being taken in the early nineteenth century by the group known as Philosophic Radicals, or Utilitarians – the representatives (and ideologists) of the emerging industrial and commercial middle class. Their objective, which was quite clearly articulated, was specifically to influence the thinking of the then radical working and artisan classes, to draw them away from ideologies that led directly to radical or revolutionary conclusions, and to persuade the workers that their real interest lay in assisting, or co-operating with, the positive and active development of capitalism. In this view, the interests of workers and capitalists were one and the same. This outlook was pressed very hard by James Mill, Francis Place and many others, and by their political representative on this issue, Henry Brougham. To propagate this view, industrialists, bankers, and others, in the 1820s attempted either to take over existing Mechanics' Institutes (early forms of which were established by working men), or to set up new Institutes (as at Manchester) under their own control. The Society for the Diffusion of Useful Knowledge (SDUK) established by the same grouping early in the late 1820s, had a similar function in terms of publications.[3]

The Mechanics' Institutes and the SDUK served a definite and clear purpose, and were (in this sense) 'appropriate' forms for activity of this kind in the period 1820-50. But as the working class became more sophisticated, more conscious of itself as a class and increasingly suspicious of external attempts at control, new means of influence had to be found. With the revival of socialism in the mid-1880s, and the increased power and organisation of the working class generally, this became the more urgent – particularly since, as already mentioned, the early socialist organisations were establishing a wide network of study circles and other means of self-education.

By this time the Mechanics' Institutes had changed their function, and no longer catered for the working class. The only initiative from above that had struck root among the working class – and in particular the Co-operative movement – was that of University Extension, which had its inception in the late 1860s as a result of initiatives emanating largely from Oxford and Cambridge. But by the end of the nineteenth century, this also was making little impact at a time when a massive upsurge of interest and concern for knowledge and education was making itself felt among workers. The weakness of University Extension, it was felt, was not only that it was inescapably middle-class in its ethos and outlook, but also that both the subjects offered (for lectures and classes), and the lecturers themselves, were determined by the University – those attending the classes had no say in the programme of studies, nor in choice of lecturers.[4]

The Workers' Educational Association (WEA), established in 1903 and specifically designed to overcome these weaknesses, adopted a much more supple and sophisticated approach. Theoretically, it was an organisation which offered tutors of university calibre, and other forms of assistance, to groups of workers who wished to study – both the choice of the subject to be studied, and of the tutors, were left to the students themselves. By this means, the early WEA hoped to overcome the suspicions of the workers and to attract them to serious, even scholarly study. As is well known, the paradigm of the WEA ideal was early established by R.H. Tawney's famous two-year tutorial classes at Longton and at Rochdale in 1908.[5]

Just at this time, however, there took place a counter-development which found dramatic expression in the students' strike at Ruskin College, Oxford. Since this was the trigger which released the movement for independent working class education in this century, culminating in the establishment of the Plebs League, the Central Labour College and in the formation of the National Council of Labour Colleges, the background needs briefly sketching.

Ruskin College had been founded specifically as a 'Labour' College by two American philanthropists in 1899. The trade union movement was represented on its governing body, which was independent of the University, though informal links were established. The students came largely from labour movement organisations. A number of these had experienced Marxist classes in Scotland and elsewhere; indeed Sanderson Furniss, a young tutor appointed in 1907, found the students 'were practically all socialists of one brand or another, and there were amongst them some of the wildest and most revolutionary young men in the country'.[6]

This was, no doubt, an exaggeration. However, just at this time concerted moves were made by Oxford University to subsume the college more directly under its aegis. This was the outcome of political developments generally – particularly the 1906 General Election which marked the emergence of the labour movement on to the political scene in a new way by which the University felt challenged to extend its role in the education of a new social class now reaching for political power. But specifically the move towards Ruskin was the outcome of an important report, 'Oxford and Working Class Education', published in December 1908, the work of a joint committee consisting of both University and WEA representatives.

This report made a number of recommendations aimed at establishing closer relations between Ruskin College and the University. Publication was followed by a sustained attempt by the University to change the character of the College, including a dramatic visit by Lord Curzon, Chancellor of the University and recently Viceroy of India. The Principal of the College, Dennis Hird, here publicly rebutted the University's proposals, Curzon turning on his heel and walking out of the meeting without replying.

The key issue for many students then at the College lay in the teaching of economics. Was this to be based on what the students regarded as capitalist apologetics, or on Marxist analyses? Indeed what was to be the direction, or thrust, of the College? Was it to equip its students to challenge the existing social order and work to transform it, or to prepare students to function within the limitations set by existing social relations?

Matters reached a head with the organisation by the students of the Plebs League in the autumn of 1908, which aimed 'to bring about a more satisfactory connection of Ruskin College with the Labour Movement'. The aim was to draw in ex-students, set up branches in industrial areas and to ensure the control of Ruskin by the workers. The *'Plebs' Magazine* (as it was originally called) was launched to propagate this outlook. The governors of the College (who included benefactors) were alarmed at the support shown for the journal and its views among trade unions. First ordering Dennis Hird to sever any connection he had with the League, they then suddenly dismissed him (at the end of March 1909) 'for failure to maintain discipline'. It was at this point that the student body (of 54) went on strike.

The outcome, as is well known, was first, the secession of a group of students (and the Principal, Dennis Hird); then, through a series of developments, the establishment of the Central Labour College, first at Oxford and later in London, as an independent institution, and the strengthening of the Plebs League (and its journal) as a body which united individual supporters of independent working class education. The movement gained strong support from two powerful unions, both at this time much influenced by syndicalism – the Amalgamated

Society of Railway Servants (later the National Union of Railwaymen
or NUR) and the South Wales Miners' Federation (SWMF). It was
around the Labour College in London, and Plebs League activities
there and elsewhere that the whole movement for independent
working-class education (IWCE as it came to be called) now
developed.

In the early 1920s both organisations, the WEA on the one hand
and the Plebs League and Labour College movement on the other,
were in the field. Proponents of the Labour College accused the
WEA of being collaborationist, particularly since the WEA was early
offered, and had readily accepted, grants from the Board of
Education (and local authorities) to finance its work. The
'impartiality' to which the WEA laid claim, in dealing with political,
economic, historical and social issues, was held up to ridicule. The
object of the WEA, it was held, was either to throw dust in the
workers' eyes (confuse them, or teach them anti-working class
ideology) or to divert them altogether from the class struggle by
holding up the ideal of self-cultivation, of pure scholarship and of the
pursuit of knowledge for its own sake. Labour College activists, it can
be said, failed to see or to recognise the educational, and indeed
political significance of 'liberal' education.

Supporters of the WEA, on the other hand, accused the early
Labour College secessionists, and the College itself, of confusing
education with propaganda, and, far from developing the intellectual
powers of students, indoctrinating them with dogmatic conceptions
about the nature of society, economic affairs, history and the class
struggle.

These two conceptions of the nature of workers' education, both of
which, as we have seen, had deep historical roots, were to come
sharply into conflict in the early 1920s, proponents of each battling
for an important prize – that of control over the education of the elite
of working class activists in the trade union movement which, at this
stage, was growing rapidly in membership, power and militancy. The
struggle over this issue, in the crucial years 1920 to 1926, forms the
focus of this essay.

(i) The Workers' Educational Association
The leading figures of the WEA – apart from its secretary,
MacTavish, and original founder, Mansbridge – came largely from
the professional middle class, particularly from university and
progressive church circles (epitomised by William Temple, later
Archbishop of Canterbury, the first President of the association who

held office from 1906 to 1922). There can be no doubt this grouping was genuinely concerned to assist working-class students to gain access to knowledge, to develop their capacity for thought and study, and to learn to apply their knowledge, if they wished, to the resolution of social, economic and political problems. R.H. Tawney, who devoted immense effort to this movement consistently, and for the whole of his life, is a case in point; G.D.H. Cole is another. Individually most of those largely involved were sympathetic to Labour's aspirations, wished to ameliorate its conditions of life, and often fully participated in efforts to do so. In particular, the WEA was well equipped and prepared to fight consistently on the issue of state education – for educational advance, equality of opportunity, and the like; at certain key moments it played a crucially important mobilising role in relation to the labour movement as a whole on this question, concentrating within itself much high-powered expertise. Nevertheless, its position led to a certain ambiguity.

Educationally, the WEA saw its role initially as making up for the defects of state education; as providing educational opportunities (at university level) for those who never had and never would have the opportunities to develop themselves intellectually at a high level. There were many among the outcast who were capable of high achievement; in any case all deserved the chance of self-development, of access to culture and knowledge. A class system of education existed; the WEA set out to soften its rigours. In so far as education was related to social change, it was through developing (or inducing) a higher rationality – the ability to see all sides of a question, that the impact of the WEA student would be felt. The way to knowledge implied 'open-mindedness', a clear impartiality on the part of the teacher on all topics that were controversial; these were the truly educative means of human and individual development. This was the standpoint taken by the WEA from its inception, under the influence particularly of Mansbridge (the founder), William Temple, R.H. Tawney, of the classical scholar A.E. Zimmern and many more.[7] It maintained this standpoint consistently, except when under critical attack from the left, as in 1925, when, as we shall see, the WEA came out with more radical slogans.

The acceptance of grants from the state followed quite logically – simply as a matter of common sense. Running classes was expensive. There was not only the hire of rooms, light and heat, travelling expenses, hire of books and general servicing – by far the greatest item was payment for the tutor. That this should be reasonably generously covered was the essential condition if the employment of university lecturers and professors as tutors was to be contemplated, and put on an administratively practical and business-like footing. Some money could be raised from affiliations, individual membership fees, donations and students' fees. But this would never come near to covering the costs involved in reasonably widespread activities. Support from the state (and local authorities) solved this problem. As we shall see, this was to be an important issue in the 1920s.

From the standpoint of the authorities, this movement was worth supporting, as R.L. Morant, Permanent Secretary to the Board of Education, decided when, after studying the problem and meeting those concerned he first offered support (or access to 'the golden stream', as he put it).[8] The WEA planned to draw heavily on university support, both organisationally and for tutors (and in the first place from Oxford); the education they offered was non-partisan and carried with it, therefore, no fundamental threat to the existing social and political order. This was how the Board of Education and the WEA saw it. 'All power to your elbow with the WEA,' wrote H.A.L. Fisher to Temple, who had sent him a note of congratulation on his appointment as President of the Board of Education in 1916. 'I shall want to help you in any way possible.'[9]

The Labour College proponents, and particularly the Marxist nucleus, saw things differently. A central aspect of Marx's teaching was that the state is not neutral as between classes; on the contrary it was seen as the expression of ruling-class interests, and this remained the case whatever the form of society and whether the dominant class was the aristocracy, capitalists or workers. On this interpretation, the function of the state is to perpetuate the rule of the dominant class. Acceptance of state support, therefore, was held directly to deny claims to impartiality on the part of the WEA. In the eyes of Labour College supporters, it indicated that behind these claims, even if unrecognised (and even if *hotly denied*), there lay the objective intention of winning the workers – in the long run – to the side of capitalism, and to acceptance of the existing economic and political system.

This did not, of course, imply that conflict between the working class and capitalism could not be discussed in WEA classes, or even express itself in practice in one form or another. But that the *general direction* of the work was one which did not fundamentally challenge the social order. The fact that known Marxist tutors were occasionally asked to take classes, conferences or schools, it was argued, could be used to support the image of 'impartiality', and was, therefore, at times necessary. This did not mean, however, that the

WEA, as an institution, did not in fact embody a definite position about the nature of society, the means of changing it, and the role of education in bringing about this change.

(ii) The Labour College movement

The other main organisation, one which rivalled the WEA for support among the working class at this time, was the Labour College and 'Plebs' movement. Plebs was the national organisation which, as we have seen, was set up originally by the Ruskin strikers to further their ends; it was also the title of their journal founded in 1909. As well as the London Labour College, with its own buildings and staff, there were by 1920 a number of local organisations known as Labour Colleges – of which by far the most influential was that at Glasgow, under the leadership of John Maclean. It was this movement that took institutional form as the National Council of Labour Colleges (NCLC) in 1921.

This movement crystallised the tradition of independent working-class education. The initial breakaway which determined the modern form of this movement involved a deliberate and conscious break with the Establishment in the form of Oxford University which appeared to the more radical students to wish to take over and to distort, for class reasons, the teaching at Ruskin College – founded as an *independent* institution and centre of working-class education. The break, significantly, took place primarily on an ideological issue – the place of Marxism in the education of the working class. The bulk of the striking students were Marxists – or at least students who recognised Marx as their philosopher, guide and prophet.[10]

With the development of radical tendencies among the organised working class before, during and immediately after the First World War, the approach embodied in the Labour College movement received considerable impetus. Shop stewards and others who had experience of this movement were already well based in the labour movement, both at grass roots level and in the leadership of some important unions, particularly the NUR and SWMF. These acted as nuclei around which the whole movement could crystallise. Inevitably this process involved opposition and rivalry with the WEA, and vice versa – all of which acted to firm up loyalties and enhance the defence of entrenched positions.

Since the basis of the whole movement was the need for *independent* working-class education and since this ideology and tendency was revolutionary and Marxist, this direction was expressed in practice by the absolute refusal to consider applying to the state for financial assistance (or, for that matter, to the universities). This independence was, in the NCLC view, the touchstone by which the value of the education offered to the working class could or should be measured.

There was however, a certain weakness in this position. Historically, independent education had been integrally linked with political organisation and political action. This was the case with the Corresponding Societies and the Hampden Clubs in the early phase, and with the educational initiatives of the socialist organisations from the 1880s. But a tendency now existed for this education, now based on Marxism, to develop separate institutions, isolated from political action. The students in Labour College classes were expected to apply what they had learned in action in their unions and elsewhere; but the College itself (and later the NCLC) was an educational, not directly a political or industrial organisation. Indeed it was seen as the *educational wing* of the labour movement, and as it developed it was built up through affiliations by trade unions – whose identity as functioning organisations, was, therefore, separate from that of the educational organisation, the NCLC.

In this separation lay the seeds of abstraction, of isolation, even of a certain scholasticism – whereby the educational activities were carried on independently from the unceasing political and industrial struggles of working people and the working class as a whole. Yet Marxism itself – as a philosophy or world outlook – is deeply and perhaps even primarily concerned with the relation between theory and practice, thought and action. This crucial aspect of Marxism was stressed by Marx himself in his famous aphorism 'The philosophers have only *interpreted* the world in various ways; the point, however, is to *change* it.'

This tendency to abstraction, or scholasticism, was certainly never intended by those involved in the movement. It may be, however, that it was endemic in the situation as it actually developed.

(iii) The Communist Party

The issue was further complicated by the foundation of the Communist Party in 1920. The Communist Party resulted from the amalgamation of various left and socialist groupings having considerable experience of education organised as an integral aspect of political action. The experience of the Social Democratic Federation (SDF) here was transmitted through the British Socialist Party; more important was the tradition of serious Marxist study brought in by the Socialist Labour Party (SLP), which had acted as the real pioneers of Marxism in the British labour movement. Many of those who had played a leading part in both the educational and the political activities of the SLP joined the Communist Party at this time; among them Tom Bell who became the first educational organiser for the Communist Party; others included T.A. ('Tommy') Jackson.

The Communist Party was avowedly based on Marxism, and came to see the education of its members in Marxism as a function of primary importance, linking it directly with political understanding and action. Educational activity, as it developed, was united with its political organisation, being based on the local or factory branch, the district and the national organisation. By 1921 there was, therefore, a third grouping concerned with working-class education taking institutional form.

In the wider field of the labour movement as a whole there were, of course, other institutions and organisations concerned, or potentially so, with education. These included the trade unions themselves and the TUC; Ruskin College which had links with the TUC; the broad Co-operative movement which traditionally regarded education as one of its functions (and from which both University Extension and the WEA partially sprang);[11] the Labour Party and the Independent Labour Party (ILP) which carried on a somewhat amorphous series of educational or social activities. The Labour Party, up to 1918, consisted of affiliated bodies (trade unions, ILP, SDF, etc.) and only accepted individual members and developed local and regional organisations in the early 1920s. Local socialist societies (as at Bristol for instance), discussion groups, parliaments and forums were widespread.

Such was the situation, then, when developments in the labour movement, particularly the syndicalist tendency, combined with increasing militancy, focused attention more sharply than ever before on the whole issue of workers' education, its organisation, perspectives, scope, and, above all, on its control.

2 The 'Heroic' Period, 1920–26

(i) Plebs League and the National Council of Labour Colleges[12]

The intention in this section is to try to bring alive some conception of the appeal and character of the movement for independent working-class education in the early 1920s – a period of sharp and prolonged industrial struggles marked by increasing class confrontation and culminating in the General Strike of May 1926. We can trace the movement as reflected in the journal of the Plebs League in 1921 and 1922.

By this time, the League was developing widespread activities, indeed there were two centres – the Labour College in London, and the League itself with its journal *Plebs*. The former had accommodation for 28 students, a plan for a block of new buildings to take 70 students with the eventual aim of 300. The two unions concerned hoped and expected that other unions would join in taking financial responsibility for this development.

Apart from this, the movement for IWCE (as it was called) was actively promoting classes in the provinces and in London. In 1919, for instance, T.A. Jackson was appointed by the miners' leader, Will Lawther, as lecturer in economics, history and philosophy to the North East Labour College Committee – a development in which another miners' leader, Ebby (Ebenezer) Edwards played a big part. This was an association of miners' lodges, trade union branches, and Socialist Societies who collectively promoted and conducted study classes in subjects (wrote Jackson later) pertinent to the economic and political struggles of the working class. Though in 'fraternal sympathy' with the residential College in London and with the Plebs League, it had at this time no direct, organised connection.[13]

Similar initiatives were taking place elsewhere, particularly in Wales and Scotland, at this time; the direction of development is well indicated in William Mellor's work, *Direct Action*, published in November 1920.[14] Mellor himself was not actively involved in Plebs activities but in the chapter on 'Education and the Class Struggle', makes his own, independent estimate of the position. After criticising the content of education within the state system for its ineffectiveness and bias (conditioned by the class system, it is 'formed to secure its continuance')[15] he turns to the field of adult education. Ruskin College, he says, 'makes no pretence of training and equipping men for taking part in the struggle of classes'. The WEA officially accepts the viewpoint that education is above the battle – in its origin it 'is a humanitarian attempt to give to those deprived of opportunities in their youth an education that shall compare favourably with that enjoyed by the more fortunate and wealthy element in society'. But the WEA does leave a good deal of scope to the students. 'They can choose the subjects they desire to study, they can suggest the authorities that shall be consulted, they can choose their lecturers and generally manage their own affairs.'

In this situation, Mellor continues, 'it is possible to get rid of the official view and to secure that the type of education given is more revolutionary than would meet with the approval of the Board of Education, of the Universities or of many of the supporters of the WEA'. By 'throwing overboard the "non-political and non-partisan" character of the organisation', writes Mellor, and 'by giving up the pretence that education takes no sides' something useful may be done. It is in just those areas where the official view has least hold that the WEA has succeeded in securing the support of the working classes. 'Places like the West Riding of Yorkshire, for instance, have managed to evade most of the regulations designed to keep the WEA in the straight path' – there, the workers do control their own education. 'Elsewhere the story is different and the dead hand of capitalism is all-powerful.' As for the Central Labour College (CLC) – this expresses uncompromising hostility to other forms of adult education. 'In season and out of season it carries on its work, and the fruits can be seen in every district in England, Scotland and Wales.'[16] The education it gives, tends, however, to a certain narrowness and 'a curiously academic view of life'. ' "Teach the workers", they seem to say, "the pure and undefiled gospel of Marxism ... and all will be well".' The CLC must 'give more attention to the creation not only of men who understand, but of men who can act'. Knowledge is power, and the power the CLC seeks 'is the power to overthrow capitalism'. 'There can, I believe', concludes Mellor, 'be no question that the future is with the CLC.'[17]

Already by 1920, then, the Central London College was beginning to be seen as an important force. The College itself, which had been closed in 1917–18, re-opened in October 1919 with 29 students, mostly from the South Wales Miners' Federation, but including some railwaymen and others.[18] New ground was being broken by the Northumberland and Durham miners, the leading figure, as already mentioned, being Ebby Edwards, an ex-Ruskin student (1908) who identified with the breakaway College and 'immediately set to work promoting independent working class education ... starting and directing tutorial classes throughout the coalfield'.[19] In the Durham coalfield Will Lawther, a student at the College in 1911–12, had taken a similar lead, also organising tutorial classes in the coalfield and support for the Labour College – Lawther was to become President of the Miners' Federation of Great Britain (1939–1945), and first President of the National Union of Mineworkers (1945–1954). This was the base from which the work developed with increasing energy in the early 1920s.

In January 1920, when organisational problems arose, a national conference was held which decided to ask the Central Labour College to take on a co-ordinating function. This had the support of the Plebs League and remained the position until the rapidity of the movement's development led to the foundation of the National Council of Labour Colleges as an independent organisation. We may trace this development in 1921 and 1922.

First, the journal itself. In March 1921 *Plebs* claimed a circulation of just under 6,500 – quite sufficient to act as an effective organisational and propaganda weapon. At its twelfth annual 'Meet' (Conference) held at Bradford in February 1921, the secretary (Winifred Horrabin) reported 800 paid up members, 30 branches, and the existence of District Councils in four centres. She urged that they should not seek a mass membership, but 'small groups of fanatical partisans, who are prepared to make the propaganda of independent working class education their main interest in life'. Two books had been published by Plebs with a print-run of 10,000 each; Craik's *Short History of the British Working Class Movement* and Mark Starr's *A Worker Looks at History*.[20]

The June issue (No. 6) carried news of developments in Edinburgh where J.P.M. Millar (later secretary of the NCLC for some forty years) and Jock Millar had brought several new classes into being and worked up much support for the Scottish Labour College. The second annual conference of the Scottish Labour College, Edinburgh district, had taken place with 100 delegates. The number of classes organised had increased from three to 21 (with 700 students), and one full-time and eight part-time lecturers appointed. Millar claimed at the conference (from the chair) that the committee was now supported by 'miners, engineers, railwaymen, printers, textile workers, wood workers, Co-operative bodies and socialist branches'.[21]

In July 1921 a strong call for the foundation of a national organisation came from the Manchester and Sheffield Labour Colleges. 'As the working class movement has developed its fighting instrument on the industrial and political fields', runs the statement, making the case for independent activity, so it has developed 'its own educational system, and where the need has been most keenly realised, classes have sprung into existence'. After a short period, these have grown so rapidly that they are entitled to call themselves a college. Several localities now own permanent premises and employ teachers. These colleges should now be linked together and the London Labour College should take the initiative.[22] The same issue reports 69 evening classes run by the Scottish Labour College, 30 of which are in the Glasgow area; 23 classes in the area served by the

Manchester Labour College, and a further 23 (with 450 students) run by the Sheffield Labour College (with 40 students following an 'intensive study class'). Sheffield reports 100 affiliated organisations and a team of lecturers on 'revolutionary periods in history' who are kept busy at branch meetings, Co-operative guilds and elsewhere.[23] Further classes were reported at Halifax, Cardiff (with 73 students) and Liverpool.[24]

In August the move towards a national organisation is furthered in a strong article from Will Lawther, stressing the immediate need for action. 'Every happening in the industrial world during the past few months has pointed unmistakably to the urgency of the need for spreading Labour College and *Plebs* teaching,' he writes. 'During the winter ahead of us the class struggle will be waged more bitterly than ever.' Nothing frightens the other side as much as 'the growth of the classes' – these are more valuable than mass meetings. 'We need the national co-ordination of classes', as proposed from Manchester and Sheffield. 'The country needs to be mapped into areas, linked up by a central organisation.' Others, whose educational aims are opposed to ours, he says, referring to the WEA, have gone further in this direction than we have so far.[25] Hence the need for action.[26]

In September, further support for the co-ordination of the work of the colleges comes from the Liverpool and District IWCE Council, and from the London IWCE Council. These district councils were set up to link together the classes started by the Plebs League in a specific area; by this time, these were gaining support from branches of unions (again on a grass roots basis) which did not officially support the Central Labour College. In October a conference called by the Bradford Labour College and Plebs classes was reported. Presided over by M.F. Titterington and attended by 50 trade union delegates the conference decided to form a Bradford and District Council for IWCE and to persuade union branches to affiliate.[27]

The November number reports that a conference on class organisation agreed unanimously to set up a National Council of Labour Colleges; it was decided to invite the governors of the Central Labour College to appoint two representatives to the Council, the Plebs League executive committee to appoint two and each area or organisation or class centre to appoint one. This number of *Plebs* contains a map of classes and labour colleges drawn by J.H. Horrabin. In this issue it was also reported that the Cardiff NUR district council was organising and financing two classes – on economic and industrial history – a precedent which earned congratulations from *Plebs* for its 'forward' educational policy, and as an example to other NUR councils.[28]

The first general meeting or conference of the National Council of Labour Colleges, which it had been hoped to hold earlier, took place early the next year in March 1922. George Sims, who was Secretary of the Central Labour College, was originally appointed Honorary Secretary of the NCLC, J.P.M. Millar being appointed Honorary Press Secretary. Sims 'disappeared' a year later and Millar was then appointed Secretary, now a full-time paid appointment, and one that Millar was to hold until 1964 when the NCLC ceased to exist as an independent organisation.[29] A directory of classes in the January 1922 *Plebs* shows the main centres of the movement to be Scotland and South Wales (where the classes were mainly run by the SWMF), but with district organisations often serving a number of urban areas in the Midlands, Sheffield, Liverpool, the North-East, Manchester, West Riding, London (about 40 classes claimed), Nottinghamshire and elsewhere. (A complete directory was published in Vol. XIV, No. 9, September 1922.) A few of these, it was reported in January, had 'already affiliated to the NCLC'.[30]

The situation, due to the way the movement had developed, was now somewhat complicated, and signs of the first rifts began to appear. There were now three institutionalised organisations in the field, all within the general movement for IWCE: the Plebs League with its journal – the original organisation in terms of time; the Central Labour College in London founded and governed by the two unions; and now the NCLC with its own governing body already heavily weighted at this time by the district or area 'Colleges' or 'Councils'. W.W. Craik, since 1920 Principal of the CLC, clearly felt later, at any rate, that the establishment of the NCLC, as a result of independent initiative was a mistake; a national organisation could have been based more effectively on the College itself. Soon, he wrote, 'ominous rifts began' between the resident and non-resident colleges, both competing for trade union support.[31] The journal *Plebs*, however, edited by J.F. Horrabin, welcomed the formation of the NCLC and saw the Plebs organisation's role as working everywhere for the extension of the NCLC, for the establishment of new classes, for trade union participation and if possible responsibility (as at Cardiff) and then the formation of yet further classes – a strategy of rolling development.[32]

The formation of the NCLC led to a rapid expansion of educational activities. Conferences were called to start new Labour Colleges, for instance at Darlington, where the strategy was to circulate all Labour bodies (a total of 300) with an announcement of the conference, to propose a resolution at the conference to set up the Darlington Labour College, to try to get all labour organisations to affiliate, and for the working body itself to affiliate to the NCLC. This particular meeting was addressed by W.W. Craik and an Executive member of the SWMF.[33] It is clear that by this time the movement was becoming well embedded in working-class organisations. In March 1922, as already mentioned, the first conference of the NCLC took place at the same time as the Plebs annual 'meet'. By now the respective organisational forms of each was becoming clear – while Plebs linked *individuals* (being solely an organisation with individual membership), the NCLC linked *organisations*, the different Labour Colleges to which local organisations were themselves affiliated. In this sense, Plebs continued as a propagandist and activist body while the NCLC was responsible for the actual work of the Colleges – or at least acted as a co-ordinating link. It was agreed that the journal should continue to be run by the Plebs League, whose Executive Committee included Raymond Postgate, Mark Starr, G.E. Sims, Maurice Dobb and three others. By this time, the journal had increased considerably in size – from 16 pages (monthly) in 1919 to 32 in 1920 and now to 48 in 1922.[34]

By May 1922, the NCLC had worked out many plans for setting up new area or district Labour Colleges, while a new pamphlet prefaced by Robert Smillie – the venerated miners' leader – was published. Wholehearted enthusiasm, an honest outlook and a 'fuller knowledge of economic, social and industrial history' is needed today by young workers, he wrote, adding that he hoped that trade union branches, and other Labour bodies, would 'contribute generously to the support of the Labour Colleges'.[35] Support for the principle of IWCE was now coming from another important union, the Amalgamated Union of Building Trade Workers (AUBTW). In June *Plebs* reported that the London branches conference of this union decided to start education classes on IWCE lines.[36] But it was at the Annual General Meeting of the AUBTW in July, that the NCLC recorded its first really important breakthrough. At this meeting a debate was arranged between speakers representing the WEA/WETUC policy (of which more later) and those representing the Labour Colleges. Both sides brought out their big guns – for the WEA/WETUC, Mactavish (Secretary), Arthur Pugh (from the steel workers' union) and G.D.H. Cole. For the Labour Colleges, Craik and Sims. This resulted (according to the *Plebs* report) in a vote supporting the NCLC's policy by a margin of 58 to 10.[37] Of the education scheme for their own members that the AUBTW founded, *Plebs* comments: 'We have every reason to be proud ... It represents in concrete form a real Labour education policy and scheme such as we have been advocating "since our day began" – educationally.' The Secretary, George Hicks, a very consistent supporter of Plebs and the NCLC, played an important part in this. At the same time disappointment was expressed at the defeat of a resolution at the NUR AGM which called for a national organisation of classes within the NUR 'whereby the education provided for our students at the Labour College can be brought to and spread among the rank and file of the union'. Such classes were already organised by the SWMF – the other Central Labour College sponsor. But this resolution was defeated by 41 votes to 27, J.H. Thomas, the union's general secretary being himself firmly opposed.[38]

Nevertheless, the August *Plebs* records the actual affiliation of the AUBTW to the NCLC: 'Our First National Affiliation', clearly marking a decisive stage in providing a firm commitment and base on the part of an important and powerful union. This was the more so in that the AUBTW – the result of a recent amalgamation – affiliated to the NCLC at the very generous payment of 1 shilling per member.[39]

New Labour Colleges were formed in the summer at Plymouth and Hull, while the Liverpool College reported as many as 125 affiliations. The councils of these colleges consisted of representatives of affiliated organisations – trade union branches, Co-operative societies, and other workers' organisations. As *Plebs* pointed out, these were not necessarily all conscious supporters of IWCE (and its principles) – and *Plebs* was now clearly aware of the danger that these principles might be forgotten as control passed out of their hands. There was a need for a body to stress the *independence* of working-class education, and a conference was to be arranged to discuss the 'demarcation' of the work of Plebs league, NCLC and Labour College. As the machinery passes more and more into the hands of officials and central executives, warned *Plebs*, the necessity for the Plebs League becomes clear. Events were to prove this to be a perspicacious assessment.[40]

By 1926 both work and affiliations had expanded enormously. In 1923, USDAW, the distributive workers' union, with 90,000 members affiliated on the more limited basis (due to stringent financial circumstances) of 3 pence per member, and in 1924 the most important affiliation – from the standpoint of the trade union movement – of the Amalgamated Engineering Union (AEU) was obtained; with over 245,000 members it was 'one of the biggest and one of the most strategically important unions in the country'. This affiliation was strongly contested by the WETUC, but was finally consolidated (after debates and discussions at the National Committee meetings – the policy-making body of the union) in 1924.[41] One of the strongest supporters of the NCLC was Jack Tanner, later President of the AEU and a national figure.

By 1923 the NCLC had gained nine affiliations from national trade unions; in 1924 22 unions were affiliated, by 1926 the NCLC were now officially running the educational schemes for 28 unions with 1,800,000 members; these included such important unions as the Transport and General Workers, the National Union of Textile Workers and the Agricultural Workers.[42] It was now organised in twelve divisions. By this time, the whole emphasis has shifted from the setting up of individual classes and colleges through the work of individual Plebs supporters, to schemes of education covering trade unions as a whole, and on the need for new affiliations of this kind. This brought a new emphasis to the work of the NCLC – particularly the correspondence courses – on material relevant to the specific concerns of trade union branch members and secretaries. Practical labour movement subjects were now established alongside the now traditional main emphasis on economic, political and social issues which had, of course, a wider significance than those subjects specifically tailored for trade unionists as trade unionists. This trend was later to be widely developed.

By 1926, then, the Plebs League had come through its testing time. Starting as a small group of individuals ('fanatics' perhaps) it had so far penetrated the rank and file of the trade union movement to have brought into being – against serious, and far better financed competition – an important organisation serving the labour movement, and especially the trade unions, as their 'educational wing'. The massive affiliations of the unions, as already indicated, opened a new phase, marked constitutionally perhaps (in spite of earlier discussions) by the winding up of the Plebs league that year – or rather its unification with the NCLC. As Kelly puts it,

> The period of most rapid advance came in the 20s especially in the years centring on the general strike of 1926. The number of classes, 529 in 1922-23, jumped to a peak of 1,234 in 1925-26; the number of students in classes reached a peak of 31,635 in the following year.[43]

The first, expansionist pioneering phase, marked by the increasing militancy and organisation of the working class through the trade union movement, was over, a phase dominated by the ideas of industrial democracy and resulting amalgamations – a movement in which Plebs supporters played a considerable part. The new phase now opening out, dominated by different considerations and influences (a period of defensive industrial struggle), was to bring new problems, and of a different order, to the educational movement.

(ii) The nature of Plebs

A few words may be said as to the nature of the movement and its leading personalities as it emerged in the 1920s. The journal itself (*Plebs*) is lively, stimulating and aggressive. For many years it carried as its main slogan or motto a phrase from Thomas Hodgskin, who fought a similar battle for independent education (again specifically on the issue of the teaching of economics) a century earlier: 'I can promise to be candid but not impartial.' This really sets the tone of the journal. Leading contributors included Raymond Postgate, J.P.M. Millar, Mark Starr, Joseph McCabe, T.A. Jackson, W. McLaine, W.H. Mainwaring, Eden and Cedar Paul, Maurice Dobb; and from the trade unions, Will Lawther, Ebby Edwards and others. The editor in the early 1920s was J.F. Horrabin, deputy principal of the Labour College in London. Occasional contributors included J.T. Walton Newbold, J.G. Crowther, H.G. Wells.

Certain characteristics are discernible in the journal even at this stage. It includes a lot of material on Marxism, on literature, economics, etc. But, in spite of the occasional trade union contributor, there is little or no reference to current political or industrial issues and struggle. Although the Plebs movement was essentially an industrial rank-and-file movement (and this was its strength), its journal was, perhaps inevitably, run by intellectuals. However this may be, the impression derived from the journal in these years is that what was being propagated was certainly independent working-class education – but independent, among other things, from the immediate and critical political and industrial struggles of the time.

As an *educational* organisation, Plebs saw as one of its most important functions the production of textbooks and other literature for its classes and correspondence students.[44] The first of these, published in 1922, was, rather surprisingly, on psychology. There followed *An Outline of Modern Imperialism* (by T. Ashcroft) and another on elementary economics (Nos. 2 and 3, published in 1922), and shortly after, W.W. Craik's *Short History of the Modern British Working Class Movement*, Mark Starr's *A Worker looks at History* and *Trade Unionism, Past and Future*, Noah Ablett's *Easy Outlines of Economics* and J.F. Horrabin's *An Outline of Economic Geography*. Other books published with the support of Plebs included Eden and Cedar Paul's *Prolet Cult*, advertised as containing a full account of the foundation and aims of the Labour College, the Plebs League, and other working class educational organisations in Britain, the Continent, Russia and America, and J.F. and Winifred Horrabin's *Working Class Education* (1924) setting IWCE aims and methods in the context of their historical evolution.

Such books filled a gap, in keeping with Plebs objectives, alongside others recommended to their students and readers, for instance, William Paul's *Labour and the War* (published by the SLP), Walton Newbold's *Capitalism and the War* (National Labour Press), John Bryan's *Essays in Socialism and War* (Communist Party) and H.N. Brailsford's searing exposé *The War of Steel and Gold* (Bell). With the development of the Labour and socialist press, socialist and Marxist literature was becoming available on a much wider scale than ever before, and in this Plebs and the NCLC played an important part.

(iii) The NCLC's attitude to the WEA

The generally aggressive attitude of Plebs and the NCLC to the WEA (and to the Workers' Educational Trade Union Committee – WETUC – by which WEA sought to provide educational facilities for the trade union movement) has already been indicated. It must be remembered that the Plebs League was originally formed in the process of breaking away from what it saw as the suffocating embrace of Oxford University, so that the WEA, very closely linked with Oxford in its inception and through the early years, was inevitably seen as a means of external control of the whole movement for working-class education. This approach is very evident in the early 1920s. There was, in particular, the persistent suspicion that, beneath all the fine phrases of Temple and others, the objective was, if not to distort, at least to neutralise the demand for knowledge on the part of the working class, and to deflect it from radical (or revolutionary) political or industrial action.

This attitude is well expressed in a comment in *Plebs* in February 1921, on a recent review of Mellor's *Direct Action* in the *Sunday Times*. This 'uttered several warning growls' over Mellor's suggestion that some WEA tutors 'did not always impart that "safe" and "unbiased" teaching in social science subjects which the WEA, as an organisation, stands for'. A week later, the comment goes on, Albert

Mansbridge wrote to express his horror at the idea of 'prostituting the educational machinery of the WEA for political and revolutionary ends'. So if any of the *Plebs* readers are still doubtful as to why it retains 'an unrelenting opposition to the WEA and all its works' they should study this phrase of Mansbridge's – and read Mellor's book.[45]

This makes clear the difficulty of overtly supporting both institutions simultaneously – as G.D.H. Cole (Mellor's colleague in his Guild Socialist stage) tried to do, although at the same time acting as the spearhead of the WEA's drive into the trade union world. It was clearly essential for the WEA that it should not lay itself open to a charge of the kind made in the *Sunday Times* if it was to receive the financial support from the state on which its entire existence depended.

Plebs was quick to fasten on to any evidence that seemed to prove the debilitating effect of 'impartial' education on the workers' struggle. A review of Sidney Webb's *Story of the Durham Miners* (1921), for instance (by George Harvey), holds that these miners, once revolutionary, have changed. In 1916, the *Times* attributed this 'change of heart' (which it applauded) mainly to 'the University-inspired teaching' which was developed widely at this time, and went on to recommend the South Wales coalowners ('the Masters of South Wales') to establish classes for the 'impartial' study of history and economics under the 'guidance' of properly equipped teachers. The *Times* hit the nail on the head, wrote the reviewer, who seemed to accept this somewhat superficial analysis. It is 'impartial' education that is responsible for the northern miners' backwardness and apathy.[46]

This point is pressed home at every opportunity. In 1922 the Liverpool WEA branch sent out an appeal for financial support. The appeal referred to 'maintaining that spirit of fellowship between different classes which is no small part of the result aimed at'. The appeal was signed (according to *Plebs*) by several WEA supporters who are 'big employers of labour'. This 'proves that the education provided by the WEA is just as propagandist, and has quite as definite a social purpose, as that provided by the NCLC' – an argument difficult to refute. One of the signatures to this appeal was that of F.J. Marquis (of Lewis's department store) who later, as Lord Woolton, and national organiser of the Conservative Party, was one of the architects of the Tory return to power in 1951.[47]

The same theme is taken up in a later article by J.P.M. Millar entitled 'The WEA Spider and the TUC Fly'. This analyses a number of bodies concerned with 'educating' the workers many of which have a direct connection with industry; for instance the Scottish Economics League (run by the Marquis of Linlithgow and a number of industrialists) which aims to 'furnish an adequate and effective antidote to the poison of revolutionary doctrine' (as disseminated, apparently, by the Labour Party!) and other similar organisations. Special attention is devoted, however, to the 'National Alliance of Employers in England' which aims to promote industrial peace by 'elementary economic teaching', and to train men 'to lead their national movements'. This body is governed by a group of industrialists (from the Federation of British Industry, FBI) and of trade unionists, among whom are named W.A. Appleton, the Rt. Hon. John Hodge (the first Minister of Labour in Lloyd George's wartime government) and Arthur Pugh (Secretary of the Iron and Steel Trades Confederation, and the leading proponent of the WEA in the trade union movement). Millar shows that several of the trade union personalities are linked with the WEA and comments on this WEA-TUC link up through the FBI with the National Alliance and its 'sinister educational policy'.[48] He adds that all (or many) of these organisations rely on the text-books of the orthodox (university) economists for their teaching, as does the WEA (Clay, Marshall, Milne, etc.), and concludes with a quotation from a leader in the *South Wales Daily News* on the WEA:

> We suggest that it [the WEA] should receive the strongest support from employers of labour, if for no other reason than that it provides an antidote and a corrective to the mischievous propaganda of the various sorts of revolutionists in our midst.

South Wales was, of course, at that time, *the* centre and focus of a militant miners' struggle, culminating in a nine-month strike or lock-out in 1923. This article was part of the counter-move against the NCLC's initiative among the trade union movement.

(iv) The Workers' Educational Trade Union Committee
That the NCLC built itself up in conflict with the WEA there can be no doubt whatsoever. This conflict was endemic in the situation as it developed in practice. The only means by which it might have been overcome (at least within the trade union movement) would have been for the TUC to take over the whole provision of working-class education for its membership, or rather, for the membership of its affiliated unions. There were moves in this direction, as we shall see, but at this stage, for a number of reasons, they failed.[49]
The bid for WEA involvement, influence (and finally control?) of

trade union education came from the WEA itself. By 1918 it was already a well established, efficient organisation, with Temple as its President, and MacTavish as Secretary.[50] It obtained financial support from the state and local authorities, and could call on the universities for its tutors. By 1920, it could claim 277 branches, to which many local organisations, including trade union branches, were affiliated (and over 20,000 individual members).[51] As a national organisation it wished to extend its influence – and what more appropriate a field than the trade union movement?

Such, at least, was certainly the view of MacTavish. It was he who (apparently) originally approached Arthur Pugh, secretary of the new steelworkers' amalgamation, indeed the approach was first made in 1918, when discussions on amalgamation were still in progress. Pugh 'gave a ready ear' to these plans and participated in working out an ambitious scheme which, from being concerned initially with the needs of one union, was finally framed to meet the needs of all. In 1919 the Workers' Education Trade Union Committee was set up to carry it through; an organisation originally consisting of seven divisions (to correspond with the steelworkers' new structure), the divisional committees consisting of both WEA and Confederation representatives, the latter being in the majority.[52]

In May 1919 MacTavish presented a full version of his educational scheme to the steel workers' executive committee.[53] This proposed the organisation of a series of weekend conferences, a residential school, study groups and classes, etc., several but not all of which were (or would be) 'recognised and assisted by the Board of Education or local Education Authority'. The whole scheme was carefully costed and it was estimated, on this basis, that a total expenditure of between £4,500 and £5,000 a year 'would give the trade union movement a system of educational provision which would be of high quality, of widespread influence and a first class investment for the future.[54]

A fortnight earlier, an official letter from MacTavish to Pugh, together with a memorandum, set out the main advantages of the scheme. This stressed the crucial issue of finance and state support which it was essential to obtain if the scheme was to be viable; the letter informs Pugh that, as a result of informal discussions at the Board of Education, there is 'reason to believe that the Board has been impressed and *providing educational work was done under the auspices of the WEA*, there is reason to anticipate that the Board will regard it as education on which grants could be paid' (my italics, B.S.). The letter goes on to suggest that this support would be unlikely to be forthcoming, if the education was 'entirely controlled by trade unions'.[55] Our scheme, MacTavish continues, therefore 'offers a possibility of developing a system of trade union education which would be jointly controlled by subscribing Trade Unions and the WEA towards which the Board may pay a grant for tuition.[56]

The key importance of external financial support is driven home in the accompanying memorandum, especially in the discussion on the difficulties of organising education work in trade unions (these are 'proverbial'). To stimulate and develop the work involves providing lectures, tutors, syllabuses, textbooks and so on; it requires developing relations with universities, the Board of Education, local authorities. But the expenses of all this, if provided solely from trade union funds, would be out of proportion to the educational advantages – while to find an adequate supply of good lecturers and tutors 'would soon prove insurmountable'. Further, good education is always expensive 'particularly if no advantage is to be taken of the National system of education to secure financial aid from the state'. Thus the cost of one tutor taking a class one night a week is from £60 to £80 per year, plus travelling and other expenses. 'The Board of Education now gives £45 a year grant in aid to an effective class, without which such classes would be impossible.'[57] Co-operation with the WEA would overcome this difficulty.

The steelworkers' union, under Pugh's guidance, accepted the scheme in a slightly modified form in November, 1919, and the WETUC was set up and began operations with this one union.[58] The WEA looked for its rapid extension to cover the trade union movement as a whole, and called a conference on trade union education in October 1920, which Pugh chaired; the conference was held at the steelworkers' headquarters in London. Of his speech, Corfield, historian of the WETUC, comments 'He spoke with a shrewd understanding of his audience. He addressed the pockets as well as the hearts of the assembled general secretaries and presidents, and demonstrated the solid economic advantages of joining the WETUC.' To meet the total cost of organising and teaching a full-scale trade union educational programme would impose 'an intolerable financial burden'. The trade unions should take their share of the grant made available for adult education from public funds.'[59]

A trade union education enquiry committee was set up from this conference, supported by sixteen trade unions while in 1921 a second union joined the WETUC – the Post Office workers (formed in 1920 from a series of amalgamations). There followed soon the railway clerks and the AESD (engineering and shipbuilding draughtsmen). In 1923 NATSOPA (a printers' union) joined, and then others, but by this time the NCLC had come into the field, gained the affiliation of the AUBTW (as we have seen) after a straight clash between the two organisations, to be followed by the AEU and other important unions. At the AEU National Committee meeting in 1924, MacTavish for the WEA argued strongly that 'the sole plausible ground for the charge against them' was that they accepted grants from the state and local authorities. But, writes Corfield, 'he refused to apologise for this'. They accepted aid 'only on condition that it should in no way hamper their freedom in teaching'.[60] But there was clearly a certain ambiguity about this stance.

This comes out also in the statement of the objectives of the original educational scheme put before the steel workers' union. The main purpose of the education is 'to provide a general understanding of the existing industrial and social order' as well as 'a knowledge of trade union history', 'technical aids to the development of administrative efficiency' and 'recreative studies to promote good feeling amongst the workers'.[61] It is difficult to avoid the impression that MacTavish and the WEA were treading a tightrope with considerable care and skill. On the one hand, for success throughout the trade union movement as it was at this period, they needed to make some appeal to the class consciousness of the workers. On the other hand, they had to preserve their own slogan of 'impartiality', or at least of non-partisanship, particularly if they were to continue to be regarded, by the Board of Education, as a 'responsible body' through which grants of public money could be distributed. Later formulations of objectives were sometimes slightly more radical. Thus Corfield claims that the objective of workers' control of industry, which was 'written into the constitution of most of the new unions' formed through amalgamations at this time, was also expressed 'albeit discreetly' in the first constitution of the WETUC. This stated that its primary object was to 'develop efficient, intelligent loyalty in the trade union movement', and added a rather long winded gloss on the phrase. Corfield comments on the 'circumspection' of this section, but suggests that underneath it 'the implications can be easily discerned.'[62] This may have been so; but the vague, generalised and frankly woolly phrases are closer akin to rhodomontade than to a clear expression of objectives.[63] That many in the labour movement remained suspicious is understandable enough – given the circumstances of the time.

With the rising militancy of the labour movement in 1924 and 1925 the WETUC also took up, in its statements, a more radical position. This was the period when G.D.H. Cole's attempt to swing the WEA towards the left and, indeed, establish it as the 'educational wing of the labour movement', reached its peak with his celebratory lecture on the 21st anniversary of the organisation delivered (somewhat ironically) in the Sheldonian Theatre at Oxford.[64] In 1924 Fred Bramley, Secretary of the TUC and 'known for his support of left or militant policies at this time' (the period of Red Friday and increasing solidarity in support of the miners), followed Temple as President of the WEA: 'a profoundly astute move' according to Corfield (unfortunately Bramley died suddenly a year later) – but this again signified the determination of the WEA to base itself more effectively in the trade union movement. In 1925, John Muir, one of the leaders of the Clydeside shop stewards' committee during the First World War, with a history of militant activity, was appointed as the WEA's national organiser for trade union education.[65]

At the 1924 TUC conference George Hicks, Secretary of the AUBTW and strong supporter of the NCLC, had made a powerful speech pressing the claims of the NCLC 'as an organisation closely committed to the workers' own struggles'.[66] This was the point at which support for the NCLC and its very specific approach to workers' education was snowballing. On the whole, support for the NCLC came from the left within the labour and trade union movement at this time – and these were in the ascendant. The right tended to go to the WEA as we have seen, and, though this is by no means the whole story, the left-right divide which now expressed itself had implications for the future – sometimes in a highly contradictory manner. However that may be, there is no doubt that the 1924 TUC conference proceedings, and particularly the impact of George Hicks's speech, caused concern within the WETUC, which had been founded to take over all trade union education. In the *Highway*, organ of the WEA, the editor, Barbara Wootton, wrote that while the Labour Colleges had 'decided views', well known to many, 'the WEA point of view is – what?'. Their standpoint had been left too long as simply the 'negation of Labour College doctrines without character of its own'. What was needed was 'a raging, tearing campaign' on behalf of their principles.[67]

The purpose of this campaign, it seems, was to wrest the initiative from the NCLC – what else? In January 1925 a manifesto was issued over the signatures of 32 leading trade unionists, including Ernest Bevin, Arthur Pugh, Clynes and Margaret Bondfield. The object of trade unionism, it stated, 'is the control of industry by the workers in the interest of the workers'. Education can do much to help reach this objective. Understanding and the development of convictions is necessary to prevent workers being misled by the press or discouraged by difficulties. For all these reasons, education is of vital importance for trade unionists – the impetus for a juster social order must come from the 'rank and file'. For this emancipation they must be intellectually awake. 'It is the business of education to assist that awakening.' Knowledge is power, concludes the manifesto; and the way to get that knowledge is through the WEA and the WETUC.[68] At no other time in their entire history had the WEA or the WETUC committed themselves to so radical a policy.

Certainly there was little about 'impartiality' there. This manifesto clearly committed the parent body – the WEA – to fully supporting a definite political and industrial policy – that of workers' control of industry.

The reaction was predictable. The *Morning Post* – the leading conservative newspaper – immediately launched a strong attack on the WEA. This organisation, it claimed (somewhat wildly), was part

> of a vast subsidised machinery for the indoctrination of youth with a certain dogma and point of view and for the equipment of street corner orators wth an armoury of phrases, catchwords, maxims and impressive passages from the works of Karl Marx and other socialist oracles.[69]

The WEA also came under a great deal of pressure from the Board of Education and the local authorities not to become involved in any scheme which openly committed it to the provision of workers' education for social and industrial emancipation. (See Roger Fieldhouse's essay in this volume, pp. 153-172.)

The WEA was forced to give an official (or semi-official) reply – and this came (appropriately) from A.D. Lindsay, Master of Balliol College, Oxford, and an active supporter of the WEA. This 'carefully worded' reply 'reaffirmed the traditional WEA standpoint'. 'The WEA', he asserted (Lindsay was a philosopher), 'were in favour of independent working-class education, but independent in the sense that it should be, as far as possible, scientific and impartial' (a blurring of categories, surely). No one, he recognised, 'could be absolutely impartial'; but it was still necessary 'to try to be as impartial as possible'. This does not mean that the WEA refused to take sides in life or social struggles; but 'by understanding things as they were, rather than as his political party would like him to believe them to be, a worker would be equipped to take sides more effectively'.[70]

Whatever may be thought of this exercise from the standpoint of precision of expression and logical argument, Lindsay's 'reply' remained only tangential to the main issue. The clear implication of the manifesto was that the education provided would arm the worker to fight effectively for workers' control of industry, and no doubt some within the WEA fully accepted this approach. Conflicts of views as to ultimate purposes, strategy and tactics certainly existed within the organisation which, generally, was highly decentralised in its functioning. But, in the outcome, this issue was not faced, and the supposition remains that this bend to the left was seen as a necessary means of retaining the loyalty, and increasing the support of active trade unionists at a particular and crucial moment. No doubt the many trade unionists whose signatures were obtained for the manifesto genuinely believed that education for workers' control was the objective of the WEA – after all G.D.H. Cole, one of the most active proponents of workers' control (in the form of guild socialism), was also one of the more ardent supporters of the WETUC, with close contact among the unions.[71]

It is difficult to estimate the impact of this manifesto in terms of trade union attitudes and actual developments. It does not seem at this stage, however, to have stemmed the advance of the NCLC – if that was its aim – nor to have seriously furthered support for the WETUC. The whole issue had, however, by now become one of serious debate at the annual congresses of the TUC, to which we may now turn.

(v) The TUC and workers' education

It is already clear that both the WEA and the NCLC had their supporters in the Trades Union Congress – both were pressing for affiliations, both offering services. Inevitably the issue came to the fore in the TUC which was already involved in the field through its sponsorship of Ruskin College. As events unfolded, it became clear that the general approach of the TUC was to find a means of unifying all general trade union education under its own control.

The issue first arose at the 1921 Congress. The recommendations of the Committee of Enquiry set up at the October 1920 Conference were given in the report of the Parliamentary Committee, together with an assurance that the Parliamentary Committee agreed with them. These concerned the co-ordination of educational activities of trade unions, encouraging all trade unions to spend some funds on these, and setting out certain general principles as to their character, for instance, the need for student control of classes, for student choice of teachers, etc. (Classes should be regarded as 'self-governing bodies', select their own subject, have the final voice in the appointment of the tutor, and should be run under the auspices of a bona fide working-class organisation.) It was also recommended that the General Council[72] of the TUC should see the Board of Education about public financial aid being made available on the lines of the Committee's recommendations.[73]

At the 1921 Congress a resolution was passed proposing that the TUC take over the two trade union colleges, the Central Labour College and Ruskin, and give effect to the recommendations of the Enquiry Committee. The resolution was moved by C.G. Ammon of the Post Office workers. It was seconded by Frank Hodges of the Miners' Federation who deplored the internecine strife in this field. Supporting speakers all agreed with the motion – it was time the TUC took this on in an organised way.[74]

So far so good, but of course complex problems were involved and all was not plain sailing; in any case, there was clearly much negotiating to be done. During the year, the Council reported in 1922, consultations had been carried on with all the interested bodies to give effect to last year's resolution, but unemployment and the general depletion of funds meant that no immediate takeover was possible if it led to increased expenditure. The matter would, however, remain under consideration.

The General Council's report for the 1922 Congress did, however, deal with the issue in some detail. In March 1922 a Committee of the General Council met the Trade Union Education Enquiry Committee; at the same time, the TUC asked all affiliated unions for information as to their educational provision. A sympathetic assessment is made of the work of the WETUC; the scheme worked out with the Confederation (the steelworkers) allows it to utilise the services of all educational organisations and institutions; thus all needs can be met while public funds are used for classes complying with Board of Education regulations. This avoids the cost of building up an educational organisation of its own, using the WEA instead, 'while retaining complete control'.[75]

Later there is a 'Group Report' which indicates considerable activity on the part of the General Council.[76] Discussions have been held with representatives of all organisations – Ruskin, Central Labour College, Co-operative Education Committee, WEA, the Scottish Labour College, NCLC and the Working Men's Club and Institute Union. All expressed approval of the 1921 resolution and of the following report and general assessment of needs. This stated that the workers want not only a specialised, but also a broad education. 'They seek knowledge, not only of economics and industrial history, but also of the general and social history of their own and other peoples, of literature, of the arts and sciences.' A broad education is necessary to give the worker 'a new sense of understanding, and therewith of power to mould the world in accordance with his human and social ideals'.

The different kinds of education needed by workers are then classified:

(1) *Training in the management of trade union business.* There is a special need for training in branch administration; the basis of trade union structure.

(2) *Training for positions as Labour representatives on local authorities and the House of Commons.*

(3) *Industrial management and Workers' Councils* – the equipment of workers for workers' control.

(4) *The training of teachers* – from among trade unionists. Universities don't always provide the best atmosphere – but a good tutor is best, even if he is anti-labour. But the best tutors should identify themselves with the students. Therefore working class tutors should be trained under conditions where 'their distinctively working-class point of view will be not submerged'.

The report then discusses briefly the specific needs of adolescents and apprentices, women and seamen, where there are particular problems now catered for by philanthropic organisations rather than trade unions.

The real need, concludes the report, is for an *inclusive* scheme, much more comprehensive than anything that yet exists, covering England, Scotland and Wales. But the cost is too great and cannot be met from trade union funds. A reasonable standard of living could not be offered to good teachers – if it could it would attract the best whose sympathies lie with the working class movement. It follows, therefore, that public money must be used. Some of the teaching that is needed (distinctively working-class in outlook) would not qualify for this support – such teaching must be financed from working class sources and run on entirely independent lines.[77]

The question is then raised as to the possibility of merging the TUC and Co-operative education schemes to help cover the cost of organisation. The Board of Education supports the educational work of the Co-op and the Adult School Union but there is no interference as regards policy. The same is true of the WEA.

An argument is then developed for the right to use public money for trade union education. Workers' schools set up by employers have been recognised for grant by the Board of Education since the 1918 Education Act – this education is biased (it is claimed). The trade union movement should also be recognised by the Board of Education as an education authority in relation to the education of their own members. The trade union movement, it is argued, through heroic sacrifices, has won itself recognised status in a capitalist state. To work to change social relations is a legitimate function. The Board of Education is a trustee of public money. Complete freedom is essential – The Board of Education in any case has nothing to do with social theories.[78]

This, then, was the argument. The report concludes by saying that further negotiations with all the organisations concerned are necessary; that the TUC must be empowered to take over Ruskin College, the WETUC and other organisations and report each year on the progress made.[79]

There was no serious discussion of the report at the 1922 Congress – probably because the go-ahead had been given the year before. But the delegates can hardly have been unaware of the financial problems involved – it was reported that the financial position of Ruskin College had grown progressively worse; with a debt of £8,000 the College had to live from hand to mouth. The income was never sufficient to meet the outlay and a deficit was running at over £1,000 per year. More adequate support was called for from the unions (in the form of scholarships – 70 students were required for economic working). Expressing a united (or compromise) approach to the different bodies or philosophies with which the TUC was now entangled, Congress voted £250 to be shared between Ruskin, its rival the Central Labour College, and the WEA.[80]

A year later the General Council reported that further discussions had been carried through with the various bodies; that they were working on plans for the future, but that the time was not ripe for united TUC control. A second interim report of what is now called the 'Joint Education Committee' (TUC General Council and Trade Union Education Enquiry Committee) had been produced, and a meeting taken place (23 May 1923) with all the bodies concerned. This report goes into the financial aspect of taking over Ruskin and the Central Labour College. There is also a long report on the education of young workers by G.D.H. Cole and a report on the Scottish Labour College, which claimed a number of district committees in the main population centres, with 84 classes and 3,005 students. The Scottish College had also conducted educational schemes for the AUBTW and miners from Mid- and East Lothian, Fife and Lancashire, and was proposing to conduct a scheme for NUDAW. Schemes were run for some 200 trade union branches and the College had the support of the principal Scottish Trades Councils, of many Co-operative societies and working-class political bodies.[81]

It was in 1924 that the whole issue was raised to a new level by a fighting speech by George Hicks of the AUBTW, who was clearly concerned at the way things were going. Hicks had been a member of SDF and later a supporter of industrial unionism; he had been, and was, a strong supporter of the NCLC and of its approach to working-class education. The General Council had reported that an advisory committee had been set up to discuss a general scheme consisting of representatives of the General Council and of individual unions together with two representatives each from the NCLC and WEA, and one each from the Central Labour College and Ruskin. Creech Jones moved a resolution urging the General Council 'to take a more active part in furtherance of working-class education' and urging adoption of a scheme in co-operation with all these bodies under the control of the TUC. He argued that the labour movement recognises that there are two schools of thought and has recognised both. Now the TUC should go ahead, take the whole thing seriously and include both directions of work under its umbrella.[82]

To this resolution George Hicks had submitted an amendment – that any scheme adopted should embody the principles of the NCLC and the CLC. The seconder of Creech Jones' resolution, J. Walker of the Iron and Steel Confederation, sharply attacked the amendment which would exclude the WEA. There is no room for difference of opinion, he said, on the laws of chemistry and medicine – these can be learned from university teachers. 'But it is when we come to that subject, namely political economy, that the trouble commences.' He did not believe that Marx had all the truth. The adult education movement owed a great deal to the WEA.[83]

In moving his amendment Hicks 'for the first time openly challenged the TUC's policy of forging unity among the existing participants'. In doing so, writes Corfield, 'he made what was certainly one of the most impressive speeches on education to be heard at Congress'. His theme was that the trade unions should break with the past. He reminded delegates of the successful advance towards independence in the political sphere. At an early stage of development they had been content to lean on the Liberal Party in politics. As they grew to maturity they stood on their own feet and formed an independent party, the Labour Party. There should be a parallel development in trade union education, he argued. The trade union movement was now strong enough to stand on its own feet in this sphere also, and provide its own education.[84]

Hicks was seconded by Ellen Wilkinson, still in her 'revolutionary' phase. The trade union movement should educate future leaders 'not in the terms of the capitalist system under which we lived, but in the terms of the coming socialist community that they hoped to establish'.

These speeches were warmly received, but an effective vote was not taken since, on an appeal from A.J. Cook in the interest of unity, Hicks withdrew his amendment 'for the time being'.[85]

The General Council, therefore, continued its discussions on the existing basis as, indeed, it reported the following year (1925) to a Congress dominated by an extremely militant class conscious approach. At this point, the trade union movement was consciously moving towards solidarity of action to protect the miners and indeed the working class as a whole against threats and actions of employers and government alike. Another factor was the disillusion felt with Parliament after the ineffective failure of the first Labour government. Resolutions were passed on the need to strengthen shop organisations to prepare for the overthrow of capitalism.

It was in this situation that the General Council, now advised by its own Education Advisory Committee which had conducted intensive negotiations with the relevant bodies during the preceding year, recommended an educational scheme that was outlined in some detail. This scheme did not affect the integrity, or independence, of any of the bodies involved (WEA, NCLC, the Central Labour College and Ruskin), but it provided for the co-ordination of their work, strengthened the position of the General Council by ensuring representation of the TUC on the governing bodies of these organisations, and also allowed the General Council to develop its own initiatives in the field of education. The agreed 'Objects' of the scheme, which, as we have seen, caused embarrassing difficulties for the WEA, stressed the need to equip workers for 'the work of securing social and industrial emancipation'.[86] Some such formulation was essential if the NCLC and Central Labour College were to be involved. This scheme was accepted at the 1925 TUC Congress in September that year, where it was also suggested that the two colleges (Ruskin and the Labour College) be taken over and transferred to the same site.[87] Later that year (1925) Lady Warwick offered her home, Easton Lodge, to the TUC as the venue of a residential college. All, therefore, seemed set fair for a considerable advance and for close TUC involvement in promoting working-class education.

It is, then, clear that by the winter of 1925 the trade unions and TUC were taking education much more seriously than had ever been the case earlier – and were responding to the pressure from two independent nuclei, each acting as an organisational centre grouping individuals particularly concerned with this aspect of trade union work. As we have seen, the necessity for education as part of a general move forward, if still seen in syndicalist, industrial unionist or even guild socialist terms (all of which were still influential and formed part of the ideology of many trade union leaders and 'rank and file'), acted as an impetus to the movement. The two rival organisations had both expanded their work in the trade union movement very greatly since 1919–20. From being embryonic, peripheral organisations, both the WETUC and the NCLC had entered into the mainstream of trade union activity while the TUC itself seemed on the edge of acting as a unifying centre.

3   The Triumph of Liberal Education, 1926–39

The General Strike, or more particularly the way in which it was brought to an end, was a traumatic experience for the British working class. Its effects were contradictory. Among a section of the workers, it led to increased political consciousness and militancy; others, whose aspirations were shattered, relapsed into apathy. Among some of the leading trade unionists, however, the failure of the strike even to achieve its immediate aims strengthened those who believed in a policy of closer collaboration with employers as the best means of achieving immediate objectives. Their object was class collaboration, and this trend was epitomised in the Mond-Turner discussions and subsequent agreement, in which leading trade unionists worked together with a powerful group of industrialists in an attempt to overcome, through 'rationalisation' and other means, fundamental economic and social problems. In the TUC both trends were represented, the militant wing being organised in the so-called 'Minority Movement'. This phase was also marked by the policy of prohibitions against Communists both in the Labour Party and the trade union movement, a policy which reached its peak in the early 1930s.

The strike had some immediate and some long lasting effects on working-class education. It was at the following TUC Congress (September 1926) that 'the movement for educational unity came

dismally and humiliatingly to a halt' (as Corfield correctly puts it).[88]
The General Council proposed that the Easton Lodge project, which
would require the sum of £50,000 from the TUC, should be supported.
But, after a long debate, this recommendation was rejected partly as a
result of NCLC pressure, but also because of the general unwillingness
to produce the money required (1 penny per member for three years)
on the part of the mass of the trade unions. This latter objection
reflected the generally depressed state of the unions following the
General Strike. Arthur Pugh, that year's President, pressed the issue
to a vote, himself recommending acceptance of the whole set of
proposals for TUC control of the field and the Easton Lodge proposi-
tion. On a card vote it was defeated by 2,441,000 to 1,481,000. This
vote marked the end of all efforts in this direction for another twenty
years.[89]

Another casualty was the Central Labour College. This depended
on scholarships for support, but so catastrophic were the effects of the
miners' strike, in particular on union funds, that this support, which
came largely from the SWMF and NUR, could not be maintained.
Appeals from both unions to the TUC made in 1927 and 1928 fell on
deaf ears. The unions were not in a position to take over or continue
these payments and in 1929 the College closed.[90] Ruskin College itself,
the originator of full-time residential education (under working-class
control) went through an extremely difficult period and only survived
through to the late 1920s and 30s by the skin of its teeth. In all these
areas the period marked a retreat.

But more important, perhaps, was the ending of the bright hopes of
the past, in terms of workers' control and syndicalist thinking as the
means to the transition to socialism. In many ways, as we have seen, it
was this which had given the ideological impetus to working-class
education – especially its independent variety. But following the
political failure of the first Labour government came failure on the
industrial front – epitomised in the inability of the trade union
movement to preserve its unity and strength sufficiently to force the
government to withdraw its policy of all out attack on the living
standards of the workers, as the means of solving the economic crisis.
Inevitably this spread a certain disillusion (speaking generally) – a lack
of clarity or wide agreement as to the means of achieving socialist
objectives. This also had a long-term negative effect on the educational
activities of the working class.

This is not to say that advances did not take place – as we shall see,
they did; and in any case the picture is never monochrome. But the
general direction of this work began to change – or to take new forms

consistent with the new situation.

Summing up the general trend during this period Kelly points to three main aspects of these changes. First, the increasing provision – and acceptance – of state aid, particularly to the WEA and the universities; second, the tendency towards a common pattern of provision as compared with earlier diversity – in particular 'the driving forces of social reform and religious service became noticeably weaker, and the motive of personal culture reasserted itself'. Both universities and the WEA now overlapped in the provision of 'general cultural courses for general audiences' – the main desire, as Kelly sees it, was for 'personal culture' and its provision was now 'dominated by the humane tradition of the Universities'.[91]

(i) The universities

The period between the wars saw the development of university Extra Mural departments on a large scale. Only three universities were involved in Extension work before the war, and these, run by rather ineffective committees, did not have departmental status. Nearly all extra mural work (apart from Extension courses) was organised and financed through the joint committees with the WEA, and took the form of tutorial classes on the lines of Tawney's original classes at Rochdale and Longton.

That universities should set up extra mural departments had been very strongly urged in the Final Report of the Adult Education Reconstruction Committee set up by Lloyd George in 1917. This committee, which had strong university-WEA representation among its members,[92] aware of the role universities could play in ensuring social stability, recommended a large increase in the expenditure by the state in adult education, and specifically proposed that the universities should set up departments and enter this field in a big way.[93] In 1920 the first of these new departments was set up at Nottingham; by 1939 all universities except three had them – a total of seventeen. The number of full-time university tutors engaged in this work (since 1924 largely financed *directly* by the Board of Education) rose from twenty in 1924 to 84 in 1939, while as part of a new set of regulations brought in in 1924 both universities and the WEA were accepted by the Board of Education as 'approved associations' or as 'responsible bodies' for the receipt and distribution of state grants. The resulting alliance between the universities and the WEA became, as Kelly puts it 'the dominant factor' in the inter-war years.[94]

Now the provision of university type teaching outside the walls of
the universities was clearly desirable in itself, both from the
standpoint of the universities themselves and of society outside. It
was the determination to break out of the narrow confines of the
universities – then scarcely attended by students with a working-class
origin – which provided the main idealist motivation for this work by
university teachers – or rather the small minority of them attracted to
teaching of this kind. Those who wished to make knowledge more
widely available were able, through university Extension, or the
university-WEA link, to make an effective, functional contact with
the working class – or at least that (small) section that ardently
wished to develop their own culture and knowledge. The conditions
in which many of these classes took place in the early days – the wear
and tear on both tutors and students – have been vividly described by
Margaret Cole. These meetings, she writes of the tutorial classes
taken by G.D.H. Cole and others,

> often involved the tutor in dark journeys in crammed local trains or tubes
> at rush hour. They were apt to take place not in purpose-built
> accomodation – or anything of the kind – but in something like a council
> schoolroom with desks made to fit infants, not grown men, hired for the
> evening from the local trades council, or in other places intended for other
> uses. One of ... Douglas's [took place] in a room sandwiched, with only
> glass partitions intervening, between a company rehearsing Gilbert and
> Sullivan and a band of army recruits learning to play the drum.

Such classes were held for two hours weekly for 24 weeks. The tutor
received £80 in payment. The devotion on the part of both students
and tutors to this work must be appreciated at its true value.[95]

But that there was a social, or political motive behind the increased
official support for this development can hardly be denied. The Plebs
League, of course, incessantly and continuously asserted that this was
so; a standpoint that was based on their early experience with Oxford
and was, indeed, the reason for their original formation. And it is
certainly the case that at periods of sharp social crisis and militant
industrial struggles, university influence was at this time seen, by
those in authority, as a stabilising influence fundamentally directed to
preserving the status quo. Confirmation of this, and the political need
for effective counter-action in the field of adult education, is to some
extent found in the ripples emanating from a sharp exchange between
J.P.M. Millar of the NCLC and Lord Eustace Percy early in 1926.

In February 1926, just at the time when the NCLC had beaten off
to some extent the WEA/WETUC campaign for hegemony and was
gaining support very rapidly indeed in the trade union movement,

Eustace Percy, as President of the Board of Education launched a very strong attack on a public occasion against the NCLC. 'Do not, however, think that education has no enemies,' he said (engaged, as he was, in his economy campaign) – 'And its enemies are not those who preach economy. Its real enemies are men like the Secretary of the National Council of Labour Colleges. I have been a non-political President of the Board of Education,' he went on, 'and I have earned the right to say this.' He then characterised Millar's position in a recent letter to *Education*, which put the NCLC standpoint that education in the social sciences must be either education for capitalism or education against capitalism, as 'spiritual wickedness'. Such activity 'stunts the mind', is more subtle than dictatorship since 'you rob men of even the desire for free speech, by stifling freedom of thought'. We all desire 'the social and industrial emancipation of the workers', claimed Percy. There is one way, the only 'charter of true education' – the promise that 'the truth shall make you free'.[96]

A week or two later, on 24 February 1926, Millar wrote to Percy.

> My Lord, a short time ago in a speech delivered at Newcastle, you made a violent attack on this organisation [the NCLC] and upon myself. In this attack you described our educational policy as poisonous and pestilential, and stated that the classrooms of our schools must be closed to such as the writer of this letter.

Millar then goes on to say that in Carmarthen and Glamorgan, under the auspices of the County Council, educational work of exactly the same kind as the NCLC carries on is being undertaken. The tutors are from the Central Labour College and the textbooks used are Plebs books. But this is no responsibility of theirs, so what is the basis of the attack? Millar concludes by saying that the NCLC's education policy is anti-capitalist and that their textbooks are anti-capitalist because 'social science unbiased by vested interests is itself anti-capitalist'.[97]

On receipt of this letter, office enquiries were immediately made through HMIs in the two Welsh counties and confidential reports submitted. Both make very interesting reading, particularly for the testimony they give to the widespread desire for knowledge in economic and social affairs, and the difficulties involved in meeting it. Thus W.T. Williams, HMI responsible for Carmarthenshire under the new (1924) Adult Regulations, minutes that the local authority is running eight classes in economic and industrial history, and that all the four tutors concerned are ex-Central Labour College students. He (Williams) has visited the classes, has not been satisfied with the procedures, and, in the course of 'long discussions' with the tutors, has laid down certain principles which must be observed if 'the classes might continue to be recognised'. These principles, he adds, have since been fully observed. (For instance, it is difficult to cavil at the use of Plebs books 'as long as they are supplemented by other books which may be regarded as authoritative'.) In addition at each visit he has 'addressed the students on the aims of adult education' – as a result two of the classes propose to apply to the University College of Swansea for university classes next session. One of the four tutors also informed him that he had a 'violent argument' with one of the professors at the Labour College in which he opposed strongly the 'class conscious' principle; this tutor is prepared to work with the WEA next session.

But even so, the HMI reports, he cannot be happy about these eight classes; he suggested to the LEA clerk that they apply to the Extra-Mural Department at Aberystwyth and Swansea to cater for them. But because of the 'embargo' upon the development of tutorial work (ironically, one of Percy's own economy measures, BS) 'no college has been able to respond'. There are already eighteen classes in the area under the university colleges of Swansea, Aberystwyth and the WEA, nine of these specifically on economics. But this does 'not at all' satisfy the need. Hence, when a college (university) or the WEA fails to meet the needs (and 'this failure of course is due purely to the Board's restrictions upon development') application is made to the Local Education Authority; but they can't supply this need, 'and, therefore, in an industrial area such as this, there will always be a grave danger of an insidious partisanship creeping in'. This minute is dated 2 March 1926,

From Glamorgan Dr Abel T. Jones reported a similar story. This, of course, included the Rhondda Valley – a stronghold of the Labour College and Plebs, but no classes had been proposed in the valley for some years.

> Several years ago classes were taken by one who is now a labour member of Parliament, but so many complaints were heard of the extreme Marxian nature of the lectures that the Director of Education considered it inadvisable to suggest the holding of such classes.

In the rest of the county, fifteen classes are held in economics or economic and industrial history. Six of these are taken by the County Council's own permanent lecturer (a socialist and Labour candidate) who 'puts different aspects of the questions fairly and scientifically'. The nine other classes are taken by eight different teachers, one of whom stated on his application form that he attended the 'London or other Labour College but left it 14 years ago'. The County Inspector looked into the matter before appointing him 'and was assured by some responsible gentlemen in the district that his extreme views had of recent years become considerably modified'.

The local authority, the HMI goes on, makes it clear to the lecturers 'that the classes are not to be used for purposes of propaganda', the local inspector visits the classes and 'on the whole the classes receive a fair amount of supervision'. But it is difficult to know what does go on, continues Jones; he has heard nothing one could 'seriously object to', but one hears 'hot stuff' sometimes from the pupils (*sic*) in the course of discussion. The practice of the lecturers, judging from the HMI's experience, 'is to attempt to modify these extreme views – at least in our presence'. About 60 per cent of the students are miners. The Glamorgan authority consider that such classes should be freely available for 'the students are likely to get a fairer presentation of the subject' than they would 'if organised by the NCLC' or others. This minute is dated 4 March 1926.[98]

These reports, submitted rapidly, indicate the care with which control was exercised, and, unwittingly perhaps, the standpoint or bias of the HMIs concerned. In submitting them to Percy, the District Inspector, G.P. Williams took the opportunity to press his views urgently on the President. He refers at the start to the fact that already in 1918 he dealt 'fully and exhaustively' with the 'educational' activities of the Central Labour College in Carmarthenshire in a confidential report to the then President (Fisher). At that time the classes were conducted in such a way 'as to be outside our official purview'; but he gleaned information about them.

> They met, or purported to meet, a strong desire on the part of the workers to know something of the science of economics which the workers regarded as being something fundamentally necessary for acquiring a right conception of what underlies present-day economic and industrial conditions. In actual practice the work done was propaganda – pure and simple ...

The Carmarthen situation is the result of a break-away by a few men who, in response to insistent demand by workers, are prepared, although themselves ex-Central Labour College students, 'to teach under conditions that the CLC do not accept' and which Millar would scarcely approve. 'In my report to Mr Fisher in 1918,' he goes on, 'I pleaded hard for the establishment of more University Tutorial

Classes in the industrial areas of South Wales.' Experience since then has proved 'clearly and definitely' that only university extra-mural classes can 'compete successfully' with CLC classes. Neither local education authorities nor WEA have done this so successfully as the universities. In quite a large number of cases, tutorial classes of universities have managed 'to snuff out entirely what had previously been a flourishing CLC class'. Members first came 'to scoff', but they 'quickly transferred their allegiance from the CLC to the university. In every instance the CLC class closed'. A section of workers in South Wales has long regarded the WEA 'as a rival to the CLC'; they will, therefore, have nothing to do with it – even now. Prominent 'labour' leaders, on the other hand, are now 'fervent advocates of university Extra-Mural classes'.

There is another complicating factor. Employers, naturally, regard the CLC with profound distrust, and, today, are not a little suspicious of the WEA. Even the recent reaffirmation by the WEA of its original policy – 'to be non-political, non-partisan, non-sectarian' leaves them a little cold. They say that 'it protests too much' and that 'qui s'excuse, s'accuse'. He then drives home his main argument: that the proper body for all this is – *the university*; and quotes in support the Report of the Commission on Causes of Industrial Unrest (No. 7 Division):

> We would further suggest that the University is the proper medium for the education of the adult, and that University Tutorial classes should be established in every centre of industry in Wales in which political economy, industrial history, and such other subjects as bear upon the conditions and interests of the workers can be studied impartially under the guidance of skilled and recognised authorities.

'I would go on to say,' he adds, 'that in the case of Wales, the very first thing to be done, when national finance permits, is to remove the embargo on the establishment, by the universities, of extra-mural classes.' This memo is also dated 4 March 1926.

On 11 March, Percy replied to Millar saying that the ex-CLC tutors concerned 'seem willingly and loyally to have accepted the view that political propaganda must be eliminated from the class work'; and that the classes were subject to inspection by the Board and/or by the local authority 'and I am glad to say that according to my information, they are not conducted upon the lines which you have publicly advocated and which I have publicly condemned'.

Nevertheless, in spite of this, more minutes are passed between officials, about making discreet enquiries, in case the matter is raised again. One HMI (W.T. Williams, Carmarthen) says he is not satisfied with the classes. He has arranged to meet all the County Council members for the industrial area to 'discuss with them the whole question of the teaching of economics. I have little doubt ... that the members will emphatically agree that the classes as now organised must cease'.[99]

Exactly what happened to these classes and tutors is not, of course, our concern; but the episode does highlight the importance now attached to the university's role in adult education. In fact, as we have seen, extra-mural departments directly financed by the Board of Education (and not, therefore, having to rely for their funds on University Grants Committee finance, the distribution of which is determined by the university) came into being throughout the country; full-time staff expanded, and grants made available to finance classes. University extension classes expanded from 360 in 1924-25 to 537 in 1937-38 while a massive increase took place in the traditional tutorial type classes organised in collaboration with the WEA. In 1918-19, 147 tutorial classes were run with 3,404 students; in 1937-38, 882 classes with 14,953 students – these were all small group classes, following courses of systematic study under the tutorial guidance of university teachers.[100] Although (according to Kelly) working class representation still remained high in these tutorial classes (about 70 per cent), it was in the changing content of their studies that the shift of interest, characteristic of this period, was most evident – the swing from the social sciences (economic and industrial history, etc.) to philosophy, psychology, literature and music. It was here that the trend towards university-dominated humane studies expressed itself.

(ii) The WEA
The tutorial classes were, of course, jointly organised by the WEA and university; so the expansion just cited must be credited to the WEA as well; indeed, tutorial classes were the WEA's original specific contribution. But there was, in addition, a wide variety of more elementary forms of study which the WEA initiated, and which was seen as an essential part of its function. These included one-year, one-term and shorter courses, and here also there was a big expansion. Between 1924-25 and 1938-39 the number of such courses tripled – from 682 to 2,172, while the number of students attending

them more than doubled – from 17,000 to nearly 40,000.[101] When R.H. Tawney took over the presidency in 1928 there were 459 branches organised in sixteen district organisations, with 11,750 tutorial class students (three year courses) and 19,000 terminal and one-year class students. By 1939 the latter figure had grown to just under 40,000 students.[102]

In the period 1925-28, when the WEA made its drive on the unions, it went through a difficult period with its officials. The lurch to the left in 1925, already discussed, was reflected in changes in both honorary and full-time officials. Temple retired in 1925 specifically to allow the trade unions to be represented at the head of the WEA, and as we have seen, Fred Bramley took his place. On his untimely death a year later his place was appropriately taken by Arthur Pugh – 'the WEA's leading ambassador in trade union circles'.[103] But he resigned in 1928, and it was at this point that R.H. Tawney took over – an academic, but a very unusual one with close links with the labour movement. In the key job of secretary, MacTavish, of working-class origin, cracked up in the mid-1920s, finally resigning in 1928; Muir then took over, though he had been working as a full-time official since 1924; on his death in 1929 the secretaryship was taken over by A.S. Firth (in 1930) who also had close links with the trade union movement, having served for seven years as secretary to the TUCs Education Department; 'but the burden of WEA responsibility was too much for him; his health failed, and in 1934, after three months' sick leave, he was advised to transfer to less exacting work'. He was succeeded by Ernest Green, a man of strong character, who, as secretary of the Yorkshire district of the WEA, had carried through an aggressive campaign against the NCLC. Green was to hold office until 1950. The total full-time salaried staff of 45 in 1927-28 increased to 56 by 1937-38.[104]

But all was not plain sailing – in the matter of bias and politics – even for the WEA. The reaction to the left turn in 1925 has already been noted and, as we have seen, the organisation had now become suspect to some on the political right. A detailed account of the WEA's political troubles at this period is given in Roger Fieldhouse's essay in this book.

(iii) The NCLC and the Communist Party

On the whole it was the NCLC that made the running in trade union (and labour movement) education before 1926, even if the WEA had powerful support and was able to call on greater resources. This is because of the greater dynamic of the Plebs/NCLC grouping, and its

much deeper roots among the rank and file. (The WEA was forced to
operate from above – through full-time officials like Pugh; even Cole
had to work in this way – from outside.) The clearer and keener
political line of the NCLC tied in directly with the aspirations and
objectives of trade unionists in general. Yet in spite of the successes
in winning the support of great unions, and in forcing the TUC to
deal with them in terms of equality with the WEA (favoured by the
General Council), all was not well; the difficulties which arose were,
perhaps inevitably, linked with the basic conception which, however
much denied in words, involved the separation of educational from
industrial and political organisation and action.

This was the core and essence of the criticism from the left – the
Communist Party, which, although small, from the early 1920s played
an important role in the labour movement. Many of the early
members of the Communist Party were fully involved in the work of
Plebs and later of the NCLC – one or two as full-time organisers
(T.A. Jackson and Frank Jackson), or as members of the Plebs
Executive (Maurice Dobb). Among these were Tom Bell who had
grown up (as it were) in the militant Marxist educational and political
organisation, the Socialist Labour Party; and who in 1922 became the
first educational organiser for the Communist Party. Bell's
assessment of Plebs is, therefore, historically important and
interesting.

'The "independence", however, which the Plebs jealously
guarded', wrote Tom Bell in his autobiography, *Pioneering Days*,
'became a double-edged weapon.' To prove this 'independence' they
eschewed all political parties. Politics and political parties 'were
analysed and dissected in the classroom in the same abstract way as
economics and English grammar'. This became a challenge to those
who wished to involve the students in political action, as the SLP
found before the war.

> It was considered a virtue amongst many of the students to remain not
> only independent on matters of education, but aloof from party politics.
> We had the mortification of seeing splendid young militants becoming
> sterilised and inert before the question of a workers' party of struggle. To
> sit back and propound the problem became the acme of revolutionary
> intelligence – a positive hindrance to the growth of a revolutionary
> workers' party. It was not until after the formation of the Communist
> Party that this challenge was taken up, and fought out.[105]

So there developed a challenge from the left. But the matter was
complicated because in fact many of the leaders of the Plebs League
joined the Communist Party on or shortly after its foundation in 1920

(for instance, Raymond Postgate and the two Horrabins). At first, all went well. Members of the newly formed Communist Party contributed to the journal (*Plebs*); in March 1921 the Executive committee of the Communist Party sent a message of support to the annual Plebs 'Meet' and to the work of the league, 'hoping for close co-operation in educational propaganda'.[106] In April the *Plebs* editor (J.F. Horrabin) reciprocated by welcoming the new journal *Communist* edited by Francis Meynell. In July R.P. Dutt contributed a closely reasoned article to *Plebs* on 'Partiality and Truth' (incidentally of a much higher intellectual standard than the general run of *Plebs* articles). But in 1922 there was a change of attitude. The Communist Party set up its own educational organisation, as part of its overall re-organisation on Leninist principles, and this led to conflict. Tom Bell put it as follows:

> Simultaneously with these [organisational] changes another innovation, for Great Britain, was made by the starting of party training groups. Hitherto, the educational side of our movement was treated as a special branch, independent of the party. Marxist teaching was carried on through the Central Labour College movement, but in practice this CLC movement made the mistake of making Marxism an academic study without showing the need for a revolutionary political party. Starting of party training groups led to disputes with the Central Labour College and especially its leading group – the Plebs League, led by party members.[107]

'We did everything possible,' continues Bell, 'to convince such prominent Plebs leaders as Frank and Winnie Horrabin and to retain them for the Party, but without success.' As Bell puts it, 'They showed themselves unable to grasp the necessity for close connection between working-class education and revolutionary struggle, and ultimately they were to drift into the opportunist ranks.' Among the Plebs leaders, however, who did grasp (and therefore presumably accept) 'the importance of this innovation of party training groups, the name of Maurice Dobb is outstanding'.[108]

'Undoubtedly the Labour College movement had done yeoman pioneering work,' continues Bell, 'but now, with a centralised Leninist party, we had the responsibility of seeing that Marxism was rescued from the barren academic manner in which it had been presented.' Bell himself was made responsible for party education and propaganda.[109]

These internal discussions led to an open breach in 1922, highlighted by two sharp attacks on Plebs by R.P. Dutt. In the May number of the recently founded *Labour Monthly*, Dutt reviewed the first Plebs textbook to be published – on psychology.

The Plebs League is the most vigorous exponent of Marxism in this country. But the Marxism that the Plebs teaches is a *non-party* Marxism. Could there be a simpler contradiction of Marxism? Marxism in this country is a branch of learning. It is a case of Marx *versus* Marxism, as if the two were rivals on the same plane. Its exponents are academic in the highest sense, in that they teach without deducing the lessons from what they teach.

No concrete results emerge from this; learning is divorced from action. 'So the first proletarian textbook in this country is a textbook on ... psychology.'[110]

To this article of Dutt's (and the Communist criticism generally) *Plebs* published a careful reply. On the one hand the NCLC is being attacked for being Communist in disguise. On the other, Plebs and the NCLC are being criticised by some members of the Communist Party for *not* supporting the party.

We want it to be clearly understood, by Communist and non-Communists alike, that our policy is now, as it always has been, *working-class control of working-class education*. We are not, we never have been, and we do not intend to be, allied to any one *section* of the working class movement.

Unlike the WEA, however, Plebs does not stand for a 'broad' view of education. 'We stand for an education aiming at assisting the organised working-class movement to overthrow capitalism.'[111]

A year later, however, Dutt followed up his first article with a bitter and violent review of the second Plebs textbook, *An Outline of Modern Imperialism* (Mark Starr). This is characterised as a 'pathetic and abject failure', as an example of Plebs' 'barren science' and abstract class consciousness which leads only to 'Labour Party vagueness'. Widening the attack, Dutt refers to 'promising young men' who are sent to the Labour College for two years 'and come back budding snobs and trade union officials' – and to the 'arid dogma' of the college. The only reason for reviewing the book at such length is 'because the Plebs teaching is still widely looked to in this country as representative of Marxism, and only when we have completely exploded that myth can we lay the foundations of the real revolutionary movement in this country'.[112]

It seemed as if open warfare between the two bodies had now been declared; the dynamic, however, coming from the Communist Party – or at least from that section of it that saw salvation in the rigorous differentiation of the party from the broader movement. It appears, however, that more moderate policies now prevailed in the Communist Party. Later in 1923 Mark Starr (*Plebs*) contributed an article to *Labour Monthly* on the TUC negotiations, a definite appeal for the NCLC and *Plebs*,[113] while in July 1923 Dutt actually praises Plebs Textbook No. 4, *An Outline of Economic Geography*, characterising it as a positive stimulus.[114] Also in 1923 *Communist Review*, the official journal of the Communist Party, takes a very positive attitude in its reviews to the books published by Plebs; for instance to Raymond Postgate's *Revolution*.[115]

This initial clash, however, certainly represented a difference of view as to the implications of Marxist theory. If, as Marx said, the point of theoretical study (philosophy) is not contemplative, but to change the world, then some organisation was necessary; for Communists, this was the Communist Party. From now on, this grouping, based on Marxism and on the left of the labour movement, set out to integrate Marxist teaching with political and industrial action. At the same time the NCLC, which in 1926 subsumed the Plebs organisation and magazine, became inevitably, through its system of representation and government, transformed into an organisation providing educational services for the unions which themselves were now mainly concerned with survival and coexistence within capitalist society. Inevitably the bite, the sharpness of analysis and the militancy characteristic of the early work of the Plebs League suffered a decline; its successor in this respect was the Communist Party, with its own 'independent' but closely structured educational and propaganda activities.

Communists, however, continued to work in the Plebs League, at least at first. At the Communist Party's Sixth Conference held in May 1924, it was reported that a Committee has been set up following the 1922 Conference, consisting of members 'who had been interested in either IWCE classes, Plebs work, or practical teaching'. It was decided not to use 'the old lecture style of education classes', but the 'question and answer' method with small groups. After discussion with Communist Party members of the Plebs Executive, 'a statement of policy was drawn up for the use of party members working in the Plebs League', also a syllabus approved for general use in IWCE classes and a list of likely Communist Party tutors compiled. It was reported that 'Party Training Groups' had now been formed in every district (London and Glasgow having the best record), that syllabuses, bibliographies, etc., were being prepared.[116] In this way the experience gained in the last twenty or more years was brought directly into the Communist Party which now had some 5,000 members and, unlike the Labour Party, saw education as an essential aspect of its work. In 1925 it was reported that 90 classes (called 'training groups') were in existence with 800 members.[117]

As for the NCLC itself, classes run under its auspices reached a peak in the inter-war years of 1,234 in 1925-26; the actual student enrolment claimed also reached a maximum of 31,635 a year later (1926-27). Thereafter there was a 'steady decline' so that by 1937-38 the NCLC was claiming 728 classes with 13,274 students.[118] On the other hand (as with the WEA) this was compensated to some extent by an increase in the number of one day and weekend schools held, and what was claimed as a massive development of correspondence courses – from now on a specific feature of NCLC provision; in 1937-38 more than 10,000 students were enrolled in such courses, which covered an extremely wide range of subjects, though how many completed them is unclear.[119] While classes declined, however, an opposite tendency also showed itself in the great increase in the number of national trade unions affiliated; this reached a total of 36 in 1937, at which time the NCLC was organised in twelve divisions, employing fifteen full-time organising tutors. The trade union influence, as already pointed out, was found to be a moderating one – and directed towards promoting more specifically professional trade union education than wider economic and social issues.

Conclusion

As indicated at the start of this essay, the period covered, 1920-26, saw both an accelerating – even explosive – expansion of new forms of working-class adult education, and a heightening of long established conflicts concerning its control, content and direction. At this period the universities entered the scene to a growing extent, while the irruption of the Communist Party added a further complexity to an already involved situation. If Plebs and the NCLC on the one hand stood uncompromisingly for an *independent* approach, championing Marxism (as then understood) as its ideological standpoint while the WEA/WETUC nailed their flag to a non-partisan pluralism, new tendencies now showed themselves which began to blur the originally sharp divisions between these two sets of organisations, each with their protagonists and supporters within and around the broader labour movement. Some crucial questions, which still require analysis, arose during this period. Developments within the WEA, for instance, took contradictory forms. In the 1930s especially, this emerged more directly as a bulwark of the Labour right, yet by the 1940s and 50s it is probably true to say that there was more Marxism being discussed and studied in the WEA (and in the university extra-mural departments) than in the NCLC which, together with the journal *Plebs*, became the voice of the more extreme right-wing in the labour movement. Nor did the Central Labour College ex-students, with the exception of Aneurin Bevan, when faced with real economic problems as Ministers and trade union leaders following the Second World War, appear capable of adopting any but Treasury policies. In the coming decades these tendencies developed further until finally, in 1964, a new situation was crystallised with the demise of the NCLC and the assumption of overall control by the TUC. These issues are analysed and discussed in later essays.

The tradition of independent educational initiatives, however, proved tenacious – deeply structured, as it was, within historic forms of the labour movement. In the following essay, Edmund and Ruth Frow, focusing on one specific area (the North-West), analyse the widespread activities that developed here immediately after the Ruskin strike and the first formation of the Plebs League in 1909, so illuminating local developments that both preceded the events covered in the main part of this essay and took place through the early 1920s coincidentally with national developments. In the following essay, Margaret Cohen analyses the growth, development and organisational changes that took place in the independent sector up to the Second World War, then focusing again on the specific area also covered by the Frows for the earlier period. In the sixth essay, John McIlroy returns to the independent movement in his analysis of overall developments in the two decades following the Second World War.

Notes

[1] For an extended analysis of these initiatives, Brian Simon, *The Two Nations and the Educational Structure, 1780-1870* (London, 1974), first published as *Studies in the History of Education, 1780-1870* (London, 1960), Chs. 4 and 5 on 'The Workers' Movement and Education', 1790-1832, and 1832-1850 respectively.

[2] This phase is analysed in Brian Simon, *Education and the Labour Movement, 1870-1920* (London, 1965), Ch. 1, 'The Rise of Socialism and its Educational Implications'.

[3] For this strand of activity, Simon, *The Two Nations*, Ch. 3, 'The Middle Class and the Education of the Workers'.

[4] The material for this and the following paragraph is derived from Chapters 1 and 2 of my *Education and the Labour Movement*; see also Sheila Rowbotham, 'Travellers in a Strange Country: working class students, 1873-1910', *History Workshop*, 12, Autumn 1981.

[5] But see R.A. Lowe, 'Some Forerunners of R.H. Tawney's Longton Tutorial Class', *History of Education*, Vol. 1, No. 1, January 1972.

[6] The Ruskin Strike and the subsequent development of the Plebs League and the National Council of Labour Colleges is analysed in *Education and the Labour Movement*, Ch. 9, 'Developments and Conflicts in Adult Education, 1900-1920'. See also W.W. Craik, *Central Labour College* (London, 1964) Chapters 1 to 5, and J.P.M. Millar, *The Labour College Movement* (London, 1979), Ch. 1.

[7] William Temple's views on the value of education for the working class are clearly expressed in F.A. Iremonger's *William Temple*, (Oxford, 1948), Ch. 5. For Temple, the WEA 'was a sacrament – a sacrament of a passion for knowledge and for brotherhood in the pursuit of knowledge ... the whole personality ... must be integrated in the pursuit of learning', pp. 80-1.

[8] Simon, *Education and the Labour Movement*, p. 309.

[9] Iremonger, p. 86.

[10] Simon, *Education and the Labour Movement*, pp. 318ff.

[11] A valuable recent study in this field is John Attfield, *With Light of Knowledge: a hundred years of education in the Royal Arsenal Co-operative Society, 1877-1977* (London, 1981).

[12] Considerable space is deliberately devoted to the NCLC and Plebs in this essay, since, until recently, the books on adult education covering this period underestimate the impact of the work of these bodies. Exceptions include W.W. Craik, *The Central Labour College* (London, 1964), J.P.M. Millar, *The Labour College Movement* (London, 1979) and to some extent A.J. Corfield, *Epoch in Workers' Education* (London, 1969).

[13] T.A. Jackson, *Solo Trumpet* (London, 1953), p. 144. Jackson gives a vivid description of his work in the North-East; he found among the Geordies kindness, generosity, quick intelligence, deep earnestness, and, among the miners, a magnificent sense of courageous solidarity. See also his description of the crammed hall for his lecture series at Chopwell on 'Principles of Socialism', with Will Lawther as Chairman, pp. 154, 161-2. For Jackson, see Vivien Morton and Stuart Macintyre, *T.A. Jackson, a centenary appreciation (Our History*, Communist Party, Pamphlet 73, n.d.).

[14] Mellor was a close collaborator and friend of G.D.H. Cole, partnering him in his Guild Socialist and trade union period before and during the war. He joined the Communist Party on its foundation in 1921, after which 'their paths drew apart'. M. Cole, *The Life of G.D.H. Cole* (London, 1971), pp. 67-8.

[15] *Direct Action* (1920), p. 127. Mellor denies that education under capitalism can be 'above the battle' – for 'truth'. Class attitudes are instilled, particularly through the teaching of geography and history. 'A child leaves the elementary schools today completely ignorant of the facts of social life in the different periods of his country's development, but possessed of an amazing collection of dates of battles and a wide knowledge of the names of kings and queens ... Any serious attempt to teach history on the struggle of various classes to raise their status and win economic freedom would be frowned on by school managers and education authorities as a departure from the truth.' Ibid., 123-5.

[16] Ibid., pp. 127-37. At this stage, the CLC was organising local provincial classes.

[17] Ibid.

[18] W.W. Craik, *Central Labour College*, pp. 108, 114.

[19] Ibid., pp. 115-6.

[20] *Plebs*, March 1921.

[21] Ibid., June 1921.

[22] Ibid., July 1921.

[23] Sheffield, of course, has been the leading centre of the very radical shop stewards' movement of 1917-18.

[24] *Plebs*, July 1921.

[25] The sharpness of the struggle ahead, writes Lawther, 'in itself will help to kill the idea of education in "the humanities" being our primary need'.

[26] *Plebs*, August 1921.

[27] Ibid., September and October 1921. Titterington had moved the full Labour Party resolution on education, comprising the 'Bradford Charter', at the 1917 Labour Party Conference, (Simon, *Education and the Labour Movement*, pp. 347-50).

[28] *Plebs*, November 1921.

[29] See Craik, pp. 134-5, on Millar; see also Millar, pp. 45 ff. for biographical material.

[30] *Plebs*, January 1922.

[31] Craik, pp. 130 ff.

[32] *Plebs*, January 1922.

[33] Ibid., March 1922.

[34] Ibid., May 1922.

[35] Ibid., May 1922.

[36] Ibid., June 1922.

[37] The September issue of *Plebs* stated that this was incorrectly reported, and that the actual vote was 59:1!

[38] *Plebs*, August 1922.

[39] Corfield, p. 18.

[40] *Plebs*, September 1922.

[41] Corfield, pp. 18-20, gives a good description of this struggle, which resulted in a clear victory for the NCLC.

[42] By 1926 several other unions had affiliated; these included the ETU, many textile unions, the furnishing trade association, tailors and garment workers, public employees, sheet metal workers, brass and metal mechanics, and others. Corfield, pp. 20-1.

[43] Thomas Kelly, *A History of Adult Education in Great Britain* (2nd ed., Liverpool, 1970), p. 283.

[44] The NCLC, when first established, began to develop correspondence courses on a large scale. By 1926 it claimed 2,700 students, and this aspect of the work developed enormously in subsequent years. Of these, Corfield says they were 'well planned and prepared, ably drafted and efficiently administered'. (p. 21). This department was later run by J.P.M. Millar's wife and partner, Christine Millar.

[45] *Plebs*, February 1921.

[46] Ibid., June 1921.

[47] Ibid., July 1922.

[48] Ibid., August 1922.

[49] This unification was finally achieved in 1964; see pp.173 ff., and Clive Griggs, *The TUC and the Struggle for Education 1868-1925* (Brighton, 1983), Ch. 7.

[50] For MacTavish see Mary Stocks, *The Workers' Educational Association* (London, 1953) pp. 40-1, 96-7.

[51] Corfield, p. 5.

52 Ibid., pp. 7-12.

53 This is reprinted in full in Corfield, Appendix 1.

54 Ibid., p. 200.

55 This surely is the message of the tortuous officialese: 'If, however, it was organised by the Trade Unions themselves, an important public principle would be involved and the Board would require to consider whether public money could be devoted to education entirely controlled by Trade Unions'. Corfield, p. 204.

56 Ibid.

57 Ibid., p. 207.

58 Ibid., pp. 12-13.

59 Ibid., p. 14.

60 Ibid., pp. 15-16, 19-20.

61 Ibid., pp. 205-6.

62 Ibid., p. 31.

63 For instance, the claim in the statement of objectives that education for trade unionism is 'if rightly understood, more comprehensive than an education for citizenship; indeed the former includes the latter' seems a somewhat tortuous way of saying that the WEA's education scheme favoured (if it did) workers' control of industry. To develop 'the great human qualities' of loyalty, intelligence and efficiency 'in the interests of trade unionism' might mean various things; one of which *might* be workers' control.

64 G.D.H. Cole, *The Place of the WEA in Working Class Education*, (July 1924).

65 Corfield, 29-30.

66 Ibid., p. 33.

67 Ibid., p. 34.

68 The manifesto is reprinted in full in Corfield, pp. 236-40.

69 Corfield, p. 34. There was also a (presumably ironic) enquiry from the NCLC as to whether the manifesto in fact meant that the WEA 'favoured an education explicitly designed to bring about workers' control'. *Ibid.*,

70 Ibid., pp. 34-5.

71 Cole's somewhat ambiguous personality – and role in this period – is well caught in this pastiche by his friend, Maurice Reckitt (from Margaret Cole, p. 84).

Mr G.D.H. Cole
   is a bit of a puzzle
A curious role
   that of G.D.H. Cole
With a Bolshevik soul
   in a Fabian muzzle
Mr G.D.H. Cole
   is a bit of a puzzle.

72 The Parliamentary Committee was renamed the General Council in 1922.

73 *TUC Report*, 1922, pp. 143-4.

74 Ibid., 1921, pp. 362-5.

75 Ibid., 1922, p. 144.

76 Ibid., 1922, pp. 187 ff.

77 Ibid., 1922, pp. 187-93.

78 Ibid., pp. 193-5.

79 Ibid., p. 196.

68   *The Search for Enlightenment*

80 Ibid., pp. 198, 416-8. Ruskin College had survived the secession of 1909, and, of course, is today still an important centre of working class education. After a difficult period between the wars, it revived after 1945 when Lionel Elvin was appointed Principal, to be followed, in 1950, by H.D. Hughes. Staff, buildings and student numbers increased substantially from this period. Students followed courses leading to the award of the Oxford University Special Diploma in Social Studies, several also gaining Honours degrees at the University. Ex-students include MPs, Cabinet Ministers, trade union and Co-operative leaders at all levels. *The Story of Ruskin College* (Oxford, 1949; third revised edn 1968).

81 *TUC Report*, 1923, p. 80.

82 Ibid., 1924, pp. 202-03, 421-2.

83 Ibid., p. 423.

84 Corfield, p. 51.

85 The vote on the amendment reported to the President was 180,000 for the amendment, and 1,188,000 against. Immediately on receiving this information, the President said 'There must be somethig wrong in those figures'. The total possible vote was 4,300,000. However, before a recount was taken (or asked for) Hicks withdrew the amendment. *TUC Report*, 1924, p. 423; Corfield, p. 51.

86 This whole episode has been acutely analysed by R. Fieldhouse, in 'Voluntaryism and the State in Adult Education: the WEA and the 1925 TUC Education Scheme', *History of Education*, Vol. 10, No. 1, March 1981. The adverse reactions of the Board of Education (Eustace Percy) and local authorities to the WEA accepting such 'Objects' and other conditions, led to ambiguity, ambivalence and much deviousness by WEA spokesmen. In this article Fieldhouse indicates that acceptance of state (and local authority) support certainly carried with it clear restraints – a matter normally hotly denied by WEA spokesmen. The scheme is reprinted as an appendix to the article cited above. For more details of these difficulties, see the fifth essay in this volume, 'Bouts of Suspicion', (pp. 153-172) and the above article by Roger Fieldhouse.

87 Corfield, p. 52.

88 Ibid., p. 53.

89 *TUC Report*, 1926, pp. 89, 181-6, 349 ff.; Corfield, pp. 53-5. See also M. Cole's chapter on Easton Lodge, of which G.D.H. Cole hoped to be appointed as Principal, in Cole, pp. 147-52; and Craik, pp. 140-4. In 1946 the TUC passed a resolution on its role in adult education and an enquiry was established (see Ch. 6).

90 Craik, pp. 145 ff.

91 Kelly, p. 286.

92 A.L. Smith was Chairman, Mansbridge and Tawney among the members.

93 The Committee reported in 1919. Among other things it recommended that the provision of liberal education for adults be regarded by universities as a normal and necessary part of their functions; that each university should establish a department of adult education; that University Extension courses should be eligible for government grants; and that joint committees of education authorities, universities, and voluntary bodies be set up. Kelly, p. 267.

94 Kelly, pp. 268-9.

95 M. Cole, pp. 108-9.

[96] Public Record Office Ed 24/593; this is taken from Percy's draft of his speech. See *Education*, 14 January 1926.

[97] PRO Ed 24/593.

[98] Ibid.

[99] Millar sent a brief reply to Percy in which he asserted that the tutors in the Ammonford area 'naturally, as all N.C.L.C. tutors would do, played a prominent part in the recent dispute, thus putting their educational policy into practice'. (16 March 1926). On this W.T. Williams (HMI) minutes: 'One tutor, who takes two classes, was concerned in the Ammonford riots, but only in a minor way. He was one of a hostile crowd, but did not play an active part. He appeared at the Assizes, but was acquitted. None of the others, so far as I can ascertain, were in any way connected with the riots.' This was within a few weeks of the General Strike. Ibid.

[100] Kelly, p. 270.

[101] Ibid., p. 273.

[102] Mary Stocks, *The Workers' Educational Association* (London, 1953), p. 102; Kelly, p. 273.

[103] Stocks, p. 101.

[104] Ibid., p. 114.

[105] Tom Bell, *Pioneering Days*, (London, 1941), p. 84.

[106] *Plebs*, March 1921.

[107] Bell, pp. 261-2.

[108] Dobb continued as a member of the Plebs EC for many years.

[109] Bell, p. 262.

[110] *Labour Monthly*, Vol. 2, No. 5, pp. 429-31. It should, however, be made clear that *Labour Monthly* was not and never became an *official* journal of the Communist Party.

[111] *Plebs*, November 1922.

[112] *Plebs*, November 1922.

[112] *Labour Monthly*, April 1923.

[113] Mark Starr, 'The TUC and Worker Education', *Labour Monthly*, Vol 5, 1923.

[114] *Labour Monthly*, Vol. 6. In 1925 the *Labour Monthly* carried an article by A.M. Robertson, Acting Principal of the Labour College, on IWCE (Vol. 7).

[115] *Communist Review*, Vol. 3 (May 1922 to April 1923).

[116] *Report of Sixth Conference of the Communist Party of Great Britain*, May 1924, p. 75.

[117] The often complex, and shifting, relationship between the Communist Party and Plebs is discussed in some detail in Stuart Macintyre, *A Proletarian Science, Marxism in Britain 1917-1933* (Cambridge, 1980, republished Lawrence and Wishart, 1987), see especially Ch. 3, *passim*. This book contains much material closely relevant to the issues discussed in this chapter, though its main focus is the nature of 'British Marxism' in this period. Jonathan Rée's *Proletarian Philosophers, Problems of Socialist Culture in Britain, 1900-1940* (Oxford, 1984) also discusses the Communist Party/Plebs relationship in an interesting way (see especially Chapter 4); this 'essay' is basically a disillusioned philosophic/historical analysis of British Marxism (especially 'dialectical materialism'). Both these books contribute to an understanding of the different tendencies discussed in this chapter, though both focus more specifically on the indigenous development of Marxist studies within the Plebs and Labour College movement and the Communist Party. The specific issue of

the relations between the Communist Party and the Plebs movement is also discussed in some detail in Andy Miles, 'Workers' Education: the Communist Party and the Plebs League in the 1920s', *History Workshop*, No. 18, Autumn 1984, and in Anne Phillips and Tim Putnam, 'Education for Emancipation: the Movement for Independent Working Class Education 1908-1928', *Capital and Class*, Vol. 10, Spring 1980, pp. 18-42. This article attempts an overall interpretation of the significance of the Plebs/Labour College movement of considerable interest.

[118] Kelly, p. 283.

[119] See *Plebs*, February 1939 and February 1959 for historical material and statistics. Figures for enrolments on NCLC correspondence courses may be misleading; there is no published information available relating to numbers completing these courses. General experience would indicate a completion rate of about one in five.

Edmund and Ruth Frow

2 The Spark of Independent Working-Class Education: Lancashire, 1909–1930

Among the students who rejected attempts by Oxford University to impose a concept of 'liberal objective' standards on the curriculum at Ruskin College in 1909 were two trade union representatives from the North-West. They had been sent by their unions so that they could gain knowledge and confidence to fit them to play a more active and, possibly, leading role in their workshop struggles. Like S.O. Davies, later an MP, they decided that they had 'had quite enough of a bourgeois and capitalist college' and dreaded to place the education of their class in the hands of people who 'had their names coupled with Lloyd George, Balfour and company, and people of this kind'.[1]

Harold Kershaw of the Amalgamated Society of Carpenters and Joiners and Jack Owen of the Amalgamated Society of Engineers were the two Lancashire men among those who responded to the call in the third issue of the *Plebs* magazine to demonstrate solidarity with Denis Hird, the dismissed Principal of Ruskin, by taking strike action. On their return to Lancashire, Harry Kershaw and Jack Owen immediately started work. Kershaw's name appears as the reporter of Plebs Meets and as tutor and Secretary of Plebs classes in the period before 1914. Jack Owen became the first Lancashire organiser of the Plebs League. He was a lively speaker with a rich fund of humour. He was an active trade unionist and during the First World War, when he went to London to work at Woolwich Arsenal, he was elected President of the London District Committee of the Amalgamated Society of Engineers. In 1920, he wrote a pamphlet, *To engineers (and other wage slaves)* to which Tom Mann wrote a foreword. Back in Manchester, he was elected to the City Council on which he served

71

until he left the Labour Party in 1939 to join the Communist Party. During the Second World War he worked as a journalist on the *Daily Worker* and contributed a weekly feature, 'Workshop Notes'. He joined the National Union of Journalists and was active on their behalf. He died in May 1957 at 70 years of age, after ten years of serious illness.

The League of Plebs had been set up to obtain control of Ruskin College in the interests of the working class and maintain it by democratic government. Having demonstrably failed in that objective, they announced that 'the object of Plebs must be to assist in the establishing of a new educational structure definitely controlled by organised Labour'.[2]

Following the strike, a Central (residential) Labour College (CLC) was established, first at Oxford and later in London, but equally significant developments followed in the localities as the strikers returned home to institute local classes in Independent Working Class Education (IWCE). The concept of 'independence' in education stressed that facts had to be looked at in a working-class way, not in that 'other way which is some-other-class-way'.[3] The motto of the Plebs League, 'I can promise to be candid, but not impartial', made the situation clear. Noah Ablett, a young Welsh miner, asserted that 'the working class must work out its own salvation'.[4] This was interpreted locally in terms of each class being financially self-supporting, and in the rejection of professional tutors and the democratic organisation of the students whereby responsibility was accepted by a more advanced member for presentation of the material for discussion. Subjects recommended for classes were sociology, history and economics and, as Edward Gill of the South Wales Miners' Federation advised, there 'should be the diffusion of ideas most likely to assist the labour movement generally'.[5] There was an implicit acceptance that the aim was not only to provide political and trade union activists with ammunition in their struggles within the capitalist system, but also to educate socialists whose objective was to change it.

It was this concept of Independent Working Class Education, born and nurtured in the heady days of 'The Great Unrest', which survived the First World War and grew into a movement that, in the 1920s was adopted by a number of influential trade unions which, while never as extensive as the activists hoped, did train a generation of men and, to a lesser extent, women to play their part in the labour movement.

It is interesting that the first record in July 1909 of a Plebs class in Lancashire was at Wigan. A poem was read out obviously in

Lancashire dialect. Mrs Taylor, who presented the poem to the class, asked for help in interpreting its meaning. It featured at a second class and the report in *Plebs* indicates that gentle leg-pulling was indulged in at Wigan because a working man, John, was able to elucidate what the host, 'a student well versed in Sanskrit, the Zend, and other ancient languages' could not comprehend. As the subject of the poem was 'Men's Occupation' and among the topics raised was that of 'kompensashun' following loss of sight, it seems likely that the students were a mixed group and included workers, who would be only too familiar with having to beg after a crippling accident, and middle-class people less likely to understand.

Classes multiplied in the North-West. Harold Kershaw was able to report to the second Annual Meet of the Plebs League in 1910 that they commenced in October and continued until April; that there were seven classes each week with a total of 150 students and that two of these had been granted scholarships to enable them to attend the Central Labour College in September.

One class, of which some records have survived, was held in Oldham in 1911. It met on a Thursday evening with the exception of Christmas and New Year. James Smith was the Secretary and there were 27 students. The tutor was Frank Jackson, a member of the Amalgamated Society of Engineers who later moved to London. Each session began at 8 p.m. and studied the economics outline drawn up by Meredith F. Titterington. One member of the class was expected to have made a preparatory study of a section of the syllabus and to open discussion on it. The hour and a half a week cost twopence and a register of attendances and payments was kept. Since the session lasted for eighteen weeks, the Oldham members paid a total of 3 shillings each.

Among the students were at least six women. It is likely that the Miss Smith who made regular attendances until the last three sessions was Alice Smith of the Lancashire Textile Operatives who, together with Mary Howarth from Bury, received a scholarship from the Women's League of The Central Labour College for full-time attendance for the year 1913-14. Returning from London, Alice Smith took over the class on philosophic logic which proved to be the most successful ever held in Oldham.[6] The attendance was the most regular of any class and 'the results of the teaching' were 'most marked'.

This complimentary report was contributed to *Plebs* magazine by fellow student, George Mearns, also a member of the 1911 Oldham class. 'The students', he wrote, 'all feel much indebted to her [Alice

Smith] for the work she has done'. This attitude towards a woman indicated that the education of women was recognised as a prime responsibility of the Plebs League. 'One of the undoubted dangers to trade unionism today, is the uneducated, unorganised woman worker,' was the assessment in an article in *Plebs*, and men like George Mearns took it to heart.[7] He encouraged Alice Smith, who later became Alice Pratt, and articles by her were published in *Plebs* during 1916. When she and Mary Howarth returned from their year at the Central Labour College in 1914, they announced that they were able and prepared to speak 'on behalf of the College to the working women of Lancashire'.

Alice Smith did not find her education easy. She continued playing a part in trade union work as well as in IWCE, but admitted in the early 1920s having nearly wept over Joseph Dietzgen's *The Positive Outcome of Philosophy* and she made an impassioned plea for a simplified textbook on the subject – something the average man 'can lap up with his Quaker Oats – something he can read (and understand) as he runs'.[8] Her difficulties probably reflected a weakness in the work of the Labour College classes which may have contributed to a narrowing of the circle of students in later years. However, her suggestion was accepted and her proposed outline for a textbook was agreed at the Bradford Textbook Conference in 1920.

Mary Howarth later became a full-time trade union official and other members of the 1911 Oldham class made contributions to the life of the town and the well-being of their fellow citizens. George Mearns was an active member of the Foundry Workers' Union both as secretary of the local branch and as a member of the district committee. Mrs Mearns, who only managed to attend the first four or five lectures, fully supported him in his work and when he died handed the records that he had accumulated to be preserved as an important part of labour history.[9]

The content of the classes run by Plebs in the North-West at this time varied considerably – including drama, dialect work and poetry. The students were young men and women who more than likely had left school to go to work half-time in a cotton mill at the age of twelve and who were hungry for education which they saw as the stepping stone to emancipation or relief from the drudgery to which they were condemned. The basic content of the classes was therefore focused on scientific socialism – the analysis of the economic situation as elucidated by Karl Marx and Frederick Engels. This not only explained the present, but showed the way forward to a better world in which working people would have control over their lives. It is interesting that many trade union officials and labour movement activists who were young workers before the First World War gained their knowledge and debating experience in Plebs league classes.

A typical example was the tutor of the pre-first World War Oldham class, Frank Jackson (not to be confused with the building trade Frank Jackson who edited *The Building Workers' Leader* and towards the end of his life worked in the Communist Party Library) whose ten-penny fare from Rochdale to Oldham was meticulously recorded in the class accounts. He was an engineer who played a part in the metal trade union. He moved to London during the war and became a part-time tutor at the Central Labour College. Jackson wrote articles and letters to *Plebs* always stressing the importance of Independent Working Class Education.

Education classes went under a variety of names. Some called themselves Plebs League Classes, some Labour College Classes or Central Labour College Classes. Until the formation of the National Council of Labour Colleges after the war, there was a confusion of identity. Students were not all of one political persuasion, nor were they all members of the Plebs League. In the Oldham class list there are eight non-members noted in the front of the exercise book which served as the register. It is a fair assumption that they were not members of the League although that is not specified.

The spark of IWCE, once ignited in Lancashire, spread rapidly. It would be an exaggeration to say that it developed into a mass movement, but it can certainly be asserted that it grew and became influential. As early as February 1912, it was reported in *Plebs* that a group of classes had been formed under the name of the Mersey District Branch of the Central Labour College. They were following a course of economics under the guidance of tutor Nun Nicholas of the South Wales Miners' Federation. The reporter was Jack Burt who was Secretary of St Helens Socialist Society. He explained that he had attended a course of lectures in industrial history given by W.W. Craik and that he then set to work and, by means of 'letters, visits, chats and lectures', had inspired the formation of classes in Wigan, Warrington, Birkenhead, Liverpool (Kensington) and Ashton-in-Makerfield. St Helens had 50 students and the others about 30. Each class was run as an adjunct of and housed by the local Socialist Society.

A fairly clear picture of the St Helens class has been preserved. Jack Burt explained that there were 'ten members of the local Labour Party Executive including two councillors, one ex-councillor, three ex-candidates for the Council, members of Labour Clubs, trade unions, and Women's Labour League, as well as members of the Socialist Society'. He added,

> Here side by side sit political Labourists and anti-Labourists and even men from rival clubs, eagerly listening to the 'tale unfolded' of exploitation and economic wrong, of social evolution and social salvation. Here Christian and Atheist, Catholic, Anglican and Non-Conformist with one consent 'hear the words of the gospel', the gospel alone that will inspire working-class solidarity and enthuse the wage-slave class with hope and courage to revolt against our oppressors.[10]

This picture of the St Helens class is continued after the war in 1920, when Robert Davies tells in his autobiography how he joined the last lecture of the session and found that a few of the members were proposing to restart the Socialist Society to which his father and uncles had belonged before the war. He found the students 'a very mixed lot'. Given the job of selling *Plebs*, he raised the sale from seven to a couple of dozen copies in two months. As a reward, he was appointed as delegate to attend a conference in Liverpool in 1920 to discuss the formation of a District Communist Party. As he remembered,

> This conference was held in the rooms of the British Socialist Party at Marmaduke Street, Edge Hill, Liverpool[11] and I remember that the Chairman was the man who had been the lecturer at the Labour College Class in St Helens. He went under the name of Jim Manus but I was told that this was not his real name as he had a good job with the Cunard Shipping Company and was afraid of being victimised. The Secretary of the conference was the secretary-lecturer of the Liverpool Labour College, Jack Hamilton.[12]

By the time the third Annual Meet of the Plebs League was held in London in August 1912 the report from Lancashire sounded impressive. Classes of approximately twenty students each had been established at Bury, Rochdale, Oldham, Waterfoot, Radcliffe, Manchester and Stockport. This list is not complete because there was certainly a flourishing group at Wigan. The Bury class had twelve local trade union or socialist organisations affiliated to it – an interesting portent of future developments.

Rochdale, centre of interest in the Co-operative movement, had a history of involvement in working-class education. It supported the well known Tawney Extra-Mural Class, it had a thriving Workers' Educational Association group as well as an IWCE class which received £6 annually from affiliation fees. In 1913, the president of the Trades Council, James Bell, took the chair at a famous debate between the exponents of IWCE and the WEA as to 'which institution provides the best education for the work people, the CLC or the WEA'. According to the report that Frank Jackson sent to *Plebs*, it was a resounding victory for the CLC.[13]

By 1913, the Rochdale classes had formed themselves into a branch of the Central Labour College. This had nine affiliated societies and a grant of 10 shillings from the Trades Council. The branch ran the classes through a General Council at which representatives from the affiliated groups and the amalgamated classes joined together to discuss policy and organisation. They had the nucleus of a well used library and Frank Jackson who sent the report to *Plebs* asked other areas to comment or add suggestions from their experience.[14]

The outbreak of war in 1914 obviously affected the work of IWCE seriously. Early that year there was a report of four classes in the Manchester area, at Sale, Hyde, Openshaw and South Salford, at which 100 students, as a result of their attendance, 'will be a finer and better equipped set of men and women capable of lighting the torch of discontent in the minds of others in the working-class movement'. For the remainder of 1914 there were no further reports from any South Lancashire classes.

The problems of the wartime situation presented a challenge to the enthusiasts who were intent on acquiring an education. Early in 1915, Rochdale, ever a leading influence, provided four lectures on four consecutive days at which W.W. Craik developed the subject of 'An Introduction to Social Sciences'.[15] With an average attendance of 23 students and a maximum of 32 they then felt confident enough to hand over the rest of the course to local lecturers. This promising experiment was followed by a course of eleven lectures on 'Philosophic Logic' given by W.T. Jones. Of the 24 students, seventeen were new and these showed 'the keenest interest all through'. Harold Kershaw gave four popular lectures on 'Philosophic Logic', presumably at a less exalted level, and followed with a course on 'The Materialist Conception of History'. As an afterthought, Frank Jackson explained that since most of the students were having to work overtime, the classes were being held on Sunday mornings. Of course, Rochdale always led the field in the education stakes, but such activity in the face of grave difficulties shows how exceptional they were.[16]

A meet was held in August 1915, but there were reports from only three South Lancashire classes, at Rochdale, Bury and Oldham. 1916 was even worse. The Central Labour College staff were called to national service and the college was forced to close. Locally, the situation was barely contained by the stalwarts willing to keep classes going in the face of severe financial and organisation problems.

Many of the Plebs League members were also members of the Independent Labour Party and refused to participate in a war which they considered to be in the interests of capital and against the interests of labour. Several were jailed for refusing military service.

This development, however, was not entirely negative, as those who found themselves in prison also found a rich soil in which to sow the seeds of IWCE. Ernest Faulkner of Hyde, for example, met some Plebeians in Leeds Gaol and, when he returned to Hyde in 1920, spent much of his life encouraging others to participate in IWCE.

Oldham succeeded in keeping its class going. George Mearns reported that Frank Jackson had again been the tutor for a course on economics and that he had 'been of very great assistance to them in unravelling the many knotty points in the subject'. Alice Smith gave an address to a local Debating Society on 'Working Class Independence in Education'. Rochdale also reported a class of over twenty students tutored by W.H. Horsfield to which twelve labour organisations were affiliated.[17]

Although the prospects of IWCE must have looked rather grim in 1916, there were two straws in the wind which augured well for the future. One was the report of the Assistant Secretary of Manchester District of the National Union of Railwaymen, Mr F.G. Temple, that his council had 'wisely decided that education, from a Labour stand-point, is an important phase of its work'. Classes had therefore been inaugurated on Sunday mornings at Manchester and Stockport at which Robert Holder, who was both a railwayman and a former student of the Central Labour College, was the tutor. Robert Holder was also visiting branches and doing propaganda work on the educational side. As Mr Temple remarked, 'Should this bloody conflict end before all our young men are sacrificed to Moloch, one can confidently look forward to a great extension of this work in the near future.[18]

The second indication of a happier future arose in letters written in *Plebs* from Ashton-under-Lyne. 'S.W.' flew to the defence of Robert Blatchford whose jingoism had offended J.F.H. (F.J. Horrabin). Horrabin accused S.W. of 'sticky sentimentality' and, rising to the bait, 'S.W.' outlined his career which ranged from work on the Canadian Pacific Railway to coal-mining in Pennsylvania. He revered Blatchford for having taught him to think. Perhaps there is a connection between 'S.W.'s' fifty years of having his 'nose applied to the industrial grindstone' and the fact that by 1922 R. Waters (his son?)

was secretary of a Labour College to serve Ashton and district.

As the war dragged to an end, there was evidence that the need for IWCE was appreciated by ever increasing numbers of people. In *Plebs* J.F. Horrabin stressed that the need for the magazine after eight years of publication was 'as great as ever'. He reminded Plebeians that they must realise 'something of the possibilities of the movement and the spirit in which it is being carried on'. Pallister Barkas commented in an article on 'Provincial Organisation' that there was

> a big push on in more places than the Somme. The Central Labour College Classes are the most important agencies at work in the Industrial Labour Movement. They will have immense influence on the future history of the T.U. Movement in this country.[19]

Certainly the Manchester classes organised by the National Union of Railwaymen with Robert Holder as tutor proved to be a resounding success. At the February District Council meeting in 1917, a resolution was passed.

> Having heard the report of the Tutorial Classes held during the last six months, we are convinced of the importance of this kind of education and the necessity for its extension among our members, in order that the new form of Industrial Organisation may be understood, and therefore made capable of meeting the problems which will confront Labour in the near future.[20]

After completing his engagement with the NUR, Robert Holder was invited to spend a month at Warrington at their expense. It was arranged that the district should be canvassed and an attempt made to get classes going elsewhere. The local British Socialist Party (BSP) invited Holder to deliver four lectures on 'The Need for Working-Class Education', and later made a grant of £3 towards the working expenses of the classes. Negotiations were opened with Widnes Trades and Labour Council which resulted in a class being formed there. Later, a second class was started in Warrington under the auspices of the Engineering Amalgamation Committee. J.H. Potter, who made the report, went on to say that classes in Warrington, Widnes and Wigan were certainties and that St Helens and Earlestown were possibilities. However, Robert Holder was called up before the arrangements could be finalised and the Editor of *Plebs* called on South Lancashire Plebeians to show their appreciation of his work 'in the best possible way – by carrying through a vigorous educational campaign'.[21]

After two and a half years of war, bubbles began to surface indicating that there was a ferment of unrest among the working class. Industrial unrest which began in the South Wales coalfield and spread to the Clyde now penetrated into Lancashire. Rank-and-file activists needed a forum where they could obtain clarity on what was happening. They also wanted to discuss the news that was coming from Russia where the Czar had been overthrown and a revolutionary workers' government later installed.

The Plebs League activists were not the only ones to appreciate the need for increased education for the working class. In a report of the Industrial Unrest Commissioners in Wales and Monmouthshire, the advice was given that the state should provide adult education of a 'broad', 'impartial' and 'humanistic' character as a corrective to all methods of study of a partisan character undertaken 'for propagandist objects'. Commenting that trade unions had supported the movement for IWCE organised in the Labour College and its classes, the commissioners pointed out that

> of late the workers have both widened and narrowed their outlook. Improvement of status, rises in wages, have all proved ineffective against the more obvious pressure of capitalist economy and the patent gambling in the necessities of life. This has been taken advantage of by teachers and leaders, and out of it has developed a form of class-consciousness increasingly powerful and deliberate of purpose. The worker as a class, has, they maintain, been exploited; as a class he must seek and win his freedom ... Thus the education which he asks for and receives tends, though intensive, to be partial ... Economics is often degraded into a gross materialistic conception of cause and effect, and the essential spirituality of education is neglected or forgotten.

Having thus stated the position with clarity and commendable insight, they proceeded to suggest 'that further facilities should therefore be granted for the spread of education and of knowledge – not knowledge in the narrow limited sense of equipment, but knowledge sought in the spirit of truth and pursued for its own ends'. *Plebs* correctly interpreted this report as a testimonial to the effectiveness of their classes and determined to redouble their efforts.[22]

Working-class education, which, in 1917, had begun shrouded in the gloom of the wartime situation, began to pick up during the year. Rochdale even offered to supply tutors to other areas from their ranks. The *Plebs* comment was that any class which 'despite the Military Service Acts having removed some of its most effective workers, can announce in this way that it has a reserve of trained and willing teachers for use where needed, is a success indeed!'[23] Both Wigan and Warrington determined to go ahead with Robert Holder while Bolton appeared on the scene with a request for interested readers to contact J. Leach if they were interested in setting up a class.

Manchester reported through George Peet at the commencement of the class year in 1917-18 that Openshaw, Salford and Stockport were in business. Moston Socialist Society, which was affiliated to the Plebs League, was organising a conference of trade union and labour organisations to be held at the Co-operative Hall in Lightbowne Road on a Sunday evening in November. The aim of the conference was to start education classes.

Towards the end of 1917 several Plebs publications were issued and these played an important part in developing the IWCE concept throughout the following decade. 1918 showed considerable gains. Oldham, for example, reported early in the year that they had 75 students on their register. This was a workshop class arranged to suit the convenience of men working on shifts.

The value of steady painstaking work was exemplified in Tom Yates. Writing from Manchester he said that during the war he had been the only Plebeian living and working in the area. But after the Socialist Society affiliated and organised a conference addressed by a comrade Claxton on economics and industrial history, requests for classes came from all round. The old man said modestly that he had not done the work, but admitted to 'pegging away at a few others till they became more enthusiastic than himself'. He ended by saying that he felt he had not lived in vain.[24]

Another significant development in Manchester was a class at Crossley Motors' factory where 109 students studied economics. In Moston the enthusiasm of the students was such that they refused to cancel classes even on the Christmas or New Year holidays.[25]

In Liverpool, a name started to be mentioned that was to become very well known over the years, John (sometimes Jack) Hamilton. He was the tutor at three flourishing classes. One was organised under the auspices of the National Union of Railwaymen, Liverpool and North Wales Council; this was held in the Birkenhead Trades and Labour Rooms in Argyle Street. Another was held at the Building Workers Industrial Union Social Club in Mill Lane, Islington, while the third gathered on Sundays at the Garston Woodcutting Machinists' Club. All three classes were studying 'The Modern Working Class Movement' and, in each case, the secretary was a long standing member of the Plebs League.

By April 1918, Manchester had taken another step forward. A Plebs District Council was formed with a literature secretary, E. Bradshaw, a treasurer, Comrade Taylor and secretary, J. McGee. Other districts were invited to follow this example in the secretary's report.[26]

On the centenary of the birth of Karl Marx in May 1918, a demonstration was organised by the newly formed District Council at which J.T. Walton Newbold, a member of the teaching staff at Manchester University, was the main speaker, supported by W. Gee, W. McLaine and others. The May issue of *Plebs* was devoted to centenary articles on Marx and aspects of Marxism.

The proposed Plebs districts were formalised at the Meet in August when it was suggested that among the seven divisions one should cover Lancashire and Cheshire. Amalgamation was in the air in the post-war years. The Amalgamated Engineering Union and the Amalgamated Union of Building Trades Workers were both formed in 1920 and the discussions which preceded their formation must have influenced the Plebs League. But the confidently expected increase in IWCE as a result of post-war activity made such rationalisation an obvious step. The pre-war development of the movement had been on a very ad hoc basis.

John Hamilton's long association with IWCE in Liverpool as well as nationally began in earnest in 1918. A conference was held in September in the Clarion Cafe in Lord Street at which J.T. Murphy[27] spoke on the general question of education and G. Jones[28] took the chair. Delegates represented 41 organisations and a bumper literature sale was reported. The 78 delegates were from such differing groups as Liverpool Trades Council, the NUR District Council, the Women's Co-operative Guild, the Fabian Society as well as many trade union and political branches. So successful was this conference that a further one was held the following month. Meanwhile, classes were being held at Liverpool, Edgehill, Kirkdale, Garston and Birkenhead.

Liverpool claimed that it was the centre of a big revival of educational interest, but it was not alone. Alex Evans of Wigan was taking two classes and said that there was 'a veritable boom of classes (or demands for classes) in Lancashire'.[29]

With such interest and participation in the classes, divergent ideas were inevitable. There was an exchange of letters in *Plebs* during October and November in which Walton Newbold supported the proposed democratisation of the League through the district organisations. He pointed out that, at the outset, the League had been formed from a 'fraternity of students, comparatively few in number and almost entirely concerned with the propagation of their ideas'. Recent industrial struggles necessitated a broadening and extension of the work. He thought that direction from the top by the Central Labour College and the Officials and Executive Committee of the Plebs League had to give way to rank and file direction.

Winifred Horrabin sprang to the defence of the status quo.[30] She put the usual case of an official who is overburdened and would be only too pleased if more rank and file assistance were forthcoming. 'We have certain principles very definitely laid down, and these principles have to be carried out.' The next thing was to get the work done 'and the Plebs has always been fortunate in finding someone willing to do four persons' work', so this difficulty was overcome. If that was 'direction from the top' or 'instruction by leaders' or even 'control by elders', anyone could 'take her share of it tomorrow!'[31] This polarisation of those who wanted central control and those who wanted the districts to develop with at least some autonomy continued and increased in intensity over the succeeding months.

Winifred Horrabin, on whom had fallen the burden of carrying on the organisation during the war years, was clearly nettled by the decision to reorganise the classes on clearly defined district lines. She wrote a reasoned article explaining why it was not quite so straight forward as might at first appear. When the Central Labour College had to close because the staff were called up, the Plebs League had undertaken the organisation of provincial classes. There was no uniformity of size or distribution of the classes. For instance, she quoted Liverpool and Manchester both of which already called themselves 'districts' and consisted of a number of classes grouped together with affiliated trade union branches. At the same time in other parts of Lancashire there were 'numerous branches entirely unconnected with either Liverpool or Manchester'. Moreover she pointed out that many classes were run under the auspices of trade unions, councils or other labour organisations. In addition there was the complication that the Central Labour College was due to reopen and that would lead to competition for affiliation between the College and the proposed Plebs League Districts. Mrs Horrabin suggested that a special conference should be held to discuss the whole question of future organisation. This point was the subject of debate at the Annual Meet in 1919 when J.P.M. Millar threw the cat among the pigeons by announcing that a Scottish Labour College was already in existence and stating categorically that affiliations from Scotland would automatically go to it.

It was obvious that the end of the war and the return of 'young men in a hurry' made some reform of the relationship between the Plebs League and the Central Labour College essential. Frank Jackson calmed some doubts by explaining that there were some classes where only one or two Plebeians supplied the motivating thrust whilst at the other extreme there were branches of the League where all students were members. Mark Starr interpreted the relevant rule as meaning that

> although the circumstances of its foundation and subsequent existence had given the Plebs a special interest in the London College, there was absolutely nothing, implied or stated, in its constitution which bound it to support one institution as against others with the same aims.

This ruling effectively ended the formative stage of development of Independent Working Class Education and marked the start of a new phase. From the end of 1919 the steady growth of classes multiplied and diversified to serve the needs of each locality.

The urgency with which men and women sought education after the war gave impetus to these developments. Many of those who obtained work felt the need to equip themselves to play an adequate part in the struggles which they were certain were before them. The impact of the Russian Revolution in 1917 acted as a spur, and the young men who had experienced war or prison determined to effect a change in society – and the quicker the better. Fresh names began to appear as class secretaries and some of these remained stalwart supporters of IWCE for many years in their turn.

The delayed re-opening of the Central Labour College in October 1919 probably helped the localities to develop. It became apparent that centres of activity were taking shape predictably in the industrial centres of Scotland, Wales, Lancashire and Yorkshire. These identifiable groupings of classes and activity obviously had to be co-ordinated and organised.

Manchester began 1919 with a lose amalgamation calling itself the 'Manchester District Plebs League'. They broke with previous practice by running a tutorial class during the summer months. The tutor was Fred Casey and he lectured on the first eight chapters of *Capital*.[32] Later, in 1922, Fred Casey published a book entitled *Thinking – An Introduction to History and Science*. On the centenary of Joseph Dietzgen's birth in 1928, Casey published *Dietzgen's Logic. A Plain Introduction to the Positive Outcome of Philosophy*. Later still, in 1933, South-East Lancashire Labour College published a collection of Casey's popular lectures as *Method in Thinking*.[33] The preface claimed that the book was 'unique as a popular presentation of the much misrepresented Dialectical Materialism – an essential part of the theoretical system for which Karl Marx was mainly responsible'.

Casey was not, perhaps, the man or woman in the street's answer to popular education, but there were other straws blowing in the wind while his students struggled with *Capital* in the summer weather. J. McGee announced in *Plebs* in May that a Labour College at which classes in Marxian economics, industrial history and social science were to be held was opening at 32a Dale Street, Manchester. The report of the opening in the June number of *Plebs* stated that 'Manchester has been successful in establishing a Labour College in the centre of the City convenient for all, whether by train or tram.' Tom Bell of Glasgow chaired a meeting at this college at which students from classes within a seven mile radius of the city were represented. There were also delegates from trade unions and other labour organisations. Harold Kershaw of Rochdale, one of the original Plebs strikers at Ruskin, outlined the subjects to be taught and indicated that as well as the traditional economics and industrial history, there would be classes in grammar and mathematics. The College was to open daily from ten in the morning until ten at night. As McGee commented, 'Great interest in the experiment was expressed and all present agreed that the College was just what was wanted in the Manchester area to arouse and to focus interest and support.'[34]

The years following its formation were, for the Manchester Labour College, very successful. 1919–20 saw 25 classes catering for 450 students. There were 24 affiliated trade unions, one Trades Council and three Labour Party Branches.[35] In the following year the subjects offered were extended to include history of trade unionism, biology, evolution, philosophy and logic. Classes, especially for trade union branches, had been developed where lantern lectures could be given 'thereby obtaining deep thinking students and intelligent trade union members'.[36]

By 1921, the narrow approach to education which had characterised the Plebs League was ended in Manchester. Summer rambles to places of interest were organised, a Students' Association was set up with its own fortnightly printed programme of events.[37] Visits were paid to the University Museum where 'object' lessons on such subjects as the development of weaving could be given with demonstrations. Moses Barritz, the music critic of the *Manchester Guardian* gave a series of evening lectures on 'The Materialist

Interpretation of Literature, Ethics, Art, Drama and Music'. This was illustrated by lantern slides and musical demonstration.[38]

Similar developments took place in Liverpool where John Hamilton worked towards his avowed aim of linking all Plebs classes in the county. At a Meet on Whit Monday at Southport, 'friends, class students and sympathisers' were invited to have 'informal chats as to propaganda, a Lancs tea and the fellowship'. The *Plebs* report of this event indicated that there had been some discussion over a resolution to link up Lancashire classes into a Plebs League District Council.[39]

Liverpool meanwhile went ahead and set up a Labour College to serve the Lancashire area, based on Liverpool. The services of J.T. Walton Newbold for industrial history and Nun Nicholas for economics had already been obtained. Although Robert Holder actually took the economics classes due to the illness of Nun Nicholas, the college went ahead and expanded. Sunday lectures were given on themes of interest at Walton College in Stuart Road. Subjects such as the 'Dreyfus Affair' were mixed with the 'Life and Times of Napoleon'.

Although Manchester and Liverpool forged ahead at a phenomenal rate in the post-war years, other classes were not idle. Rochdale, the old faithful, began the 1920 season with 50 students and increased their *Plebs* order on the strength of it. Harry Brownjohn, an old member of the Salford class, had moved to Fleetwood in search of work.[40] The group which responded to his appeal to Plebeians within reach of Fleetwood to join him in a class had an interesting history over the years. The students clubbed together and bought a piece of land which they used as a communal allotment growing their own fruit and vegetables. They built a hut in which they were able to hold classes and discussions. Their educational work was always of a high standard because most of them were victimised activists from Manchester or Salford who had considerable industrial and political experience. In Bury Fred Casey initiated a class consisting of women most of whom were teachers.

The growing maturity of the IWCE movement was reflected in 1920 in two important conferences. The first was held at the Labour College in Manchester in January. The object was to 'discuss and exchange ideas upon the needs of classes and the most useful ways of co-ordinating and developing their work'. The two days' discussions ranged over aspects of organisation such as the payment of tutors, the use of visual aids and the supply of textbooks.

The second conference was held in Bradford in April and it arose out of the questions raised at Manchester on the content and supply of suitable texts for use with classes. *Plebs* reported:

> If the Conference held at Bradford April 17-18 was not quite so breathlessly busy as the Manchester Conference in January, it none the less settled the matters it set out to settle, and marked another stage in the task of organising and co-ordinating the movement for Independent Working Class Education in this country.[41]

Although the post-war years were marked by the growth and increasing maturity of the movement, there was a development of divergent ideas. Possibly it was inevitable that there should be a clash of interests between the newly formed and rapidly developing Districts and the freshly opened Central Labour College after 1919. The provincial classes expected help from the CLC which it was not in a position to give. National tutors were expected to travel to local classes when there were plenty of local students well able to act as lecturer. Frank Jackson, never one to mince words, told provincial students:

> some of the older students of our classes would be doing a better service to the movement and to their fellows if they prepared themselves to conduct a class in their own locality instead of merely discussing the possibility or otherwise of being able to finance a full-time lecturer. Some of these people will sit and argue for hours to prove their knowledge of Marxism, and yet plead inability to take a class.

He ended his letter by reminding would-be revolutionaries that 'Man is a product of conditions; but if he stands aside when favourable conditions present themselves he is not going to get rid of economic and social bondage.[42]

Discontent, however, continued in the district and it was voiced in a joint statement issued by Manchester and Sheffield Labour Colleges. These took exception to the tardy recognition by the Central Labour College of the actual existence of local Labour Colleges. After listing the benefits which would result from co-ordination of the Labour Colleges, they called for a national organisation to be set up. Strong support was given to the joint statement from the North-East, from Liverpool and from Robert Holder who had moved to London and was a member of the London Council of IWCE.[43] This groundswell moved the Executive Committee of the Plebs League because they announced that the subject of the Annual Meet at the Clarion Club House at Yardley in Birmingham would be that of class co-ordination, and not teaching methods, as advertised.

The conference decided to set up a national organisation without asking anyone to do the work of co-ordination for them. This was an obvious crack at the Central Labour College and was taken to be so by W.W. Craik. He thought that the Plebs League and the Labour Colleges ought to have directed their energy and influence to building up support for the Central Labour College. Setting up a National Council of Labour Colleges, in his view, would in effect kill the residential college and reduce the provincial ones. Later, he wrote:

> The separate existence and claims of the two institutions led to a competition for trade union support that was, in the end, to facilitate, first the demise of the Labour College and, very much later, the disappearance of the NCLC itself as an independent entity.[44]

At the time, however, there was no way Craik could have foreseen the complex of events that ended the movement for Independent Working Class Education as such.

The five members of the interim executive elected at the conference were John Hamilton of Liverpool, J.P.M. Millar of Edinburgh, T.D. Smith of Wolverhampton and one representative each from the Plebs League and Central Labour College.[45] The aim of the organisation was 'to bring together the various colleges, districts and groups already in existence, with a view to extension and mutual help'. Liverpool and District Labour College was the first to pay the affiliation fee to the National Council and was closely followed by Manchester, Rochdale and the other North-West groups that had been building up support since the war.

One well documented instance of the problems that beset those who tried to develop IWCE is that of Ernest Faulkner of Hyde. He arrived in Hyde when he was released from Leeds prison where he had been serving a sentence as a conscientious objector to military service and took lodgings with Mr and Mrs Binyon with whom he lived for over forty years. He had met proponents of IWCE in prison and immediately set about trying to start a group locally in Hyde. He joined the Plebs League in January 1921. He wrote to individuals in Hyde from the Binyons' address:

                                          46 Bennett Street
                                          Newton,
                                          Hyde,
                                          Cheshire.
                                          Thursday Dec 8/21
Dear Comrade,
Initiative taken room engaged and meeting called and will be held on Dec

15/21 Thursday next at 7.30 p.m. in an ante room of the P.S.A. Market St. Hyde.

There is no institution in the town prepared to work a programme of Independent Working Class Education. Therefore Comrade if you realise what Marx and his teachings mean to your class, I invite you to come to the above meeting and we will endeavour to put into working the above programme.

Yours faithfully
Ernest Faulkner

P.S. Should you be unable to attend, I will be obliged if you will inform me.[46]

The class conscious citizens of Hyde apparently failed to respond to the call, so Faulkner sent a similar appeal calling a meeting in the Lower Hall of Hyde Socialist Church, George Street on 5 January 1922. He signed himself, 'Yours in the Workers Cause'.[47] After this second failure, Ernest Faulkner apparently abandoned Hyde and attached himself to Ashton and District Labour College[48] from which he was sent as delegate to the South-East Lancashire Area Council when it was formed in March 1922. Throughout his life, he worked for worker education and became an active member of the local Co-operative Society. For several years after his death in 1963, a commemorative lecture was held in his memory continuing the educational work which he had faithfully carried out over the years.[49]

Possibly the most important item discussed at the first Annual Conference of the newly formed National Council of Labour Colleges (NCLC) which was held in the Clarion Clubhouse at Handforth in Cheshire in March 1922, was a draft scheme initiated by the Amalgamated Union of Building Trades Workers to institute education classes for all their members.[50] This will be discussed shortly.

Plebs was adopted as the official organ of the NCLC and the Plebs League, which was to affiliate to the council, was given the responsibility of co-ordinating and assisting individuals and organisations which were not affiliated to the council. A resolution expressed willingness to co-operate with the Workers' Educational Trade Union Committee, or any similar body, providing that 'the definite and avowed aim' should be the education of workers to equip them to participate in the class struggle. The opinion expressed by the majority of IWCE supporters was that the WETUC was another name for the Workers' Educational Association which, in their view, was a vehicle for the propagation of anti-working class ideas. The concept of 'impartial' education was foreign to the understanding of

Plebs, whose motto 'I can promise to be candid but not impartial' echoed the sentiments expressed by the Ruskin strikers in 1909.

The basic principles on which NCLC classes were to be instituted were that all classes and tutors should be entirely controlled by trade unions, Trades Councils or other working-class organisations and that the definite and avowed aim of all such classes must be the education of workers to participate in class struggle with the ultimate objective of ending the capitalist system of government.

The major policy changes in the organisation at national level did not affect grass-roots planning. Throughout 1922 reports were sent in from South Lancashire classes which continued to expand and develop. Both Rochdale and Oldham had set up Labour Colleges and both made significant contributions to IWCE.

Oldham had long set the pattern of encouragement for women students. Alice Pratt, one of the original class, published an article in *Plebs* in January 1922, in which she raised the problems of technical training and questioned whether the working class took the subject seriously in a rapidly developing technological society. She suggested that trade unions should undertake specialised training for future leaders, an idea which gave rise to a number of letters in subsequent issues – including one from Ernest Faulkner.

In 1922, Leigh and District were running four classes in the Labour Party rooms; Rochdale had three classes and four fully qualified lecturers, all of whom were active trade unionists – two woodworkers, an engineer and weaver. Altrincham Council for IWCE was formed in January 1922 and by April already had two classes running. The tutor was Ellis Redfern who was to play an important part in the movement for some years ahead. Liverpool, always a pace setter, had prepared sets of slides which were available for hire or purchase with a synopsis lecture attached. Manchester meanwhile, concentrated on producing wall charts and had a Committee of eight to run the College. Ashton Labour College was 'doing well, thank you', while in Fleetwood, Harry Brownjohn, the long serving stalwart, was Secretary of the District.

While this basic grass-roots activity built a solid foundation on which the movement could expand and grow, other developments were taking place which were to influence the history of the young NCLC.

Evidence had for some time pointed to an increasing interest in education on the part of the trade unions. From the beginning, the Central Labour College had been supported by the South Wales Miners' Federation and the National Union of Railwaymen. Locally, the railway union had undertaken responsibility for classes in several localities before and during the war. But the scheme put forward by the building workers at the Annual Meet of the NCLC was of a more far-reaching character. The scheme called 'Our Next Step – Education' was issued on 1 January 1922. It set out the arguments for education as well as the historical background to the need for independence. The centre cartoon on the pamphlet showed three arrows on target. They were labelled 'Union in Industry', 'Workers Own Political Organisation' and 'Independent Working Class Education'. Arrows which failed to reach the target were 'Liberalism', 'Local Craft Unions', and 'National Craft Union', 'Co-partner Politics', 'Co-partnership in Education' and 'Elementary School Education'. The workers' need for education arises out of their industrial and political needs. The kind of education they want, therefore, is one which will fill those needs. Education could 'be no more free from bias than the worker can be free under capitalism. The only question is – What sort of bias? Bias against the workers, or for the workers?'

The subjects suggested as suitable for workers to study ranged from history, economics and the science of reasoning to psychology, economic geography, English language and literature and public speaking. The union reasoned that the Central Labour College, with its two year intensive course, would provide the specialists to become activists in the movement whilst the local Labour Colleges would ensure that all 'keen trade unionists' could obtain a general education. The pamphlet ended with the Vowels of Victory: '*U* and *I*, mate, have got to *A*gitate, *O*rganise and *E*ducate.' Ernest Faulkner, in his margin notes of the NCLC Conference agenda reminded himself that a local version of the national leaflet would be useful.

The AUBTW, in fact, now affiliated to the NCLC, who agreed to implement the programme.

To deal with the added responsibilities imposed on the organisation by the building workers education programme, the South Lancashire NCLC groupings decided that they needed greater co-ordination. Rochdale Labour College took the initiative and moved a resolution calling for an area council of the NCLC to be set up to deal with the demands of the building workers and, moreover, that the council remain in being apart from that immediate objective. Ernest Faulkner covered his agenda with pencilled notes so that his report to Ashton should be as full as possible.[51] The newly formed council secretary was Ellis Redfern and the building workers' representative was Luke Fawcett. By June, the council was sufficiently in business to send out the call to a meeting on notepaper headed 'South East Lancashire Area Council affiliated to the National Council of Labour Colleges'.

At the First Annual Delegate Conference of the Amalgamated Union of Building Trade Workers held in July, the point of view of the WEA, the Labour College and the NCLC were presented.[52] George Sims, in putting the Labour College case, quoted Lord Robert Cecil's reply to a remark made by Ben Tillett, the dockers' leader who was by that time a Member of Parliament, 'I am surprised at a prominent Labour Leader saying "education is the thing"; why, the people who are governing you are educated.'[53] Lord Robert made the Labour College case for them. 'Education has got to be specific,' argued Sims. The Labour Colleges were concerned with education which consisted of working class subjects taught in a working class way. As a result of the debate which followed, a resolution was passed which stated that:

> This conference agrees that the educational subjects taught at the National Labour College and in their classes are beneficial to the workers and serve the best interests of this society. It recommends that all members selected for educational courses be sent to the National Labour College.

Following the conference, a meeting was held between the AUBTW and NCLC which drew up a scheme of work and a reading list of useful pamphlets for beginners. These indicated the divisional secretaries to whom applicants for courses should write for information. For Number 8 Division this was Luke Fawcett of Chorlton on Medlock.[54]

In October 1922, Ellis Redfern sent out a call to a meeting at Manchester Labour College which was to discuss not only the AUBTW scheme but also the proposed education programme for the Amalgamated Society of Woodworkers (ASW), South-East Lancashire District.[55] Woodworkers had a long history of encouragement for their members who wanted to undertake further education. As early as the 1860s, branches were advised to set up technical classes to provide the theoretical knowledge pertaining to their craft. When technical education was taken over by the state, the union encouraged their members to undertake education which would enable them to 'take their share in the control of industry, which will be the next democratic advance'.[56]

Following that meeting, the NCLC, the AUBTW and the Amalgamated Society of Woodworkers (ASW) in South-East

Lancashire entered into a partnership in which the unions promised to provide the finance and the NCLC the tutors and organisation of classes.[57] Later the ASW nationally set up a scheme similar to that of the national AUBTW by which 1 shilling per member was allocated for education. But the South-East Lancashire District of the Woodworkers seems to have started local negotiations without waiting for the national agreement.

In a report given to the NCLC South-East Lancashire Area Council meeting in 1923, Ellis Redfern reported that a joint education committee of the ASW, the AUBTW and the NCLC had been set up. Moreover, the South-East Lancashire Council had extended its field of operation to include Bacup, Rawtenstall, Haslingden, Todmorden and their respective districts. In his report to the Number 8 Division of the AUBTW in March 1923, Redfern commented that there was 'reason to be pleased with results of the winter session'.[58]

In Redfern's report there was an indication that those who paid the piper perforce called the tune. He said that much had been done to make the lectures suitable for the average trade union member – but more needed to be done. Among the 40 courses there had been fifteen on industrial history, ten on economics, four on economic geography, seven on the science of understanding, three on evolution and two on sociology. The subject of imperialism, he explained, had been treated in the history course.

Trade union support continued. Lancashire frequently led the way and local trade unions took action before national agreement was reached. Manchester and Salford Trades Council passed a resolution promising 'greater financial and moral support to the Manchester and District Labour Colleges'. The National Union of Distributive and Allied Workers sent out a local canvass to ascertain if there was sufficient interest to initiate a scheme. Rochdale Labour College had secured the affiliation of the Weavers' Amalgamation while the Lancashire District of the National Union of General Workers had a resolution before its District Meeting in July 1923 calling for support for the NCLC.

Nationally, the Amalgamated Engineering Union passed an education rule which stipulated support for IWCE, while the National Union of Distributive and Allied Workers had also agreed to inaugurate a scheme similar to that of the AUBTW.

This considerable change in circumstances called for reorganisation of the NCLC and accordingly it was agreed to divide the country on the divisional basis used by the building workers. This seemed the most suitable way of conforming with trade union arrangements. Number 8 Division was suggested as comprising Lancashire, Cheshire, North Wales and North Shropshire. This covered fourteen existing Labour Colleges and it was the largest division in the country in terms of affiliated organisations. John Hamilton became the education organiser for the division. He had already proved himself as a man of outstanding drive and ability and the subsequent success of the division was further proof.

John Hamilton had a long history in the working class movement when he took over the Divisional Secretaryship. During the 1914–18 war he became organiser of the militant Building Workers Industrial Union.[59] This was formed in 1914 largely as a result of the frustration felt by bricklayers and masons after an unsuccessful strike. The union was short-lived. The policy of the union was against war and many of the members found themselves in prison as conscientious objectors. The union was virtually finished in 1916 which was fortunate for IWCE because John Hamilton immediately turned his enthusiasm and energy to education. He became in turn a class tutor, the education organiser of the Liverpool Council for IWCE, secretary of the Liverpool Labour College, national chairman of the NCLC and secretary of Number 8 Division of NCLC. He also became a Liverpool City Councillor and later an Alderman.[60] He was a foundation member of the Communist Party in 1920. John Hamilton not only taught and organised, he wrote polemical literature. In *Industrial Unionism, What It Is and What It Isn't* he explained the basic principles on which Industrial Unionism was founded.[61] 'All the trades and crafts, regardless of age, sex or race, engaged in the production of a given commodity' are represented in one trade union. In 1926 when the miners were engaged in their struggle against starvation following the General Strike, he wrote *The Class Struggle in the Mining Industry*[62] which had a foreword by Arthur Cook, the Secretary of the Miners' Federation of Great Britain. This was published by the Plebs League in two editions and the proceeds of the sale of one edition went to the Miners' Relief Fund.

John Hamilton's Report on the Liverpool Labour College for the year ending April 1923 gives some indication of the amount of work involved at local level at that time.[63] In spite of the industrial slump having seriously affected the finances of the college there were 130 affiliated organisations. 1,000 students had enrolled with an attendance of between ten and 70 in each class. Hamilton drew attention to the Labour Party Conference resolution which placed on record 'its appreciation of the work of the Labour Colleges' and urged organisations to 'support the work of the Colleges in their work of educating the workers for their task of overthrowing Capitalism'.[64] He also called attention to the new AEU rule which allowed grants to be made to colleges and institutions 'having for their object Independent Working Class Education'. He ended his report by telling the students that 'the importance of our educational work to the industrial and political movements is slowly receiving recognition'. Rhetoric, he asserted, was 'all very well in the heat of a campaign, but sound knowledge and a "reason for the faith that is in you" make the most effective and lasting weapons'.

In addition to his teaching and organisational activity John Hamilton offered his services to Luke Fawcett. He wrote in January 1923:

> If I can be of any assistance, by addressing mass or branch meetings of the members, to help in resistance to the building bosses' demands you can count on my service. Saturdays or Sundays being most convenient owing to my class work during week-nights.[65]

Those lectures were time-consuming. For example, in 1923 he gave twelve lectures on elementary economics at the National Union of Distributive and Allied Workers' rooms in New Ferry. On Sundays he lectured at the Independent Labour Party rooms in Birkenhead to students from the National Union of Railwaymen and he repeated the lecture, on economics, at Liscard on Monday evening. In the first half of 1924, he took an economics class at Liverpool Labour Club and in the second half of 1924-25 he was teaching Industrial History in the Co-op Rooms in Birkenhead while 'Modern Problems' were discussed on Tuesdays at Queensferry. On Sunday mornings in that year, he taught the Carters' Union members in economics and took the same subject with a class at Garston on Monday evenings. On Wednesday he was at Islington at the Sheet Metal Workers' office where he took industrial history. On Thursday evenings, by arrangement with Blackburn Labour College together with Blackburn Trades Council and Labour Party, he took a class on local government.[66] In addition to these local commitments he lectured at the Summer School on 'The Organisation and Structure of the NCLC.'

John Hamilton was an innovator in more ways than one. He pioneered the use of visual aids in the form of lantern slides which he made himself. He instituted summer classes in which students studied economics, industrial history and the history of trade unionism. There was no fee for these classes but students were expected to act as lecturers if called upon in the following winter session. Advice was given that students should concentrate on one of the topics and, if unable to attend, take a correspondence course instead.[67] By the end of the 1924 session, Hamilton had arranged that students from the AEU, AUBTW, NUDAW, NUR, Liverpool and District Carters and Motormen, and members of the sheet metal workers', plasterers' and tailors and garment workers' members could attend Liverpool Labour College without paying a fee. John Hamilton was not typical. He was far above the average Labour College tutor. His enthusiasm and energy, however, were typical of many who gave their services to the cause of IWCE and whose contribution was gratefully remembered by thousands of students who benefited from his classes.

The number of trade unions which supported the NCLC between 1924 and 1939 increased annually. This had a snowball effect locally where classes had to be increased to meet the demand. It also eventually led to changes in the content of the education provided. The fare offered in Plebs League classes proved heavy for some trade union stomachs. Ellis Redfern wrote to Luke Fawcett as early as February 1922 pointing out that attendance of AUBTW members was 'much behind what we desire'.[68] He was not alone in his disappointment that students failed to take advantage of the schemes in large numbers. John Hamilton also appealed to Fawcett suggesting that the AUBTW Divisional Council arrange for a meeting of each branch to be addressed jointly by an Area Council member and a delegate from the NCLC Division. He suggested that the Labour College speaker should speak on a topic such as 'The Past, Present and Future of Trade Unions' as that 'seems to be the only way to stimulate interest and it is best done systematically through your Divisional Council'.[69]

Divisional council meetings recorded continued growth in trade union support and further necessary ironing out of the organisation. Changes in teaching methods were tried. The Joint Education Committee advertised a course of six lectures based on the textbook *Outlines of the History of the Modern British Working Class Movement* and promised adequate time for discussion after the first two lectures. A meeting in February 1924 sent Ellis Redfern and John Hamilton to the National Annual Meeting to be held in Leeds in May. John Hamilton was found to have been underpaid and was given £20 a year extra to bring him up to the agreed national minimum. Area reports at the meeting indicated growing support from trade unions and Co-operative societies and also that the North-East Lancashire Labour College had been re-formed. Tutorial classes were arranged for the summer months, weekend schools were planned and it was agreed that the Division should send a group to the national summer school at Blackpool in August.[70]

The steady growth continued. The number of organisations affiliated with an educational scheme increased from nine in March 1923 to 29 in December 1930. The national pattern was reflected locally. Even the disastrous year of the General Strike in 1926 only resulted in an overall loss of one, but the Associated Society of Locomotive Engineers and Firemen as well as ten miners' unions were forced to suspend their educational activities following the dispute.

The increase in activity is shown in the Annual Report of the South-East Lancashire Area in 1926.[71] At the Annual Area Conference held in the Milton Hall, Manchester, in September 1925 there were 174 delegates from 87 organisations which included thirteen Trades Councils. The Conference was told that 4,000 students had attended 63 lecture courses in the area. By 1929 the number of Trades Councils affiliated to the Area Council had increased to 29. The main North-West trades of engineering, textiles, transport and building were well represented. Only mining seems missing from the lists.

Although all appeared to be well at national and area level in the 1920s, grass-roots struggles continued. All did not run smoothly for Ernest Faulkner. Having arranged with Hyde Socialist Church to hold Plebs League Branch classes in a room at the Church for 1 shilling a session, only 5 shillings had been paid in the seven months up to July. Faulkner kept meticulous accounts showing the contributions to class funds and the expenses incurred. His total expenditure for the year to July 1923 was just under £2 and he carried cash in hand of 11 shillings and 6 pence forward to the following year.[72]

The main class in Hyde in 1925 was on labour history and in 1926 on economics. These were held at the Co-op Hall in Charles Street at 7.30 on Friday evenings beginning the first week in October. The fee for the twelve lecture course was 2 shillings and 6 pence but, of course, members of affiliated organisations with education schemes attended free. Tutors were given guidance in duplicated notes to help them in the registration and organisation of the class. An attendance register was to be kept, noting the way that a student progressed so that reports could be sent to their sponsoring organisation. The class was to begin and end punctually and should not exceed one and a half hours. Students should be encouraged to buy text books and *Plebs*.

The tutor was asked to fill in monthly report sheets to be sent to the local organiser who, in the case of Hyde, was Ellis Redfern.[73]

Unfortunately, Redfern and Faulkner did not always achieve that happy state of co-operation that would have made their respective tasks run more smoothly. It is possible to detect a lack of confidence on the part of Ernest Faulkner and some irascibility by Ellis Redfern. After a somewhat acrimonious exchange of letters early in the decade, they seemed to settle down and managed to conduct affairs amicably but without obvious enthusiasm for each other.[74]

However, Ernest Faulkner continued to take an interest in IWCE. In 1927 he attended the summer school at Kiplin Hall, Scorton in Yorkshire where he met a miner from the anthracite coalfield in South Wales. They corresponded after returning home and the Welshman told him that he and his friend had been refused work when they presented themselves on the Monday after the school. They were informed that as they had gone away without obtaining the manager's consent they were deemed to have left. They were allowed to start after a couple of weeks but on a shift that operated alternate weeks. Therefore they had to miss one class in every two. The disgusted miner commented:

> It is hellish to have to fight for the return of a job you hate, because every sane-minded miner hates to work in the unnatural atmosphere of a coal pit. But the economic factors of the capitalist system binds every workman to his respective job whether he approves of it or not.

He ended by saying that it would give him the greatest pleasure to keep in contact by correspondence. 'Ideas', he said, 'are like money. They are for circulation and not accumulation.' He wished Ernest Faulker 'every success in the struggle towards emancipation'.[75]

While he remained secretary of the Plebs League class, Faulkner turned his attention to other avenues of activity after his disagreement with Ellis Redfern.[76] He spent much of his time and energy in the Co-operative movement. When John Hamilton wrote a textbook for the distributive workers' union in 1925, he raised some points with him for clarification. John Hamilton wrote, 'Of course the Co-op movement has tremendous potentialities, and does act as a sort of reformist movement within the present social system.'[77]

Although the rift between Redfern and Faulkner was apparently patched up (Redfern addressed a letter to Comrade Faulkner in 1925, and ended 'best wishes, Ted')[78] Owen Binyon in fact took over the necessary liaison between the Hyde class and the Area while Faulkner acted more as a back-room adviser.

The increase in trade union affiliations certainly led to some dilution of the more abstruse aspects of the IWCE courses; it did not, however, weaken the determination of some students to dig deep into the knowledge they believed would lead them to power. A training class was held in the summer of 1927-28. It was of fourteen weeks' duration on Friday evenings from April to July. The eight students were expected to undertake both written and oral work. Average attendance was seven and each student received a satisfactory report. Each gave at least one lecture and submitted written work. Ernest Faulkner reported at the end of the course, 'All students will agree with me when I say that this form of a class method is one of the best ways of learning and hope you will agree to another class being set up on the subject of economics by the same method.'[79]

While the proposed economics session was being planned, the students met weekly on Thursday evenings at 8 p.m. to discuss topics agreed between themselves. The first was in August when they discussed 'Citizenship and Christianity'. The literature list for the month is of interest. During August, T. Hawkins took four copies of *Plebs* and four of the *Communist*. He also bought a copy of Fred Casey's *Methods in Thinking*. Four more students each took four copies of *Plebs*. Two ordered W. Winwood Reade's *The Martyrdom of Man* and one took a copy of Lenin's *Left Wing Communism* as well as a copy of the pamphlet by Hamilton, *Co-ops and Socialism*.[80] By any standard, the eight enthusiasts must have emerged from their exposure to self-education with increased confidence and ability to play a part in the political scene. Many of those who became MPs or trade union leaders after 1945 had undertaken similar exposure to IWCE in their younger days.

After 1929, Ellis Redfern left Manchester to take up a post as area organiser for Nottingham. Ernest Faulkner increasingly devoted his time to the Co-operative movement with considerable success. The Hyde class, however, which must have been one of the longest lived in the NCLC, continued to be active throughout the 1930s.[81] Albert Knight became the area organiser when Redfern left and his captaincy of the IWCE ship led it into fresh waters.

A study of development in a locality has an intrinsic interest and value, but a full understanding of local events has to be gained in conjunction with a knowledge of the national scenario. The development of two opposing and contradictory methods by which the desired change from capitalism to socialism could be conducted led to the Labour Party calling for a gradual evolution of the state whilst the other saw the state as a standing conference of trade unions.

This latter concept of industrial syndicalism was the motive force actuating the Ruskin students in 1909. The development of events during the period up to the outbreak of the First World War fuelled their belief and made IWCE appear to answer the need for an informed and confident leadership of the working class. The positive aspect of syndicalism was its advocacy of organisation by industry and a realisation of the need for social change. Its negative aspect was the failure to appreciate the role of the state. These trends of socialist thought were reflected in the classes which the Plebs League conducted before the war. The content of the early classes sought to supply the need for trained and disciplined activists willing and able to conduct the class struggle. The subjects studied were intended to lead to a deeper understanding of the struggle and enable the student both to play a more active part and to pass on his knowledge to others with a snowball effect.

There is no question that this education was for the truly dedicated. It reflected the trends that went to form the Plebs League, the convinced Marxist socialists of the Social Democratic Federation and the various syndicalist groupings. They shared a limited outlook but also a confidence in the efficacy of education and that was the star that guided their support for IWCE.

After the war, the workers were on the offensive. The Russian Revolution had a traumatic effect and there was a belief that socialism was around the corner. The IWCE movement was caught up in the movements which called for larger groupings with more influence. The newly formed trade union amalgamations realised that they had a responsibility to fill the educational void that so many of their members fell into. The new associations and amalgamations of the post-war years led to changes in the outlook of the IWCE movement. Both the organisation and the content of the classes changed to meet the need.

With the formation of the Communist Party in 1920, many of the active workers for IWCE found themselves with new tasks and less time. The more rigid and dogmatic approach of the older socialists towards teaching economics and working-class history was relaxed. A less formalised approach to the subjects became necessary to fulfil the needs of the trade unionists who came into the movement when their unions organised education schemes. Paradoxically, this broadening of the content tended to remove the significant difference between IWCE and the other bodies catering for workers' education, and so the seed of eventual decline was sown.

Eden and Cedar Paul, two of the most active Plebeians, wrote in 1921:

The WEA and Ruskin College idea that 'Knowledge is Power', that bourgeois culture administered to the workers in suitable doses, will supply all proletarian needs, is demonstrably false. But other departments of knowledge besides economics must be wrested from the bourgeoisie, refashioned, and used for proletarian ends.[82]

The NCLC recovered from the blows delivered by the General Strike. It continued to run classes and a successful correspondence department. The content continued to broaden out embracing more aspects of human knowledge until the historic differences between the WEA and the Labour Colleges tended to pale into insignificance. Stage by inevitable stage the NCLC lost its independent soul and eventually in 1964 when it merged with the Trades Union Congress Education Department, it lost its independent organisation.

The question is, has the social change for which the stalwarts of the Oldham class and the Hyde class, the Liverpool and Manchester Labour Colleges, the Number 8 Division of the National Council of Labour Colleges and the trade unions which supported them, been achieved? Or will the flame of Independent Working Class Education need to flare again to guide the people along the path to emancipation?

Notes

[1] S.O. Davies, *A Socialist Faith*, (Dyfed, 1983), p. 46.
[2] *Plebs*, March 1909.
[3] Amalgamated Union of Building Trade Workers. Education Scheme. Front cover. June 1922.
[4] *Plebs*, March 1909.
[5] Ibid.
[6] Philosophic Logic: Classes were based on Joseph Dietzgen's work *The Positive Outcome of Philosophy*, translated by Ernest Untermann in 1906 and by W.W. Craik of the Central Labour College in 1928 (both editions were published in Chicago); also available was Dietzgen's *Some of the Philosophical Essays on Socialism and Science, Religion, Ethics, Critique-of-Reason and The World-at-Large* (Chicago, 1907).
[7] *Plebs*, September 1914. Annual Report of the Women's League.
[8] Ibid.
[9] Now at the Working Class Movement Library (WCML).
[10] *Plebs*, February 1912.
[11] The Communist Unity Conference was held in 1920 and was the formation conference of Merseyside District.
[12] R.W. Davies, 'Pages from a Worker's Life', *Our History*, No. 23, Autumn 1961.
[13] *Plebs*, May 1913.
[14] Ibid.

[15] Ibid., March 1915.

[16] Ibid.

[17] Ibid., March 1916.

[18] Ibid., December 1916.

[19] Ibid., January 1917.

[20] Ibid., April 1917.

[21] Ibid., July 1917.

[22] Ibid., September 1917. For these commissioners see Brian Simon, *Education and the Labour Movement, 1870-1920*, p. 335.

[23] *Plebs*, September 1917.

[24] Ibid., January 1918.

[25] Information on the Crossley Motors' Class from tape recorded interview with Audrey Ainley, 1976, and from letters from Harry Ingle to E. Frow 26 February 1975 and 26 January 1975. Crossley Motors had a strong shop stewards' committee a number of whom were Plebs; among them were Harry Ingle, Jack Halstead, Fred Flood and Jack Munro. See R. and E. Frow, 'Munro, William John (Jack)', in Joyce M. Bellamy and John Saville (eds), *Dictionary of Labour Biography*, 1984, Vol. III, p. 189.

[26] *Plebs* April 1918. 'Comrade' Taylor was apparently not known by name to the person submitting the report, probably J. McGee.

[27] Jack Murphy was a Mancunian who went to Sheffield during the First World War and became a leader of the Shop Stewards' Movement. See Edmund and Ruth Frow, *Engineering Struggles: Episodes in the Story of the Shop Stewards' Movement*, (Manchester, 1982).

[28] G. Jones is not known as an activist and reference to him has not been found elsewhere.

[29] *Plebs*, October and November 1918.

[30] *Plebs*, November 1918. For a brief biography of Winifred Horrabin see W.W. Craik, *Central Labour College*, (1964), p. 101.

[31] Ibid.

[32] For a delightful account of Fred Casey and his idiosyncracies see Stuart Macintyre, *A Proletarian Science: Marxism in Britain 1917-1933*, (Cambridge, 1980), pp. 134-8.

[33] Casey's publications included, *Thinking*, (Labour Publishing Company, London, 1922), *Dietzgen's Logic*, (Manchester, 1928), and *Method in Thinking* (Manchester, 1933).

[34] *Plebs*, March 1919.

[35] *Plebs*, June 1920.

[36] Manchester and District Labour College Annual Report and Financial Statement, August 1921.

[37] Manchester and District NCLC Students' Association Programme 1929.

[38] Moses Barritz. For the story of his encounter with H.M. Hyndman see T.A. Jackson, *Solo Trumpet*, p. 84.

[39] *Plebs*, May 1919.

[40] Conversations with Harry Brownjohn of Kelmscott, Pilling Lane, Preesall, Lancs., who died in 1965.

[41] *Plebs*, May 1920.

[42] *Plebs*, August 1921.

[43] The London Council of IWCE was the equivalent of the Labour Colleges in the provinces, but because the Central Labour College was sited in London, the Plebs used the alternative title. It was one of the formative associations of

the National Council of Labour Colleges.
[44] W.W. Craik, *The Central Labour College*, (London, 1964), p. 126.
[45] *Plebs*, November 1921.
[46] Manuscript letter in WCML.
[47] Ibid.
[48] Membership card in WCML.
[49] E. and R. Frow, Ms Lectures, WCML.
[50] Leaflet, Building Trades Workers' Education Scheme, June 1922.
[51] MS notes on NCLC Conference agenda March 1922, WCML.
[52] *Report*, First Annual Delegate Conference, Amalgamated Union of Building Trades Union (AUBTW), July 1922.
[53] Quoted by George Sims in his address to the First Annual Delegate Meeting of the AUBTW July 1922. *Report*, p. 18.
[54] AUBTW Education Scheme, 1922, WCML.
[55] Card, E. Redfern to R. Waters, October 1922, WCML.
[56] S. Higenbottam, *Our Society's History: Amalgamated Society of Woodworkers*, (Manchester, 1939), p. 111.
[57] Typescript Report, NCLC South-East Lancashire Area to AUBTW, February 1923, WCML.
[58] Typescript Report, 31 March 1923, Redfern to AUBTW, WCML.
[59] Raymond Postgate, *The Builders' History*, (London 1923), p. 430.
[60] Information supplied by Alderman John Hamilton (junior).
[61] John Hamilton, *Industrial Unionism*, (Building Workers' Industrial Union, London, 1917).
[62] John Hamilton, *The Class Struggle in the Mining Industry*, (Plebs League, 1926), Foreword by A.J. Cook. Profits to Miners' Relief Fund.
[63] Liverpool District Labour College Annual Report, April 1923, WCML.
[64] *Labour Party Conference, 1923*, p. 245.
[65] MS letter Hamilton to Fawcett, 20 January 1923, WCML.
[66] Liverpool and District Labour College Class Syllabus 1923/24/25, WCML; National Union of Railwaymen, Liverpool and North Wales Council, Education Classes Syllabus 1923, WCML.
[67] Duplicated letter Liverpool and District Labour College, March 1924, WCML.
[68] MS letter Redfern to Fawcett, February 1922, WCML.
[69] MS letter Hamilton to Fawcett, 28 November 1923, WCML.
[70] Minutes No. 8 Division Council Meeting NCLC, February 1924, WCML.
[71] South-East Lancashire Area NCLC Annual Report ending 31 March 1926, WCML.
[72] MS Balance Sheet July 1923, WCML.
[73] NCLC South-East Lancashire Area Class Lists 1925-26, Notes for Tutors, WCML.
[74] Typed letters Redfern to Faulkner, 19 and 28 September 1923, WCML.
[75] MS letter D. Jones to Faulkner, 6 October 1927, WCML.
[76] Information supplied by Mrs Binyon and the late Dennis Herrick of Hyde.
[77] MS letter Hamilton to Redfern, 5 February 1925. WCML.
[78] MS letter 'Ted' to Faulkner (n.d.), WCML.
[79] MS Report of Training Class 23 April-31 July 1928, WCML. This fourteen week course was for the dedicated student who was prepared to act as tutor on future courses. Although it looks highly academic in content, much of the course consisted of prepared leading statements which were followed by

discussion. It was intended that there should be maximum student participation.

80 MS Report to Training Class meeting and MS Accounts August 1928, WCML.

81 NCLC Division 8 Programme of Classes October-December 1936; CLC Annual Report year ending 31 March 1937, WCML.

82 Eden and Cedar Paul, *Communist*, 7 May 1921.

Margaret Cohen

3   The Labour College Movement Between the Wars: National and North-West Developments

The years immediately after the General Strike saw fundamental changes in the movement for IWCE. The NCLC underwent decline and retrenchment before recovering overall student numbers in the 1930s. In 1927, however, classes which had multiplied in the post-war period started a fall which, apart from a few minor checks, was never reversed. This decline was accompanied by a further weakening of the autonomy of the constituent colleges and a considerable strengthening of the central power of the national executive which was dominated by the leaders of the affiliated trade unions. The residential branch of the movement, the CLC, whose future prospects as part of the Easton Lodge scheme had seemed bright before the strike, was forced to close in 1929 when its two main supporting unions withdrew their funds. Graduates of the CLC made a considerable contribution to the labour movement in general as trade union and political officials and MPs, but their two years of full-time study of the core IWCE subjects – Marxist economics, dialectical materialism, working-class and industrial history, economic geography – made their contribution vital to the continuing development and relevance of the IWCE movement. The closure of the college played no small part in the failure to establish a British school of Marxism firmly rooted in the labour movement.

It is frequently held that in this period the NCLC ceased to challenge capitalism by providing education for fundamental social change and simply became an efficient trainer for a moderate trade union movement operating within the system. A.J. Corfield in his history of the WETUC asserts that the ideological differences between the two organisations became insignificant and quotes an assurance by the NUGMW's right-wing executive to its 1930 conference that the NCLC's 'Communistic ideals had for all practical purposes been expunged'.[1] Brian Simon has argued that it was the educational activity of the Communist Party and not that of the NCLC which 'represented [the] continuation of the traditions of IWCE'.[2] This essay considers these claims by examining the work of the NCLC first nationally, then locally in the South-East Lancashire Area from the late 1920s until the outbreak of the Second World War. The next looks at the rival educational organisations set up by Communists in the early 1930s.

I The NCLC – The National Picture

In the aftermath of the General Strike, the IWCE movement, like other labour movement organisations, faced the problem of falling numbers and income and hostile legislation. During 1926 the Labour Colleges locally and nationally had wholeheartedly supported the miners' cause. Issue after issue of *Plebs* contained reports of activities in mining areas, articles by miners' leaders and assessments of the strike by politicians and trade unionists critical of both the government and the TUC. Classes were held for miners during the long months of the lock-out, their scale being reflected in the high student numbers for 1926–27.

By 1927, however, the miners had been forced to return and the government and employers pressed home their advantage. The trade union Act passed that year banned sympathetic strikes, drastically altered the law on picketing, jeopardised trade union funds in the event of 'illegal' strikes, limited state employees to house unions, and substituted 'contracting in' to political funds for the 'contracting out' of the 1913 Act. Total trade union membership fell, with the numbers affiliated to the TUC going below 4,000,000 for the first time since 1916. Union funds were in a parlous state. Many had completely spent the sums set aside for industrial disputes and had been forced to borrow from their friendly benefit monies. Some employers took the opportunity to sack militant shop stewards and branch officials.

In the circumstances the left could not effectively challenge the TUC General Council's appeal for co-operation between trade unions and employers. It is ironic that the chairman for 1927 was George Hicks, one time member of the SDF, a founder and London secretary of the Building Workers Industrial Union and later first General Secretary of the AUBTW, which he persuaded to affiliate to the NCLC and finance scholarships to the CLC. The following year the TUC endorsed the Mond-Turner agreement which laid the basis for the collaboration between employers and the trade union leadership which characterised the period. Yet Ben Turner, the chair for 1928 who gave his name to the agreement, had signed the 1925 WETUC manifesto which stated that trade unionism stood not only for the 'improvement in the conditions of the workers within the limits of the existing system, but for the creation of a new and juster social order'.[3]

The NCLC was faced with a declining income as trade union membership fell. Ten miners' unions and ASLEF disaffiliated in 1927, and, though the losses were more than offset numerically by new affiliations, these included limited schemes for schools, branch lectures and reduced-fee postal courses which were entered into grudgingly for low payments with unions which had agreements with the rival WETUC.

The Plebs League, too, was in financial difficulties due to a decline in sales of its magazine *Plebs*, its pamphlets and books such as the Plebs Outlines series which were the basic texts of Labour College classes and correspondence courses. The NCLC took over responsibility for the publications and the League's debts. This gave Millar (the General Secretary) and the national executive control over the content of *Plebs* as well as over the list of books and pamphlets produced for the movement.

The position of the WETUC was more advantageous as it operated through the grant-aided WEA. The government looked favourably on it, allowing civil service unions to affiliate under the 1927 Act to the WETUC but not to the NCLC, and continuing a grant to the WEA of over £6,000 a year. That the WEA in its turn was expected to provide acceptable workers' education was confirmed for IWCE critics by Lord Eustace Percy, President of the Board of Education, when he agreed in the House of Commons with a fellow Tory that WEA classes 'ought to be closely watched' and added, 'I have watched and am watching them.'[4] However, despite being able to offer education schemes at subsidised rates, the WETUC gained no new affiliations between 1926 and the autumn of 1930 when the National Union of Printing, Bookbinding and Paper Workers joined.

In 1929, the CLC closed as its two major supporting unions were no longer willing or able to back it without wider trade union funds. The South Wales Miners' Federation (SWMF) was virtually bankrupt and, though the position of the National Union of Railwaymen (NUR) was not so parlous, it had benefited less from the CLC. Fewer than a half of the NUR's graduate students had found work on the railways due to the companies' reluctance to re-employ them. On the other hand, the majority of the SWMF's graduates were able to return to the South Wales coalfield – frequently as check-weighmen elected by their fellow miners. Millar points out that at one time all but one of the South Wales' Labour MPs were ex-CLC students.[5]

The CLC in the 1920s suffered from a series of disputes. There was student dissatisfaction with the quality and limited content of lectures, resentment at the rigid rules imposed by the college authorities, a scandal over the misappropriation of funds followed by the resignation of the Principal and disputes which parallel those between the Communist Party, the Plebs League and the NCLC.

All sections of the Labour College movement saw their role as a purely educational one: providing students with the theoretical weapons for the class struggle. The Communist Party argued that revolutionary theory was inseparable from revolutionary practice and that the Labour Colleges distorted Marxist theory by separating it from political action.[6]

By 1924 the split between the Communist Party nationally and the established IWCE movement was complete and the following year 800 out of a total of 5,000 CP members attended classes organised by the Party Training Department. The breach, which, as will be discussed later, was largely ignored by Communists in Lancashire, strongly influenced Communist students at the CLC. Albert Knight of the NUR who started his two-years course early in 1926 remembered it being punctuated with 'skirmishes between the Communists and anabaptists as we called them'.[7]

In 1928 seven Communist students were expelled from the CLC for refusing to take part in the college's celebrations to mark the centenary of Joseph Dietzgen. The study of Dietzgen, once regarded as essential for serious labour college students, had declined by the late 1920s, and only the South-East Lancashire College and the CLC held centenary celebrations. Communist criticism of Dietzgen intensified after the publication in 1927 of the first English translation of Lenin's *Materialism and Empirico-Criticism* and his article 'Joseph Dietzgen' both of which, whilst recognising Dietzgen as a unique worker-philosopher who independently developed the theory of dialectical materialism, criticised confusions in his writings which gave 'concessions to idealism and agnosticism'.[8]

Millar recalled how, in 1929, on hearing of further activities of a group of Communist students at the CLC, Tom Pocock of the NUR, the secretary to the governors, exclaimed 'this is, along with a lot of other things, about the bloody end'.[9] It was later that year that both the NUR and the SWMF withdrew their financial support, so forcing the college to close. Despite a slight rise in employment, stimulated in the main by the boom 1920s which preceded the Wall Street crash, and a corresponding increase in trade union membership, no other unions were willing to take over responsibility.

In this period, the Communist Party which, like the Labour Party and trade unions, had experienced a fall in membership after the defeat of the General Strike, underwent a further disastrous decline. In response to instructions from the Communist International the party adopted the policy of 'class against class' which characterised the Labour Party as the third capitalist party and regarded social democratic and fascist governments as merely different forms of capitalist rule, both equally dangerous to the working class. The non-Communist political and industrial leadership of labour movements were described as 'social fascists', staunch defenders of capitalism, who conned the working class by proclaiming a commitment to socialism. Any alliance or co-operation with them was thus against the interests of the working class. Conditions throughout the capitalist countries were, it was claimed, 'objectively revolutionary' and the rank and file were ready to be led to revolution. The role of Communist parties was to expose the social democrats and provide the necessary revolutionary leadership by being at all times in the vanguard of class struggle. Acts of protest by working-class people were mistakenly interpreted as precursors of the revolution and responded to with inappropriate revolutionary slogans which helped the right in its portrayal of Communism and Marxism as alien and suspect. Party membership fell by 80 per cent from 12,500 in January 1927 to 2,500 in 1930–31. In the circumstances the Communist Party was in no position to develop its educational work.[10]

The NCLC experienced considerable growth in 1930–31 despite the disaffiliation of two unions, due in the main to the affiliation of the NUR. The number of students undertaking correspondence courses more than doubled to 6,600 and the number of day schools and lectures were higher than in 1927–28. There was a further setback in 1931 when the AEU cut its payment from £1,000 to £250 and withdrew from the postal course scheme, though numbers, in fact, grew over all. Economies were made by the executive which included reducing the number of areas and organisers in both the North West No. 8 division and in the Scottish No. 10 Division from three to two and requiring organisers to mark correspondence course papers without additional payment. The reorganisation in the North-West took place when John Hamilton, the Liverpool and West Lancashire organiser, resigned and so Joe Crispin of the North area and Albert Knight of South-East Lancashire became the organisers of the enlarged Western and Eastern areas. The 'surplus' Scottish organiser, James Younie, was transferred to head office in London.

John Hamilton was a stone-mason by trade and had worked in the United States with Bill Bowers, the 'rolling stone', on the building of Harvard. Whilst there, he had become a member of the Industrial Workers of the World, a 'wobbly'. On returning to Liverpool, he had helped to found and became the secretary of the militant Building Workers' Industrial Union. He married and his only son, John, became the Labour leader of Liverpool City Council in the 1970s and 80s. During the war he was a conscientious objector, hidden by his family. In 1919 he helped to found and became the first secretary of the Liverpool Labour College and the following year joined the new Communist Party. He was elected president of the NCLC at its founding meeting and was appointed the organiser for Liverpool and West Lancashire. He found himself increasingly at odds with Millar and his methods which, according to his son, he felt were killing the movement at its grass roots. John Hamilton remembers how his father trailed round the area, frequently with heavy lantern equipment on public transport, giving classes and lectures to trade union and Labour Party branches, Trades Councils and co-operative societies only to return late at night to complete, in his view, irrelevant forms for head office. His work, he considered, was inhibited by gross underfunding – the local colleges being sacrificed in order generously to finance costly correspondence courses and a well equipped and staffed head office.[11] After leaving the NCLC, John Hamilton was elected to Liverpool City Council and later became leader of the Labour group. He earned his living as an insurance agent, an occupation to which many Labour councillors turned as employers were unwilling to give time off for council business. Jack Jones, a student and voluntary tutor in the Liverpool Labour College in the late 1920s and early 1930s was conscious of much criticism of head office and remembers that 'we kept Millar out of Liverpool while Jack Hamilton was organiser and afterwards'.[12]

In his book, *The Labour College Movement*, Millar wrote that the organisers, especially those originally appointed to local colleges like John Hamilton, resented their loss of independence, the imposition of central control, the tight overseeing of expenditure and the time-consuming administration demanded by head office which thwarted their political ambitions. He also claimed that they were prejudiced against Christine Millar as a married woman receiving a wage at a time when women frequently had to give up work on marriage. No doubt such prejudice existed, though he failed to add that organisers' wives who helped with labour college work received no payment at all.

The transference of James Younie to head office in 1931 lead to events which Millar subtitled 'Civil War Begins in the NCLC'.[13] Younie later claimed that he became disturbed by the poor relationship between the office staff and Millar, the amount spent on office equipment, the preferential treatment given to Christine Millar which included allowing her to arrive late for work virtually daily and paying her additionally for correspondence course scripts marked in office time. He reported these matters in confidence to a meeting of the organisers' association, but a member, Morgan Phillips, the man frequently credited with first saying that the Labour Party owed more to Methodism than Marxism, told Millar and Younie was dismissed.[14] He appealed to the executive which set up a committee of enquiry to which he made a lengthy submission including affidavits from John Hamilton and two other former organisers that they had left the NCLC because of the 'head office attitude'. The committee gave its full backing to Younie and was highly critical of Millar alleging that he had treated Christine with 'favouritism', that he had 'interrogated' potential witnesses, that the previous year's absence book had been destroyed and that he had made alterations to the salary book. The executive received this report and set up a joint committee which recommended Millar be removed from the position of General Secretary and given the new post of National Organiser and that Younie should be reappointed as an organiser when the next vacancy occurred. Before any of this could be acted upon, the NCLC found itself in severe financial difficulties. The executive then set up a sub-committee to look into the whole affair yet again which started work immediately and issued a report in the small hours of the next morning backing Millar but agreeing there had been 'slackness in the keeping of records'.

It was the findings of this sub-committee which were accepted by the 1932 Annual Conference where the leaders of the big unions spoke strongly in favour of Millar with John Jagger of NUDAW blaming the crisis on the NCLC divisions which, he claimed, were 'a law unto themselves' and not prepared to 'take the discipline of national and central control'.[15] One of the critical organisers, Albert Ellis, claimed that as the three reports had not been circulated, delegates had only a hazy idea of the facts and that the vote for Millar was more an expression of support for the movement in difficult times than an endorsement of his actions.[16]

The executive consolidated the central control of the affiliated unions by introducing a new constitution which gave the unions a block vote of one for every £50 paid in affiliation fees, the local colleges one for every 200 students and the divisions one for every 400 students. On this basis the AUBTW had more delegates than the divisions. Organisers could no longer represent their divisions but would be able to meet an executive sub-committee before each annual conference to discuss working conditions, etc. The few organisers of the original Labour College areas still paid locally were to be paid nationally. An attempt by the Glasgow area of the Scottish Labour College to retain local independence was quickly quashed.[17]

Thus the organisation which had been founded thirteen years earlier to bring together local colleges 'with a view to extension and mutual assistance' without infringing their autonomy submitted itself, to use John Jagger's words, to the 'national and central control' of the affiliated unions. Younie, needless to say, was never offered reinstatement, and Ellis added a disturbing postscript – that five senior members of the head office staff who had given evidence against Millar were sacked on the grounds of economy.[18]

In the same period the Labour Colleges' old adversary, the WEA, was facing problems with regard to its role as a provider of working-class education. After also suffering a fall in numbers in the wake of the General Strike, it was experiencing an overall growth in student numbers but a fundamental change in their social composition. Albert Mansbridge, the founder of the WEA, had stressed that 'the first condition of the power and life of the Association was that at least three-quarters of its members should be actual labouring men and women'.[19] By 1932 only one-third of its students were manual workers and this is reflected by the growth in popularity of such subjects as literature, drama, art appreciation and music.[20] Another trend in this period was the decline in the number of students who became members of the WEA. Until the mid-1920s, students were normally also branch members but by the late 1930s less than half were members, indicating a decline in commitment to the aims of the WEA with an increasing proportion of students viewing it as merely another provider of adult education.[21] In his 1931 presidential address, G.D.H. Cole viewed these trends with disquiet, asserting that the WEA 'must meet the special needs of the working class' and that 'its heart must be a working-class heart, as long as there is such a thing as the working class'.[22]

The NCLC continued to press home its argument that the WEA could not serve the needs of the working class as it provided an 'extension' of governing class education in a misleading working-class wrapper. Ever mindful of the attraction of the grant-aided WETUC schemes to cost-conscious trade union leaders in a period of recession and declining membership, editorials and articles in *Plebs* pressed home the WEA's close connection with the reactionary establishment compared with its own independence as an integral part of the labour movement. They cited the BBC's invitation to the WEA to join the Central Council for Broadcast Adult Education;[23] the award of charity status with the accompanying tax exemptions;[24] the receipts of monies from trusts which, like the Carnegie, were the product of the exploitation of fellow trade unionists, the continuing government and local authority grants,[25] the enforcing of the 1927 Act (the 'Blacklegs' Charter') which permitted civil service unions only to have WEA schemes,[26] and the WEA's special relationship with the universities which were seen as reactionary purveyors of orthodox capitalist education whose members had never returned a Labour MP.[27]

On its tenth anniversary, Millar wrote that he considered the NCLC's particular contribution to the IWCE movement had been its success in persuading many unions 'to look upon affiliation to the NCLC in the same way as ... affiliation to the Labour Party or the TUC'. It also, he added, had shown the important part that correspondence courses could play in workers' education, turning 'the state postal system into a vehicle for spreading Marxism'.[28] Certainly the WETUC, despite its advantages, trailed behind the NCLC. By 1935 when union membership was growing with the recovery of the economy and more unions were affiliating to both the WETUC and the NCLC, the number of WETUC classes was 200 compared with 753 NCLC classes and similarly schools students numbered 4,325 compared with 15,649 and correspondence course students were 527 compared with 6,827.[29] Correspondence courses had been introduced by the WETUC in conjunction with Ruskin College in 1931 with a certain reluctance as Ernest Green, the General Secretary, considered them 'one of the most expensive and, unless properly controlled, one of the least effective methods of education', which were no substitute for the 'discipline of classwork and discussion'.[30] The numbers were small, according to Corfield, because Green insisted on the courses meeting the WEA's traditional high standards.

It was on the question of standards that the WEA counter-attacked. The education versus propaganda battle, of course, had been going on since the foundation of the Plebs League. For those critics who accepted that the NCLC was to a certain extent an educational organisation, the lack of written work by class students and the fact that class and correspondence course tutors were not academics were seen as evidence of low standards. The jewel in the WEA's crown was the three-year tutorial class which demanded regular attendance and written work from students. Throughout the period under review, however, these courses only accounted for a minority of WETUC work and Corfield gives no indication as to the numbers undertaking or completing these courses. There is just one reference to the early 1920s when the newly appointed tutors in Scotland and Wales reported only one class of eighteen students satisfactorily meeting attendance and written work requirements.[31] The content of shorter WETUC classes is impossible to assess as much depended upon individual tutors, though, of course, as grant-aided classes they had to pass inspection. The content of NCLC classes is, however, readily available as the majority were based on the Plebs outlines in such subjects as economics, imperialism, economic geography, psychology, European history and the earlier books by Mark Starr and W.W. Craik on working-class history and Fred Casey on philosophy. The outlines were 'first drafted by one hand, then discussed and revised by an editorial committee'.[32] Each book was divided into chapters which would provide the basis for a class with further reading suggestions given at the end. This answers Mary Stock's jibe in her history of the WEA that the Webbs' *History of Trade Unionism* was recommended as a supplement to W.W. Craik's *History of the Modern Working Class Movement* – it was regarded, quite correctly, as further reading once Craik's basic text had been studied.[33] This open method in practice encouraged lively participation. Ex-students who attended both NCLC and WEA classes in the period contrast the noisy cut and thrust of Labour College classes with the respectful silence during the lecture with question and answer only at the allotted time of WEA classes.[34] The much-criticised 'unorthodox qualifications'[35] of the Labour Colleges' worker-tutors meant that students could argue with them on a basis of equality in the same manner as they would in their trade union or party branches.

Labour College tutors were not entirely untrained. In 1930 Millar wrote in *Plebs* that prospective tutors needed to get a good background in social and industrial history, economics and economic geography. Reading must start with the Plebs textbooks and recommended further reading and then continued with *Ethics and History* by Karl Kautsky, *Puritanism* by C. Meilly and *The Theoretical System of Marx* by L.B. Boudin. He advised them to attend local NCLC tutor training courses and to begin teaching with a single lecture, perhaps on the need for IWCE to a trade union branch or Co-operative society and also, if possible, to take correspondence courses in the subjects to be offered. Economics should not be taught until the students had undertaken extensive study, Marxist economics being 'no easy subject to learn and still less easy to teach'.[36]

He summed up the strengths of the voluntary tutors – who were predominantly skilled manual workers – as being that, as workers themselves they understood the workers they taught, that they had learnt much of their social science from experience, and that, unlike many professional teachers, they thoroughly enjoyed teaching. The reasons he saw for there being so few professional teachers in the NCLC were that these would jeopardise their chances of promotion by participation, that they were paid generously for WEA and LEA work, that they neither knew nor were willing to make the effort to acquire knowledge of Marxism, and that they were 'chained' to orthodox conceptions of education which caused them to gravitate to the WEA – 'the Outpatients' Department of the universities providing orthodox educational salves for proletarian sores'.[37]

Certainly any professional teachers who volunteered for NCLC work would have had to be willing to undertake further study since their academic qualifications in no way prepared them for many Labour College courses. Ellen Wilkinson said at the NCLC annual meeting in 1924, 'Although I had taken a degree in history at Manchester University, I was astonished to discover when I came into contact with the Labour Colleges how little real history I had been taught.'[38] The value of peer-teaching in adult education has had a certain vogue amongst academics recently, particularly in relation to the enormous educational problems in the third world. Academic attacks on the standard of NCLC tutors quite correctly stressed the value of full-time study but also contained a certain element of professional defensiveness and an ignorance of the broad labour movement.[39] Any academic who is active in that movement learns to respect the intellectual ability and analytical skills of many of their comrades with few, if any, formal educational qualifications.

In 1933 the NCLC achieved a breakthrough in the Co-operative movement when it reached an agreement with the Co-operative Union, the movement's central organisation which had long been connected with the WEA. Millar claims that its value was above all financial bringing with it association grants paid by the CWS and SCWS.[40] Individual Co-operative societies were, of course, autonomous and whilst many were affiliated to the WEA, many others had affiliated to local Labour colleges from their inception. Labour colleges allowed free or reduced fee entry to classes, supplied speakers and tutors for lectures and courses to Co-operative organisations like the guilds and benefited from the free use of Co-operative halls. In the South-East Lancashire area, affiliation varied from year to year depending on the political complexion of the elected education committees. Much of the local work with women students took place in the rapidly growing, radical and vigorous Women's Co-operative Guilds.

In the same year a Communist IWCE competitor – the Marx Memorial Library and Workers' School – was founded. The suggestion to establish a permanent memorial to Marx in London came at a conference held in March 1933 to mark the fiftieth anniversary of his death, which contained, according to Millar, all the exhibits from Moscow denied to the London Division of the NCLC for its Marx commemorative exhibition. The new school ran classes in the library premises in London but also offered to provide tutors for study circles in trade union branches and other working-class organisations which it asked to affiliate.

In an editorial attacking its new rival entitled 'The Disunited Front', Millar claimed that if the organisers truly believed in their party's call for a united front they would be urging people to join their local labour colleges.[41] He reminded readers of the *Daily Worker*'s refusal to accept NCLC advertisements. These included one for *Socialism's New Start: A Secret German Manifesto* written by socialists working underground in Germany, A.L. Williams' *What is Marxism?* and an edition of *Plebs* containing an article on Trotsky.[42] Though criticism of Communist Party activities and publications continued to appear, Communists continued to work as voluntary tutors for their local colleges and to contribute to *Plebs* throughout our period. Communist writers for *Plebs* included J.D. Bernal, T.A. Jackson, Maurice Dobb, R. Page Arnot, John Lewis, Hyman Levy, Walton Newbold, Ivor Montagu and Ralph Fox. The progress of the Marx Memorial Library's Workers' School, which will be discussed in the next essay, to a certain extent mirrored the Communist Party's recovery. Though membership of the party rose from 2,500 in 1930–31 to 6,000 in 1935 and reached 17,539 by 1939,[43] Communist activities in popular anti-fascist, anti-imperialist, peace and other left-wing movements allowed little time for systematic study.

The *Plebs* attack on fascism which started with Mussolini's rise to power, continued throughout the 1930s, its analysis being basically Marxist. The April 1933 edition which was entirely concerned with 'Hitlerism', had on its cover a cartoon by Barlow of a hideous ape in a business man's pinstripe suit holding in its paw a human 'democratic' mask entitled 'Capitalism takes off its mask'. The editorial underlined this view of fascism as an extreme form of capitalism in which its true nature is exposed. In contrast, the official Labour Party and TUC view was that fascism and Communism were merely two different forms of dictatorship and it failed to analyse the different roles of the working class within them.[44]

Marxists, however, disagreed over the strategies to defeat fascism. Much of the work on fascism in the NCLC was carried out by refugee socialists including Edward Conze, Peter Petroff and Maria Saran who wrote articles in *Plebs* and tutored classes and schools. Their position was strongly anti-Communist and they strongly opposed the Popular Front policy. *Plebs* carried articles both for and against the Popular Front though editorially did not support it.[45]

It is not only the *Plebs* analysis of fascism which shows it retained its Marxist standpoint, but equally its analysis of imperialism, with articles and cartoons particularly on Japanese, British and American imperialism. Colonial freedom movements like the India League were supported and their leaders contributed articles.

The recovery of student numbers experienced by both the NCLC and the WETUC was checked in the late 1930s, in part, by the growth of activity in anti-fascist, peace and other left-wing groups. The Left Book Club which started in 1939 had a membership of 40,000 and 730 local groups in 1937 and this increased to a membership of 57,000 with 1,200 local groups by 1939.[46] Groups met fortnightly or monthly to discuss the club's current choices. Large rallies were also organised, addressed by left Labour and Communist leaders such as Stafford Cripps, Aneurin Bevan, Harry Pollitt and Willie Gallacher. Whilst a high proportion of the membership was of professional and white-collar workers, it also included a number of those manual workers who might previously have attended their trade union financed classes. Frank Allaun, convenor of the Manchester Left Book Club, remembers that it contained a 'considerable number of trade unionists'.[47]

Student numbers in Labour College classes were also affected by the large amounts of overtime being worked in the years immediately before the war. The radio and the appeal of increasingly luxurious cinemas also had an influence, as did the housing boom which caused many skilled manual and white-collar workers to move to the new council and speculatively built estates, frequently served by poor public transport with few, if any, meeting places.[48]

The 1930s saw an overall change in the direction of the NCLC's work with correspondence course students, who accounted for only 8 per cent of total course and school students in 1930, having risen to 30 per cent by 1939. These courses included practical labour movement subjects like chairing meetings, local government, public speaking and three levels of English – the advanced involving article writing and labour journalism. Traditional IWCE courses continued and in 1939 these included three levels of economics with Marxian economics at the advanced level, economic geography and imperialism, imperialism and world problems, history of the British working class, industrial history of modern Europe, the scientific way of thinking, social history and socialism.

There is no doubt that the ideological differences between the orthodox education of the WEA and that characteristic of the NCLC, which Corfield claimed to be insignificant by the late 1920s, remained in existence throughout the 1930s. In certain aspects of its work in local colleges, in some of its correspondence courses and in its excellent magazine, *Plebs*, the NCLC still 'represented [the] continuation of the tradition of IWCE'.[49] Its independent stance was more than a hollow appeal to labour movement chauvinism. However, the nationally affiliated unions which dominated the national executive expected their educational organisation to provide the training essential for their members as part of a large, complex labour movement in an advanced capitalist society. This gave rise to a difference of emphasis. Arthur Woodburn, in his presidential address in 1939, claimed the major achievement of NCLC had been to provide 'a great body of "informed" and "trained" members ... in every position in the labour movement from efficient branch member to general secretary and MP',[50] while the Scottish organiser, C.L. Gibbons, gave priority to the more fundamental IWCE objective – 'to shake and remove the capitalist outlook received from orthodox education' and 'to instill a socialist outlook' by teaching students to think scientifically. Stimulating students to be active in the labour movement, he added, was a product of this process.[51]

It was the provision of costly correspondence courses to meet the training and educational needs of the nationally affiliated unions that, according to many local activists, starved the local colleges of funds and prevented them from developing appropriate IWCE initiatives to meet the changing circumstances in their areas. In the next section we look at the work of one of these colleges – the South-East Lancashire Labour College – in the period under consideration.

II *The South East Lancashire Labour College, 1927–39*

The collapse of the General Strike, the remorseless defeat of the miners and the quiescence of the trade union leadership was as bitter a blow to supporters of IWCE in the South-East Lancashire as elsewhere. The immediate decline in activity, however, was sharper, with class student numbers collapsing from 1,602 in 1926 or 5 per cent of the national total to 648 or 3 per cent of the national figures in 1929. The number of locally affiliated organisations fell from 103 to 83 and the number of classes put on for labour movement organisations halved with those for Trades Councils and trade union branches being most affected. Only the numbers of students attending day schools and lectures remained fairly steady. Classes continued to be run throughout the industrial areas from Bacup and Rawtenstall in the north to Altrincham in the south, and from Oldham and Stalybridge in the east to Horwich in the west. The central premises in Dale Street, Manchester, had been closed on Millar's instructions as he considered the shabby basement unsuitable for the Labour Colleges' new role as a national educational organisation seeking the support of general secretaries and their executives. Unfortunately the funds for more prestigious premises were not forthcoming from head office and the Manchester college lost its meeting place, its library and the focal point for its activities.

The trade union movement in the area was facing fundamental changes with the old staple and highly unionised industries of cotton, coal, general engineering and textile finishing in long-term decline causing high unemployment in towns like Oldham and Stalybridge. By contrast in the southern parts of the area around and to the west of Manchester there was a growth in the electrical wiring, cable, supply and engineering industries, and also in paint and varnish manufacturing, furniture making, road transport and clothing which had overall a lower level of trade union organisation. It was the long-term unemployed trade unionists who had worked in the staple industries, particularly the engineers with experience as shop stewards, who from the early 1920s organised and provided the effective leadership for the National Unemployed Workers' Movement in South-East Lancashire – one of the movement's most active areas.

In September 1929 Ted Redfern, who had been organiser since the foundation of the NCLC, transferred to the East Midlands area, and was replaced by Albert Knight, a young CLC graduate. Bert Knight came from Lydney in the Forest of Dean where at the age of fourteen he had started work as a porter for the GWR. His father who was also a railwayman and a keen union member ensured that he immediately joined the NUR. By the age of eighteen, Bert was secretary of the Lydney Trades and Labour Council. He was influenced by older union men who were Supporters of 'Clarion' and the ILP and by books from his union branch's library including Bellamy's *Looking Backward*, Blatchford's *God and my Neighbour*, Tressall's *The Ragged Trousered Philanthropist*, Morris's *News from Nowhere*, several titles by Jack London and the Webbs' *History of Trade Unionism*. In 1925 at the age of 22, he won an NUR scholarship to the CLC, but did not take up residence until January 1926 as the NUR was hesitating about continuing to support the college. Bert thought that whilst the disruptive behaviour of some Communist students of the CLC was given as the immediate reason for the NUR's doubts, J.H. Thomas, the NUR General Secretary, was fundamentally anti-Marxist and opposed to the college and its curriculum based on Marx, Engels and Dietzgen. Other students at this time included Morgan Phillips, Len Williams and James Younie. After completing his course, Bert returned to his job as a porter with the GWR and to his trade union and political activities. He also worked as an NCLC voluntary tutor and travelled round the area persuading trade union branches to affiliate locally and to support classes. Two years later, in 1929, he became the full-time organiser for South-East Lancashire.[52]

The following year, Bert married Winifred Hopkins, a teacher from his part of the country. Winifred's father was a railwayman and her mother an active Co-operative Guild woman, a founder member of the Labour Party and a candidate for the local Board of Guardians who had organised a successful march of the unemployed on the workhouse to demand that relief vouchers could be cashed at the Co-op as well as with private traders. Winifred had won a scholarship to grammar school and whilst still at school had attended NCLC classes in industrial history and thinking and had become interested in Esperanto through visiting a socialist commune in the Cotswolds. She and Bert were students at the same time in London where she attended a teacher training college. Winifred taught for two years before having to give up on her marriage. After arriving in Manchester she became an unpaid, virtually full-time worker for the NCLC. The front room of their house in Eccles was the area's office where Winifred undertook the main burden of the clerical work and in the evenings she gave lectures to Co-operative Women's Guilds and Labour women's sections. She also attended tutor training courses and became a tutor of courses held for Women's Guilds on co-operation and modern economic problems. The South-East Lancashire Labour College was very fortunate in its choice of Bert Knight as it got two enthusiastic, intelligent young workers for the price of one.[53]

Student numbers in Labour College classes, however, continued to decline. Class students for the year ending March 1930 were 573, less than one third of the number enrolled in 1926, and day school students were down to 67 compared with over 300 only the year before. To halt the decline, Bert Knight encouraged the formation of student associations and invited tutors to join a tutors' council to overhaul lecture courses and prepare new ones.

Since the opening of the Dale Street premises, Manchester students had organised a programme of summer activities – mainly hikes – helped with refreshments, publicised the college programme, persuaded their organisations to affiliate and recruited new students. Harry Ingle, the Manchester secretary, had been one of the college's first students and had trained as a tutor in economics. He was an engineer at Crossleys and later Metro-Vickers in Trafford Park. Like many other NCLCers, he was also active politically and in his union. In the mid-1930s he was elected to Salford Council and, a few years later, moved to London to work for the research department of the AEU. The loss of many of its most active and able tutors to other labour movement organisations was a constant problem for the South-East Lancashire Labour College.

By the spring of 1930, five students associations had been formed and the centre pages of the annual report were used to publicise their summer programmes organised jointly with the college. It is worth looking at these in detail, as, whilst the number of schools increased and the subjects changed, the pattern remained the same until the mid-1930s.

In May there was an intermeet with West Area students at Newton-le-Willows Labour Club with Fred Casey, the area's best known tutor, speaking on 'The Theory of Scientific Thinking' with tea provided by the club. In June another intermeet was arranged with Yorkshire students at Hardcastle Crags, Hebden Bridge. Seventy students met at the entrance to the Crags, climbed up, had a picnic lunch and listened to Fred Shaw, the Yorkshire organiser, talking on 'Modern Problems'. They were then free to talk or ramble before walking down to Hebden Bridge Trades Hall for tea and an evening lecture by Bert Knight on the stock exchange. Also in June, a residential school was held in Blackpool at which Fred Shaw spoke on 'Local Authorities: Their Growth under Capitalism' and John Hamilton, the West area organiser and Liverpool councillor spoke on 'The Local Government Act, 1929: The Public Assistance Committee' and 'Municipal Enterprise in Germany and Austria' illustrated with lantern slides of Viennese housing schemes, etc. Bed and breakfast accommodation was 4 shillings and 6 pence a night, meat teas an extra 1 shilling and 9 pence, while the three lectures cost 1 shilling. In July students again met up with Yorkshire comrades for a ramble. This time from Edale to the Winnats, Castleton where they had a picnic lunch and heard a Yorkshire tutor, A.C. Lygo, talk on international relations. They then walked back to Edale for tea. The last school of the summer was at the Stockdove Hotel in Romiley, beyond Stockport. Jack Brewin, a firehose weaver who was an active trade unionist and vice-chair of the Lancashire and Cheshire Federation of Trades Councils, lectured on psychology and social science. Jack, who had joined the Dale Street classes in the early 1920s, was the main psychology tutor, and illustrated his talks with a number of visual aids which he made himself. He was elected to Salford Council in 1933 and left for a job with the LCC Fire Department a couple of years later. His talk, which was given in woods near the hotel, was followed by tea and a musical evening at the hotel.

Manchester students organised rambles in the summer of 1930. There were rambles from Hayfield to Edale, from Glossop to Hayfield, from Edenfield via New Hall, Wagh's Well and Deeply Dale and back, and, for less hardy students, a gentle ramble in the flat Cheshire countryside from Altrincham to Bollington. Other student groups organised their own activities in addition to those of the centrally organised schools. There were musical evenings, local rambles – a favourite with Bolton students, for example, being Rivington Pike – and small study groups whose topics included the latest Soviet five year plan and Bogdanoff's *A Short Course of Economic Science*.

The tutors' council overhauled lecture courses, prepared new ones and developed tutor training courses. In the summer of 1930, five 50-week training courses were started. The most influential member and grand old man of the council was Fred Casey.

Fred Casey was born in Bury in 1876, the eleventh child of an Irish Catholic tailor and his wife.[54] He left school at the age of twelve and went with the family to Ireland for eighteen months before returning to Bury. He worked in the office of a canal company for a few months before joining a plumber's shop. At seventeen he fell at work, severely injuring his leg which became infected and had to be amputated. After just over a year's convalescence he started an apprenticeship with a watch repairer with whom he worked for several years before being laid off at the age of 26.

As a boy he had taught himself to play the violin and took on what he described as 'small engagements'. With the extra money earned he paid for books and tuition in harmony, counterpoint, composition and instrumentation. After ten years study, he wrote orchestral works, orchestrations for songs, some dance music and two masses. All his music was performed but not published. Many ex-students claim that he played second violin for the Hallé Orchestra but there is no record of this in his papers.

After being made redundant, he opened a small business of his own. He had no funds to buy a stock of jewellery and watches for sale and was simply a repairer. The shop hours were long, causing him to give up his music. It was, he wrote 'economically crushed out of me'. He started to read a combination of physics, astronomy, biology and philosophy as well as rationalist literature. At 29 he married but his wife died only fourteen months later. Shortly after his marriage, he left the Catholic church, his beliefs having been 'spoilt' by his reading of rationalist literature. As a result over half of his customers took their work elsewhere.

After his wife's death he joined the local socialist society, trained its choir and studied Marx and Engels with great difficulty. For him the 'great questions' were only settled when the Rochdale and District Labour College ran a class in Bury on Dietzgen's *Positive Outcome* tutored by W.W. Craik who was later principal of the CLC. 'That altered everything,' he wrote. 'I had found something after my own heart.' In 1912 he won the Rochdale Labour College Scholarship to the CLC but could not afford to take it up. Instead he took a CLC postal course in political economy, married again and started teaching economics. He found his students experienced as much difficulty as he had in understanding Marx and fell away discouraged. He decided to devote himself to 'simplifying and expounding', and over a number of years developed his 'Economics for all' course which became the accepted syllabus for the South-East Lancashire area.

He found that in discussion his students raised a number of philosophical questions on the 'morality and legality ... of socialising

the means of life'. He started to teach 'Thinking' using Dietzgen's
Positive Outcome as the text but found that worker students had as
much difficulty with that as with Marx's *Capital*. He developed a
twelve-lecture course which afterwards formed the twelve chapters of
his book *Thinking*, published by the Labour Publishing Company in
1922, together with wall charts of such minute complexity that
students would have needed a watch-maker's glass to decipher them.
The book was reprinted in 1927 and there was also an American
edition in 1926 published by Charles Kerr of Chicago. Sales in
America were only fair according to Kerr, as the American labour
movement was in the hands of reactionaries, but a number of copies
had been exported to Japan, Russia and China.

'Economics for All' was published in serial form in four journals
with a joint circulation of 22,000 including one in braille. It was not
published nationally either by the Plebs League or the NCLC. To the
young middle-class intellectuals of the Plebs League in London who
felt it was time to put 'Old Joe' Dietzgen 'on the shelf', Fred Casey
stood for a period of IWCE which they considered they had
superceded. Bert Knight felt that Casey never got the recognition he
deserved from the NCLC nationally, partly due to the fact that he
was a self-educated working man and also because he represented the
continuation of a strong, local independence disliked by Millar and
the national executive.

All students on tutor training courses in the South-East Lancashire
area had to undertake training in Casey's 'Method in Thinking'.
Casey would take six or seven students at a time. He would divide his
lecture into six sections and deliver each section slowly. He would
invite a student to come to the front and deliver it in his or her own
words and so on until the lecture was completed. The students then
went home and rewrote the whole lecture in their own words and
returned the following week prepared to deliver it. One student
would be asked to give his or her lecture and Fred Casey and the
other students then asked questions. Fred Casey claimed that
throughout he was guiding the student 'as to his *method of
approaching* the question'. The students then returned home and
rewrote the lecture in the light of what they had learnt from the
question and answer session. This was then given to Fred Casey to
comment upon. The procedure was then followed again with the
following five lectures. Casey claimed that this method enabled him
to correct students according to their 'special needs' and 'to bring
them all to a *unified concept* of dialectical thinking.'[55]

A revised and extended 'Method in Thinking' series of lectures was published in 1933 by 'voluntary tutors and others attached to the South-East Lancashire Labour College'. In their preface the publishers, whilst highly recommending the book as a unique popular presentation of Dietzgen, were careful to make clear that the publication was a private undertaking unconnected with the NCLC. The book sold well in the North-West but was largely ignored by the NCLC nationally. Tommy Jackson, Casey's old adversary, was so incensed on reading it that, though suffering from acute neuralgia, he immediately jumped out of bed and started to write a refutation.[56]

Whilst Fred Casey was stern and a hard task-master in class, he was not totally devoid of humour as alleged by Tommy Jackson and quoted by Stuart Macintyre. Nor was he reduced in the 1930s to giving talks on 'Proletarian Logic ... to increasingly unlikely audiences such as the Oldham Health Society'.[57] In fact, he continued to be one of the busiest tutors throughout the 1930s and, on the day the Second World War broke out was addressing a day school organised in conjunction with Eccles Trades Council with over 70 students.

He apparently had a mischievous, dry wit and his strict adherence to vegetarianism followed a period in his fifties when his health suffered due to failing eyesight and obesity which severely affected his mobility on his artificial leg. Far from estranging himself even from his own supporters, as Macintyre alleges, the writer found he was still remembered with affection in the area over twenty years after his death. One ex-student sent a poem which was printed and sold at sixpence a copy in his home town of Bury to raise money for Aid for Spain.

> Bald, but not bald,
> Flecked with virgin white.
> Somewhat subjective, personal perspective
> Something, in fact, of a blight.
> Talking down, simplifying,
> Critical frown, amplifying,
> Discreet, dissembling, rather dry –
> Need, Oh need, we ask him 'why'?
> Twisting questions, turning phrases,
> dispelling mists with further hazes,
> 'Read your Marx' (whimsical look)
> 'I too have written a valuable book
> In it you will also find
> The eternal oneness of my mind.'

After the war at the age of 73, he published *How People Think* and continued to be active in IWCE. In a letter to a friend in 1947 he wrote that he was teaching two lecture courses in Oldham and Manchester on the history of philosophy, tutoring a summer school for the North Yorkshire Labour College and giving a public lecture on the British labour movement for the Heywood Labour Party. His book received what he described as a 'mean' review by Millar who ordered only 50 copies for the NCLC postal book service, took eight months to pay and then passed on additional orders to Casey who incurred the cost of postage. When he was 80 he claimed that he would be 'giving up teaching and travelling', following a twelve-lecture course in Birmingham of two lectures a day on six consecutive Sundays. He added that despite his exhaustion the teaching of scientific thinking remained his chief interest. 'The more I teach Dietzgen's Theory of Understanding,' he wrote, 'the more it seems to me to be "the goods".' A week or so later his artificial leg gave way whilst he was climbing the stairs at home and he ended up on the hall floor pinned down by a heavy grandfather clock. In a letter which belies his alleged lack of humour, he described how he and his wife coped and how 'by 12pm we got grandpa standing up, ticking'. Fred Casey died in 1959 at the age of 83. His wife was active in the labour movement in her own right as a local councillor and, in 1944, she became the first woman in its history to be elected a director of the then flourishing Bury Co-operative Society.[58]

The winter session 1930–31, during which a dispute between Fred Casey and Sam Knight took place, marked a turning point for the South-East Lancashire College. Classes, day schools and lectures started to grow as did affiliation fees from local organisations. In December 1930 the joint students' associations held a reunion with A.J. Cook, the miners' leader, speaking on 'Can Empire Free Trade Solve Britain's Economic Difficulties?' followed by tea, dancing, rebel songs and a play performed by the Eccles Students' Dramatic Group entitled *Oration over the Dead Body of a Miner*. The 'oration' was a parody of Mark Antony's famous funeral speech in Shakespeare's *Julius Caesar*.[59]

The event was so successful that for the rest of the 1930s the annual conference at which the annual report was presented took a similar format, with a national speaker like Ebby Edwards of the SWMF or Harold Laski, followed by tea and entertainment. Some years there were plays, like the Nelson and Colne Players' production of *Power and Poverty* written by W.J. Throup the Nelson Labour agent, and on other occasions there were lantern slides or an exhibition which were always followed by dancing and singing. The event was held in the large hall at the main Downing Street premises of Manchester and Salford Co-operative Society.

The turning point in the decline of the South-East Lancashire

Labour College in the winter of 1930–31 came surprisingly at a time when the area was suffering disproportionately from unemployment caused by the world crises. By the end of 1930, unemployment of insured workers in a slightly larger area of East Lancashire and Cheshire surveyed for the Board of Trade by Manchester University had risen to 31 per cent whereas the national figures never exceeded 22 per cent throughout the crisis. The cotton industry was the worst hit with unemployment rising three-and-a-half times and accounting for half of all unemployed in the area. Electrical engineering and the shirt and underclothing making-up industry came next with unemployment trebling, whilst in distribution, general engineering, textile finishing, tailoring, printing, chemicals and rubber the numbers doubled.[60]

The experience of unemployment, or of seeing whole areas like the huge industrial estate at Trafford Park virtually close down, invoked in many a feeling of outrage at the cruelty and absurdity of the capitalist system and a determination to replace it with socialism. Against the national trend South-East Lancashire Labour College numbers grew again for the year ending March 1932. Class students at 1,346 were only 60 short of the 1927 figure and, from accounting for just 3 per cent of the national total in 1930, rose to 8 per cent in 1932. Day school students were higher than in 1926 and attendance at lectures reached 6,000 exceeding the previous highest figure by 1,500. Unemployed students whose trade union membership had lapsed got free access to classes through other affiliated organisations which included Labour and Co-operative parties, Labour League of Youth, Labour Clubs, Co-operative Societies, Co-operative Men's and Women's Guilds, ILP Branches, the Clarion Cycling Club and a Labour Fellowship. Others gained free access through 28 local labour movement organisations, mainly Labour Parties, with which joint courses were arranged. There was no attempt to provide therapeutic courses for the unemployed and it would appear no demand for them. Half of the winter's 64 classes were in Fred Casey's 'Economics for All', both elementary and advanced, and in his 'Method in Thinking': all of which made considerable demands on students.

In the year ending in the spring of 1933 class student numbers rose to 1,510, less than 100 short of the peak 1926 figures and representing over 8 per cent of the national total. Day school students were nearly treble and the numbers attending lectures to labour movement organisations more than double those of 1926. Local affiliation fees rose to £110 from 83 organisations, nearly £30 more than in 1926. The annual report declared triumphantly that its work 'Independent

Education based on the works of Karl Marx', was the only way to prevent a repetition of the disaster which befell the labour movement in 1931.

In the summer of 1933 a women's tutor training class was started in Salford. The NCLC, both tutors and students, consisted overwhelmingly of men, like the labour movement it served. Millar estimated that overall there was one woman student to every twenty men. It is likely that the average would have been higher in South-East Lancashire with a high proportion of women workers in the affiliated textile unions and the Tailor and Garment Workers' Union and with its large number of Co-operative societies whose Women's Guilds were growing rapidly. In the summer of 1932, two of the area's women students travelled to the United States on Bryn Mawr Scholarships and Hannah Russell of the Tailor and Garment Workers' Union and a member of the women's tutor training class, went in 1934. The Bryn Mawr Summer School for Women Workers in Industry, which ran for eight weeks during the famous college's summer break, had started in the early 1920s and was organised jointly by the college and by representatives of working women. 'Women workers in industry' were defined as 'women working with the tools of their trade, and not in a supervisory capacity' – waitresses, saleswomen, teachers, etc. were excluded.[61] On returning Miss M. Aughton of Nelson became a NCLC tutor and Hannah Russell left the area in 1936 to become a full-time organiser for her union in London. A number of Co-operative Guild women who undertook courses went on to hold office in their Co-operative societies and in the guild itself with two ex-students, Mrs E. Beavan and Clara Bamber, becoming guild presidents. There were a few women named in the announcements of tutors and students elected to local government and, from interviews with ex-students, it would appear that many more took on political and trade union office at branch level.

There were no courses developed specifically for women students and only three schools were concerned with the position of women in our period. Of these, two were given by Sylvia Pankhurst in Nelson and Manchester in 1935 when she addressed both on 'The Struggle for Women's Emancipation' and 'The Position of Women Today', chaired by Mrs E. Beavan who had been both president of the Co-operative Women's Guild and a suffragette. The third was a weekend school attended by 130 students held in the Manchester and Salford Co-operative Society's residential centre in Altrincham in 1934, when Peter and Irena Petroff spoke on 'The Position of Women in Russia' and 'Education in Germany'. Peter Petroff had been Under Commissar for Foreign Affairs under Lenin and left for Germany following disagreements with Stalin. There he met and married Irena who was a director of education for a district of Berlin until the Nazis took power. The couple fled to France after being tipped off that they were to be arrested. Friends later helped to get their two young daughters across the border and reunited the family. The Petroffs aroused much controversy at the Altrincham school with their critical assessment of the position of women in Russia, being fiercely attacked by Communist students.

The dramatic rise in student numbers did not continue for the year which ended in the spring of 1934, though both the numbers of class students and attendances at lectures were maintained with only day school students falling significantly. Owing to the decline in class students nationally, the South-East Lancashire area's share of the national total rose to its highest point: nearly 9 per cent. In 1934 the area was reorganised with the relatively inactive areas of South Cheshire and North Wales being transferred to the Liverpool and North Lancashire area and the active cotton-weaving area of North-East Lancashire, including Blackburn, Nelson, Burnley and Accrington, being added to the South-East Lancashire College's area.

The following autumn the area faced a number of problems. The rapid growth of the previous years had to a large extent been financed by persuading local organisations, approximately half of which were Labour parties and Labour Leagues of Youth, to sponsor courses. The fall in such courses from 32 the previous winter to eighteen is virtually accounted for by the decline in the number of Labour Party organisations willing to pay for them. An additional factor was that there was a change in the demand for courses with the previously most popular subjects of economics and 'Method in Thinking' being replaced by 'Modern Problems', 'The World Today' and 'History of Socialism'. The college did not have sufficient tutors in these subjects to meet the increased demand and so some courses requested by local organisations could not run. The perennial tutor problem was exacerbated by the loss of a number of experienced tutors due to Labour successes in the autumn local elections, or people moving to jobs in the south, and also the loss of some young promising tutors to the Communist Party. Hugh Scanlon, later General Secretary of the AEU who enters his education in *Who's Who* as 'Stretford Elementary School and NCLC' joined the Communist Party at this time and stopped attending classes which, he says, were regarded as 'anti-Communist'. The North Lancashire area posed particular problems which resulted in Bert Knight travelling there three nights a week to take classes. That winter too the area lost in part the services of Winifred Knight who was expecting her first child, putting the main burden of organising the enlarged area on Bert.

The sharp fall in the number of Labour Party organisations sponsoring courses may have been influenced by the college's inability to provide tutors for courses on current topics but must also have been affected by preparations for the first General Election since the disaster of 1931. Selection of parliamentary candidates was made that autumn – in fact, Bert Knight was selected for Rusholme, Manchester. It would appear that the defeat of 1931 shocked some local Labour parties which had an uncharacteristic interest in political education but that, with the prospects of recovery, they reverted to being primarily organisations to get Labour candidates elected to local councils and Westminster.

It was classes and class student numbers which declined, not day schools whose students nearly trebled or attendance at lectures which increased by 500. The growing demand for courses to develop knowledge and understanding of current world problems, particularly the threat posed by fascism in Europe, could be met as far as day and weekend schools were concerned by a number of refugee socialists, mainly Austrian and German, who travelled the country giving lectures to labour movement organisations. There were sufficient local tutors to meet the growing demand for single lectures. The newly trained women tutors spoke mainly to co-operative organisations and Labour Party branches. A third lantern was purchased and used widely both with sets of slides made by the NCLC nationally and also with ones devised locally on such subjects as 'Fascism in Austria and Germany', 'Russia Today' and 'Manchester Municipal Enterprise'.

By 1935 unemployment in Britain as a whole had fallen to 15 per cent and in industrial Lancashire to 18 per cent, but this figure included the North Lancashire weaving district which remained high at 26 per cent despite a fall in population. The government's programme particularly benefited engineering in the Manchester area with the majority of contracts being placed within fifteen miles of the city. The economic recovery of this area and its accompanying growth in population and building boom posed problems for the local Labour College. Often the only public buildings in new areas were schools which they were not allowed to use. Also, there was frequently a time lapse between the initial development and the establishment of labour movement organisations. The new estate of Wythenshawe in South Manchester, to which Bert and Winifred Knight moved, was an exception. They and four others founded the Labour Party branch there in September 1934. By the first AGM in February 1935, there were 600 members and delegates voted to affiliate to the NCLC. Classes were held in a large manor house on the edge of the estate which the Labour Party rented from the city council. Amongst the first students were two future Labour leaders who became associated with the right and became members of the House of Lords – Jack Cooper, Wythenshawe's first Labour councillor who was later General Secretary of the GMWU; and Alf Robens, later an MP, Chairman of the NCB and of Vickers, who remembers Bert Knight as an 'excellent' and 'exceptional' tutor.[62]

In the spring of 1935 Bert Knight prepared a report on the changing situation for the Divisional Council.[63] He argued that if the decline in classes was to be reversed, the policy of relying on outside organisations to sponsor classes to meet expense should be abandoned. Instead, the South-East Lancashire Labour College itself should promote and fund all classes. Additional finance would be needed to appoint workers to carry out local advertising and organisation and also to enable the area to pay rent for suitable rooms, to meet the cost of advertising courses and to promote all aspects of the college's work. Despite the improved situation of the NCLC, no additional finance was forthcoming. Millar took the view that 'more educational work could be done by adding new postal courses than by appointing new organisers.'[64] After the problems with organisers in the early 1930s and the strengthening of central control in the revised constitution passed the previous year, he and the national executive were hardly likely to encourage local initiative.

In appointing Bert Knight in 1929, the NCLC unintentionally had acquired two organisers for the South-East Lancashire area, both Bert and his wife, Winifred. The record of their joint work suggests that a vigorous, grass-roots organisation could have been rebuilt in the 1930s if a higher proportion of the affiliation fees paid nationally had been allocated to the districts. With additional funding, initiatives could have been taken in the new industrialising areas, particularly of the Midlands and South-East. A strong commitment to local work at head office would also have resulted in the development of new syllabuses in response to changing demand. As it was, over-pressed organisers wanting to offer new courses were obliged to turn to those written for correspondence courses.

In the summer of 1936 Bert Knight became an organiser for NUPE

and moved to Chester. He and Winifred regarded their years in
Manchester as among the most rewarding and fruitful of their lives.
But their warm memories were tinged with bitter disappointment that
local work, by being starved of funds, was allowed to run down with
the resultant loss of a basic understanding of Marxism within the
Labour left.

Jack Owen took over as organiser a few months later. He was born
in Ardwick, Manchester, at the turn of the century and, after a basic
elementary education, was apprenticed to engineering at Armstrong
Whitworths. Like so many others he became unemployed in the early
1920s and joined the NUWM where he met comrades who introduced
him to Gorton Socialist Society. The Society was originally a branch
of the Clarion Cycling Club but broke away when Robert Blatchford
turned 'jingoistic' in the First World War. There he attended classes
on Marxism, enjoyed the social activities which, of course, including
cycling, and met his wife, Alice, whose mother threw her out on
learning that she was to marry 'that bolshie'. He joined a tutorial class
in Dale Street, run by Fred Casey, and became a voluntary tutor.
After some years of unemployment, he managed to get work at the
Manchester Corporation tram car works as a turner where he worked
until being appointed organiser for South-East Lancashire. He was a
quiet conscientious man, well liked by tutors and students.[65]

During the summer of 1936, in response to a national executive
decision, there was a reorganisation of the area involving the
establishment of seven local colleges, but, without additional funds
this change was merely cosmetic. The numbers of class and day
school students declined for the next two years but recovered in 1939
as did those of the NCLC overall and the WETUC. The divisional
council considered that the decline was due in part to the labour
movement being preoccupied with events abroad. In a reference to
the growth of anti-fascist organisations and the Left Book Club, they
referred to a growing tendency to form new organisations which they
considered resulted in needless duplication of activities and a
tremendous waste of workers' time and energy. They decided to call
upon trade union leaders to do all they could to persuade their
members to leave 'these mushroom organisations'. The increasing
amount of overtime being worked was also blamed.[66]

One bright spot was an influx of young engineers from Trafford
Park following an apprentices' strike in 1937; 50 of them attended an
economics class in Eccles given by Fred Flood, one of the original
Dale Street students. But few of these or indeed other young students
appear to have committed themselves to the IWCE movement.

There were only sufficient numbers for one tutor training course to run in 1937 and 1938 and for two in 1939. This was not enough to compensate for the loss of trained tutors, and, as they were all held in the south of the area, the problem of tutors in North Lancashire remained acute. Branch lectures fell by two-thirds from an attendance of over 10,000 in the year ending 1936, to just under 3,000 in 1939. In part, this must have been due to the amount of overtime being worked, to the development of suburban housing estates which lengthened travelling time and made members keen to keep branch meetings as short as possible and, perhaps, as standards of living improved, to a move towards the 'instrumental collectivism' which Goldthorpe and Lockwood argue was the basis of trade unionism among the affluent manual workers in Luton in the 1960s.[67]

Although the decline in activity in South-East Lancashire in the late 1930s was sharp, it merely brought the area into line with national developments – the share of class students being only slightly less and that of school students and those attending lectures somewhat more than in 1926.

The South-East Lancashire Labour College in the period between the defeat of the General Strike and the outbreak of the Second World War was remarkable for regaining and in some aspects even surpassing its 1926 level of activity. Yet at no point did the National Executive, faced with a steady decline in class numbers, seriously reconsider its heavy financial commitment to correspondence courses. Millar's assertion that more educational work could be achieved by adding correspondence courses than by appointing new organisers did not hold true in this period. In 1936, for example, the writer estimates that nearly two thirds of the NCLC's income was spent on only 7,000 correspondence course students and central administration whereas the one third allocated to local colleges provided a service for 15,000 class students, 16,000 school students and those attending single lectures.[68] Faced with this gross underfunding and the impossibility under the new constitution of the local colleges combining to defeat the National Executive's policy at the annual conference, it is hardly surprising that many able voluntary tutors decided they could serve the labour movement more effectively in other ways and that young men and women turned to other progressive organisations. As argued earlier, the NCLC did continue to be a provider of IWCE as well as of practical labour movement training courses, but in the process of asserting strong central control, the union leaders on the national executive discouraged local initiative and stultified the movement.

Notes

[1] A.J. Corfield, *Epoch in Workers' Education: a History of the WETUC* (London, 1969), p. 41.

[2] Brian Simon, *Education and the Labour Movement, 1870–1920* (London, 1974), p. 340.

[3] Corfield, op. cit., p. 33.

[4] *Annual Report* of the South Lancashire Area of the NCLC for the year ending March 1928, p. 3; Albert Knight papers.

[5] J.P.M. Millar, *The Labour College Movement*, (London, 1979), p. 92.

[6] Stuart Macintyre, *A Proletarian Science, Marxism in Britain, 1917–1933* (Cambridge, 1980), pp. 81–5, and Andy Miles, 'Workers' Education: the CP and the Plebs League in the 1920s', *History Workshop*, no. 18, 102–114.

[7] Organiser South-East Lancs, NCLC, 1929–1936. Albert and Winifred Knight were interviewed on four occasions between December 1977 and Albert's death in December 1979. Subsequently Winifred has given two interviews, clarified numerous points in telephone conversations and letters and has read and confirmed the final draft of this essay.

[8] Reprinted in *Labour Monthly*, February 1927.

[9] Millar, op. cit., p. 97.

[10] For a brief account see James Klugmann, 'The Communist Party from Class against Class to the Popular Front', in *Culture and Crisis in Britain in the 1930s*, J. Clark, M. Heinemann, D. Margolies and C. Snee (eds), (London, 1979), pp. 22–7.

[11] Interview with John Hamilton in Liverpool, July 1980.

[12] Letter from Jack Jones, 26 February 1980; see also Jack Jones, 'A Liverpool Socialist Education', *History Workshop*, No. 18, Autumn 1984, pp. 92 ff. Jack Jones was later General Secretary of the Transport and General Workers' Union.

[13] Millar, op. cit., p. 109.

[14] Morgan Phillips was later General Secretary of the Labour Party.

[15] In October 1923, two years after its formation, the NCLC reorganised the affiliated colleges into eleven divisions based on those of the AUBTW. Most divisions had one organiser, but those with a number of large constituent colleges were divided into areas with an organiser for each area – for instance the North-West No. 8 Division and the Scottish No. 10 Division, both of which had three areas and organisers.

[16] For the two accounts see Millar, op. cit., pp. 109 ff. and Albert Ellis, *A Secret History of the NCLC* (Birmingham, 1937), pp. 10 ff.

[17] Millar, op. cit., p. 114.

[18] Albert Ellis, op. cit., p. 13. The matter was taken up by their union, the Association of Women Clerks and Secretaries.

[19] A. Mansbridge, *An Adventure in Working Class Education* (London, 1920), p. 19.

[20] S.G. Raybould, *The WEA: The Next Phase*, (London, 1948), p. 102.

[21] J.F.C. Harrison, 'The WEA in the Welfare State', *Trends in Adult Education*, S.G. Raybould (ed.) (London, 1959), p. 6.

[22] *Plebs*, April 1931.

[23] Ibid., September 1931.

[24] Ibid., May 1932.

25 Ibid., December 1933.
26 Ibid., December 1933.
27 Ibid., May 1931.
28 Ibid., June 1932.
29 Corfield op. cit., p. 248; *Education For Emancipation* (NCLC, London, November 1935), pp. 6–7. But see p. 70, note. 119.
30 Corfield, op. cit., p. 67.
31 Ibid., p. 58.
32 H. Lyster Jameson, *An Outline of Psychology* (London, 1921), Preface.
33 Mary Stocks, *The WEA: The First Fifty Years* (London, 1953), p. 89.
34 Interviews with students of the 1930s, including Sam Banks of Swinton, Harry Lees of Stockport, Annie Taylor of Sale, James Bisley of Chester, Lord Fred Lee of Newton le Willows.
35 Stocks, op. cit., p. 19.
36 *Plebs*, March 1930.
37 Ibid., May 1930.
38 Quoted in Millar, op. cit., p. 264.
39 R. Peers, *Adult Education* (London, 1958), p. 160; T. Kelly, *A History of Adult Education in Great Britain* (2nd ed., Liverpool, 1970), p. 283; J.F.C. Harrison, *Living and Learning* (London, 1961), 297.
40 Millar, op. cit., p. 117.
41 *Plebs*, May 1934.
42 *Ibid.*, December 1933.
43 Noreen Branson, *History of the Communist Party of Great Britain, 1927–41*, (London, 1985), p. 188.
44 See Michael Newman, 'Democracy versus Dictatorship: Labour's Role in the Struggle against Fascism, 1933–6', *History Workshop*, No. 5. Spring 1978.
45 *Plebs*, October 1935, February 1937 and April 1937.
46 See Betty Reid, 'The Left Book Club in the Thirties' in Clark *et al.* (eds), op. cit. See also John Lewis, *The Left Book Club: an Historical Record* (London, 1970), p. 7.
47 Letter dated 14 September 1984.
48 At the NCLC Annual Conference, 1935, the organiser for the South East Lancashire area urged members to press councils to build meeting places on new estates.
49 Simon, op. cit., p. 340.
50 *Plebs*, October 1939.
51 C.L. Gibbons, 'The Training of Tutors', *Plebs*, January 1937.
52 Interview with Albert Knight.
53 Interview with Winifred Knight, March 1980.
54 Fred Casey papers, Ruskin College Library, Oxford, Box 9; letters Fred Casey to Eugene Dietzgen, 16 January 1926 and 7 February 1929; W.W. Craik to Fred Casey, 7 August 1912 and 25 July 1913. Interview with Albert and Winifred Knight, December 1977. Albert Knight's papers. Information also from numerous ex-students including Harry Haslam, Arthur Millwood, Harry Lees, James Disley and Elisabeth Wood. For an excellent critical account of Fred Casey's writings, see Stuart Macintyre, *A Proletarian Science* (Cambridge, 1980), pp. 134–8.
55 Letter, Fred Casey to Joseph Dietzgen, 27 February 1929 (Box 9, Fred Casey papers, Ruskin College Library).
56 T.A. Jackson, *Solo Trumpet*, original manuscript, pp. 111–3. Working

Class Movement Library.

[57] Macintyre, op. cit., pp. 134–6.

[58] Letters in Fred Casey papers, Ruskin College Library, Box 9, dated 15 April 1947, 6 July 1955, 3 August 1955 and 8 October 1955. Poem from H. Haslam. Information about Mrs Casey from Margaret Withington.

[59] Copy in the Working Class Movement Library.

[60] *An Industrial Survey of the Lancashire Area (excluding Merseyside)*, made for the Board of Trade by the University of Manchester, (London, 1932).

[61] Margaret T. Hodgen, *Workers' Education in England and the United States* (London, 1925), p. 227.

[62] Letter, 16 January 1980.

[63] NCLC Acc. 5120, Box 84, National Library of Scotland.

[64] J.P.M. Millar, *The Labour College Movement* (London, 1980), p. 139.

[65] Information from his lifelong friend, Fred Flood, 31 March 1980.

[66] Minutes of meeting at the Thatched House Hotel, Manchester, 5 March 1938. NCLC Acc. 5120, Box 84, National Library of Scotland.

[67] John H. Goldthorpe, David Lockwood, Frank Bechhofer and Jennifer Platt, *The Affluent Worker in the Class Structure* (Cambridge, 1971), pp. 166–70.

[68] Albert Ellis, op. cit., p. 61, for national income; South-East Lancashire Labour College Annual Report for area grant, multiplied by fifteen, and assuming all fifteen areas received a similar amount.

Margaret Cohen

4   Revolutionary Education Revived: The Communist Challenge to the Labour Colleges, 1933–1945

In the autumn of 1933 the NCLC, long used to combating the education versus propaganda claims of its major competitor, the WEA, faced a new challenge from within the independent working class education movement. The Marx House Schools in London and Manchester were set up by Communists who considered that the Labour Colleges had abandoned the historic independent working-class education objective of preparing workers for power, and 'too often ... merely trained workers as officials and leaders who became false to the ideals of the [working-class] movement'.[1] They wanted to establish workers' schools in which the Marxism taught would include the recent developments made by Communists, particularly Russian Communists, which the Labour Colleges largely ignored.

This essay traces the history of these Marx House Schools from 1933 until their closure in 1945 and assesses the extent of their contribution to IWCE. As in the second and third essays, a detailed study is made of developments in the Manchester area.

The decision to establish a Marx Memorial Library and Workers' School in London had been taken earlier in the year when a group of Communist intellectuals in the Labour Research Department, with the support of the publishers Martin Lawrence, set up a Commemorative Committee to mark the fiftieth anniversary of Marx's death with 'a fitting memorial in the form of a centre of working-class education to the greatest thinker and revolutionist of all time'.[2] The committee organised a conference and exhibition attended by 190 delegates from London trade union branches, Trades Councils and Labour Party, ILP, and Communist Party branches and

137

put before it a resolution, which was passed unanimously, that the memorial should take the form of a Marxist library and workers' school.

An appeal for money was launched under the auspices of the Labour Research Department with Clive Branson in charge. Within a few months sufficient funds to buy premises outright were raised – the major contribution coming not from the labour movement but from two benefactors in one of whose names the title deeds were held. The property purchased at Clerkenwell Green had long been associated with progressive organisations. In the 1870s it had been the home of the London Patriotic Club and from 1893 was used by the Twentieth Century Press which printed William Morris's *Justice* and large numbers of socialist pamphlets. *Iskra* was printed there for twelve months in 1920-3, when Lenin was in London, with formes made by an emigrant Russian compositor. In 1922, the press moved to new premises in Southwark and the building had a variety of tenants until 1933.

The committee also appealed for gifts of books and pamphlets to establish the library which was to have sections of both Marxist and non-Marxist works on political philosophy, economics, history (especially working-class history) and science. About 3,000 had been donated by the time the library opened.

Robin Page Arnot, who had been secretary of the Labour Research Department, was appointed Principal of the school. He was a leading Communist intellectual who had joined the party in 1920. In 1925 he had been imprisoned under the Emergency Powers Act but was released in time to play an important role in the General Strike in the North-East. He was also a long standing member of the Communist Party's Central Committee and one of its delegates to the Comintern in Moscow in the late 1920s.

The school and library opened in October 1933 with an inaugural public lecture by the veteran Tom Mann on 'The Life of Marx'. Classes were held in the evenings. There was one three-term course in political economy and the rest were ten-week courses consisting of 'Marxist Newsreel', giving a Marxist interpretation of current affairs, 'The Russian Revolution', 'Trade Unionism: Its Recent History and Problems', 'How Socialism can be Achieved' and 'What Every Worker Wants to Know – An Elementary Course in Marxism'. Class tutors included J.R. Campbell, the Red Clydesider and ex-editor of the *Worker*, Bill Shepherd chief sub-editor of the *Daily Worker* and John Mahon a leader of the Minority Movement who was later sent to Spain as a Political Commissar. Weekly Sunday lectures ranged from 'Marxism in India', given by Ben Bradley, one of the Meerut prisoners, to 'The Films' by Ivor Montagu, the film-maker and a founder of the Progressive Film Institute which became famous for its documentaries of the Spanish Civil War.[3]

The syllabuses of some class courses were printed and offered with a tutor to study circles for discussion, or to individuals and groups as correspondence courses. No tutor training courses were run but the tutors offered to study circles were in the main Communists who had undergone party education. Workers' study circles were inspired by factory study circles in the Soviet Union. The role of a circle leader was described by 'a Soviet propagandist on Marxism-Leninism' as being to 'conduct his class in such a way as to rouse the *activity* of his students, so as to teach them to *undertake independent work*, to accustom them to make independent contributions to the discussions ... bookishness must be eliminated'.[4]

Marx House Bulletins were published from March 1934 giving reports of activities, announcements of forthcoming events and containing one or two articles of interest to Marxists. They consisted of a few duplicated sheets produced on the school premises and costing a few pence.

In 1935 an impressive fresco was painted in the Library's reading room by Viscount Hastings who had joined Marx House as a student. He had recently returned from Mexico where he had studied under Diego de Rivera and he adopted a similar heroic style and strong colours. The subject was 'the symbolic representation of the working class breaking the chains of the capitalist stage'.[5] In the centre is the head and shoulders of an archetypal worker (male, of course!) behind whom the rising sun forms a halo. He is flanked by Robert Owen, Engels, Marx, Lenin and William Morris. On the left foreground are Chartists and on the right contemporary workers, whilst in the centre falling churches, banks and the Stock Exchange represent the crumbling of the old order. In 1966 the mural was covered and the space in front covered with bookshelves. Andrew Rothstein, a post-war librarian wrote 'opinions were and remain divided as to whether this was a loss or a gain'.[6]

Student numbers grew steadily and by 1936 there were 1,533 individual members but only 45 affiliated organisations, mainly at branch level. Apart from students attending classes and lectures at Marx House itself, there were 67 discussion circles, 32 correspondence course students and a summer school. There had not been the necessary breakthrough in the Co-operative, trade union or political movements, except for the Communist Party, for the school to be firmly established. In fact, nearly half its income in 1935 came from 'a few good friends'.[7]

Regular exhortations were made to supporters to build up Labour movement affiliations, but little was done by the school to develop out-reach work. There were no prospectuses published, no tutor training courses held, no voluntary organisers appointed and no regular news of study circles was printed in the *Bulletin*.

Marx House School, Manchester, had rather different origins to its London counterpart. It was opened in January 1934 by four Communist working men: Sam Knight, a water board employee; Jimmy Claxton, a plumber; Larry Finlay, a tool-maker; and Marcel Bouttier, a Frenchman known as C.H. White who is thought to have settled in Manchester after taking part in the Black Sea Mutiny of 1919 led by André Marty and who earned a precarious living from language tuition in between his many political activities.[8] The Manchester school had no leading Communist intellectuals to give lectures or to act as tutors and compilers of syllabuses and no generous benefactors to provide premises. The four self-taught men, or (to use the ugly jargon term) autodidacts,[9] launched their workers' school, wrote a wide-ranging two-year tutor training course, compiled syllabuses, ran courses on a variety of subjects and met their expenses as best they could by charging a few pence per student per class.

Knight, Claxton and White were all ex-tutors of the South-East Lancashire Labour College. They left in 1930-31 when a new basic dialectics course – Fred Casey's 'Method in Thinking' – was introduced which included an attack on Communist Party policy.[10] They continued to teach Marxism to a variety of organisations including some newly formed workers' study circles, but considered that this piecemeal activity did not 'help the revolutionary movement in the Manchester district very much'.[11]

Marx House School, Manchester, was to be the central organisation on which an effective network of workers' study circles could be built to provide revolutionary Marxist education free from the distortions of Caseyism. It would train tutors, plan syllabuses and provide study materials but, at that stage, a central school running classes and lectures on the London model was not envisaged.

In January 1934 the school opened in a room in C.H. White's house opposite the central Co-operative premises in Downing Street. Nineteen students including four women were enrolled for an ambitious two-year training course which, the founders claimed, would 'transform their previous knowledge from a more or less parrot-like form into scientific reasoning'.[12] The first year consisted of 25 lectures in physics and astronomy, geology, biology and sociology, and in the second, political economy, the works of Marx and Engels, the works of Lenin and the everyday struggle of the present revolutionary movement. Although each subject was presented by one of the four founders, the lectures were a collective effort, based on material collected by all four and a final draft agreed by all. Where possible all the lecturers attended the classes but took care not to dominate the discussion. At the end of each year the lectures were typed and a copy handed to each student.

The following July, the founders felt sufficiently well established to write to the *Daily Worker* appealing to readers in the Manchester area to form their own study circles and affiliate to Marx House. A summer day school was held at the Clarion Club House in Handforth addressed by Robin Page Arnot.

As in London, modest progress was made. By April 1937 central premises had been obtained in Water Street and a technical department established which produced all the school's teaching materials. There were 126 individual members whose 2 pence a week provided the school's main income but only eight affiliated study circles, which were mostly Labour Party organisations, and two two-year training courses in Manchester and Bury. A Sunday Forum was running successfully – the 'Unity Campaign' bringing in speakers from previously hostile organisations.[13]

The two-year training courses had not produced many active study circle leaders. The school, in fact, had only eleven trained tutors on whom the full burden of teaching fell. Over half of the 70 students who had enrolled in the central classes since 1934 had dropped out or left the area. Others worked long hours or lived at a distance. Two attempts had been made to offset the school's failure to attract organisations away from the Labour College by trying to develop links with those which did not have NCLC schemes. The first was in the autumn of 1936 when the Left Book Club, whose membership in the Manchester had risen to 700 in only six months,[14] indicated that a number of members wished to study Marxism. Marx House school organised a sixteen-week introductory course and Collets Book Shop sent out specially printed syllabuses to all Left Book Club members. In the event only three students turned up to the first class! A similar poor response occurred when leaflets outlining the school's activities were distributed at a series of public meetings organised by the Communist Party. The annual report claimed that people who showed an interest were 'not directed to the Marx School ... though

... the present Unity Campaign conclusively points that this should have been the proper course to take'.

In late 1937 two of the founders left the school and this, together with the failure to keep newly trained tutors, meant that the school had to curtail its activities. It moved to cheaper premises in Bridge Street and stopped training courses but continued to give classes to outside bodies, to hold the Sunday Forum and even introduced a successful class in Esperanto.[15]

The two founders who left the school were Sam Knight, who returned to his native Cardiff, and Larry Finlay, who was elected to the District Committee of the AEU. As mentioned in the previous essay, the loss of trained tutors was a constant problem for the IWCE movement. Tutors were lively, intelligent men and women who were also active in other labour movement organisations. Often the fact of their studies in workers' education led to their being selected as candidates for political, trade union and Co-operative office. Some firms also had a policy of promoting such workers thereby effectively removing them from labour movement activities.[16]

At some time in the summer of 1938, a decision was made by the remaining tutors not to re-open Marx House School in the autumn. The closure was due to the failure to build up sufficient labour movement affiliations, to hold a viable number of trained tutors and to get the whole-hearted support of the Communist Party in the Lancashire and Cheshire district. The older labour movement organisations of the left – and we must remember that those of the right favoured the WEA – remained in the Labour College movement, and the newer growth organisations, consisting of the peace and anti-fascist movements and the Left Book Club, were more interested in immediate issues than in systematic study. The broad syllabus of the tutor training course was excellent and the typed lectures that have survived are of a high standard. It compares favourably with the two-year full-time course at the Central Labour College. It was, perhaps, unrealistic, given the inevitable high wastage rates, to tie up so many of the school's limited resources in this course. However, what was achieved was considerable. Sam Knight and his comrades must be one of the last groups of elementary-school educated workers in Britain to set up, teach and write all the material for courses in Marxism.

Despite the growth in Communist Party membership, the London school also experienced a decline in the second half of 1937, due, according to the annual report, to increased activity in connection with Spain and the growth of the Left Book Club discussion groups.

A deficit of £125 was incurred. Once again wealthy supporters dipped into their pockets and a problem which in Manchester could have proved terminal in London was simply a minor set-back.[17]

The school responded by offering short five-week classes mainly on current issues and tutored by leading marxists. They included William Rust on the 'Recent History of Spain', Palme Dutt on 'War and International Politics' and 'British Empire and Peace', Allen Hutt on 'Post-War History of Britain', J.B.S. Haldane on 'Heredity', Emile Burns on the 'Class Structure of Britain', John Gollan on 'Youth', John Lewis on the 'History of Philosophy' and John Strachey on 'Political Economy'.[18]

For the growing number of intellectuals joining the Communist Party and those developing an interest in Marxism, Marx House published two *International Book Reviews* which provided a guide to the growing body of Marxist literature being published throughout the world.

In 1939 the school was reorganised into faculties of history, philosophy and science and 'set itself the task of establishing a People's University' which would develop in students the 'fullest scientific understanding necessary for building a future society'.[19] Three distinguished professors headed the Faculty of Science – the physicist J.D. Bernal, the biochemist J.B.S. Haldane and the mathematician Hyman Levy. In the winter of 1939-40 they organised a twenty-week series on popular science with the aim of bringing 'science to the understanding of the common people' as T.H. Huxley had done in his famous 'Lectures to Working Men'. Unfortunately the war interrupted their plans and the London Blitz caused the cancellation of the entire winter programme for 1940-41.

In the summer of 1940 the London school sent its honarary librarian, Edward Charles, to Manchester in what appears to be its only successful attempt to develop a provincial school. Charles, or Professor E.C.E. Hemsted as he was known in Manchester, was a recent recruit to Marxism, which he claimed he had been driven towards by sheer intellectual logic. He was, Frank Williamson recalls, 'a dominating character, an excellent lecturer and a wonderful theoretical Marxist'.[20] He was one of those colourful, wealthy, middle-class eccentrics the labour movement attracts from time to time. He claimed to have been vice-chancellor of the University of Hyderabad, tutor to the children of the Emperor of Japan and a writer of short stories.[21] He made his own clothes and furniture, bound books and devised a method of chicken rearing which resulted in record egg production. Although sent to Manchester by the

London school, Hemsted, always totally convinced of the correctness of his own position, soon grew to distrust Alex Massie, the London secretary, and discouraged links with the parent organisation.

The second Manchester Marx House School was launched in September 1940. Rooms were rented in the Corn Exchange and a working committee of Communists was formed to undertake the day to day work of the school. There were two full-time members – Molly Broadbent, the organising secretary, and Hemsted, the educational secretary, whose private income enabled him to give his services free. Course syllabuses and material were, in the main, first written by Hemsted but then discussed and revised by the working committee.

Ten-week tutor training courses were organised, and by May 1941 eighteen tutors were active out of a total of 38 trained. They were responsible for the formation and organisation of 22 groups and the tutoring of 24. Two ten-lesson correspondence courses were offered in 'Political Economy' and 'Capitalism and War: Socialism and Peace' and, by May, 41 correspondence groups had been set up, mainly in Manchester, South-East Lancashire and Cheshire with a total of between 400 and 500 students. Duplicated course lessons were sent to the groups weekly or fortnightly and it was suggested that these be read aloud a paragraph at a time with a pause for discussion. At the end of each lesson were questions for discussion and a list of reading material. With the last lesson of the course, Hemsted wrote a letter suggesting that the group might undertake further correspondence courses. If the group was ready for a more advanced study of Marxism, there were readers' guides to aid members in the reading of Marxist texts, or if members wished to study any other subject, study guides and individual classes would be prepared.

Tutorial classes were also held. In May 1941 classes in 'Basic Marxism' were given to a group of twenty engineers contacted through the People's Convention Committee and another to a small group of artists. A third tutorial class was held in 'Office Routine' for 'new members of the working committee and close associates' which covered 'the ordinary methods and techniques of organisation against the background in which Leninists work'.[22]

During the summer of 1941, members of the working committee became alarmed at the gulf that was developing between Hemsted and the Communist Party and insisted that discussions be held on relations between Marx House and the party. As a result it was agreed that Marx House would become the official educational arm of the Lancashire and Cheshire District whilst also continuing its work in the wider labour movement.

In the following month (June 1941), the school campaigned to extend its activities in both areas. Communist Party branches were urged to affiliate and to run classes for their 600 new members, to put on advanced courses for members of longer standing and to persuade other local organisations to put on Marx House classes. Trade unions, factory committees and co-operative organisations were offered courses and tutors. 80 courses were held in the last quarter of 1941 – half on elementary and advanced Marxism and half on aspects of the Soviet Union and the war. It is not clear what proportion of these were specifically for the Communist Party, but a letter from Marx House to branch secretaries in December states that the education department was 'gravely concerned about the apparent lack of interest in education throughout the Party'.[23] In addition there was a number of very successful classes and factory discussion groups some of which were attended by 'well over 100 workers'.[24] Six day schools were held in Manchester and surrounding towns with speakers including Palme Dutt, Hyman Levy and J.B.S. Haldane.

Finance of the Manchester school was unorthodox. Professor Hemsted's view was that deficits did not matter: to sell a lot one had to spend a lot. Within a few months of opening the school had a debt of £130 due to maintaining a central office and a paid full-time secretary, purchasing office equipment and Professor Hemsted's insistence on expensive publicity material. The financial problem was eased by renting cheaper premises at 62 Downing Street, using two rooms and letting the other four, and, of course, by the rapid growth of classes and affiliations. These were sufficient to reduce the debt to £77 by the annual general meeting in April 1942.

In the summer of 1942, Professor Hemsted left for Cornwall after disagreements with the district Communist Party and the committee set about the formidable task of paying off the rest of the debt. It doubled affiliation fees, issued an appeal fund and, it was hoped as a temporary measure, dispensed with its full-time paid secretary. The burden of organising the day-to-day work of the school, planning programmes and contacting organisations fell on the part-time members of the committee, most of whom had jobs and other labour movement commitments. In the circumstances it is hardly surprising that the school was not able to maintain its early high rate of growth. Frank Williamson remembers particularly the extensive educational work that the school continued to undertake in the large factory branches at Metro-Vickers in Trafford Park and Gardeners in Eccles.

The economy measures were not sufficient to solve the school's financial problems which were exacerbated the following winter when income from classes fell as students found it increasingly difficult to attend central classes due to wartime conditions. Day schools flourished and the committee decided to concentrate on them. They were, however, expensive: halls had to be hired, speakers' costs had to be met and as much publicity as for a whole programme of classes had to be produced and distributed.

In April 1944 the school's working committee recommended that the Manchester school should become a constituent part of Marx House, London, providing suitable financial arrangements could be made. In June it became Marx House, Manchester Branch. It continued to plan its own programme which consisted of only two central classes, monthly day schools, two summer schools, classes for affiliated organisations, occasional lectures to outside bodies and two Sunday evening showings of progressive films.

At the end of the war the Manchester school was closed as a result of a national decision of the Communist Party that Marx House should cease direct educational activity. In the euphoric atmosphere of 1945 it was felt that there was no longer a need for a separate 'respectable' educational organisation to present Marxism-Leninism to the wider labour movement. Its closure was viewed with little regret by the local Communist Party leadership who always disliked the fact that it was not subject to party control.

In 1944 the working committee assessed the Manchester school's educational provision as being basic in standard but given by tutors of high quality. Certainly the correspondence courses and tutorial class material which survive are well planned, thorough and free of jargon. The school provided an educational service for the growing numbers of Communist Party members whose branches accounted for over half of its affiliated organisations. The few trade union or Co-operative affiliations tended to be with branches or guilds. There was one breakthrough at regional level when the North-West Region of the Fire Brigade Union affiliated in 1943, but despite considerable effort by Marx House, which organised tutorial classes and day schools for the union, it did not reaffiliate. The South-East Lancashire Labour College remained the major provider of IWCE in the area.

The London school's lectures and classes continued to be severely affected by wartime conditions after the London Blitz had caused the complete cancellation of its winter programme in 1940-41. The popular Sunday evening lectures were replaced by occasional short series held in large central halls. Classes continued to be offered but fewer ran and student numbers fell. Bombs damaged the central premises causing the school and library to be moved to nearby Doughty Street in late 1942. The library offered a limited service there until the flying bomb raids when it was packed up and sent to Nottingham for storage by the Nottingham Co-operative Society.

Affiliations grew from 64 in 1939 to 182 in 1944. As in Manchester, the majority were Communist Party branches but some headway was made in the trade union and Co-operative movements. In 1944 the London Region of the Fire Brigade Union affiliated and the National Union of Shop Assistants, Warehousemen and Clerks' annual conference adopted a post-war education scheme which put Marx House on the same footing as the WETUC and the NCLC. Under the scheme members would be able to choose between the courses offered by the three organisations. There were also two affiliations by Co-operative societies – the London society in 1942 and the Nottingham society in 1944. Many Co-operative guilds which did not affiliate took up Marx Houses's offers of speakers and tutors. Maggie Jordan, who was assigned to develop links with local societies, tirelessly travelled the country giving talks.

In 1941 the faculty of science decided to give priority to developing educational work with scientists in the hope of recruiting them to the anti-fascist struggle.[25] They organised symposia and day schools on political issues to which scientists had a special contribution to make, such as racialism, science and technology in the Soviet Union and Hitler's New Order in Europe. The first symposium on Engels: *Dialectics of Nature* and *Origin of the Family, Private Property and the State* was held at Caxton Hall in August 1941 with an average attendance of 400 at each of the three sessions and a total of 700 overall.[26]

The most important wartime contribution to IWCE by the London school was its provision of educational materials. Syllabuses of class courses had been printed throughout the 1930s and offered to study groups. In 1941 sales of the three syllabuses in print rose dramatically. 5,000 copies each of *Scientific Socialism* by Joan Thompson and *Leninism* by Palme Dutt were sold within two months and had to be reprinted and a similar number of a new edition of *Introduction to Political Economy* by R. Page Arnot were also sold.[27] The *Marx House Bulletin* for August 1941 claimed that this unprecedented rise in demand came from newly formed workers' study groups and discussion circles particularly in London, Lancashire and Scotland.

Edmund Frow considers that these consisted partly of Communist Party branches whose numbers were increasing and partly of groups

formed by Communists with their workmates and fellow trade unionists. Factory branches were growing. By April 1942 there were 109
branches in the Lancashire district alone with 1,925 members. Even a
small factory branch with members in different workshops could form
several study groups. Members of the forces also used the syllabuses in
informal discussion groups and they are even said to have been used
unofficially in army education.[28]

The October *Marx House Bulletin* contained an article on 'Methods
of Work in Study Circles', and a *Guide for Tutors* was published in
December which dealt in 'particular detail with the "question and
answer" method of handling classes'.[29] 160 prospective tutors had
completed a series of five tutorial classes by the following February but
no indication was given of the number who were active.[30]

New syllabuses were rapidly prepared and, by the summer of 1942,
Marxism and War by Dona Torr, *Socialism in Practice* by George
Rudé and *Problems of Trade Unionism* by Allen Hutt were available.
Two syllabuses were specially produced for railway and building
workers – *Railways and Railwaymen in the USSR* by Peter Kingsford of
the Railway Clerks Association and *Problems of the Building Industry*
by David Percival of the Association of Building Technicians. These
were followed by *India* by H. Palmer, *Women in Industry* by Joan
Thompson, *Economics of Capitalism* by Maurice Dobb, *Imperialism
and the People* by Frank Verulam, *Chartism* by Salme Dutt and lastly,
in time for the 1944 local elections, *What You Need to Know on Local
Government* by Michael Shapiro.[31]

Sales remained high throughout the war years and the more popular
syllabuses went into several editions. *Economics of Capitalism* which
was published in November 1943 sold 12,500 copies in just over twelve
months whilst *Imperialism and the People* and *Chartism*, which were
published in the spring of 1944, sold 5,000 copies each by the end of the
year.

The syllabuses were pocket-sized, paperback booklets costing a few
pence. In all except Dutt's *Leninism*, the text was divided into lessons.
Some gave guidance to study circles by asking questions for discussion
and distinguishing between essential and further reading whilst others
simply had a list of further reading at the end of each lesson. *Leninism*
was, in fact, a study guide to Stalin's *Foundations of Leninism* with an
introductory essay by Dutt. Read on their own, the syllabuses would
give a very brief, very basic introduction, but if the further reading was
conscientiously studied, a reasonable coverage of the subject could be
achieved. Much, of course, would depend on the availability of books
and also on the study-circle leader.

In November 1942 Marx House started to publish a fortnightly *Educational Commentary on Current Affairs* in association with the *Daily Worker*. Each issue dealt with a topic of current interest to the labour movement. It covered the background, assembled the relevant facts and figures, summarised arguments and policies and suggested further reading on the topic concerned. The *Commentary* was bought by trade union and Co-operative committees to be used as speakers' notes, by discussion groups and members of the forces.[32] Sales, which totalled 2,000 in the spring of 1943, rose to 3,400 by December 1944 and to 5,000 a year later. Issues of special interest to labour movement organisations were reprinted and sold as leaflets. *A Century of Co-operation* and *Why you Should be a Co-operator* jointly sold over 50,000 copies to Co-operative societies. One society distributed the latter with its bread round and another gave it to members with dividend notices.[33]

Marx House, London, was closed in the summer of 1945 as a result of the same change in Communist Party policy which closed the Manchester school. Its annual general meeting in April set up a sub-committee 'to consider the work of Marx House in relation to the further development and expansion of Marxism in this country'. It reported that Marx House's role as a provider of education was virtually limited to the London area, that its output as a publisher of educational materials for the labour movement was sporadic due to lack of capital, that the library had in practice taken second place and that its basis in the labour movement was very weak. The only remedy to these weaknesses would be to compete against the NCLC and the WEA: organisations with which the Communist Party's new policy was to have 'friendly association'. It recommended that Marx House should be built up as a central national library of the literature of the labour movement. The report was overwhelmingly accepted and a move to keep the school open as a tutor-training organisation was defeated.

Marx House, London, was most successful in the 1930s as a prestigious central school with classes and lectures given by many of the country's leading Marxists. Its failure to develop as a national IWCE organisation based on study circles was in part due to its own lack of commitment to out-reach educational work. No voluntary tutors or organisers were trained and no forums by which tutors and students could communicate with each other were established.

In the war years the school's printed syllabuses helped to meet the desire of growing numbers in the labour movement and armed forces to learn more about Marxism. They provided excellent, basic summaries but, again, the school's organisers failed to ensure that the needs of inexperienced worker tutors and students were met. All syllabuses should, like George Rudé's *Socialism in Practice*, have included questions for discussion and have given advice on essential and further reading.

The courses provided by all three schools were, in the main, short and elementary. Attempts to introduce longer, more systematic study were not successful. A sizeable number of students dropped out of the two-year tutors' training course offered by the first Manchester school and only three Left Book Club members were interested in its sixteen-week course in basic Marxism. The London school soon dropped its one-year course in political economy and an attempt in 1941 to launch a certificated 'Fundamentals of Socialism' course for study circle students based on printed syllabuses was unsuccessful.[34]

At the founding conference of the London school in 1933, a woman delegate stated that 'Capitalists realise the importance of women and use them for cheap labour; the workers must equally realise their importance and turn it to another purpose.'[35] However, all three schools, like the labour colleges, offered courses to women on an 'equal' basis with men and failed to develop strategies which took into account women's additional inequalities.

Overall the Marx House schools made a valuable contribution to the IWCE movement. They primarily offered Communist education and their failure to become the major provider of IWCE in their areas paralleled the failure of the Communist Party to displace the Labour Party as the natural party of the left in Britain.

The Marx Memorial Library continues to provide an excellent resource for the labour movement. It was reopened in 1949 at 37a Clerkenwell Green after the extensive war damage to the building had been repaired. The closure of the school effectively doubled the space available for the reference library and enabled the creation of a reading room and offices for the librarian and secretary.[36] A programme of evening lectures on Marxist classics, philosophy, history and literature was held. Since 1949 occasional lecture series and individual lectures have been organised. The library now contains over 100,000 books, pamphlets and periodicals. It has specialised collections on the International Brigade and the Spanish Civil War, the Hunger Marches, Ireland, the Third World, the John Williamson Collection of US material, the J.D. Bernal Peace Library and the James Klugmann collection of radical and Chartist literature.

Notes

[1] Report of an Exhibition and Conference held at Conway Hall, Red Lion Square, London on Saturday, 11 March 1933. Marx Memorial Library.
[2] R. Page Arnot, first principal of Marx Memorial Library and Workers' School, quoted in Andrew Rothstein, *A House on Clerkenwell Green*, (London 1983), p. 73.
[3] Course Prospectuses and Programmes, Bulletins, Annual Reports and other papers File 1d. Printed syllabuses Box A14. All in Marx Memorial Library. Biographies from Noreen Branson, *History of the Communist Party of Great Britain*, (London 1985), p. 346.
[4] Reprinted in *Marx House Bulletin*, October 1941.
[5] *Marx House Bulletin*, November 1935.
[6] Letter to Carol McKenna, 28.1.76. Marx Memorial Library, File 1d.
[7] *Marx House Bulletin*, March 1935.
[8] E. and R. Frow, *The Communist Party in Manchester 1920-6* (Manchester 1979), p. 73.
[9] Stuart Macintyre, *A Proletarian Science*, Cambridge 1980.
[10] For Fred Casey's account see Proceedings at the Tutor Council, 17 January 1931, NCLC Box 38, File 2, National Library of Scotland, and letter to J.P.M. Millar 10 December 1935. Fred Casey Papers, Ruskin Library, Box 9. For Sam Knight's account see *Communist Review*, August 1931, p. 322.
[11] First Report of Manchester Marx House School, July 1934, Larry Finlay Papers, Working Class Movement Library.
[12] Ibid. Of the nineteen students, seven were Communist Party members, four in the ILP, four were in Co-operative Guilds and four were unattached.
[13] Annual Report, Marx House School, Manchester, April 1937, Finlay Papers.
[14] Letter from Frank Allaun who was the Left Book Club Convenor in Manchester, 14 September 1982.
[15] Treasurer's Report, Marx House School, Manchester, April 1938. Finlay Papers.
[16] Interview Albert Knight, December 1977.
[17] Annual Report for 1937, Marx House, London. Marx Memorial Library, File 1d2.
[18] Prospectuses for October-December 1938 and January-March 1939, Marx House School. Marx Memorial Library, File 1d.
[19] Prospectus Autumn-Winter 1939-40. Marx House, London. Marx Memorial Library, File 1d.
[20] Frank Williamson was Treasurer of Marx House, Manchester from 1940. He gave interviews and lent his papers.
[21] An Edward Charles won the Best British Short Story Prize for 1932 for *A Great Bunch of White Lilac*. Short Story Index.
[22] Reports to the Working Committee, October to December, 1941, Marx House School, Manchester.
[23] Letter from the Organising Secretary, December 1941, Frank Williamson Papers.
[24] *Marx House Bulletin*, London, May-June 1942.
[25] Barbara Ruheman, Report to the Faculty of Science, 1943, Marx Memorial Library, File 1d.

[26] Andrew Rothstein, *op. cit.*, p. 76.

[27] *Marx House Bulletin*, August 1941.

[28] Interview with Edmund Frow, 17 August 1987.

[29] *Marx House Bulletin*, London, December 1941.

[30] *Marx House Bulletin*, London, February 1942.

[31] Syllabuses, Marx House, London. Marx Memorial Library, Box A17.

[32] *At Your Service: Educational Commentary on Current Affairs*. Published Alex Massie, Marx House Library, no date. Frank Williamson Papers.

[33] Annual Report, Marx House School, London, 1944. Marx Memorial Library, File 1d.

[34] *Marx House Bulletin*, London, August 1941. Under the scheme students would study the three syllabuses in print (*Scientific Socialism, Introduction to Political Economy*, and *Leninism*) and the three in the process of publication (*Socialism in Practice, Problems of Trade Unionism* and *Marxism and War*). They would receive a Marx House Certificate if they attended 80 per cent of classes, produced written work to a satisfactory standard and made relevant contributions to group discussions.

[35] Report of an Exhibition and Conference held at Conway Hall, Red Lion Square, London on Saturday, 11 March 1933, p. 5. Marx Memorial Library.

[36] Annual Report, 1946. Marx House, London, p. 3.

Roger Fieldhouse

5   Bouts of Suspicion: Political Controversies in Adult Education, 1925–1944

For much of the period covered in this essay an anti-fascist 'semblance of unity' existed which obscured many of the ideological divisions in British society, particularly in the society of intellectuals and the Labour movement to which adult education belonged. A broad popular-front consensus bred a tolerance of political opponents. Communists, socialists, social democrats, liberals, even conservatives were sometimes caught up in the same anti-fascist net. Certainly there was a popular-front unity which was quite unlike the later fragmentation of the left.[1] However, there *was* an alternative ideology of the right which was more prevalent in the world at large than in the world of adult education. On occasions the right was stirred out of its complacency precisely by this semblance of unity on the left, and this was sometimes reflected in attitudes to adult education:

> At a time when the distinction between democratic and revolutionary socialism, between Labour and Communist parties, was still blurred in most people's minds, the working-class idealism of the WEA, with its political overtones, frequently led it to be regarded with suspicion, despite its care in proclaiming itself 'non-party political'. Indeed, throughout the inter-war period there were recurrent bouts of suspicion.[2]

Therefore, although the Board of Education files,[3] which contain correspondence, interviews, annual returns, HMIs' reports and all the other records of relations between the Board and the adult education 'Responsible Bodies'[4] from the mid-1920s onwards, reveal very little in the way of political controversies, from time to time there were nevertheless controversial incidents which reveal the political sensitivity of this adult education work. Perhaps one of the most revealing was the WEA's involvement in the proposed TUC education scheme in 1924-25 which is referred to briefly in the first essay in this volume.[5]

The formation of the Workers' Education Trade Union Committee by the WEA and the Iron and Steel Trades Confederation in 1919 and the foundation of the National Council of Labour Colleges (NCLC) by the Labour Colleges and the Plebs League in 1921 had heralded a fierce battle between the WEA and NCLC for the educational heart of the trade union movement. After several years of insults and bickering between the rival organisations the TUC general council established an education advisory committee to try to resolve the conflict. The committee invited its various constituent bodies to submit plans for a co-operative trade union education scheme 'under the control of the general council'. In July 1924 the WEA responded with a proposal which, although emphasising the association's non-doctrinaire educational tradition, envisaged a constitutional amendment which would put its policy *under the control* of direct representatives of the working-class movement. In September the TUC passed a WEA-backed resolution in favour of a co-operative educational scheme subject to 'such measure of control (by the general council) ... as is considered necessary in the interest of workers' education'.

At the instigation of the NCLC, which doubted the WEA's ideological commitment to independent working-class education, the TUC advisory committee persuaded the WEA to agree that the purpose of the scheme should be 'equipping the workers ... in the work of securing social and industrial emancipation' – an anti-capitalist and distinctly subversive objective.

The proposal was ratified by the WEA in May 1925 and by the TUC in September, but even before the scheme had been formally agreed, the WEA was being accused of becoming a Marxist or communist propaganda machine. The WEA reacted to these criticisms by attempting to minimise the political significance of the scheme, claiming that it implied no real change in its work. On occasions, representatives of the WEA deviously adopted modified terminology which introduced a degree of confusing ambiguity about the aims and purpose of the scheme.

The WEA also claimed that the scheme was a compromise to prevent the TUC from establishing a fully-fledged Marxist educational scheme under the influence of the NCLC. In July 1925

R.H. Tawney explained to leaders of the County Councils Association that the scheme was not altogether to the WEA's liking, but it was the price they paid for securing recognition of WEA classes by the TUC. In default of the agreement, Tawney suggested that the TUC may well have set up its own separate educational organisation which would have been far more subject to the influences of the Marxian wing of the labour movement. Three months later, A.D. Lindsay, the influential Master of Balliol, told Lord Eustace Percy, President of the Board of Education, that the scheme was really an attempt to prevent the TUC dismissing both the WEA and the NCLC and starting an educational scheme of its own, with most undesirable consequences. 'If the WEA is not allowed to enter into this agreement and at the same time retain the support of the Education Authorities, then I am afraid the only result will be a great swing to the left in educational matters.' The TUC scheme was thus represented as a compromise to prevent this happening 'and all the objectionable phrases in that agreement' sprang from that compromise. Understanding this 'makes a considerable difference to the way these phrases ought to be interpreted'.[6] However, these arguments did not convince all the sceptics and critics. For nearly a year following the publication of the agreement in March 1925 the WEA found itself subject to a barrage of threats and criticisms from its friends, partners and paymasters, as well as its enemies.

One of the most influential critics was Alderman Sir Percy Jackson, Chairman of the West Riding Education Committee and leading member of the County Councils Association and the Association of Education Committees. He not only disliked the stated aims of the scheme, and the trade union movement's apparent controlling influence, but also the other clauses of the agreement which implied that courses would be exclusively for trade unionists; restricted the source from which tutors could be recruited; and required the WEA to try to ensure that all its tutors would be members of a trade union or professional organisation. He believed the Agreement represented a surrender by the WEA to the control of a new committee on which the hated NCLC would be represented. He saw in this a grave risk that the Association was exposing itself to be captured, or to be used for the purpose of propaganda, by the Labour Party, and indeed by the Marxian wing of the labour movement.

During the remainder of 1925, the local authority associations and individual local education authorities continued to express doubts as to whether, under the circumstances of the TUC agreement, they could continue to grant aid to the WEA.

Meanwhile, on behalf of the government, Lord Eustace Percy insisted that courses of study assisted out of public funds must have no connection with the tenets of any political party and the teaching given must be free from any flavour of political propaganda, and that there should be no restrictions in the recruitment of tutors or students. This not only comprehensively undermined the proposed scheme, but also the WEA's traditional commitment to *working class* adult education, which went back to its founding principles. Moreover, as Lindsay pointed out, it was impossible to avoid all tenets of the political parties without excluding almost all socially relevant subjects, and that absolute freedom from political bias required a degree of impartiality which no tutor could be expected to possess. Lindsay claimed that although the WEA tried to avoid political bias, no one is absolutely impartial in practice and, what is more important, people's views about what is impartial vary. They ultimately compromised by agreeing that the teaching 'must *aim* at freedom from party bias and from any flavour of political propaganda', but Lindsay was less successful in arguing that it was legitimate to expect WEA tutors to have experience or understanding of working-class life and sympathy with working-class aspirations. This was a fundamental ideological principle about the identification of the adult education movement with working-class interests which the Conservative Lord Eustace Percy stoutly resisted.

Indeed, as the summer of 1925 wore on, Percy's attitude hardened for a number of reasons. By September he was encouraging the local authorities to 'assist the Board in ascertaining the character of the WEA classes' and to think of replacing them where they were deemed unsatisfactory. Although hesitant to undertake this task unless they had full control, the local authority associations decided to set up a sub-committee to look into the scheme in October 1925. When it met on 16 December, it adopted the conditions that had been hammered out between Percy and Lindsay, and also insisted that grant-aided classes should be open to inspection by local educational authorities, or their representatives, who would also have the power to approve (or disapprove) syllabuses and tutors. These conditions undoubtedly amounted to a diminution of the liberties previously enjoyed by the WEA, particularly its specific identification with the working class, and represented a significant increase in the local authorities' control over WEA classes.

The scheme itself never came to anything. The agreement was never implemented. The trade union movement had more urgent things on its mind during the early months of 1926, and more pressing problems after May! The WEA and NCLC continued to bicker and to compete for trade union support. But this in no way invalidates the conclusion that the reactions of the Board of Education and the local authorities to the scheme did demonstrate the limitations of the WEA's independence by making explicit what had long been said of the WEA, that its privileged position was conditional on good behaviour, and that its vital funds were conditional on its 'impartial' blend of education not unduly upsetting the social *status quo*. The authorities took the opportunity of this incident to clip the wings of the WEA by imposing a very restrictive interpretation of the agreement and establishing a more effective machinery for supervision and control of grant-aided classes, always with the threat of the withdrawal of grants if the WEA did not meet their conditions.

In fact, some local authorities acted as if the scheme had come into operation and used the powers allotted to them. Bolton Education Committee, under the influence of its very dominant Conservative chairman, had been suspicious of the WEA as a 'hot-bed of socialists' for the previous decade. It now jumped at the opportunity to withdraw its grant on the grounds that the WEA had indeed become a socialist propagandist agency for the TUC. The Bolton WEA branch organised a vigorous campaign for the restoration of its grant, abetted by the staunchly Liberal *Bolton Evening News*, by Canon Carpenter, the Vicar of Bolton, who admonished the town councillors from the pulpit on Mayoral Sunday, and by one of the WEA's respected elder statesmen, William Temple, Bishop of Manchester, who addressed a public meeting in the Co-op Hall attended by more than 300 people. Temple spoke of the value of the WEA in providing working people with a chance to take a responsible part in politics and public affairs and warned that if responsible people were not given this help, then working-class organisations might fall into the hands of 'irresponsible people'. He was echoing the warning given by other WEA leaders to Lord Eustace Percy and the local authority associations, and it was heeded in Bolton where the publicity did much to rehabilitate the WEA. The Education Committee restored the grant the following year.[7]

In Edinburgh, the local education authority (which under the Scottish system was the sole source of public finance) decided to support the new 'Edinburgh Workers' Educational Association' which had seceded from the National Association in January 1926 in protest at its involvement in the TUC scheme.[8] Two months later, in March, the East Riding County Council attempted to interfere in the WEA's choice of subjects and tutors, much to the annoyance of the

Yorkshire District.[9] These were the practical and immediate manifestations of the WEA's loss of independence. The longer-term and less tangible sense of caution induced by the affair is not so easy to document, but was accurately foreseen by Lord Eustace Percy when he remarked during the controversy that it was his view 'that £100,000 spent annually on this kind of work, properly controlled, would be about the best police expenditure we could indulge in'.[10]

However there is no doubt that the protracted negotiations over the TUC education scheme had left a residue of suspicion and this was reflected in Board of Education investigations into alleged NCLC infiltration of LEA classes in Carmarthenshire and Glamorgan in 1926, described in detail in the first essay in this volume (see pp. 52-57), which claimed to identify suspicions about the WEA's political reliability on the part of both employers and the local education authorities.

A year of so later, the HMIs were discovering some of this alleged 'extremism' in Responsible Body classes in the North of England. In a 'Report on Adult Education in Yorkshire for the Period Ending the 31 July 1927' the HMIs complained that literature was too often treated as a discussion of social problems, and they tartly noted that '*Oliver Twist*' is not a scientific treatise on Poor Law Reform'. The history classes in Yorkshire were reported to be 'in danger of encouraging that habit of facile speculation and superficial generalisation which it is one of the purposes of the study of history to correct', while in Lancashire and Cheshire the following year it was reported that

> comparatively inexperienced tutors ... devoted too much time to a popular treatment of the lists of wrongs suffered by the working classes. Instead of discussing cause and effect relationships, there was a tendency to teach such topics as the Poor Law, Factory Acts, Chartism, and trade union history, [while] vital national issues were never discussed.[11]

Clearly, the HMIs were not happy about this concentration on political and social topics of particular interest to working-class students, which were likely to offer a rather different lesson from the national issues they had in mind.

In 1930 the WEA South-Western District tripped over the line of acceptable orthodoxy and fell on its face in Torquay, when it attempted to dissolve the local WEA branch and form another, more closely linked to the trade unions. At a full meeting, members of the existing branch, some of whom claimed to be the 'reverse in political views of Labour', vigorously opposed the move as undemocratic and unconstitutional. They were supported by Alderman Johns, who stated he had come as representative of the Local Education Committee, and by W. Bennett, MP. Suspicion that the district was attempting a political coup was repeatedly expressed. 'There is a deliberate attempt to bring in a side issue of politics into this movement, to make the WEA part of the labour movement in Torquay,' stated one member heatedly. What the district was apparently trying to do was to create a branch which more accurately reflected the WEA's commitment to working-class education. But the coup was unsuccessful and the meeting broke up in uproar. Bennett raised the matter with the Parliamentary Secretary but he was advised to discuss it quietly with the WEA national officers. The Board of Education watched discreetly from the touchline to make sure the game did not get too rough, but refused to become directly involved. HMI Owen was asked for his opinion about the incident and was sent off to make further discreet enquiries. But he was told to avoid trouble because 'the more we can keep out of these local disputes, the better'.[12]

This incident well illustrates the subtle role of the officials of the Board of Education in controversial incidents at this time. As far as possible they kept out of any conflict, adopting the role of neutral umpire which enabled them to warn the Responsible Bodies if they appeared to be stepping too far out of line, but also to protect them from misguided or merely prejudiced right-wing attacks, such as the following incident, although in this case the politicians bypassed the officials, who were therefore powerless to defuse the situation.

The incident arose out of a day school on the development of Russian industrialism, held at Chatham in April 1933, and run jointly by the WEA Medway Towns branch and the Chatham Divisional Labour Party. The tutor was H.L. Beales who had considerable experience of adult education in both the Yorkshire and London districts (and who, as lecturer and later reader at the LSE, became one of the leading economic historians of his time, and an active member of the Extramural Council and Joint Tutorial Classes Committee in London for many years). The day school was attended by a representative of the Conservative Party South-Eastern Area Agents' Association who clearly went as a spy, not a student. His contentious report accused Beales of being 'not only a Socialist but an avowed Communist [who] was not afraid of airing his views' on the subject of the daily life of the Russian people. Beales had the temerity to defend Russia from the attacks which had been made in the national newspapers and to support the present system in Russia. He gave 'a very flowery atmosphere of the advantage of living under the Communist regime'. It was also deplored that the tutor was apparently an atheist. Other objections were raised to the 'supply of political literature available of a Socialist and Communist character', particularly the *Daily Worker* which appeared to be read by most people present between the lectures; to the presence of Hugh Gaitskell, the prospective Labour candidate for Chatham, and the open association with the Chatham Division Labour Party; and to a resolution denouncing the government's attitude on Russian questions which was carried unanimously by a meeting of those who remained behind after the day school was closed. This report was subsequently discussed by the Conservative Party South-Eastern Area Agents' Association which was also informed about certain WEA activities at Folkestone. They decided to send the report to all MPs in the area and also to party headquarters so that further evidence of 'socialistic control of classes' could be obtained – sufficient to warrant the matter being raised in the House of Commons with a view to eliminating the socialistic propaganda or stopping the WEA's grant. At least three local Conservative MPs (Sir Park Goff, Sir Philip Sassoon and Waldron Smithers) raised the matter with the President of the Board of Education, Lord Irwin, or his Parliamentary Secretary, H. Ramsbotham. Sassoon's consti-tuency association, Hythe, also sent a resolution to the Board, expressing alarm at the WEA Medway Towns branch's political activities: 'and in view of the state grant received by the WEA, respectfully suggests to the President of the Board of Education that a close enquiry is necessary into the activities of the WEA'. Ramsbotham summoned Ernest Green, the WEA General Secretary, and told him 'that it seemed grossly improper that a body which received grants from the Board of Education for its tutorial classes, and which claimed to be non-political, should hold what was practically a political meeting in conjunction with the local Labour Party'. Green apparently accepted the Conservative Party agents' criticisms without demur and undertook to administer a severe warning to the culprits and to ensure that this sort of impropriety did not occur again. Lord Irwin told the MPs he hoped this warning would suffice to stop this sort of thing.[13]

The extreme Tory atmosphere in Kent did tend to breed suspicion and complaints about the views and activities of adult education tutors. According to Lord Wigg, who was the WEA's honorary area organiser in East Kent between 1931 and 1935, there was a constant stream of such complaints.[14] One of the causes was the anti-capitalist and pro-Russian attitude of A.T. D'Eye, an Oxford staff tutor, who began teaching in Canterbury in 1931. D'Eye's unrestrained and unambiguous admiration of the Soviet Union embarrassed both the WEA and the Oxford Extramural Delegacy on a number of occasions in their relations with the local authority.[15]

In West Sussex, concern was expressed about the life-style of J.R. Armstrong who became a part-time WEA organising tutor in 1932, and a full-time member of Southampton University College extramural staff in 1936. The Bohemian social habits and extreme political views of some of the inhabitants of Armstrong's home at Storrington before the war caused a considerable amount of gossip amongst his rather staid conservative neighbours. On several occasions the County Director of Education felt obliged to warn J.H. Matthews, the WEA District Secretary, that Armstrong's activities were causing offence. What would now be regarded as an unexceptional communal life-style was frowned upon in pre-war rural Sussex, especially when it involved nudism or when the Education Committee discovered that a young woman whom they were paying as a model at Worthing College of Art was living with a man in Armstrong's house. Armstrong himself explained that

> we kept a rather open house and a number of friends who stayed with us were or had been members of extreme left-wing groups, some being German refugees ... other friends were members of the Peace Pledge Union or eccentrics who had attracted some measure of attention.

He also gave a home to Jomo Kenyatta, and befriended two young Trotskyists who quite seriously asked if they might house a secret printing press in his house.[16]

At Nottingham Professor Peers had to defend one of his tutors, Arthur Wells, who was no political extremist, against complaints about a lecture he gave at Derby in which he stated it was possible to have a strike of capital as well as a strike by workers; and that he thought this might be what was then happening. At Leicester, there was much head-shaking about James Cameron while he was a staff tutor at Vaughan College because it was felt he somewhat ardently advocated his communist views (at least until his conversion to Catholicism). At Liverpool, Mary Hickley was criticised by HMI Dann for being 'a staff tutor very much in the Labour interest', although she was also considered quite incompetent, and was eventually dismissed by Liverpool. (She then took a job as a Conservative organiser!)[17]

HMI reports on classes provided by Hull University College in 1933 and Birmingham University and the West Midlands WEA

District in 1934 were highly critical of their academic standard and some of their political bias, in much the same way as the reports on Yorkshire, Lancashire and Cheshire had been in 1927-28. The HMIs criticised the perjorative use of the terms 'nationalism' and 'imperialism' in two international relations extension lecture courses at Hull, and were much more critical of 'intemperate' written work by students in several international relations classes in Birmingham and the West Midlands.

> Many controversial statements were presented as self-evident truths ... Such tolerance as was displayed consisted only too often of the spurious type that is based not so much on belief in the *bona fides* of other nations as in an unreasoning distrust of the writer's own country.

It was implied that the tutors were partly to blame for not challenging the students' prejudices. They needed to be not only highly qualified in knowledge, experience and temperament, but also of a 'judicious habit of mind'. Students in literature classes were again criticised for being too keen to discuss social and economic problems suggested by the tutors' summary of the subject matter, and there were two instances of WEA classes in which thoughtless and intemperate statements were encouraged rather than checked by the tutors. There was also a philosophy tutor who allowed popular economic theories to go unchallenged in his classes. The general feeling expressed in the reports was that there was altogether too much intemperate, perjorative and injudicious bias being permitted if not encouraged by the tutors.[18]

One interesting aspect of the Board of Education file on the Birmingham and West Midland classes in 1934 is the difference between what the Board's officials were prepared to condemn privately and what they considered fit for more public knowledge. A minute paper referring to HMI Grierson's original report notes that a certain paragraph

> casts a rather livid light on the sort of nonsense that – I suppose invariably – goes on in some of these adult education classes and I don't doubt that it is useful to call the attention of RBs [Responsible Bodies, ed.] to it. But I should imagine that if this report ever got into the hands of the uninitiated and unsympathetic, this passage might supply popular material for attack on adult education work in general.

The offending passage refers to a trade union tutor, O.G. Willey, who taught sessional and terminal classes in modern economic problems, and was also engaged in political organising. The Board minute considered it 'rather surprising that the tutor in question was appointed to take classes of this nature; it would be asking too much of him to expect strict detachment and impartiality in the treatment of his subject'. The Board's officials seemed particularly anxious to delete the reference to Willey's political activities because they had burnt their fingers in such cases before. The HMI agreed that the offending paragraph about Willey should be omitted because 'he had a poor mind, but his intellectual integrity is not in question'. The passage does not appear in the final printed report.[19] This provides another illustration of the Board's officials protecting the RBs from political attacks.

In 1938 it was HMI Dann's turn to criticise a tutor's 'intemperance' – in this case R.H.S. Crossman's, who at that time was Dean of New College and a part-time tutor for the Oxford Delegacy of Extra-mural Studies. At the annual conference of the British Institute of Adult Education in September 1938, Crossman returned to a theme he had aired earlier in the year in the WEA journal, the *Highway*: that university methods and concepts of education were faulty in themselves and unsuited to adult education, often creating a gulf between the tutor and his class; while 'academic standards' could paralyse students' capacity for action and render good trade unionists useless to the labour movement. He hinted that the Board of Education favoured the academic approach because it thought that it thereby turned adult education students into politically innocuous bystanders. Dann abhorred this 'intemperate speech' and also condemned G.D.H. Cole for speaking 'as though he considered that the function of the voluntary body were to provide education exclusively for the working class' – thereby confirming that the battle fought between A.D. Lindsay and Lord Eustace Percy in the summer of 1925 about whether or not it was legitimate for the adult education movement to be specifically committed to the working class had been won by Lord Eustace and that, at least in the eyes of the HMIs, this fundamental ideological principle had been displaced by the view that grant-aided Responsible Bodies should be universal providers for the whole community. Dann noted that both Crossman and Cole were offending against this official orthodoxy.[20]

These were not major clashes. No action was taken. Indeed, there is little the Board of Education could have done about Crossman or Cole. But Dann's remarks do reveal how there was this continuing suspicion and feeling of unease – and a continuous watchfulness.

A year later Cole again appears in the picture, although not at the centre of the stage, when the South Berkshire Conservative

Association agent, C.F.R. Bagnall, wrote to their MP, Brigadier-General H. Clifton-Brown, about the scandalous activities of the WEA in Thatcham:

> Once more I have to complain about the WEA at Thatcham. A meeting was held on Thursday, June 1st in that district and a lecture given by Mr Jardine of Andover. The chairman was Mr Cole, a well-known local socialist. Once more a tub-thumping speech was given on Communism and the Russian system. The reports that I have received indicate that the lecture was in no sense educational but merely a piece of left-wing propaganda posing as such. Mr Jardine gave a lecture at Newbury to the League of Nations the other day and protests at that meeting were made on account of its extreme Communist views. Russian institutions through the whole lecture were compared favourably to British institutions and the usual left-wing claptrap produced. I have some notes on the lecture if they are required. It really is scandalous that money should be granted by the Berks County Council to support what are really only Socialist meetings in Thatcham. It is only fair to say that generally speaking, in this part of Berkshire, Thatcham is the chief offender and that in Woodley, for example, the lectures are more moderate and educational.
>
> Would it be asking you too much to draw the attention of the Board of Education once more to the activities of this branch of the WEA? Either this organisation is a Workers' Educational Association, or it is vehicle for left-wing propaganda. If it is the latter, as is undoubtedly the case at Thatcham, grants of public money should be withdrawn from it.
>
> I am sure you will agree with me that something should be done with regard to this matter.[21]

One of the common characteristics of such complaints is clearly evident in this case. It is based either on hearsay, or on what the lecturer said *at a different place and time* – in this case at a League of Nations Union lecture where he presumably would have been fully entitled to engage in political propaganda. He may have given another tub-thumping speech on communism and Russia to the WEA at Thatcham but it is possible that the reporter's own political perspective, combined with the socialist reputations of the chairman and lecturer, made a legitimate lecture seem like a piece of left-wing propaganda. However, it was good enough for the General, who passed the complaint on to the Board of Education, but there is no evidence that the Board did anything more than quietly file it.

Berkshire was part of the Oxford extramural empire. In another part of that empire, in North Staffordshire, George Wigg took over as WEA district secretary in 1937. Apart from the financial and administrative problems of the district, he had to deal with numerous complaints about the political activities of some tutors. These stemmed very largely from the intrigues of John Thomas, the senior resident tutor in the district, who encouraged students to report any examples of tutors' political bias to local Conservative councillors; or would himself feed councillors with ammunition for accusations. (As Cecil Scrimgeour rather euphemistically says in his history of the North Staffordshire district, Thomas's 'overflowing energy and enterprise were not always easy to live with'.) Complaints flowed in about Stephen Swingler and other tutors whose youthful enthusiasm for good causes resulted in their making political speeches, attending protest meetings, helping to organise strikes and being involved in all kinds of political activities. For tutors in adult education it has never been easy to draw the line of demarcation between private political activity and work, especially if their job involves organising and/or teaching courses in politically relevant subjects. It has caused many disputes. It brought endless trouble in those politically tumultuous years leading up to Munich and beyond, to war. Wigg claimed that there were very few weeks when he did not have some complaint to deal with. These were not always from arch-Tories: the local trade union officials and Labour councillors in Stoke were just as liable to complain about tutors' political activities and opinions – such as Scrimgeour's pacifism – if they did not agree with them.[22]

At Cambridge, the insistence of one extramural lecturer, F. Elwyn Jones (who later became a Labour Lord Chancellor), that he include references to a popular front in his syllabuses; and the enthusiasm of another, John Hampden Jackson, for Finnish, Estonian and Latvian resistance to the encroachments of the Soviet Union, attracted criticisms from HMI Jack from time to time. Jack was also involved in investigations into another Cambridge tutor, Maurice Bruce, whose reference to the 1919 Amritsar massacre as a decisive factor in influencing Gandhi's attitude against the British administration in India, at a class at Wellingborough in 1939, was misreported in the local paper and caused the local Conservative MP, Wing Commander A.W.H. James, to suspect Bruce of raising trouble about the government's Indian policy. James asked the Board of Education to obtain a satisfactory explanation, threatening otherwise to raise the matter in the House of Commons. Jack was dispatched to Cambridge to question Geoffrey Hickson, Secretary of the Cambridge Board of Extramural Studies, about Bruce, and to examine Bruce closely about his views.[23] The episode does illustrate how vulnerable adult education was to criticism and political pressure if it was believed – in this case erroneously – to be purveying political views that threatened the Establishment, especially in such controversial areas as the question of Indian independence.

The outbreak of war not unnaturally increased the political pressures and strained the interpretation of objectivity even further, especially in the field of international relations and current affairs. The war brought much closer to the surface the conflict that always existed between what tutors might conceive of as objective scholarship and what the Establishment paymasters might consider to be the national interest.

In the early months of 1940 HMIs Jack and Dann submitted reports to the Board of Education on the problem of controversial topics in adult education. They were anxious for the Board to realise the inflammable nature of many of the topics dealt with in adult education, including 'international relations, causes of the war, the character of the peace, federal union and so forth'. 'Such topics if indiscreetly handled either by accident or design on the part of the lecturer might easily give rise to a storm of protest accompanied by questions in the House which the Board would find extremely embarrassing,' warned a Board official in a minute paper circulated internally in May 1940. It was also noted that the Board had received 'various letters from individuals complaining of certain tutors in this connection. We have *mostly* been able to satisfy ourselves that in these cases the complaints could be answered,' but it was necessary to realise that 'The temper of people is easily roused at present and with the increase of casualties and danger may become more readily roused still.'[24] This was a clear warning that the adult education movement should be even more careful not to stray beyond the permissible boundaries.

This cautiousness was apparent in Wales when a tutor supported an application by one of his students for exemption from military service as a conscientious objector by stating that the applicant's views were consistent with those he had previously expressed in a WEA class. The tribunal chairman demanded to know whether WEA classes were teaching pacifism. It is doubtful whether he, or public opinion, was altogether placated by the tutor's claim that students were at liberty to express their views in the class.[25] Another example of the difficulties that arose during the early part of the war occurred in Cornwall, where a class had to be stopped after the tutor and one of his students came to blows about their opposing views.[26]

The Board of Education minute warned that indiscretions and embarrassment were a very real danger, 'especially in view of the left-wing character of so many of the lecturers and their disciples'. It was not considered possible for the Board to prohibit classes in these subjects, which were of course matters of the liveliest interest at that time. But it was suggested that the Board should issue to the Responsible Bodies 'a very carefully worded circular stressing the necessity of treating such topics objectively and impartially and of avoiding any ground for complaint that the Board are encouraging an anti-national point of view'. (It is interesting to see such an overt example of equating the national interest with objectivity and impartiality.) It was also suggested that it should be intimated 'that any lapse from propriety would jeopardise payment of grant'. However, despite the acknowledged problems, which were liable to be increased with the extension of adult education lectures to HM Forces, and despite the added advantage that the warning should not only obviate any cause for complaint 'but would be a very useful weapon of defence in the event of any complaint arising'; nevertheless, it was decided that a directive from the Board would precipitate trouble. 'The Board would be charged by some extremists with a desire to limit free discussion,' especially as it had no actual evidence of improprieties that it could produce. Instead, it was decided to encourage the Responsible Bodies 'to pass on a word in season to their lecturers and tutors'. At a meeting on 21 May, representatives of the Responsible Bodies were warned that

> at the present time more than ever is the subject of 'International Relations' and related subjects full of inflammable material and it therefore behoves RBs to see to it that syllabuses are without doubt defensible from the scholarship point of view and that the tutors are not only qualified in scholarship but are judicious persons ... 'Freedom' of lecturers is limited by scholarship and judiciousness of mind.[27]

Of course, what was considered judicious was itself a value judgement.

The representatives of the Responsible Bodies appreciated the importance of this informal warning, and within a month the Central Joint Advisory Committee on Tutorial Classes (CJAC) issued a statement by Sir Walter Moberly (Chairman of the Central Advisory Council for Adult Education in HM Forces and of the University Grants Committee) on 'The Handling of Controversial Subjects in Wartime'. There is internal evidence indicating that the statement was drafted or approved by the Board of Education before being issued by the CJAC. The statement recognised that frank and free discussion of controversial subjects was one of the very things Britain was currently fighting for, but also warned that this would inevitably cause particular difficulties in wartime when 'any attempt at objectivity and detachment in discussion is apt to seem unpatriotic'.

In such circumstances, extra caution and discretion were called for. A tutor was not expected completely to bury his personal opinions on burning issues which came up for discussion. 'But it is his business to avoid propaganda, conscious or unconscious, and to be scrupulous not to use the class as a means of making converts to his own beliefs, whether popular or unpopular, or to allow it to be so used by the class members.' (The last phrase was a late insertion into the document, adding further to the tutor's demanding obligations – he was already required to guard against unconscious bias!) Failure to put this principle into practice ('we all accept this principle in theory') would imperil freedom of discussion throughout the whole field of adult education at this difficult time, warned the statement, so the Responsible Bodies should impress on tutors 'the exceptional demand which will be made in wartime on their sense of responsibility'.[28] Thus, tutors were exhorted to show a 'patriotic' objectivity and a sense of responsibility which paid due deference to what the Establishment defined as the national interest in wartime.

Acting in the spirit of these wartime directives, Major Peto MP raised the sort of embarrassing question in the House of Commons in November 1942 that the Board of Education had earlier envisaged, and tried to prevent. He asked R.A. Butler, the President of the Board of Education, whether he had considered the statement made at the Labour Institute at Kettering on 3 October by the acting President of the WEA (H. Clay) and 'whether he will take steps to ensure that no such partisan or contentious political pronouncements are made in future by officials of grant-aided bodies'. Butler was able to dismiss this question quite easily by stating that 'the acceptance by a body of grant from the Board in respect of its educational work should not be taken as placing a limitation on the right of free speech enjoyed by its officers and members,' but the question had nevertheless been raised.[29]

Two years later, Sir Robert Topping, General Director of the Conservative and Unionist Central Office, was roused by a report of the 1944 WEA annual conference in the *Daily Herald* to write to Butler to ask about the WEA's grant. He was 'curious to know what grants the WEA did receive from the government and how they are expected to use them'. The Board's explanation about grants of up to 75 per cent of teaching costs for courses under adult education regulations, plus exceptional grants for wartime work, apparently allayed his suspicions.[30]

Earlier in 1944, the HMIs' adult education committee expressed concern that with the growth of informal adult education during the war, there had been a downgrading of the premium on tutors' qualifications, with a resultant decline in educational conduct and objectivity. The inspectors warned that unless the articles requiring tutors to be suitably qualified were retained and enforced, they 'could not give the Board guarantees that what it was aiding was educational in character and free from party-political bias'.[31] They did not like the less academic informal work which was growing in popularity in the WEA and many extramural departments for the same reason that they had not liked Crossman's attack on academic standards and Cole's identification with the working class at the British Institute of Adult Education conference in 1938: it was intemperate and politically less reliable, or orthodox.

In September 1944 G.F. Hickson, the secretary of the Cambridge Board of Extramural Studies, was called upon by Butler to explain the political activities of adult education lecturers in the Cambridge area once more: in particular, the activities of Douglas-Smith who was regarded by the Board of Education as somewhat unsatisfactory in this respect. HMI Jack prepared a brief for the Minister, explaining that Douglas-Smith was an old-established tutor with serious academic qualifications and many years of unexceptionable teaching in the Bristol area before the war.

> But during the war something seems to have affected his judiciousness. In particular he was very much antagonised by Lord Vansittart's views about Germany. Not that he sympathises with the Nazi outlook – he hates it; but he, I think, objects to broad condemnation of the German *people*. He feels strongly about this and social affairs generally and I think his emotional balance has been upset by the war ...[32].

It does not appear to have occurred to Jack or anyone else at the Board that it might have been their judiciousness and emotional balance that had been upset by the war, and that Douglas-Smith's refusal to swallow the Churchill-Vansittart hysterical hatred of everything German was a rational and valid viewpoint if the mistakes of Versailles were not to be repeated after the end of the Second World War.

It appears that one of the complaints about tutors' political activities that Butler made to Hickson concerned Butler directly: the Labour Party prospective candidate for Butler's constituency of Saffron Walden was a lecturer employed by the Cambridge Regional Committee for adult education in HM Forces. Other complaints apparently referred to WEA rather than extramural tutors because a fortnight later F. Jacques, the WEA District Secretary, wrote to

Butler to assure him the WEA would not be used as a vehicle for any party-political campaign, but this did not altogether satisfy Butler. In early December, Jacques again wrote to Butler, offering to discuss his concern about the WEA in Essex. The next day, a WEA deputation informally met Butler, and Tawney took the opportunity to assure him that the WEA did not engage in political propaganda.[33]

There were undoubtedly other occasions when the Responsible Bodies or tutors stepped a little too far out of line.[34] Other episodes have no doubt gone unrecorded or undetected. But even so, it is not a story of constant conflict. For most of the time the boundary between the legitimate and the unacceptable was appreciated by all concerned. The incidents that did occur were often petty and of little consequence. But they were just serious enough, and just frequent enough, to ensure that temperance, responsibility and judiciousness (to use the terms favoured by the HMIs) and an acceptable orthodoxy did prevail.

In the semblance of ideological unity, which surrounded adult education during much of the 1930s, there had been relatively little controversy or political conflict, although there were some complaints about left-wing tendencies, or too close an identification by the adult education movement with the working class or the labour movement, or too much attention being paid to specifically working class interests. During the war, there was undoubtedly greater concern about how controversial topics were dealt with in adult education, but this concern still did not give rise to major incidents. It was the outbreak of the Cold War that really brought the simmering conflict of interests to a head, first at Oxford and in the North Staffordshire district, and then all over the place in the late 1940s when the liberal tradition of adult education was besieged by Cold War anti-Communism in the extramural world, in the WEA, in the adult education exported to the colonies and in the civilian adult education provided for HM Forces. Then there was a real danger that the perceived need to preserve western 'free', 'democratic' society from Communism would eliminate the liberal approach which aimed to give students access to a whole range of arguments and to develop their critical faculties so that they would question all assumptions, formulate alternative interpretations and come to their own conclusions about the important issues of the day. The fear that this liberal tradition would be subverted was sometimes justified. McCarthyite proscription of tutors and ideas revealed some very illiberal tendencies within the Responsible Bodies and their paymasters at this time, as has been fully described elsewhere.[35]

Notes

[1] See, e.g. S. Spender, *The Thirties and After*, (London, 1978), pp. 13-33, and R. Williams, *Politics and Letters* (London, 1979), pp. 33-41.
[2] M. Bruce, 'A Fair Field Full of the Folks', *David Crowther Memorial Lecture* (Sheffield University, 1974), p. 12.
[3] Public Record Office (PRO), ED.73/1-100.
[4] The university extramural departments and the WEA were known collectively as the 'Responsible Bodies'.
[5] For a full account of this incident and full reference to the primary sources, see R. Fieldhouse, 'Voluntaryism and the State in Adult Education: the WEA and the 1925 TUC Education Scheme', *History of Education*, Vol. 10, no. 1 (1981), pp. 45-63.
[6] PRO, ED.24/1913 & 1915 and B. Jennings, *Knowledge is Power: A Short History of the WEA, 1903-1978* (University of Hull, 1979), pp. 37-8.
[7] Information from Frank and Tom Benson; F. Benson, letter to *WEA News*, n.s.15 (Autumn 1978), p.2 and 'History of the WEA', in *WEA News*, n.s.16 (Spring 1979), p. 2.
[8] Jennings, *Knowledge is Power*, p. 34.
[9] PRO, ED.24/1915; WEA National Committee minutes (March-July 1926); Jennings, *Knowledge is Power*, p. 36.
[10] PRO, T.161/186/S.17166, Lord Eustace Percy to Walter Guiness, 7 October 1925.
[11] Quoted in J.A. Blyth, *English University Adult Education 1908-1958: A Unique Tradition* (Manchester, 1983), pp. 77 and 84.
[12] PRO, ED.73/38, local newspaper cuttings and Board of Education papers relating to the WEA South-West District.
[13] PRO, ED/24/1916, newspapers advertisements, report by a representative of the Conservative S.E. Area Agents Association, and correspondence.
[14] Lord Wigg, interview with author, 10 January 1980.
[15] For full details of the controversy over D'Eye, see R. Fieldhouse, *Adult Education and the Cold War: Liberal Values Under Siege* (University of Leeds, 1985), pp. 26-7 and 31-2.
[16] J.H. Matthews, WEA Southern District Secretary 1921-1952: interview with author, 9 April 1980; J.R. Armstrong, correspondence with author, 25 February 1980; E.J. Feuchtwanger, *The Department of Adult Education, University of Southampton 1928-1978* (University of Southampton, n.d.), p. 4.
[17] E. Eagle, interview with author, 8 March 1980; J. Allaway, interview with author, 19 December 1979; PRO, ED.80/26, report by HMI Dann on the case of Miss Hickley.
[18] PRO, ED.73/1, 11 and 41, reports on Hull University College adult education work, 1933, and Birmingham University and West Midland WEA adult education, 1934.
[19] PRO, ED.73/1, Board of Education minute paper referring to HMI reports on Birmingham University and West Midlands WEA, and the final report (1934).
[20] PRO, ED.80/22, HMI Dann's report on annual conference of the British Institute of Adult Education, 16-19 September 1938; *Highway* vol.30 (1938), pp. 113-4. Five years earlier, Board of Education officials had shown similar

disapproval when HMI Boothroyd reported that the differences between classes provided jointly by Hull University College and the WEA and classes provided by the Hull Extension Lectures Committee was that the former were provided for working men and the latter for non-working men. 'I think that the public would be shocked, and properly shocked, by this frank admission that a class can be composed of workers or non-workers but not both.' (PRO, ED.73/11, report on Hull University College adult education work, 1933.)

[21] PRO, ED.80/22, C.F.R. Bagnall, South Berks. Conservative Association agent to Brigadier-General H. Clifton-Brown MP,5 June 1939.

[22] Lord Wigg, interview; C. Scrimgeour, *Fifty Years A-Growing: The History of the North Staffs District of the WEA* (Stoke-on-Trent, 1973), pp. 48-54.

[23] M. Bruce, 'Reminiscences Extramural 1932-41', Cambridge University Library, BEMS 38/31, pp. 22-3; Bruce, interview with author, 1 November 1979 and correspondence with author.

[24] PRO, ED.80/23, minute paper on Adult Education Controversial Topics, May 1940. (The theory of 'federal union' gained some popularity in the 'phoney war' period, as an easy antidote to war. It was based on the assumption that wars arose from the rivalry between sovereign states, and therefore to abolish state sovereignty and replace it by a Federal Union of States would abolish war.)

[25] *Caernarvon Times*, 12 January 1940.

[26] PRO, ED.80/23, minute paper on Adult Education Controversial Topics.

[27] Ibid. Since the Nazi-Soviet Pact of 23 August 1939, and particularly since the decision by the Central Committee of the British Communist Party on 4 October to oppose the war, Communists and fellow-travellers were understandably suspected of being enemies of Britain.

[28] PRO, ED.80/23, C.J.A.C. Statement by Sir Walter Moberly on 'The Handling of Controversial Subjects in War-Time'.

[29] *Highway*, Vol. 35 (1943), p. 58.

[30] PRO, ED.80/26, Sir Robert Topping to Rt. Hon. R.A. Butler, 21 November 1944 and Board of Education reply to Topping, 27 November 1944.

[31] Ibid, observations concerning the new adult education regulations prepared for consideration by the Inspectors' Adult Education Committee, 9 March 1944 (revised 11 April 1944).

[32] Ibid, arrangements for G.F. Hickson to meet R.A. Butler on 29 September 1944 and brief prepared for Butler by HMI Jack.

[33] Ibid, F. Jacques to Butler, 18 October and 4 December 1944 and note of WEA deputation to Butler, 5 December 1944; PRO, ED.80/27, Board of Education memo, 29 January 1945.

[34] For an analysis of the political constraints imposed on the civilian contribution to adult education for H.M. Forces during the war, R. Fieldhouse, *The Political Education of Servants of the State*, (Manchester, 1987), Chapter 5.

[35] See R. Fieldhouse, *Adult Education and the Cold War: liberal values under siege*, Leeds Studies on Adult and Continuing Education (1985).

Part II, 1945–1988

John McIlroy
6 The Demise of the National Council of Labour Colleges

Introduction

The twenty years after the war are normally thought of as comprising two very different periods, 'the age of austerity' and the era of 'you've never had it so good'. All attempts at periodisation engender simplification. The boom of the 1950s and 60s was uneven, while its disintegration has touched different groups and areas in very different ways. None the less, taken in general terms, the two decades under consideration here witnessed important social and economic changes of which full employment, the establishment of the Welfare State, the nationalisation of basic industries and rising living standards were only the most important.[1]

As in any period, social classes were undergoing change and recomposition.[2] Key strongholds of the working-class movement suffered rapid and enduring decline. The numbers employed in mining and quarrying declined from over 1 million before the war to 660,000 in 1964. In textiles, the drop was of the order of half a million, whilst the 550,000 rail workers of the 1930s had shrunk to 396,000 by the 1960s. As manufacturing industries declined, service industries expanded. This process was accompanied by a growing shift from manual to white-collar employment. The managerial and professional category grew from 14 per cent of the workforce in 1931, to 17 per cent in 1951 and 19 per cent ten years later. Clerical workers, some 7 per cent of the workforce before the war, grew to 11 per cent in 1951 and 13 per cent in 1961. Between the early 1950s and the early 1960s, the proportion of women in the workforce grew from 31 to nearly 36 per cent.

The decline in traditional working-class communities and the different experience of work that the changes in the occupational structure provided for different strata were important for the working-class movement. For example, throughout this period a manual worker was twice as likely to be a member of a union as a white-collar worker, whilst women, because of the occupations they entered, tended to be less well organised than men. Unemployment was rarely much above the 1 per cent mark after the 1940s and in the 1950s and early 1960s, real wages were rising at around 2 per cent per year. By the end of this period nearly half of all houses were in owner occupation, 11 million homes had television (almost non-existent in 1939) and there were 8 million cars on the roads compared with 2 million in 1947. The increased equality of opportunity that the 1944 Education Act, which raised the school leaving age to fifteen and established the principle of free secondary education, represented, was an important gain for the working class. By 1964 there were a million more secondary school students than in 1945. The number of university places had more than trebled.

These changes, the product of economic reorientation and new and intelligent political strategies, all stood in stark contrast to the inter-war period. There was – also in contrast with that period – a decline in political activism and a softening of class consciousness and class conflict. This was reflected in the return of Conservative governments in three successive elections; the decline in Labour Party and Communist Party membership; the stagnation of trade union membership after the 1940s and the minimal strike rate.

None the less, despite the limited and temporary respite a victorious war and conversion to Keynesianism gave the British economy, Britain remained a capitalist society. Inequality, class and exploitation remained realities in the affluent society, and political and industrial struggles continued to be part of working class experience.[3] In the mid-1950s, two-fifths of all private property in the UK was estimated to be in the hands of 1 per cent of the adult population.[4] Four-fifths of all share capital was held by only 1 per cent of the adult population, and nearly all the rest by a further 9 to 10 per cent.[5] The evidence suggested that redistribution of income through the taxation system and through welfare measures represented redistribution within, rather than between, social classes.[6] Despite increases in consumption, as late as 1964 47 per cent of all households lacked a washing machine, 66 per cent were without a refrigerator and 63 per cent had no car.[7] Given the relatively backward technology of British industry, work continued to be an intensely oppressive experience for the majority.[8] In 1938 the ratio of gross profits to all employment incomes was 1 to 4.5 and, by 1965, 1 to 4.2.[9] The share of wages in the national income remained roughly the same as in the previous century at around 42 per cent.[10] Despite the 1944 Education Act and the expansion of further and higher education, the vast majority of workers' children went to work at fifteen. Moreover 96 out of 100 working class children were eliminated from education by the age of 17 and 'at 11-13 a professional or managerial family's child had nine times as high a chance of entering a grammar or independent school as an unskilled worker's child'.[11]

The contradictions of this period imposed grave strains on the organisations established in the first half of the century to meet the educational needs of the workers in their struggles to change society. Both the NCLC and the WEA were affected by the decline of activism and by greater educational mobility. These bodies had grown up in the mould of opposition to the economic and political status quo. They had hardly come to terms with the changes a majority Labour government brought to their operations before they were faced with the fact that a high proportion of the leadership and of the rank and file of the labour movement apparently accepted that capitalism had solved its problems and now provided the trade unions with a satisfactory role in society. Much of what the WEA and the NCLC had struggled for, it was claimed, had now come to pass. What, if any, was to be their role now that their original mission was largely accomplished?

Changes in the labour movement also produced changes in its educational philosophy. The pre-war position could well be summed up by the statement put to the TUC in the early 1920s as the charter of a unified scheme of workers' education. It declared that,

> in providing educational facilities for the workers it is important to realise that whilst they need certain specialised forms of education, their needs are by no means confined to such specialised training. The workers want knowledge both for the immediate and practical purposes of the labour movement and, also, as a means of enlargement of their mental and social outlook. They seek a knowledge, not only of economics and industrial history, but also of general and social history of their own and other people's literature and of the arts and sciences.[12]

In different ways and with different emphasis both the WEA, in alliance with the universities, and the NCLC, as the custodian of independent working class education with a Marxist bent, had sought to provide an education of this breadth and unity.

Now the demand from the labour movement was increasingly for education to make the system work, rather than education to change the system, education which took the status quo as largely given and concentrated on maximising success within it. The post-war decades were to witness a conscious separation of the specialised training for immediate and practical purposes, from the broader knowledge required to understand and change society; and the progressive downplaying of the latter. This reaction by the trade union leadership to their post-war position in society further eroded the Marxist tradition of the NCLC and the liberal approach of the universities and the WEA, already weakened by the transformed economic and political climate.

Throughout this period working-class education took on a narrower utilitarian stamp. Despite the enhanced social role of the labour movement, its education remained a very small scale enterprise, marginal to the real concerns of the movement. It never broke out of its limitations to become a considerable minority movement, let alone anything on the scale of, say, the Scandinavian model. Indeed, by the end of this period, there is a loss of the sense of a *movement*. The NCLC is extinct and the WEA's working-class education increasingly takes place on an institutionalised basis as part of a national trade union system of training. None the less, if this was not a period of success, thousands of students and tutors struggled to maintain and develop past traditions and make them relevant to changed circumstances. They kept alive the ideas of 'education for social purpose' and of 'really useful knowledge'. The old tradition was weakened and it was distorted, but in very unfavourable conditions it did survive.

Trade Unions and Trade Union Education

A greater emphasis on the training of union officials to improve their performance and to encourage their identification with union purposes and policies had become apparent as part of the reorientation of the movement after the General Strike. Such training was perceived quite sharply as a union function, not the prerogative of the NCLC or the WEA. The TUC viewed its encouragement as one of the services it could directly provide to help create a more professional, better organised movement, distanced from what it saw as the disastrous flirtation with direct action that had characterised the first quarter of the twentieth century. This design was given some small substance by the programme of summer schools and day schools sponsored by the TUC via the trades council machinery from 1929.[13]

The TUC had a clear and coherent conception of their specific role in the post-war education of trade unionists. This was stated in precise detail as early as 1944. Their responsibility was to stimulate

> ... greater provision of trade union technical education which only the movement itself can provide. There is no desire to compete with the well established work of the NCLC, the WEA and Ruskin College. The aim of the TUC is to fill a gap which they believe to exist. While the educational bodies named cater especially for the working class student their approach is quite rightly a general approach ... This work of general equipment is by no means underestimated by the General Council and they would wish to see it continued under the auspices of the organisations named. The General Council take the view, however, that the time has come when the TUC itself should provide facilities for training those who are to serve as officers and active members of the movement. It will be noted at once that the approach in this case is more specific and immediately suggests the methods of technical education. This kind of training, the General Council believes, is the special responsibility of the TUC to provide.[14]

The TUC's approach was formally a balanced one. It saw itself as moving into unoccupied space and filling a vacuum. It conceived of the liberal and political provision of the educational bodies as quite different from role training. The latter required a distinct and specialist approach. It aimed not, as the NCLC and WEA did, at all union members but at the activist, specifically the official. It sought to develop not a greater understanding of social, political and economic processes in the union or among Labour Party activists, but, rather, to give the official greater efficiency as an administrator, negotiator, organiser and adviser.[15] There was, therefore, no need for friction or competition with the educational organisations.

The TUC's view was supported by contemporary commentators. One observed that:

> the solid academic type of adult education has its place – a very important one – but the trade union movement will be well advised to concentrate still more on the practical educational needs that face its workers ... They must be educated as *trade unionists* well versed in the practical details of their job with full understanding of the legal and technical problems they will have to meet.[16]

Another commentator felt that:

> Education in trade unionism has been rather more neglected ... General
> trade union structure and methods are fairly widely taught but there is still
> too little education in the problems of individual unions, the practical
> work of the different categories of trade union officer and the element of
> management studies. On the whole, it will be seen that the neglected
> topics are generally those for which the unions themselves could best
> provide through their own educational schemes.[17]

A veteran of workers' education agreed that this gap required
plugging and added that the unions would need 'to keep the ultimate
control of this type of activity in their own hands. They certainly
cannot afford to hand it over to colleges or universities, although they
can and should make use of both'.[18]

In line with this philosophy the General Council announced its
intention of establishing, as soon as a cessation of hostilities
permitted, a training scheme for officials and active members. This
new initiative required a big expansion in TUC provision. At the end
of the war, the TUC was running a summer school attracting 150
students and ten-day and weekend schools in conjunction with trades
councils. A TUC Educational Trust had already been established in
1943, with dividends accruing from the *Daily Herald*. The 1944
Congress carried a resolution urging the establishment of a
residential TUC training college: to set the new scheme on a firm
footing Allen Winterbotham was appointed as Director of Studies.
The General Council did their utmost during this period to publicise
and popularise the need for technical training and to demarcate its
ambit. It was, they constantly emphasised, to be 'essentially practical
in character'.[19]. The courses, therefore, would deal with industrial
and trade union history, union structure, trade union administration,
negotiations, accountancy and legal issues. They were to be mounted
at Congress House. Teaching was to be undertaken by the Congress
House administrative staff rather than academics, supplemented by
politicians, civil servants and trade union leaders as visiting
speakers.[20]

The experience of the summer schools was to be utilised. The latter
had been conceived as a conveyor belt for Congress House policies, a
means of ensuring the identification of activists with those policies,
rather than as a means of stimulating critical examination of them.[21]
This, too, was the bent of the new scheme. 'It was now necessary',
Citrine felt, 'for trade union officials to be trained in the concrete
application of the policy and principles of our movement.[22] Bevin

had long believed, against the background of his problems with the rank and file in the docks and on the buses, that

> ... the lay members must be conscious that there are certain things they cannot do, and that they must leave the officers to carry out the tasks in which they are employed to specialise, the lay members supplementing this work and, thereby, making a very happy combination.[23]

It has been observed that Bevin anticipated what other trade union leaders were to think about education[24] while Cole claimed that Deakin, Bevin's successor, shared with him a sharp distrust of intellectuals but attached more importance to training.[25] Training was important not only to improve performance but to improve performance within an accepted framework and, it was argued, 'that cannot be done by academic forms of education frequently at variance with the policy of the movement'.[26]

The TUC was, therefore, determined to ensure Congress House control over future developments. The NCLC, still feeling the loss of the Central Labour College, pushed a proposal for a residential college which it projected as a joint venture between Great Russell Street and Tillicoultry (headquarters of the NCLC). Its overtures to the TUC were firmly rebuffed. It was made clear that any residential college must be under 'the undivided control of Congress'.[27] It was noted at this stage that there was a school of thought 'entrenched in Congress machinery which thinks that all trade union education should be provided by Congress'.[28] The background here is important. Trade union membership had increased from 4.39 million in 1933 to 9.3 million by 1948. Trade unionists who represented 22.6 per cent of the workforce in 1933 made up 45.2 per cent of all employees by 1948.[29] The war years had confirmed the re-emergence of an extended network of shop stewards.[30] Labour was in power. The need for professionalisation of the union apparatus supported by Citrine and Bevin since the 1920s was greater than ever. The conditions for moving forward were now present and an extension of collective bargaining gradually occurred. The policies of the TUC, moreover, required the loyalty of the rank and file. The TUC accepted the continued illegality of strikes after the end of the war and the government used troops to break industrial action on a record number of occasions. As the Cold War developed, the TGWU joined the General and Municipal Workers Union in proscribing Communist office holders, sacking nine officials, including a TGWU member of the TUC General Council. From 1948, the TUC was involved in trying to hold the line on 'voluntary' wage restraint and was opposed by the CP and the left in the unions.[31] In this context, the utility to the General Council of training at Congress House in 'the concrete application of the policy and principles of our movement' requires little emphasis.

Nonetheless, the TUC at this stage were not completely myopic with regard to 'technical training'. They specifically stated that active trade unionists required *in addition* 'that liberal education in the social studies essential to any member who intends to engage effectively in trade union activities'.[32] And in this wider provision they saw a specific niche for the universities. A special trade union course was initiated at the London School of Economics. The TUC saw this venture as advanced provision for those who held or wished to hold senior positions. It was intended to provide 'a wide background and an equipment of theoretical knowledge which will stand the trade union officer in good stead in his practical work'.[33] This course was full time but an evening variant was organised on a three years basis and this model spread to other universities. The TUC gave these courses serious support. Winterbotham went to Glasgow to explain the course there to local trade union bodies.[34] The TUC saw this kind of endeavour as 'a very promising field for co-operation'[35] and viewed the position as one of 'joint control' with syllabuses agreed between universities and the TUC.[36]

There was, however, opposition to this development from sections of the left. The Communist Party supported the establishment of training schemes within the unions.[37] There was also hostility to the universities and support for TUC education on the grounds that it took place within and was controlled by the movement. The courses at universities came under fierce attack in terms already familiar. One critic commented, 'his own experience of Glasgow University was this, that if one took a course of economics one got the orthodox economics while Marxian economics was ruled out entirely'.[38] NCLC-influenced trade unionists supported the TUC initiatives as 'independent working class education'.

The response of the General Council was predictable: 'the universities were the property of the people and they would be foolish not to avail themselves of any opportunities provided there'.[39] The members of the LSE course were soon following past traditions and unanimously demanding that Marxist economics should be taught as part of the course.[40] As the Cold War developed it would be hardly surprising if the TUC saw the growth of the training scheme as preferable to an expansion of wider forms of education. That scheme was under their direct control. And its restricted subject matter rendered it more amenable to isolation from the cut and thrust of political controversy which workers' education was pledged to stimulate.

The TUC certainly applied minimal energy and enthusiasm to prosecuting the resolution of the 1946 Congress which reopened, for the first time in two decades, the question of a comprehensive scheme of workers' education. The resolution, moved by the NUM and influenced by the Communist Party, required TUC co-ordination of the work of the NCLC, WEA and Ruskin College. The NCLC, in response, proposed the take-over of itself, the WETUC and Ruskin to provide integrated TUC provision. The WEA made the minimal suggestion that competition between the organisations could be softened and controlled by the establishment of a central TUC fund which could be used to finance the educational bodies. Taking two years to report, the TUC Education Committee proposed no action. They rejected what – given the WEA's wider interests – nobody had seriously suggested: an amalgamation of all four bodies. They then discarded the possibility of the TUC taking over the trade union education of the WEA, the NCLC and Ruskin on financial grounds. They felt that trade union members would not be prepared to pay the extra levy of 3d a head that a co-ordinated scheme would require: they recalled the way the unions had voted down the 1925 Easton Lodge Scheme on similar grounds. The proposal for a centralisation of finance was rejected on the grounds that it would involve the TUC in greater administrative costs without providing any real rationalisation. Competition between the NCLC and the WEA, the General Council now felt, had advantages in providing unions with a choice of educational provision.[41] Finally and interestingly, in the light of later developments, the report's author, Winterbotham, argued that 'concentration would possibly (and indeed probably) give it [workers' education] an authoritarian or totalitarian twist which could easily degenerate into mere propaganda instead of education'.[42]

The use of the common TUC technique of listing every possible disadvantage to the exclusion of even obvious advantages in order to legitimise a preconceived position of inertia, led the NCLC- and CP-influenced unions to move reference back of the report. This was defeated. There can be little doubt that 'the TUC had killed the 1946 resolution as they wanted things to stay as they were'.[43] Whilst finance was a factor, a major motivation was the TUC's absorption in consolidating their own training provision and avoiding the distraction and dissension a unified scheme would entail. More systematic training of officials rather than workers' education was very clearly their first priority. British empiricism was coming into its own. As one speaker at the Congress commented in the debate: 'You cannot tackle an administrative job by using the name of Marx, Lenin, Lloyd George or anybody else. You have to get down to brass tacks.'[44]

Yet it was clear that the new training scheme was not an answer to demand from the ranks. In 1947-48 the courses at Congress House attracted only 70 students. Only half the places available were taken up and the General Council were claiming that 'Education is being treated as a Cinderella.' What was the use, they inquired, of spending more money on a co-ordinated scheme when their own basic training was not being used?[45] That the scheme was created from above as a project of the leadership was demonstrated by the fact that again, in both 1949 and 1950, the TUC were expressing concern at low recruitment. The lay officials apparently did not want to be trained.[46] Indeed, almost every Congress in the early 1950s saw General Council members valiantly attempting to drum up business. The basic four-week training courses were supplemented by the introduction of short courses on industrial relations, negotiations and management techniques aimed specifically at shop stewards and members of Joint Consultative Committees. But as Congress House continued to complain that few unions were supporting the scheme – eleven out of 186 which were eligible sent students in 1950-51 – and as special publicity failed to produce the goods, the position was reviewed.[47]. The conclusion was that the unions were likely to support shorter courses; four weeks was too long. The basic course was, therefore, reduced to two weeks, while the specialist courses now ran for a week each.[48]

The thrust of the TUC provision can be seen from the initiation of the courses in production and management. The impetus came from the desire to train stewards to implement the TUC policy of increasing production and the establishment of a TUC Production Committee. The courses covered such matters as work study, payment systems, job evaluation, scientific management and the organisation of production. They were intended to provide a technical grounding but also to give an understanding of and breed sympathy towards the General Council's position. It would, nevertheless, be erroneous to believe that the provision was as narrow as TUC training in the 1980s. The TUC reading lists for this period encompass a wide range of political, economic and sociological literature. And whilst the approach in the courses on trade unionism was an institutional one, the use of books by Barou, Cole and Cole and Postgate meant that *issues* were inevitably part of the discussion, a process limited by later developments.[49]

The advent of the Conservative government presaged no great change at Congress House. In 1931 the TUC had been represented on one government committee. By 1950 they were represented on more than 60 such bodies.[50] They asserted that it was 'our long-standing practice to work amicably with whatever government is in power'.[51] The Minister of Labour, Monckton, convinced the government that every initiative in the field of industrial relations should carry 'the greatest possible measure of TUC approval and concurrence'.[52] In return, the TUC leaders ensured that 'the cautious and moderate policy which they had pursued under the Labour government was maintained under the Conservatives'.[53]

TUC educational emphases continued to reflect this position. As the TUC increasingly became part of state policy making and as satisfactory social change developed, so training for service was seen as more important than education for social change. From time to time this occasioned disquiet. One critic observed that, in the TUC courses, 'too much attention can be given to what one might call patching up capitalism and not enough to helping us to fight capitalism'.[54] The basic response of the unions, however, was one of apathy.

None the less, in 1956 the TUC decided to extend the small provision it had established. At this time the TUC was providing what it termed 300 'student weeks'. This was to be stepped up to 1,200 student weeks. Part of the TUC's new headquarters was to be opened as a training college and the scheme was to be financed by an increase in union affiliation fees. Unions were to be allocated places on the basis of their membership. The opening of the college was accompanied by a meeting of general secretaries and affiliates of more than 50 unions. Its purpose was to impress upon them the need for greater support. The new system of financing courses helped the TUC 'to fill them up'.[55] In the first year of the new system 632 out of 812 available places were taken up – a big improvement on the late 1940s.[56]

As well as leading by example the TUC also saw its task as proselytising in the unions. They offered to advise affiliates on shop steward training[57] and called on all unions to provide training for officials.[58]

The biggest union, the Transport and General Workers' Union, had appointed an education officer in 1938.[59] By 1947 it was spending

£7,544 on education and by 1954 nearly five times that amount, £34,764.[60] The union had started a correspondence course in 1940. The most important post-war development was the system of schools organised for the union by the WEA from 1950. However, only around 500 students attended the schools each year in this period. The union also supported some NCLC work. Whilst its educational expenditure might be seen as slight, it was justified on the grounds of low take-up by its members.[61]

The General and Municipal Workers' Union with a membership of well over 800,000 was, in 1947, spending only £7,000 on its educational facilities. From 1949 it developed one-month courses at eleven technical colleges and several universities focusing on industrial relations, management skills and communication techniques. The union provided some 90 courses in the first two years. Thereafter, demand and provision declined and was derisory by the mid-1960s. Instead the union concentrated on internal provision. In 1958 an education officer was appointed and developed a scheme based on linked weekend schools taught by union officers leading to one week courses for shop stewards and branch secretaries at the union headquarters. In 1964 this scheme was put on a more efficient basis when the union's training college opened at Woodstock.[62] USDAW (the shop workers' union) was affiliated to both the NCLC and the WETUC but began to run its own summer schools from 1951, tutored by its own officers. Its disaffiliation from the NCLC in 1958 led to the appointment of its own full-time education officer and a growth of internal provision. As in other unions great importance was attached to its correspondence course. The ETU (the electricians' union) coherently developed its own scheme, opening a training college at Esher in 1953.[63] The engineers, in contrast, relied almost totally on outside provision, limiting themselves to a small series of weekend schools. The different areas of the mineworkers' union provided a varied pattern. From the 1940s the Communist Party-dominated South Wales Area developed full-time courses of between six and twelve months at Coleg Harlech. Long-standing tensions with the NCLC led to disaffiliation in 1956. Dissatisfaction with Coleg Harlech, which was viewed unfavourably as a path for activists into higher education, motivated its replacement, in 1958, by a fifteen-week day-release scheme. The Scottish Area ran an annual two-week summer school, whilst other areas increasingly became involved in long day-release courses with university extra-mural departments.[64]

Provision in the unions, therefore, varied and was influenced by wider political concerns. The foundry workers, for example, broke with the WEA because of that body's objections to left wing tutors. It created its own scheme of summer and weekend schools dealing with economic and political issues. But even where provision reflected such issues it tended to be small scale. The Post Office Engineering Union, for example, one of the smaller national unions, emphasised liberal as well as practical subjects. However, only 450 places were provided annually for nearly 100,000 members.[65] A powerful NCLC union such as the National Union of Railwaymen by 1960 was, annually, mounting only five one-week schools involving in total a little over 100 students and tutored by the union's own members. The trend of development could be seen from the decision in 1957 to cut down on the previous range of subjects and concentrate on branch administration, largely book-keeping, industrial law, collective bargaining and work study.[66]

More and more unions began to accept that 'trained leadership at all levels is the key to the efficiency which the organisation must have to give proper service to its members'.[67] As local and plant collective bargaining, the number of stewards and the variety of functions demanded of them all grew, so unions tended to see education more and more as something 'intended to benefit the unions directly by improving the performance by branch officials and shop stewards of their jobs for the union and by increasing their loyalty to the union'.[68] Education in these terms was seen as increasingly important in influencing the elite who took part in union leadership at all levels. Education carried out by officials or sympathetic educators at union training colleges could have an impact out of proportion to the numbers involved. So, for example, when the ETU established their training college, an educator sympathetic to its leadership was appointed.[69] When he retired and his assistant, Les Cannon became an opponent of that leadership, the college was closed, allegedly on financial grounds, to facilitate his removal and then, after a decent interval, re-opened. Once installed in leadership himself, Cannon appreciated the importance of the college in training activists, made it an instrument of his policies and never missed an opportunity to lecture personally.[70]

By the mid-1960s, nineteen unions covering 5 million members had appointed a full-time education officer or required an officer to spend a substantial amount of time on these duties.[71] A rough estimate made during this period was that the total amount spent on education by the unions had increased from around £250,000 a year in the late 1950s to around £350,000 in 1964. But it was pointed out that progress was uneven and concentrated on unions which already made significant provision.[72] At least until 1960 the majority of unions relied on the NCLC, the WEA and the universities for the majority of their educational provision. The TUC and individual unions, however, had laid the foundation for a small but influential core of specialised trade union education in which the TUC possessed an important role and which was philosophically and organisationally distinct from the broader workers' education in which the unions had interested themselves in the past. This development was to have an important impact on those voluntary organisations which had created the broader provision. Would the new technical training or trade union education usefully complement workers education? Or would the two, in reality, be in competition?

The Demise of Independent Working Class Education

The post-war period saw a strengthening of tendencies noted earlier in the NCLC's development: centralisation of control, a move towards more practical trade union education and an increasing distance taken from Marxism and the left.[73] With the election of a Labour government and with Parliament packed with MPs and Ministers associated with the Labour Colleges, among them the influential NCLC President, Arthur Woodburn, a new turn was articulated. It was now urged that,

> from being principally concerned with fostering an anti-capitalist viewpoint independent working class education had had to concern itself with the more difficult task of engendering a constructive socialist outlook and providing a training necessary to the intelligent grappling with the vast and complex problems confronting this country and the world.[74]

A 'constructive socialist outlook' meant in practice encouraging a dogged loyalty to the policies of the Labour government even in the face of working-class opposition. From 1946 Millar was justifying Labour's austerity measures, stressing the need for a productivity crusade and arguing that greater redistribution of income would do little to improve the condition of the working class.[75] Marshall Aid was essential for a renovated economy. Wage restraint was acceptable given the increase in the social wage Labour's reforms had engineered. As international tensions developed, Soviet policy in Europe was criticised, together with opposition to Marshall Aid.[76] The Truman Doctrine was justified on the grounds of the Soviet

Union's expansionist appetites. By 1950 *Plebs* was editorialising that: 'The issue which dominates the world is the struggle between the Democratic West and the Communist East.'[77] There could be little doubt as to its firm support for the Cold War.[78] What was involved was not merely support for Labour but a determination that NCLC education should create an understanding and acceptance of its policies. The development was from 'education for emancipation' to 'education for responsibility'.[79]

Such an approach was bound to attract criticism. Millar's support for increased productivity led one NCLC student to inquire: 'Have not the workers produced enough without having professed socialists joining the speed up gang?'[80] Labour, the critics complained, was solving the economic burdens of British capitalism by making trade unionists work harder for less money. The evidence did not justify the charges of Soviet aggression. The Labour government's policy was a long way from that of a socialist administration.[81] Millar's retort was that, whilst the Britain of the late 1940s was not a socialist state, only containing elements of such a state, the government was doing its best in very difficult circumstances. It therefore deserved understanding and loyalty.[82]

Opposition to the line that *Plebs* was taking came to a head at the NCLC's Annual Conference at Scarborough in 1950. The position of the leadership was attacked by Communist Party supporters, McLennan of the electricians and Grahl of the Fire Brigades Union. The NCLC leadership, it was claimed, was no longer concerned with the establishment of socialism, merely with supplying justification of the maintenance of capitalism. *Plebs* was full of the ideas of class collaboration and critical articles were being suppressed by the General Secretary. The NCLC, a Trotskyist asserted, had broken with its past espousal of 'scientific socialism'. The response was predictable. The advent of the first majority Labour government, it was argued, had 'naturally made necessary a re-examination of many of the speeches, articles and views that might have been acceptable in the past'. The role of independent working-class education should involve 'looking into old prejudices and pet theories'. The NCLC was 'bound to reflect the democratic socialist philosophy of the British trade union movement'.[83]

Cutting with the right wing grain in the unions and on the NCLC executive in the 1940s and 50s, Millar was unassailable. Much of the policy direction was in the hands of a small reliable executive sub-committee. There was a moderate majority on the unevenly attended executive. Annual conference was not allowed to debate 'administrative issues'. Motions on key issues, including the dismissal of organisers, were regularly ruled out of order. Millar's orientation towards the union leaders as part of his strategy of winning more union schemes and more finance required a reciprocal response from the NCLC in reflecting those leaders' requirements. This was made easier by the anti-Communism of both himself and Arthur Woodburn, discernible two decades previously. [84] The formulations 'independent working-class education' or 'education for the labour movement' can easily evade complex and unresolved questions of exactly who is finally to control that education and whose interests it is to serve, in a movement split by political and material conflicts. But certainly in the kind of conditions prevailing in the 1940s and 50s, any independent organisation which has put all of its eggs in the basket marked 'educational arm of the unions', and which lacks any alternative base, was bound to come to some *modus vivendi* with the existing leadership of those unions – generally on the latter's terms. Pressures did not need to be overt. Self-discipline was far preferable. But the right-wing trajectory of the union leadership, supported, on the whole, by the members, exercised strong influence on the NCLC leadership in a period very different from the rank and file upsurge of 'The Great Unrest' and the Bolshevik Revolution.

Yet at the same time as it was moving to the right, the NCLC attracted the attentions of left-wingers. The organisation remained relatively open on the ground. Given the difficulty of attracting activists it could not be too fastidious in its choice of organisers and tutors, although clashes did occur. However, Millar's leadership, assaulted in earlier periods, attracted little organised sustained opposition now. The Communist Party had turned itself decisively against the NCLC as a reformist body in the 1920s and counterposed to its activities their own education programme. In 1944-45 the party moved again towards the adult education bodies. However, whilst individual members continued as voluntary tutors, as Tommy Jackson did, and numerous young members took NCLC courses, like Lawrence Daly did, and while CP supporters in the NCLC-affiliated unions fired broadsides at Millar's pontifications, developments in the NCLC were still seen by the Communist leadership as of marginal importance.[85] In 1948 the party was talking of the NCLC's 'conservatism' but arguing that workers should not abstain from its programme, indeed they would find within the NCLC and WEA classes a new interest in Marxism.[86] As the CP's turn to opposition to Labour and the TUC leadership developed, language more reminiscent of the pre-war vilification was the order of the day. Trade unionists were warned against '... the flood of class collaboration material that is poured out by the General Council of the TUC, by the Labour Party and through the educational attacks of the WEA and the NCLC'.[87] Many CP intellectuals were entrenched in the universities and greater opportunities were perceived there. Attention was also paid to the unions' own initiatives which strengthened the party view that the NCLC was not 'alive to the educational needs of the movement'.[88]

The Trotskyists provide another interesting case in point. *Plebs* had provided a major forum for discussion amongst British socialists of the struggle of the left opposition in the USSR.[89] One of the founding fathers of British Trotskyism, Henry Sara, had been prominent in the NCLC from the early 1920s. In a situation where the CP officially had turned its face away from the Labour Colleges whose own leadership was, moreover, increasingly anti-Communist the NCLC provided a fertile field for small propaganda groups.[90] In the 1940s two Trotskyists, Bob Briscoe and Karl Westwood, were employed as Divisional Organisers in addition to Sara. On the break up of the Revolutionary Communist Party two of its full-timers, Frank Ward and Jock Haston, were also appointed to the staff. Whilst they quickly moved to the right, as did Raymond Fletcher, another NCLC organiser with a Trotskyist past, many other Trostskyists were active in the NCLC during these years.[91]

Yet these left-wingers seem to have involved themselves minimally in creating an organised opposition to the line the NCLC was taking. This was related to Millar's organisational stranglehold and partly to the fact that the movement was not Millar. Whilst the view from the top was that workers needed the NCLC to understand and to accept Labour's policies and problems, serious educational work in which a variety of approaches were discussed and debated took place in the classes and schools.[92] Moreover, increased interest in the Labour Colleges from 1947 was a product, not of strength but of the increasing weakness and disorientation of the Trotskyist movement.[93] As their activities in the unions decreased, voluntary lecturing came to be seen as a means of establishing contacts and making propaganda. There was little desire to disrupt a framework which made useful work possible.

Despite the rightward political drift, the basic tenets of the NCLC's ideology remained formally in place. The WEA, it was claimed, was about as independent of the capitalist state as the police force was.[94] The news that 'WEA tutor becomes Conservative political agent' and that Conservative Central Office was recommending WEA courses in

an educational handbook were greeted with glee.[95] Antagonism
between the two organisations was sustained by a series of clashes. Of
particular note was the WEA's attempt to exclude the NCLC from
international links. The NCLC had attended the pre-war conferences
convened by the International Federation of Trade Unions from its
formation in 1922. When Ernest Green convened a meeting to
establish an International Federation of Workers' Educational
Associations, the NCLC was not invited. Millar's argument, that
many of the foreign organisations were as similar to the NCLC as the
WEA, seemed justifiable. But it took all of his persistence before the
NCLC was admitted, amongst much acrimony.[96]

The flames of enmity towards the universities were also carefully
nurtured. The progress of the abolition of university Parliamentary
representation was followed with acute interest. The TUC's decision
to support the LSE course caused particular consternation. The
NCLC's supporters unsuccessfully moved reference back of the
proposal at the Congress. Was the trade union movement so
'educationally incompetent', it was asked, that they need to send
their activists to what NCLC activist, Syd Bidwell, termed the
London School of Capitalist Economics? The reactionary economic
views of Professor Paish were commented on with relish.[97]

In an extended statement, the NCLC reiterated its hostility to
education financed by the state. State backed institutions, it was
argued, could be trusted to teach arithmetic without capitalist bias,
but not history or economics. It was permissible for the labour
movement to send its children to university to be trained as scientists
or doctors or lawyers. It must train its activists not in university or
WEA classes but in the Labour Colleges where they would be taught
philosophy, history and economics from the vantage point of their
own class and their own interests.[98]

None the less, the problems of recruiting organisers and students
and running fast to stand still in an under-resourced and overworked
organisation led to some re-examination. Many of the members of
the NCLC executive, particularly those on the left, asked why the
organisation should not become a responsible body. The proposal
was rejected but, interestingly, on the tactical grounds that it might
cause problems for the government and, in the event of a Tory
administration being returned, would provide only a temporary and
compromising respite.[99]

Instead, renewed attention was given to the question of TUC
rationalisation. This project was pursued in full awareness of the
possible dangers. It was argued that 'even the most highly centralised

scheme of trade union education should provide that those responsible for the education work should be given a substantial measure of freedom'.[100] The relative autonomy of the universities, maintained despite state finance, was suggested as a model:

> to have the universities echoing the last Act passed by Parliament, or the immediate policies of the government, would not be a healthy position. In the same way, to so organise trade union education that it would automatically reflect the last decisions of Congress or the current policy of the General Council would be equally unsatisfactory. Workers' education, under such circumstances, would on the one hand be propaganda in the narrow sense and, on the other, lose a great deal of its spirit and, therefore, its power to excite interest, to attract students and to stimulate thought.[101]

This prescient concern to avoid the dead hand of bureaucratic control was frequently reiterated. It would be fatal, it was argued, if any TUC-controlled scheme should 'remove from workers' education *the active socialist essence and freedom to question*'.[102] In this context, the NCLC forcefully pursued rationalisation as the answer to its problems. This produced some controversy. How was it possible for the NCLC to lie down with the much execrated WEA in the TUC bed?[103] Millar's view seems to have been that there was no chance whatsoever of the WEA liquidating an organisation, now far from limited to trade union organisation and enmeshed with the Ministry of Education and the local Education Authorities, into a TUC scheme. He always believed that the WEA's trade union arm, the Workers' Educational Trade Union Committee, was a weaker vessel than the NCLC and would constitute little threat in an amalgamated organisation. However, he underestimated the extent of the TUC's move away from support for wider education towards advocacy of more specialised training.[104]

The problem was that the push towards more immediate educational concerns, orchestrated by the TUC and stimulated by objective economic and political conditions, was bound to influence 'the educational arm of the labour movement'. Moreover, the argument that there was a need for a reorientation, 'a difficult change for a movement cradled in strife', taken with the NCLC's view that 'emancipation is in the course of being achieved by democratic means so that it is now essential to give workers training in management and administration',[105] was bound to influence the content and approach of independent working-class education. Indeed, the emphasis on TUC rationalisation was, to some degree, dictated by the understanding that the burgeoning TUC scheme could be a dangerous competitor to the NCLC.[106] If the NCLC did not get involved in the more practical area of trade union education then, as the latter developed, it would, in all probability, be outflanked.

Certainly the NCLC did not, in this period, draw a line between the older workers' education and the new trade union education. It did not, in practice, accept the distinction made by the TUC that the former constituted the province of the voluntary organisations and that the latter should be left to the unions. Conceiving itself as the unions' educational agency, in a more formal institutionalised and subordinate way than its pioneers would have thought possible, the NCLC sought to involve itself as much as possible in training in skills and techniques. Rather than attempting to develop an alternative to the conception of education increasingly held by the union leaders, Millar sought to cater for those conceptions.

From the beginning, it was asserted, 'our curriculum has included subjects of importance to the technical side of trade unionism'. Courses in public speaking, chairing meetings, law and branch administration were cited as evidence.[107] As part of the new awareness of the shop steward that the war had engendered, the NCLC developed a postal course, 'Shop Stewards and Workshop Representatives and their Functions', which was also used in classes. The disappointment at the failure of the TUC to rationalise trade union education seems to have strengthened the more directly instrumental approach.[108] This was further reinforced when, in the aftermath of the 1948 Congress, Millar turned unsuccessfully towards the Labour Party. The failure of this initiative laid to rest for the foreseeable future the important conception that education for working-class activists should encompass both the industrial and the political wings of the movement. Whilst the NCLC, until its demise, catered for Labour Party activists, working-class education would, henceforth, focus largely on workers as trade unionists.[109]

The importance of training for shop stewards was stressed by the NCLC as the 1940s developed.[110] In 1948, courses on industrial management were introduced, again influenced by the Labour government's productivity drive, and were soon regularly provided for the engineering workers' union.[111] The programme also covered courses on local government for councillors and electioneering for Labour Party activists. The NCLC claimed that its work had a far more practical orientation than that of the WEA.[112] NCLC groups even took the Training Within Industry courses originally sponsored by the Ministry of Labour.[113] The introduction of courses on work study produced fierce criticism from the left; it was again claimed that the NCLC was supporting speed-up. In its heyday, independent working-class education, it was argued, would have analysed Taylorism in Marxist terms, not inducted workers into its techniques. The response was that union activists needed knowledge of management techniques and a critical approach *was* being taken.[114]

In 1946, the NCLC provided 748 classes involving 12,514 students, 206 day and weekend schools involving 11,747 students and 1,722 Branch lectures covering 52,827 members. There were 15,835 postal course students and five summer schools involving nearly 500 students. By 1950, there were 900 classes involving 15,275 students, 245 day and weekend schools involving 11,434 students and 2,680 branch lectures covering 80,591 members. There were 18,718 postal course students and eleven summer schools involving 636 students. By 1950, 43 trade unions with 3.2 million members had full schemes with the NCLC and six unions representing 2.4 million workers had limited schemes. The WETUC, in comparison, had 38 unions covering 4 million members affiliated, while a further ten representing 230,000 members were affiliated to the WEA alone.[115]

This position represented a minor triumph for the small, overworked NCLC staff. In 1946, for example, there were fifteen full-time organisers, three full-time tutors and one full-time winter tutor. The staff at the head office involved in administration and the postal courses was between 25 and 30.[116] The complement in this period was often less. With salaries around £400, organisers were hard to come by. Voluntary tutors only paid their expenses also had little financial incentive. Turnover was a problem. Because of the political orientation of the staff that were acquired, many became MPs or union officials.[117] But there were important limitations in terms of depth and duration. More and more of the courses were of six rather than twelve two-hour meetings.[118] There was little opportunity for sustained detailed study and little attempt at an integrated interlinked programme. Written work in the classes was extremely rare.[119] The NCLC was still strong on reading: 'It is the NCLC's job to encourage workers to get the habit of literature buying and reading.'[120]

It was still possible to attend classes where the basic laws of Marxism were recited in mechanical fashion.[121] However, from 1946 the NCLC ran an annual national school on teaching methods and the divisions followed suit.[122] Some of the organisers were critical of discussion methods and argued that they were no replacement for lectures. Proponents largely accepted this: discussions were not an alternative, only a supplement.[123] It was asserted that there was still too much lecturing and that the 'solid' hour's lecture followed by question and discussion was still the common pattern. It was argued that 'the NCLC has certainly too closely followed university lecture methods'.[124] It was high time 'all of us engaged in education work in the NCLC dealt with the tyranny of the unbroken hour's lecture'.[125]

The return of a Conservative government seemed to reinforce rather than reverse these tendencies. There was support from Tillicoultry for the TUC line of working with the Tories and avoiding any disruption of the economy.[126] Millar backed a strong defence policy, supported German rearmament and again urged the need for a modernised trade union movement to accept its responsibilities. Bevanism was apparently the product of old and outdated prejudices.[127] These 'prejudices', it was claimed by the opponents of the NCLC leadership, were in reality the very stuff of socialism which Millar was all too eager to jettison.[128] The NCLC, its critics asserted, was very strong on the Ruskin College strike and the reactionary nature of the WEA. But socialism was now part of this glorious past. Marxism, they argued, was, in practice, irrelevant to its activities in the 1950s. If its present course continued there would be no problem burying the hatchet with the WEA.[129]

The NCLC's move towards more practical work was clearly underlined when the Report of the 1953 WEA Working Party was described as 'excellent' and worthy of publication as an NCLC pamphlet.[130] This was portrayed as the WEA rather than the NCLC changing its spots. None the less, attacks on the universities continued. They were, to some degree understandable, given the attempts of prominent adult educators to pretend that the NCLC did not exist and to slight its valuable efforts.[131] Yet there was some self-congratulation in the face of the WEA's continued failure to attract manual workers. The NCLC, in distinction, claimed on its own statistics that more than 80 per cent of its students in the early 1950s were from that category.[132]

The Conservatives' second electoral victory in 1955 was the occasion for some heart-searching. Fletcher argued the need for change in terms of the Labour Party's revisionism and was answered by John Archer who claimed that the old problems and the old necessities still existed.[133] Millar provided a stark contrast with the past leadership of independent working-class education. When the NCLC was criticised on the grounds that its basic argument was

> that the labour movement's task was to get rid of the 'capitalists'. I said that if any NCLC voluntary tutors were still living in the dark ages like that, I should be glad to have their names so that I could arrange for the organisers to take them off the tutorial list until they went through an

extensive refresher course.[134]

When one of the organisers advertised a tape-recording of a Bevan speech for use as a discussion device in classes, and the press sensationalised the matter as part of the general witchhunt, Millar ordered its withdrawal. He stated,

> ... it is essential that the NCLC should confine itself to its job as the labour movement's education organisation and should take care to avoid giving the impression that any of its representatives are interfering in matters of trade union and Labour policy.[135]

Matters reached a head when Archer, who had involved a number of Trotskyists in the work in Leeds, was the subject of complaints related to the TGWU-Stevedores Union battle in the docks. He was summarily dismissed because, it was claimed, 'he had involved the NCLC in the dispute and had rendered it impossible for him to be considered an objective and impartial teacher, and so had made it impossible for him to function as an NCLC organiser'.[136] This new invocation of impartiality could be viewed as yet another clear attempt to lay down yardsticks and to prove the NCLC's credentials to the trade union leaders as a safe, mainstream educational agency. It prompted again the question: were the unions any less committed to limits on education – different limits perhaps – than the state?

Moreover, real concern was by now developing in the NCLC about the tendency of unions to create their own education schemes. More than 100 unions were associated with neither the NCLC nor the WEA. The intensive propaganda war had been unsuccessful in the sense that not one union had deserted the WEA for the NCLC. Life in the NCLC was a running battle for more students and more money from the unions. The threepence a head affiliation had been set pre-war. The loss of the South Wales miners was an unpleasant reversal, the problems with the ETU a further warning and the desertion of USDAW a major blow.[137] The NCLC was now in serious financial trouble. It had become clear that there was little chance of getting the big unions like the TGWU and the GMWU to affiliate. Not merely were they divided between the NCLC and the WEA: their major commitment to education was now through their own increasingly well-established schemes. Millar realised that the tendency for union education to possess a more immediately practical orientation would increasingly lead the unions to make it an internal service and control function.[138] What had always appeared an uphill struggle could now be seen as a labour of Sisyphus.

Hence rationalisation became more and more urgent. Despite protestations of good health it was seen as the only answer to deepening financial and organisational problems. From 1956, there began the effort which was to lead to the establishment of the co-ordinated TUC scheme.[139] By that year the NCLC was mounting 769 classes with 11,631 students, 230 day and weekend schools with 8,468 students, 2,468 branch lectures covering 66,762 members. There were 15,832 postal students and eleven summer schools catering for around 600 students. More than 90 unions were affiliated.[140] Whilst these figures maintained the levels of the post-war period, they represented a falling away from the pre-war situation, particularly in terms of relationship to working-class activism.[141]

The NCLC was isolated from what were increasingly perceived as the mainstream developments, particularly the long day-release courses which were seen as the universities at last making an overdue attempt to mobilise their resources – resources which the NCLC simply could not match, for working class education. The fact that important sections in the WEA and the universities were moving, as the NCLC wished to move, into skills training, helped to weaken the old antipathy. Declarations that it was possible for the NCLC to work with the WEA were made,[142] while the WEA itself was prepared for 'a number of concessions' and it could be said from their side that the 'controversy was moribund or close to it'[143].

It was difficult now to see the organisation as, in any determined sense, Marxist or even left-wing. It was a broad church, representing all shades of opinion in the labour movement.[144] Michael Foot, Ian Mikardo and Bevan himself spoke at schools but so did Crosland and Jenkins. Members of Labour's right wing, such as Dennis Healey or Rita Hinden, contributed to *Plebs* and so did the purveyors of antagonistic educational approaches such as Hugh Clegg and Allan Flanders. The organisers and the voluntary tutors tended towards the left and the leadership right until the end maintained a formal commitment to Marxism. On the NCLC's booklists, *Anti-Dühring* and Conze's *Introduction to Dialectical Materialism*[145] kept company with Horrabin and Millar on working-class education and more practical texts such as Citrine's *ABC of Chairmanship* and Frank Allaun's *Your Trade Union And You*. But the increasing mellowing towards respectability was perhaps summed up by the fact that the basic popularisation, *What is Marxism*, was written by A.L. Williams who, by this time, was the national agent of the Labour Party while another NCLC'er, Morgan Phillips, was General Secretary. The

NCLC's Marxism was increasingly 'Marxism for Holy Days', formulaic politics devoid of any related activist content. Socialism was something to keep the troops going in the present, its gradual implementation – *for* not *by* the working class but by Labour governments – indefinitely postponed. The central task of the NCLC was the routinist strengthening of the unions.

None of this is intended to denigrate the NCLC's achievements, particularly in relation to the qualitative degeneration of trade union education in the last two decades. The NCLC at least carried the flag for a philosophy still relevant in this period: the insistence that activists in the labour movement needed a training in trade union techniques, not at the expense of, but as part of, a training in politics, economics and philosophy if they were to be the agents of progressive social transformation. Moreover, its classes and schools provided an arena in which experienced cadres and new activists could read, think and discuss the problems and issues of the period. What was increasingly *not there*, at least as far as the unions and most students were concerned, was any deep sense of the NCLC's political distinctiveness.[146] In the early 1950s, one observer pointed out that there was no important matter of industrial or political principle dividing 'NCLC unions' from 'WEA unions'. As for the organisations themselves, 'they each had a fair representation of conflicting viewpoints'.[147] In the heat of the onslaught on the LSE course it was announced that all bar one of a particular intake had been NCLC students; and similar comments were made about Ruskin.[148] As in the pre-war period, many activists attended NCLC or WEA provision either promiscuously, or by accident of region or union, rather than by design and with a clear awareness of the distinctions.

As the 1950s moved to their close, even the most cherished totems, such as the differences with the universities and the WEA, were moved further back into the closet. The curriculum which had evolved consisted largely of provision on practical trade union issues and political and economic matters of current prominence or concern, rather than rigorous training in the principles of economics, politics, philosophy or history. Some bewailed 'the absence of serious class studies in the field of social studies'.[149] Labour history was now 'rarely taught'.[150] Veterans argued that NCLC classes 'no longer provide to any substantial degree the knowledge indispensable to the intellectual equipment of the workers for the conquest of political power by the workers'.[151]

Observers from the universities also felt that 'Marxism is no longer central to the teaching of the NCLC'.[152] Whilst the impact of the push towards training by the TUC had had an impact on the NCLC, and brought the two bodies closer together, 'The efforts of the unions themselves and the TUC are concentrated almost exclusively upon the technical training of trade unionists and this is largely also the role of the NCLC.'[153] The defence was now more tentative than in the past. All of this, Millar retorted, was not the NCLC's fault. Students had voted with their feet. They had 'tended to concentrate more and more on the practical subjects and have not given sufficient attention to the background subjects, much to my personal regret'.[154]

There was further criticism – the NCLC had only partially maintained its initial objective and had allowed a 'drift to utiliterianism'[155] and more sweeping indictments: 'all discussion and activity seems to be based on developing capitalism. Social ownership is very rarely mentioned. Social change and the transformation of a society appear to have been thrown overboard'.[156] The NCLC, it was argued, was a completely different body now from that of the 1920s': it had deserted principle to win the union barons.[157] The response was to point to the postal courses in history, economics and socialism, claim rather hollowly that a majority of union leaders were now socialists compared with a minority in the 1920s, and reiterate the difficulties of attracting students to serious study.[158]

The exhaustion of the NCLC, with its lantern lectures and quiz competitions for the J.P.M. Millar Cup in a world of relative prosperity, family cars and television, was apparent by the start of the final rationalisation offensive. The events of Hungary and Suez and the Soviet Communist Party's 20th Congress led to a new interest in Marxist ideas as witnessed by the Wortley Hall Conference, *New Reasoner, Universities and New Left Review*.[159] But this found little resonance in *Plebs* – which by this time was publishing 'Where Marx Went Wrong' – or in the Labour Colleges classes.[160] The children of this small upheaval looked elsewhere. On the level of ideas the NCLC was caught in a 1940s time warp. Whether a different approach might have garnered a more ample harvest we shall never know. But the key question, apart from philosophy, was financial resources, or rather the lack of them. The Labour Party was simply not interested in education for its members. The unions were not prepared to pay for the NCLC's *kind* of education.

The attitudes of the Communist Party had not helped. With the exception of brief interludes, its leadership had displayed either hostility or disinterest. The right-wing thrust of Millar and Woodburn cut the NCLC off from the energy and activism, essential to voluntary organisation, which only the left could supply. The pressure for orthodoxy generated by a strategy which attempted to serve unenthusiastic or suspicious unions in a period of capitalist stability finally took its toll. The TUC and the unions' espousal of a particular conception of education gave focus to these pressures. Moreover, in a sense the NCLC got the worst of both worlds. It continued to embody the democratic idea that students in a class should control that class. Its curriculum did remain wider than most of the union training schemes. But when, for example, USDAW argued on disaffiliation that they wanted a scheme which paid 'more regard to present day needs and conditions'[161] they were stating what many unions felt: that the NCLC's continuing attachment to broader education was dysfunctional to the training of their officials in the techniques of representation.

To this double bind was added the problems, particularly in generating new resources, of an ageing, centralised leadership. Throughout this period, the 'colleges', themselves, were in a faltering state. Failure to attract groups of volunteers meant that months of effort from an organiser could vanish overnight when a college secretary died or dropped out. If Millar did not accept that the NCLC had been allowed 'to degenerate into a family concern'[162], he did accept that there was a problem of renewal and thought it best to press rationalisation, whilst the NCLC still possessed some negotiating purchase.[163] The successful 1957 resolution on rationalisation moved by the NUR with the NCLC's support illustrated the NCLC's continuing attempt to marry together training and education. In the words of the mover,

> It is all very well to make a more efficient trade union officer at the negotiation table but we have still got to keep clearly in mind the need to educate in order to emancipate and to do that we still require to continue consideration of the social sciences.[164]

The succeeding years were to show that the TUC did not share that conception.

Notes

[1] For general background see J. Cronin, *Labour and Society in Britain 1918-1979* (London 1984), Chapters 8-10; J. Hinton, *Labour and Socialism: A History of the British Labour Movement 1867-1974* (Brighton 1983), Chapters 10 and 11; H. Pelling *A History of British Trade Unionism* (Harmondsworth 1963), Chapters 11 and 12; G. Dorfman, *Wage Politics in Britain 1945-67* (London 1973); K. Middlemass, *Politics in Industrial Society*

(London), 1979, Chapter 14; R. Miliband, *Parliamentary Socialism* (London) 1979, Chapters IX and X; N. Harris, *Competition in the Corporate State: British Conservatives, the State and Industry 1945-64* (London) 1972; M. Jenkins, *Bevanism Labour's High Tide, The Cold War and the Democratic Mass Movement* (Nottingham), 1979; R. Eatwell, *The 1945-51 Labour Governments* (London) 1979; L. Panitch, *Social Democracy and Industrial Militancy* (Cambridge) 1976, Chapters 1-5.

[2] The following section is based on A.H. Halsey (ed.), *Trends in British Society Since 1900* (London) 1972; B.R. Mitchell and P. Deane, *Abstract of British Historical Statistics* (Cambridge) 1971; G. Routh, *Occupation and Pay in Great Britain 1906-79* (London) 1980; G.S. Bain (ed.), *Industrial Relations in Britain* (Oxford) 1983, particularly G.S. Bain and R. Price 'Union Growth: Dimensions, Determinants and Destiny' pp.3-33 and D. Deaton, 'Unemployment', pp.237-62.

[3] For some of the trade union struggles that did go on under the affluence see, for example, V. Allen, *Militant Trade Unionism* (London) 1966; H.A. Clegg, R. Adams, *The Employers Challenge* (Oxford) 1957; D. Widgery, *The Left in Britain* (Harmondsworth), 1976, Chapter 4; and see footnote 1.

[4] J.E. Meade *Efficiency Equality and the Ownership of Property*, (London) 1964.

[5] *Economist*, 15 January 1966; 2 July 1966.

[6] J.L. Nicholson, *Redistribution of Income in the United Kingdom* in C. Clarke, D. Stuvel, 'Income and Wealth', Series X, London, 1964, p.61.

[7] *Family Expenditure Survey*, 1964, quoted in R. Blackburn 'The Unequal Society' in R. Blackburn and A. Cockburn (eds), *The Incompatibles: Trade Union Militancy and the Consensus* (Harmondsworth) 1967, p.34.

[8] See, for example, K. Coates, 'Wage Slaves' in Blackburn and Cockburn (eds), op.cit., pp.56-92.

[9] Quoted in Blackburn and Cockburn (eds), op.cit., p.25.

[10] E.H. Phelps-Brown, E.P. Hart, 'The Share of Wages in the National Income', *Economic Journal*, Vol.XII, 1952.

[11] A. Little, J. Westergaard, 'The Trend of Class Differentials in Educational Opportunity' in *British Journal of Sociology*, Vol.15, 1964, pp.301-11.

[12] Statement to 1922 Trades Union Congress on proposed unified trade union education scheme quoted in TUC *Report*, 1960, p.168.

[13] See. J. McIlroy, 'Adult Education and the Role of the Client – The TUC Education Scheme 1929-80', *Studies in the Education of Adults*, Vol. 17, No. 1, April 1985, pp.33-58.

[14] Trade Union Congress *Report*, 1944, p.92.

[15] TUC *Report*, 1944, p.37.

[16] N. Barou, *British Trade Unions* (London) 1947, p.30.

[17] J.D.M. Bell, 'Trade Unions' in A. Flanders, H. Clegg, *The System of Industrial Relations in Great Britain* (Oxford) 1954, pp.188-9.

[18] G.D.H. Cole, *An Introduction to Trade Unionism*, (London) 1953, pp.201-2.

[19] TUC *Report*, 1944, p.311.

[20] See the comment that it was not feasible to have full-time teachers 'with probably an academic rather than a practical approach to some of the problems which have to be dealt with in the course of these classes', TUC *Report*, 1950, p.557.

[21] McIlroy, op.cit.

22 TUC *Report*, 1946, p.449

23 Quoted in V.L. Allen, *Trade Union Leadership* (London) 1957, pp.84-5.

24 Ibid and see also pp.243-5.

25 G.D.H. Cole, 'What Made Bevin Tick?' *Tribune*, 12 July 1957. The TGWU leadership was also hostile to the NCLC; J. Jones, 'A Liverpool Socialist Education', *History Workshop*, Autumn 1984, p.96. No matter how strenuously the NCLC strove to distance itself from the left it could not convince many on the right.

26 TUC *Report* 1946, p.450.

27 Letter from the TUC to NCLC, 5 February 1945, Minutes of the NCLC Executive Sub-committee, 7 February 1945, Accession 5120 2nd Deposit, National Library of Scotland.

28 Ibid.

29 G.S. Bain, R. Price, 'Union Growth Dimensions, Determinants and Destiny', in Bain (ed.), op.cit.

30 R. Croucher, *Engineers at War*, (London) 1982.

31 For a good account see Panitch, op.cit., Chapter I; also Miliband, op.cit., Chapter IX; V. Allen, *Trade Unions and Government*, London, 1960, Chapter XV.

32 TUC *Report* 1951, p.170.

33 TUC *Report* 1944, p.9.

34 TUC *Report* 1948, p.141.

35 TUC *Report* 1949, p.143.

36 TUC *Report* 1944, p.318; TUC *Report* 1948, p.151. A more practical explanation of the TUC's support for the work with the universities in this period is that they received advice that if the dividends from the *Herald* were used for a TUC college they would be subject to tax. If they were used to provide scholarships to universities they would not. TUC *Report* 1943, pp.72-3.

37 See R. Fieldhouse, *Adult Education and the Cold War, Liberal Values Under Siege 1946-51*, (Leeds) 1985, p.11.

38 TUC *Report* 1944, p.316.

39 Ibid., p.331.

40 TUC *Report* 1947, p.357.

41 TUC *Report* 1948, pp.155-62.

42 Ibid., p.347.

43 Ibid., W. Kenyon.

44 Ibid., p.348.

45 Ibid., p.350.

46 TUC *Report* 1950, p.395.

47 TUC *Report* 1951, p.539; TUC *Report* 1952, p.467.

48 TUC *Report* 1953, p.162.

49 Throughout this period the TUC published a comprehensive 15-page *Trade Union Book List*. Today any list of books is absent from TUC Basic Education materials.

50 J.D.M. Bell, op.cit., p.180.

51 TUC *Report* 1952, p.300.

52 Cabinet Memorandum 1951 quoted in *Times*, 14 January 1986.

53 H. Pelling, op.cit., p.235.

54 TUC *Report* 1952, p.467.

55 H.A. Clegg, R. Adams, *Trade Union Education ... A Report for the WEA*,

(London 1959), p.58.

[56] TUC *Report* 1958, p.165.

[57] TUC *Report* 1949, p.144.

[58] TUC *Report* 1957, p.165.

[59] This section draws on General and Municipal Workers *Union Training and Education* (London 1966); WEA *Trade Union Education: Report of a Working Party* (London 1953); H.A. Clegg, R. Adams, op.cit., *Plebs* and *Highway*.

[60] V. Allen, *Trade Union Leadership*, op.cit., p.244.

[61] R. Fletcher, 'Trade Union Democracy', *Plebs*, November 1952, p.244.

[62] General and Municipal Workers ... op.cit.

[63] For one view of these developments see J.P.M. Millar, *The Labour College Movement* (London 1979), Chapter VIII.

[64] H.A. Clegg, R. Adams, op.cit., pp.62-64. The authors erroneously date the breach with the NCLC in 1947. See also, H. Francis, D. Smith, *The Fed* (London 1980), p.447-8.

[65] J. Banks, 'Labour Education's New Role in Britain', *Industrial Relations*, Vol. 5, No. 2, February 1966. Information from Jim Fyrth, April 1987.

[66] Clegg, Adams, op.cit., p.64.

[67] General and Municipal Workers Union, op.cit., p.20.

[68] Clegg, Adams, op.cit., p.71.

[69] J.O.N. Vickers, who was a member of the Communist Party, and who had worked at the Oxford Delegacy for Extra-Mural Studies, see passim and Fieldhouse, op.cit., Chapter 3.

[70] See O. Cannon, J.C.R. Anderson, *The Road From Wigan Pier* (London 1972) – viz, 'Whenever an agreement was signed Les always tried to arrange for the company concerned to send representatives to a joint course at Esher to study precisely how best to work it out ... Les usually gave up part of his Sundays to the college to address new courses as they assembled and he would spend a weekday lecturing if he thought a course particularly important,' p.267.

[71] TUC *Report* 1965, pp.105-7.

[72] Banks, op.cit., p.75.

[73] S. McIntyre, *A Proletarian Science: Marxism in Britain 1917-1933* (Cambridge 1980), Chapter 3.

[74] Quoted in J.P.M. Millar *The Labour College Movement*, op cit., p.132. The dominance of Millar in this section is justified by his dominance of the NCLC in this period. As has been observed 'rarely does an individual place such an imprint on an organisation'. R. Challinor, Review of J.P.M. Millar *The Labour College Movement*, op cit., *Bulletin of the Society for the Study of Labour History*, No. 39, Autumn 1979, p.106. Woodburn's role, however, should not be discounted. One view is that the NCLC President was 'in a sense Millar's intellect. He exercised a great deal of influence on him politically', F. Ward interview, December 1986. For Woodburn see W. Knox, (ed.), *Scottish Labour Leaders 1918-39: A Biographical Dictionary* (Edinburgh 1984), pp.284-9.

[75] See, for example, 'The Importance of Productivity of Labour', *Plebs*, January 1946. 'Austerity Real or False', *Plebs*, March 1947. S. Watson, 'The Coal Crisis', ibid.

[76] Editorial, *Plebs*, July 1947; H. Fox, 'American Trade Unions and Marshall Aid', *Plebs*, March 1948; J.P.M. Millar, 'The Brass Tacks of the Economic

Situation', *Plebs*, April 1947.

[77] Editorial *Plebs*, January 1951.

[78] J.P.M. Millar, 'The Facts Behind the Cold War', *Plebs*, March 1948; J.P.M. Millar, 'Labour and Western European Unity', *Plebs*, July 1950.

[79] See for example, Annual Conference Minutes, 1948,'50,'51,'52, 'The great safeguard is education ... the type of education provided by the NCLC ... Trade Unions without an educated membership are vulnerable to anti-Labour Propaganda,' Woodburn, *Annual Conference Minutes, 1949*, National Library of Scotland, op.cit.

[80] ... and was the voice of IWCE to 'get back to the crusading spirit it had before 1945 or, is it to go on being a recruiting sergeant for the capitalists and their friends in the Labour Movement?'. Letter, W. Owen, *Plebs*, May 1952, c.f. ' ... it is your and our job to support this government but for goodness sake let us see a kick in the old socialist dog sometimes', Letter, C. Marshall, *Plebs*, January 1950.

[81] See, for example, letters, C. Bruce, *Plebs*, September 1947; I. Morris, *Plebs*, April 1948; H. Green and I. Morris, *Plebs*, May 1948; T. King, *Plebs*, November 1949; J. Gasson, *Plebs*, December 1949.

[82] J.P.M. Millar, 'The Brass Tacks of the Economic Situation', op.cit., reply to T. King, *Plebs*, November 1949; reply to Gasson, *Plebs*, December 1949; also the letters from T. Nixon, J. Thomas supporting Millar in *Plebs*, May 1948.

[83] 'The NCLC's Parliament', *Plebs*, July 1950; Minutes of A.C., 1950.

[84] For background see, S. McIntyre, op.cit.; A. Phillips, T. Putnam, 'Education for Emancipation: The Movement for Independent Working Class Education', *Capital and Class*, 10, Spring 1980; J. Rée, *Proletarian Philosophers: Problems in Socialist Culture in Britain*, 1900-1940 (Clarendon Press 1984), Chapter 4. R. Lewis, *Leaders and Teachers: the Origins and Development of the Workers Education Movement in South Wales, 1906-40*, Ph.D. thesis, University of Wales (Swansea 1980). See Woodburn's attack on the CP: *Minutes Annual Conference, 1949*; A. Woodburn, 'Communists and their Tactics', *Forward*, 23 September 1950.

[85] For example, from 1943 to 1949 Jackson attempted to combine speaking tours for the party with lecturing for the Labour Colleges. He was often attacked from both sides. Daly took NCLC correspondence courses in English Grammar, Social History and Trade Unionism and read *Plebs* regularly. Rée, op.cit., pp.76, 122, 129.

[86] For the CP turn to a Mass Marxist Education, see *Communist Policy for Britain: Report of the 18th National Congress*, November 1945; *Marx House Bulletin*, October 1945. For the return to Marxist education provided directly by the party see *Communist Policy To Meet the Crisis: Report of 21st National Congress, 1948*; *The Battle of Ideas*, 1948; D. Garman, 'Trade Union Education', *Labour Monthly*, September 1948. Garman was the educational secretary of the Communist Party at the time. The article was actually written by Jim Fyrth of the Party's adult education group.

[87] J. Klugmann, 'Party Educational Programme for 1952-3', *Communist Review*, September 1952, p.281; cf 'Party Educational Programme for 1953-4. Adopted by the Political Committee of the Communist Party' *Communist Review*, October 1953. For the CP's own programme of courses in this period see D. Garman, 'The Place, Content and Materials of Marxist Education', *Communist Review*, December 1948.

[88] Garman, 'Trade Union Education', op.cit.

[89] For an account of this see S. Bornstein, A. Richardson, *Against The Stream: A History of the Trotskyist Movement in Britain 1924-38*, (Socialist Platform 1986), Chapter 1. For Trotsky's attitude to the NCLC see London Division, 'The Karl Marx Exhibition', *Plebs*, February 1933.

[90] For Sara see S. Bornstein, A. Richardson, op.cit; S. Bornstein, A. Richardson, *War and the International, A History of the Trotskyist Movement in Britain 1937-1949* (Socialist Platform 1986); R. Groves, *The Balham Group: How British Trotskyism Began* (Pluto Press 1974); A.J.P. Taylor, *A Personal History* (Hamish Hamilton 1983).

[91] For Briscoe see M. Shaw, *Fighter for Trotskyism: Robert Shaw 1917-1980* (New Park 1983); For Westwood see S. Bornstein, A. Richardson (i) and (ii) op.cit; for Haston and Ward see ibid., also J. McHugh, B. Ripley 'The Neath By-election 1945: Trotskyists in West Wales', *Llafur*, Vol.III, No. 2, Spring 1981. Others employed as full-time organisers with a Trotskyist background were John Archer, Duncan Hallas and Syd Bidwell.

[92] *Plebs*, July 1947, p.106, cf Millar's valedictory view that education was a vehicle by which workers would learn acceptance of the policies of Labour governments: 'the grave misunderstandings which arose between the Labour government and the unions during the period 1967 and 1970 might have been less serious had the TUC, the Labour Party and the co-operative Movement sensed the opportunity to build up an educational programme designed to enable supporters to face up to the obsolescent structure of the trade unions, the vulnerability of the national economy and the possibilities offered by the EEC', Millar, 'The Struggle for Socialist Education', *Plebs*, Summer 1969.

[93] J. Hinchcliffe, 'The NCLC', *Party Organiser*, January 1948.

[94] J.P.M. Millar, 'The WEA and Independence', *Plebs*, February 1945.

[95] *Plebs*, May 1947 and July 1950.

[96] WEA Correspondence, Box 21, op.cit., National Library of Scotland.

[97] See, for example, 'The TUC and Educational Independence', *Plebs* November 1944. There were, however, a number of communications from those who argued that workers could benefit from a university education. See, for example, J.H. Lloyd, *Plebs*, December 1944; G. Tweedie, *Plebs*, February 1943.

[98] 'What the NCLC Believes', *Plebs*, April 1944.

[99] 'The Present Position of Workers Education', Executive recommendation to NCLC Conference. *Annual Report*, 1946. This decision meant that the NCLC, increasingly purveying responsible education without responsible body status, was faced with a relatively well subsidised WEA able to use WETUC as a loss leader. This further constrained the NCLC's bargaining power with the unions. *ESC Minutes*, 12 December 1952.

[100] 'The TUC and Workers Education', *Plebs*, October 1946.

[101] Ibid.

[102] J.P.M. Millar, 'Why Not Rationalise Labour Education?', *Plebs*, 6 June 1947.

[103] The Communist Party, on the other hand, was strongly in favour of links with the WEA and of the NCLC becoming state financed. See G. Hitchings speech, NCLC Annual Report, 1946.

[104] J.P.M. Millar, 'Labour Education in a Socialist State', *Plebs*, August 1947. See also J.P.M. Millar, *The Labour College Movement*, Chapter VIII.

[105] J. Wood, 'What is the NCLC?' *Plebs*, November 1950.

[106] See 'The Present Position of Workers' Education', op.cit.

[107] Ibid.

[108] For the NCLC's reaction to the 1948 failure see J.P.M. Millar, 'The TUC and Trade Union Education', *Plebs*, September 1948; J.P.M. Millar, 'The TUC and Trade Union Education', *Plebs*, October 1948.

[109] J.P.M. Millar, *The Labour College Movement*, Chapter VIII.

[110] A class was run at a Reading factory as early as 1946. *General Secretary Report to EC*, 31 May 1946. 'Trade Unions and Industrial Management', Editorial, *Plebs*, December 1948; S. Swift, 'Training Today's Trade Unionists', *Plebs*, November 1949; 'Training of Shop Stewards', Editorial, *Plebs*, December 1949.

[111] Millar, *The Labour College Movement*, Chapter VII.

[112] Swift, op.cit.

[113] EC Minutes, 18 March 1950; GSR to ESC, 16 March 1951.

[114] See *Socialist Leader*, 26 May, 2 June, 10 June 1951; 'Think Again Mr. Sadler', Editorial, *Plebs*, June 1951; 'Come, Come Mr. Sadler', Editorial *Plebs*, July 1951; J.P.M. Millar, 'One Telescope and Two Blind Eyes', *Plebs*, August 1951. See on the management courses, J.P.M. Millar, 'Facing up to Realities: A New Advance in Trade Union Education', *Plebs*, October 1950.

[115] NCLC *Annual Reports*; J.P.M. Millar, *The Labour College Movement*; H.A. Turner, 'The NCLC, The WEA and the Unions', *Plebs*, December 1951. The question of the NCLC's statistics is a vexed one. The best view appears to be that there was exaggeration and that this was also true of the WEA to a lesser degree. Interviews with J. Archer, S. Bidwell, F. Ward, December 1986; February 1987.

[116] Millar, *The Labour College Movement*, p.139.

[117] From this period, for example, Eddie Milne, Ray Fletcher, Syd Bidwell, Will Coldrick became MPs. Haston went to the ETU and Ward to USDAW and then the Labour Party. Almost *all* the organisers were parliamentary or local candidates at one time or another.

[118] EC Minutes, 31 May 1946; Meeting between ESC and organisers, 6 May 1947.

[119] EC Minutes 31 May 1946.

[120] GSR to ESC, 12 December 1947.

[121] Interview, F. Ward. Dietzgen's disciple, Fred Casey, was still lecturing for the NCLC into the 1950s. His book, *How to Think* reviewed in *Plebs* sparked off yet another controversy, see C. Gibbons, *Plebs*, August 1949; J. Owen, *Plebs*, October 1949; C. Gibbons, *Plebs*, November 1949. For Casey see Macintyre, op.cit., Chapter 6; Rée, op.cit., Chapter 4. See also pp. 84-85 and 122-126 of this volume.

[122] A. Murie, 'The Discussion Method', *Plebs*, December 1946. Minutes ESC, February 1946.

[123] See correspondence from B. Briscoe, J. Thomas, *Plebs*, January 1947; A. Murie, *Plebs*, February 1947.

[124] J.P.M. Millar, 'Getting It Across', *Plebs*, February 1954.

[125] Ibid., p.47.

[126] 'To endanger Britain's economic stability is to attack the working class; we want to play our full part in keeping the productive machine turned up to its maximum efficiency,' A. Woodburn, Minutes AC, 1952.

[127] J.P.M. Millar, 'Let's Watch our Prejudices', *Plebs*, May 1952.

[128] J. Grahl, 'Millar Massacred', *Plebs*, August 1952; J.P.M. Millar, 'The

Corpse Replies', ibid.

[129] C. Sleigh, 'Does Plebs Face The Facts?', *Plebs*, September 1952.

[130] J.P.M. Millar, 'Is the WEA Changing its Policy?', *Plebs*, February 1954.

[131] See, for example, the acrimonious debate in 1951 between Millar and the Director of Glasgow University Extra-Mural Department, *Plebs*, August 1951; *Plebs*, September 1951.

[132] J.P.M. Millar, 'Manual Workers and Trade Union Education', *Plebs*, May 1951.

[133] J. Archer, 'Is Socialism out of Date?' *Plebs*, October 1955; R. Fletcher, 'Is Socialist Fundamentalism Out of Date? A reply to John Archer', ibid.; c.f. R. Fletcher, 'Where Marx Went Wrong', *Plebs*, January 1957.

[134] J.P.M. Millar, 'NCLC'ers at Ruskin', *Plebs*, September 1956.

[135] GSR to EC, 19 March 1955.

[136] EC Minutes, 17 March 1956.

[137] R. Clements, 'USDAW Breaks with NCLC', *Tribune*, 9 May 1958. Financially the NCLC was 'torpedoed', Millar to J.A. Birch, 13 March 1958. The NCLC had suffered a loss in both 1956 and 1957, ibid.

[138] See Millar's comments, particularly on the 'satisfactions of direct control', 'What Next in Trade Union Education?', *Plebs*, June 1957.

[139] J.P.M. Millar, 'What's Wrong with Trade Union Education?', *Plebs*, August 1957.

[140] Millar, *The Labour College Movement*, pp.267ff.

[141] NCLC, *Education for Emancipation*, 1930.

[142] J.P.M. Millar, 'What Next in Trade Union Education?', op.cit., pp.123, 124.

[143] Clegg, Adams, op.cit., p.44.

[144] c.f. H.A. Turner, op.cit., G. Brown, 'Independence and Incorporation: The Labour College Movement and the Workers Educational Association Before the Second World War' in J. Thompson (ed.), *Adult Education For A Change*, (London) 1980.

[145] Conze was seen as another break with Dietzgien proletarian philosophy and the traditions of independent working class education. His work was seen as 'an academic study of scientific method shorn of intrinsically proletarian or socialist ambitions', Rée, op.cit., p.44.

[146] See footnote 144.

[147] Turner, op.cit., p. 17.

[148] Millar, 'NCLC'ers at Ruskin', op.cit., p. 196.

[149] Letter from J. Jones, *Tribune*, 27 May 1960.

[150] 'The NCLC and Labour History', *Plebs*, July 1963.

[151] W.W. Craik, *Central Labour College* (London) 1964 p. 156.

[152] H.A. Clegg, R. Adams, *Trade Union Education* ... op.cit., p.44; c.f. the view of an organiser in a reasonably buoyant area: 'courses in Marxist subjects were few and far between'. Letter from J.C. Connell to author, March 1987.

[153] R. Peers, *Adult Education, A Comparative Study* (London) 1958, p.167.

[154] J.P.M. Millar, letter to *Tribune*, 27 May 1960.

[155] F. Moxley, letter to *Tribune*, 7 December 1961.

[156] H. Bill, letter to *Tribune*, 14 December 1962.

[157] H. Wicks, letter to *Tribune*, 21 December 1962.

[158] J.P.M. Millar, letter to *Tribune*, 28 December 1962.

[159] See, for example, J. Saville, 'The XXth Congress and the British Communist Party' in R. Miliband and J. Saville (eds), *The Socialist Register*, (London)

1976, pp.1-23; M. MacEwen, 'The Day The Party Had To Stop', ibid., pp.24-42; M. Heinemann, '1956 and the British Communist Party', ibid., pp.43-57; D. Widgery, *The Left in Britain 1956-68*, op.cit., pp.43-97.
[160] R. Fletcher, 'Where Marx Went Wrong', op.cit. A year later Fletcher went to work for the WEA.
[161] R. Clements, op.cit.
[162] E.S. Napier, letter to *Tribune*, 16 May 1958.
[163] Millar, *The Labour College Movement*, p.148. Millar's view that the NCLC was in a 'strong position', ibid., p.156 seems wishful thinking. The views of organisers differed. Some thought the NCLC could have continued, A. Murie to author, March 1987. Others that 'the NCLC was played out', Connell to author, op.cit. This appears the best view.
[164] TUC *Report*, 1957, p.390.

John McIlroy
7 The Triumph of Technical Training?

In the universities the immediate post-war years constituted a period of expansion, but one which failed significantly to affect their class basis.[1] Despite intensified pressures to serve the economy, British universities remained small-scale elite institutions.[2] By the late 1940s, almost all universities had established extra-mural departments. Their new directors quickly announced that 'they could not regard their services as available exclusively to any one organisation or section of the community',[3] that they must attempt to provide the full range of university studies, that they could not concentrate on liberal education and that they had a particular role to play in refresher courses for professional and vocational groups.[4] Changes in the Ministry of Education regulations from 1946 enabled the new departments to compete with the WEA across virtually the whole range of provision.

In 1951-52, the total number of courses mounted in extra-mural departments was 4,064.[5] By 1963-64, this had grown to 6,055. There were 83 tutors employed in 1945-46, 244 in 1951-52 and more than 300 by the mid-1960s. Joint provision with the WEA had fallen by the end of this period to under 40 per cent. Courses became shorter and less rigorous. The number of three-year tutorial classes increased by under 20 per cent, of one year courses by more than 150 per cent and of courses of even shorter duration by a massive 250 per cent. Moreover, the subject pattern changed: subjects such as archaeology, religion, language and literature, the sciences and psychology became entrenched in the programme at the expense of the traditional social studies. And there was a growth of provision for professional groups.

By the early 1950s one extra-mural director could state,

... university extra-mural work is developing into a public service for the benefit, not of the educationally underprivileged section of the population, but increasingly for those who have received the advantages of a full-time education ... increasingly the emphasis is on the further education of the products of the grammar schools, technical colleges and universities.[6]

Surveys carried out in the 1950s and 60s confirmed this view, the most extensive claiming that only 8 per cent of those attending extra-mural classes and only 12 per cent of those attending joint university/WEA classes were drawn from the lowest occupational groups.[7] In its evidence to Robbins, the University Council for Adult Education commented that,

... the welfare state and the affluent society have combined with the disillusioning effect of political events since the 1930s to blunt the edge of that social and political idealism which provided much of the dynamic of adult education in the first quarter of the twentieth century.[8]

Although there was extensive heart searching about these developments,[9] it is clear that the universities in this period devoted a tiny fraction of their resources to extra-mural work, despite the socially regressive pattern of university entrance. And that the extra-mural departments, themselves, lavished only a fraction of that small pittance on the education of workers and on helping the WEA.

Similar problems were affecting the WEA.[10] 66,570 students had attended WEA classes in 1938-39. The Association underwent an immediate post-war boom and numbers increased to an all time high of 111,351 students in 1948-49. A decline then set in, bottoming out at around 80,000 students in the mid-1950s when the WEA's participation in day release courses produced a small increase of around 30 per cent over the following decade. Membership declined to the 30,000 mark in the mid-1950s when around 60 per cent of students were not members of the Association. Almost fifty tutor organisers had been appointed by the end of the 1940s and by 1960 the figure was 75.[11]

The expansionism of the extra-mural departments was viewed with concern by the WEA who criticised 'some elements in certain universities' in their evidence to the Ashby Committee which reported on adult education in 1954.[12] This was a response to suggestions that the WEA should cease to be a teaching body. 'Let the WEA produce the students, the universities can provide for them.'[13] By the mid-1950s the main initiative lay with the universities.[14] According to certain extra-mural directors, the WEA was 'a survival of obsolete class distinction'.[15] There was also, now, competition from the local education authorities. And, like the NCLC, the WEA and specifically the WETUC were also faced by competition from the TUC and the individual unions.

Attention focused on the decline of manual workers in WEA classes.[16] They had constituted over 30 per cent of all students in the 1930s, 24 per cent in 1945-46 and around 15 per cent by the mid-1950s. The long three-year tutorial classes which had been the central vehicle in the WEA's crusade for educational emancipation were also in sharp decline. As with the universities, there was a change in the subject matter of provision. Despite the attempts by Raybould and his supporters to insist on a continued emphasis on social purpose, rigorous, sustained education and a close relationship with the labour movement, there was an increasing feeling during this period that ' ... the undermining of the ideal of social emancipation by welfare economics had slowed down the main dynamic of the WEA'.[17]

It was possible to write with conviction of 'that profoundly middle-class institution – the WEA'.[18] Although the WEA periodically asserted the central role of workers' and, increasingly, trade union education in its activities, by the mid-1960s it had, in fact, become a general provider of adult education. Its branches bore little intimate relationship to working-class communities. The changes in its constitution, so that its objective became to stimulate and satisfy the demands *of adults* for education (not, as hitherto, *workers*), and the creation of automatic membership for all students, were a product of the weakening of 'The Great Tradition'.[19]

There, were, however, those who sought to develop working-class education in the universities and the WEA. The WEA had taken particular note of the wartime work of the Army Bureau of Current Affairs and the Army School of Education, the emphasis on a wider audience for adult education and new methods centering on discussion techniques.[20] They were also influenced by the Ministry of Labour which sponsored courses for shop stewards adapted from the American *Training Within Industry Scheme*.[21] A further influence was the approach taken in US union education which was already strongly based on the inculcation of industrial relations skills.[22]

These emphases found some resonance in the 1944 WETUC Report, *Workers' Education and the Trade Union Movement – A Post-War Policy*, which looked for a large-scale expansion of work with trade unionists. It envisaged a continuation of the pre-war thrust of long courses in politics and the social sciences as the core of future provision. But it also recommended ancillary, shorter, more informal, classes for new members. And it urged study circles, based on union branches, and provision specially for the youth. There was an interest in union technical education, not because it was thought that the WEA should be directly involved; indeed, it was explicitly stated that 'the WEA makes no claim to specialisation in a function which is quite properly the responsibility of the trade union movement'.[23] It was, rather, the unions themselves which should 'provide more opportunities for what might be called the technical approach to trade union problems'.[24] Interest was shown because it was felt that this developing field would 'throw open opportunities for them [the WEA] to provide education in the social and economic background which would be necessary to give balance and perspective to that training'.[25]

This stance overestimated the demands that were to develop. There was soon unease at what was seen as a slightly disappointing response.[26] There were, therefore, attempts to integrate the work of the WETUC more closely with that of the Association and, in 1949, the WETUC Divisional Committees were replaced by trade union advisory committees for each WEA District. The official position of WETUC remained that the WEA's job was to provide workers' education for trade unionists. Yet they found a lack of interest perceived as connected with the scholastic rigidity of the tutorial class approach. There were, therefore, those whose concern for greater relevance was leading them to examine, and to hope to exploit more fully, provision related much more directly to union functions. The General Secretary of WETUC claimed in 1951 that,

> The WEA has repeatedly stated that in trade union education it is primarily concerned with providing a broad liberal background of knowledge, leaving the more 'specialised' and 'technical' provision to the TUC and to the unions themselves. It would, however, be difficult to distinguish sharply between what is liberal and what is specialised and technical and there is undoubtedly something of a 'no man's land' which there may be some danger of neglecting.[27]

The unions possessed an interest, under-resourced as they were educationally, in attracting the growing tutorial labour force of the educational bodies to help in cultivating this area.[28] Certain tutors' sympathy with trade unionism and concern at the academicism of orthodox provision inclined them in this direction. They realised, however, the dangers of opposition from those who would see talk of a 'no man's land' as casuistry and assert that there was 'the liberal' and there was 'the technical'. This position was underpinned by the fact that the WEA took pains at the time to ensure in its schools that the practical side was dealt with by full-time officers, and the wider background by WEA tutors.[29] Those who wished to move the WEA from the broad workers' education to the narrower trade union education were careful to seek legitimacy, and successfully moved the 1951 Annual Conference to establish an inquiry into the WEA's future role in educating trade unionists.[30]

A similar and overlapping searching was apparent in the universities. For those, like Cole, who still asserted in the 1940s that 'I am damned well not interested in adult education. I am interested in workers' education,'[31] the obvious arena to turn to was, again, the trade unions. Initially this group, like Vickers, who worked for the Oxford Delegacy in Staffordshire, saw little wrong with the content and form of the traditional evening class in economics, politics and trade union issues supplemented by day and weekend schools. These just required to be brought to the workers *as trade unionists*. 'The key to the development of working class education lies in the development of a network of classes corresponding to the existing organisation of trade union branches and shop stewards committees'.[32] Existing provision should not yet be written off, for it had not been adequately exploited. This approach was supported at Leeds by Raybould who argued the need to recruit trade unionists 'not as individual members of classes composed of students drawn from the public at large, but in groups already associated as members of the same union branches'. It was also useful to 'begin with a study of the position or history of the particular industry or organisation with which the students are associated'.[33]

The LSE evening course, followed at Glasgow, was in the traditional three-year tutorial mould. The Nottingham Trades Council requested a similar course with the university and Manchester, Liverpool and Southampton were soon involved. By the early 1950s, however, both recruitment and drop-out were causing problems, and this led to a further examination of alternatives to the tutorial class.[34] As early as 1947, Frank Pickstock was urging the need for a new approach if Oxford was to renew its influence in the new welfare state. The TUC-supported classes, he argued, were general social science courses, not trade union education aimed at 'training men specifically for the exercise of trade union functions'. What was needed was a curriculum more related to the specific problems of trade unionism to create, in classic Oxford terms, 'both an intelligent rank and file and an intelligent local leadership'.[35] Pickstock's concern at the lack of links between the university and trade union leaders and the lack of suitable tutors for more practical provision was a factor behind the summer schools run at Queen's College in this period. Pickstock himself conducted a course in 'Practical Trade Unionism' in 1947-48 covering issues such as preparing a speech, conducting a meeting and reporting back to members. As a result, he felt work had to be adapted to students who wanted direct results in terms of an enhanced ability to perform a particular role in a union. Courses on 'The Future of the Aluminium Industry', based on a particular company, and 'The Future of the Motor Industry', based on the Cowley works, were successfully mounted. A sessional course for TGWU members was 'conducted on experimental lines with vocational interest, a high degree of student participation and the use of techniques such as role playing'.[36]

Other departments such as those at Hull, Newcastle and Durham, had turned directly to the unions and developed courses with the General and Municipal Workers Union which sought to broaden out from a consideration of union problems to a wider examination of economic and political issues.[37] A survey of extra-mural provision found a variety of courses: 'The Development of Trade Unionism', 'Trade Union Studies', 'Economics for Trade Unionists', 'Joint Consultation', 'Trade Union Law' and 'Modern Political Problems' were just some of the titles. There was a strong feeling amongst the tutors that subject matter required to be strongly related to the problems of the students, which were seen in limited terms. 'To generalise, I would say that trade union students who attended would prefer to study specific trade union problems rather than social problems.' Students wanted to know more about industrial relations 'as distinct from general knowledge of economics, politics, etc.' Consequently it was felt that tutors needed more detailed practical knowledge, '... a knowledge of day to day trade union activities is essential for a tutor. Without this I would many times have been floored by a question ...'; '... the tutor will have a great deal of difficulty unless he has some acquaintance with the conditions in the industries'. However, the aim of most of the tutors remained to mobilise the experience of the class and show how to relate it to general principles.[38]

Leeds put particular effort into their tutorial class programme. They ran classes preparatory to three year tutorials in both 'Industrial Relations' and 'Trade Union Studies'. The former term 'was interpreted in a wide sense, leading to discussion of political and sociological problems'. The books used, however, like those on nearly all courses on 'Trade Union Studies' at this time, were of a strongly institutional nature: Flanders' *Trade Unions*, Clegg's *Democracy and Nationalisation*, the government's *Industrial Relations Handbook*. The success of the course was measured for the providers by the fact that the students at the end requested a tutorial class in Social Philosophy. 'Trade Union Studies' was designed to harness the 'semi-vocational' interest of a group of steelworkers from a variety of unions. The first half of the course was 'essentially bread and butter, dealing with collective bargaining disputes, wages and the cost of living index', most of these issues being considered from the viewpoint of the unions involved. The second half of the course dealt with 'the trade unions' role in national economic and political life'.[39] There seemed to be wide disparities in the production of written work. 'The idea of writing always met with strong resistance' in a Leeds class on economics recruited from Wakefield Trades Council.[40] The Cowley carworkers, it was claimed, produced 93 pieces of written work.[41]

Whilst the avowed intention was to use more specific provision to bring trade unionists into the traditional tutorial classes, there was a growing feeling that those classes were too abstract, too formal and too alien to working-class experience. Campbell, another Oxford tutor in the Midlands, saw the mass of workers as indifferent to traditional tutorial classes because

> ... we have set the educational pattern in terms of a world which is not their's and tried to make them into fit replicas of that world. Unwittingly, we have often disparaged and insulted their values. We have assumed a condescending air of patronage ...[42]

Campbell also argued for courses aimed at particular groups of workers, sited in working-class areas with syllabuses tailored to particular concerns and tutors 'who speak their language'. Lecturing and limited discussion should be replaced by less formal teaching, eschewing 'the petty tyrant pedagogues who have well nigh sealed their minds against awakening curiosity'. He warned that a continued attempt to make extra-mural education march to the beat of intra-mural provision 'could only result in the progressive elimination of representative workers from our ranks'.[43]

Alan Bullock argued the need for tutors sympathetically to understand the life experience of their students as well as conditions in local industry, and to mix socially with students outside the classroom.[44] Richard Hoggart suggested the need to make a positive effort to seek out working-class students. But to soft-pedal what a university was about and evade issues of standards by provision which made few demands on students was, he asserted, self-defeating. The absence of workers from university courses might require 'a radically different approach in teaching working class people from the one we are used to, an approach which aims all the time at starting from and connecting with working class experience.'[45] It was no good patronising workers with provision that required little effort. He felt it particularly 'scandalous' that the method most used 'is still the "one hour lecture – one hour discussion" ', a method which, he argued, was 'often irrelevant and ineffective'.[46]

What seemed to be emerging, however, from all this searching was not an attempt to approach the worker as trade unionist, in order to penetrate the cultural experience of the working class and ignite a new understanding of social processes, but – at this stage only a tendency – a turning towards a professional trade union education at one with the 'professional role' approach of extra-mural departments. Hitherto, courses were taken by the generalist tutor in the PPE mould. Now appointments were made at Birmingham and at Sheffield in 'trade union studies'. A similar post was established at Leeds. Raybould noted the development of the study of industrial relations in universities and saw it suitable for adult students as long as it was treated in a broad not a technical fashion.[47] And Oxford looked towards the research of internal academics such as Clegg and Flanders to be applied to their extra-mural programme.[48] The growing specialisation and buds of professionalisation were marked by a conference in 1952 on 'The Teaching of Trade Union Studies' held in Oxford and attended by 27 university and WEA tutors.[49]

The same year the Universities' Council for Adult Education (UCAE) drew attention to developments in this area. 'The age', it intoned, was one of 'education for industry ...' What is 'variously called Economic and Industrial Problems, Industrial Relations and Trade Union Studies', it noted, was receiving special attention and had attracted 'a considerable amount of thought and experiment since 1945'.[50] The need was for a wider appeal to the trade unionist '... to be made along new lines given the decline in manual workers in tutorial classes and the extended social role of the unions'.[51] Already at this stage the UCAE was justifying this appeal in terms of economic and social need and 'responsibility'. The growth of trade union education was specifically related to the general development of training in industry. In comparison with tutorial classes 'a different approach is required'.[52] Expansion was already sufficient to justify high hopes, tempered with caution. 'The trade union class may prove the modern counterpart of the earliest tutorial class as a contribution to the further education of the responsible trade unionist, or it may only be a passing boom.'[53]

However, problems had already emerged. Education which addresses itself to trade union issues can always run foul of leaders who see discussion of union policies and alternatives to existing policies as subversive of their position and tutors who stimulate such discussion as external meddlers in union affairs. In the atmosphere of the Cold War, with divisions over wage restraint, nationalisation and rearmament, the problem was an acute one. Fieldhouse has recently documented the impact of this on the burgeoning university-WEA trade union education.[54] The background was a prolonged debate in the *Highway* on whether it was possible for Marxists to be objective and whether they should be involved in the adult education movement: '... eddies of McCarthyism in Leeds, Liverpool, London, Birmingham and Manchester belie the claim that the Cold War did not enter the portals of the university'.[55]

In London, problems were created for a Communist tutor because the trade union work was regarded as particularly sensitive. At the Oxford Delegacy, around one-third of the full-time staff, including the secretary Thomas Hodgkin, were members of the Communist Party or fellow travellers. The situation was viewed with concern not only by Pickstock who was secretary of the Tutorial Classes Committee, but by the WEA who saw Hodgkin as invading the field of trade union education which they acknowledged as their own. Complaints from the unions and the TUC, filtered through the WEA, led to formal inquiries into the 1948 Queen's College Trade Union School and the teaching at the Delegacy's Wedgewood Memorial College. Whilst the allegations concerning lack of objectivity were not upheld in relation to the summer school, continued attempts were made to stop left-wing tutors participating. At Wedgewood College, the contracts of the warden and another tutor were not renewed. The pressures led to Hodgkin and other staff departing and broad conformity being re-established.[56]

Of course, one means of at least limiting this problem is to move away from education towards narrower training. By 1952 the growth of the more practical orientation was causing some concern to defenders of liberal education. Courses that extra-mural departments were mounting for the GMWU had led Newcastle to argue that 'more attention to practical problems of work and of trade unionism is called for than can appropriately be given by an extra-mural department'.[57] They suggested, therefore, that the courses 'could be better done in a technical college'.[58] Durham, on the other hand, was well satisfied and drew attention to the high quality of the work. This problem, and this division of opinion, was to develop as time went on. The UCAE was not prepared to deliver a firm verdict. On the one hand, it felt that while some attention to practical problems was required in trade union courses, if the practical eliminated or severely curtailed the liberal approach the extra-mural departments 'should leave the field to others ... until suitably liberal classes are formed'.[59] On the other hand, there might not be any necessity to withdraw or succumb to narrow training because 'a fundamentally liberal approach may be devised which does not overlook practical illustration'.[60]

These tensions were also reflected within the WEA. The 1953 Report of its Working Party on Trade Union Education represented an important victory for 'practical trade union studies'. The report recommended an emphasis on skills and participative learning methods and careful experiments in pilot areas.[61] This influence was reflected in the curriculum of the WEA's TGWU summer schools which were soon under attack from supporters of liberal adult education as constituting a simple training exercise in union administrative activities – the province of the unions not the WEA.[62]

The defence argued that the training approach was designed to relate directly to broader issues.[63] This account, later embodied in Tony Corfield's *Epoch in Workers Education*, is not borne out by a study of the syllabus or the franker, contemporary statements of its proponents. Unions needed both skills training and broader education, but resources were shifting towards the latter. The unions' cannibalisation of WEA resources was personified by Corfield's transfer from Temple House to Transport House. From there he argued that

> the first thing to say about trade union education today is that it is no longer primarily concerned with education, at least not in the sense in which the WEA and the extra-mural departments have usually understood it. The greater part of union expenditure goes upon training rather than liberal studies ... The purpose is to prepare members to deal in a specific way with prescribed problems or to find a pre-determined route through given surrounding; the purpose of liberal studies by contrast is to teach men and women to plan a route for themselves. Training is a closed circuit – education is the open road.[64]

The new instrumentality also affected extra-mural departments, particularly Oxford, where the view was increasingly that trade unionists imbued by a new love of skills were 'not yet ready' for political and economic studies. Frank Pickstock, whose conceptions of working-class education were every inch as partisan as those he so bitterly opposed on the left, linked up with academic reformers. They emphasised that

> The contribution which education is able to make to improving workplace industrial relations will be most effective when both sides are well versed in 'the rules of the game' and share a common understanding of what are after all their joint institutions.[65]

This joint-interest conception prompted Oxford, financed by the Leverhulme Trust, to concentrate on the stimulation of industrial peace through the preparation of documentary materials which could overcome the tutors' lack of knowledge of specific industries and which would develop stewards skills in operating established industrial relations procedures.[66] There were distinctions between the internal union focus of the WEA and the industrial relations emphasis of the Oxford approach. But the small number of tutors encouraged cross fertilisation and the extension of practical orientations was stimulated by Hugh Clegg's influential 1959 Report on the WEA's experiments in the pilot areas.

It was the promptings, both of those who wished to see a move towards a greater emphasis on the safer and more acceptable training, and those who wished to overcome the perceived lack of relevance of traditional provision without dissolving liberal adult education into technical training, which led to the emergence of day release courses. As the 1950s developed, many tutors felt that the amount of time spent recruiting for evening courses returned a low ratio of results to effort. The continuing problems can be seen from the collapse of the Leeds programme and the fate of the TUC-sponsored tutorial classes, so that by 1954 only Liverpool and London were persevering with this model.

Holding the Line: Day Release Courses 1950-64

Day release for workers to attend university courses was not an innovation. A scheme had been established at Nottingham University in the early 1920s which secured unpaid release for two days a week. Mineworkers attended certain internal courses together with special classes provided by the extra-mural department and went on to degree examinations. The scheme was funded by the Miners' Welfare Adult Education Joint Committee and was revived after the war.[67] In 1952 a reorganisation of the welfare arrangements in the coal industry provided an opportunity for restructuring.[68] The Nottingham department had been exercised by a decline in manual-worker students, particularly miners, and felt the need for provision more tailored to their needs than the tutorial classes.[69] It is also claimed that the director wished to disabuse critics of the belief that he was a supporter of ephemeral provision for the middle classes.[70]

A new one-year course of one day a week for 30 weeks was introduced in 1954, greatly helped by links with former students, and supported by the NCB and the Nottingham NUM. It was aimed at all workers, not simply union officials and not just the 'high flyers' but those who, it was hoped, would stay in the industry and provide 'a steadying, constructive and thoughtful element in local leadership'.[71] The response was overwhelming, with 168 applications for 30 places leading to two parallel courses. By the end of the decade, a cycle of two one-year courses and three three-year 'follow on' courses running each year involving 120 students had been established.[72] In 1961, provision was restructured and all students had a minimum two-year course with a smaller number going on to a two year follow-on course.

The Derbyshire Area NUM President, Bert Wynn, had been a student on the pre-war Nottingham course and prominent in local left-wing politics, as were two of the tutors in the Sheffield department. As a result of their collaboration, and the problems the director was experiencing with forming tutorial classes for miners, an experimental one-year course was mounted by Sheffield for the Derbyshire miners. It proved so successful that it was extended in 1954 to the Yorkshire Area NUM with three-year courses running in both regions.[73] After 1956, to accommodate a greater number of students, the Yorkshire course was reduced to 72 days release although the Derbyshire course remained as it still does, the most intensive experiment in trade union liberal education, providing for 120 days release over a three-year-period with two days a week study in the second and third years. Payment of wages was initially undertaken by the NUM, later by the NUM and NCB jointly. Again, the demand was so great as to encourage Sheffield to involve Leeds, that department mounting its first course in 1957. These courses were all, eventually, mounted in conjunction with the WEA. But the initiative came from the universities and whilst the WEA tutors were involved, it was in a minority role. On the whole, the WEA was very much a junior partner.[74]

The exponents of these courses saw them as an adaptation of liberal studies to a new, improved and extended format. Nottingham emphasised that what we want to do in day release courses is ordinary extra-mural work of the traditional kind. The only difference between these courses and the bulk of our other work is that we are fortunate to have the students in the daytime instead of the evening. Otherwise, all the traditional yardsticks apply ... the courses are grounded firmly in liberal studies; they are non-specialist and non-vocational ...[75]

The courses were designed to create 'awareness and understanding of the problems facing industry and the trade unions today and to relate them to their economic and political background'.[76] It was felt that they afforded 'all the advantages of the good tutorial class',[77] and the director at Sheffield, Bruce, claimed them as 'essentially an adaptation of traditional tutorial class methods to new conditions'. However, they had

the enormous advantage that the students came to them fresh and that they could, therefore, be expected to tackle their work seriously ... the ground covered and the work done were far greater than in normal courses.[78]

The curriculum focused initially on economic history, industrial relations and communication skills. However, as time went on, 'special attention [was] devoted to topics such as arbitration and negotiation procedure and techniques employed such as role playing and case studies'.[79] The approach was to 'start with an examination of the economic, political and social facts of life as the coal miner experienced them and to move steadily from there to theories, problems and policies'.[80] One tutor found himself for some time regurgitating his PPE training until he realised how to use and restate the knowledge in a way which related to the students' experience. Gradually, the time given to project work and to discussion increased.[81] Another teacher felt himself free to

experiment with participatory methods, with individual and group project work, and with more ambitious use of the class for research, despite the fact that the previously prevailing style of working class education had been over formal and academic.[82]

All was not sweetness and light. One tutor was troubled by the lack of self-discipline on the part of some participants in discussion. He felt that 'the most serious obstacle to an objective assessment of some ideas was the belief that Marx could not be wrong'.[83] Some tutors found it a struggle to get their students to appreciate 'the relevance of theory' and 'to lift their eyes above the horizon set by the problems of their own industry'.[84] Others took a more practical, but in reality, value-laden approach:

suspicions of orthodox economic theory had to be met by the use of a practical test and this we found in the work of the Coal Board. Could we explain Board policy in terms of orthodox economic theory? If the Coal Board wanted an alternative policy could they really find the answers to their day to day problems in the writings of Marx and Lenin? Using this as a starting point we worked through the important reports on the coal industry in so far as they dealt with price policy, the organisation of production, and limitations on the supply of additional productive resources.[85]

There was clearly a diversity of ideology and approach between tutors and between departments. But, overall, this provision had a breadth and a depth lacking in the more technical approach we have examined. At its best, the early day-release work made a serious attempt to relate established knowledge to the subjective concerns of the students, whilst attempting to enlarge their experience, not simply reflect it. Williams describes the attempt to come to terms with problems of content and methodology:

> ... the students became accustomed to hearing lectures and taking notes but the formality was not rigid. The pattern of an hour's lecture followed by an hour's discussion was avoided as far as possible. The lecture was frequently interspersed with discussion and in this way would occupy the whole two hours of the morning session.

Often, particularly in the afternoons,

> the students were divided into groups to inquire into a specific problem. Each group appointed its own chairman and secretary and drew up a report which was later discussed by the class as a whole. Towards the end of the course, the tutors arranged a mock collective bargaining dispute ... After a fortnight of research and analysis they presented their cases ... it was a useful exercise in which the students were able to learn some economics at the same time as they were gaining confidence in preparing cases and presenting them in public. It was, of course, equally important that students should be able to express themselves well in writing. In this connection, the periods of individual tuition were invaluable. The students were asked to write one formal essay each fortnight and any tendency to use faulty arguments or emotional language was ruthlessly exposed by the tutors.[86]

While, therefore, 'some elements of the new trade union education found their way into the courses'[87] this provision was broader and remained far more within the framework of liberal adult education (they were not, of course, confined to union representatives) rather than trade union training. The syllabus and reading list of the longer courses at Sheffield by the mid-1960s are impressive. The course commenced by examining the local organisation of trade unions with special reference to mining, then moved on to national organisation, culminating in a section on trade unions in society, once again attempting to examine, but go beyond, immediate concerns. There was a range of reading relating to legal reform and the Donovan Commission. But there was also an extensive range of books recommended related to the history of mining and trade unionism; conventional texts by Clegg, Flanders and Roberts on industrial relations: all Vic Allen's books; Harrison on unions and the Labour Party; Coates' and Topham's book of reading on industrial democracy; Pelling on history; Wedderburn on labour law. The syllabus could be expected to give a good grounding in industrial relations while developing its political and economic dimensions.

The second year dealt with the economics of the nationalised industries. The aim here was to focus on coal but set it within its wider framework and to use this focus to teach basic economic concepts. Once again, the movement was from the particular to the general. An examination of the size and administrative structure of the nationalised industries, their pricing, investment and wages policy and their relationship to political decision-making led into a discussion of the allocation of wealth in society, covering the factors of production; the nature of capital; employment incomes; the price mechanism and the tax structure. An examination of patterns of employment led into a wider consideration of the aims of British economic policy, economic growth and the causes of unemployment. The final section was entitled 'Britain in the World Economy'. The texts listed included the general textbooks by Lipsey, Samuelson, Harrison, Hicks and Prest; Barber's *History of Economic Thought*; Cole and Postgate; Ashton on the Industrial Revolution; Skidelsky and Galbraith on the slump; Marx, Keynes – indeed books from all perspectives, on all aspects of economics.

The third and final year dealt with the structure of modern society, politics and government, communications in modern society and the reform of industrial relations. Once again, the book lists were extensive and equivalent to those used on degree courses.

The descriptions of the course work and the impressive and sustained achievements of the students in going on to further education and replenishing local union and political leadership, is both impressive and sustained.[88] In 1963-64, the Sheffield courses were described by the HMI's as 'an outstanding venture in adult education'.[89]

There was suspicion and hostility from some quarters. For example, a report was presented to the Yorkshire Area Executive in 1960 which warned of the dangers of 'the clerks taking over the union'.[90] But the general view of the teachers was that union officials had shown 'a scrupulous respect for the freedom of the tutors to devise their own syllabus'[91] or, as another tutor said, 'There was never once a suggestion that Bert Wynn would try to make us do anything.'[92]

There could be little doubt about the success of this experiment. Of course, it developed in a nationalised industry. Despite the history of conflict there were at this period strong links between management and union. Although the increasing pressure of technical training showed itself, the tutors were able to ensure that '... the teaching of skills does not become isolated from the academic side of the course but is integrated with it'.[93] As one famous miners' leader said, years later, of the course at Leeds, 'It taught me to think and to question. I began to dissect everything that came my way in minute detail so that I could argue.'[94] Indeed, the courses answered a variety of different interests. For many tutors they represented an opportunity to renew the links between university and labour. For extra-mural directors they provided a guaranteed flow of students immune from the vicissitudes of the individual canvass and the messiness of WEA branch recruitment. The quality of the courses was soon demonstrated and the UCAE was soon talking of work 'reminiscent of the legends of the early heroic days of tutorial class work'.[95]

This reputation was soon underpinned by the powerful flow of students – against the original intentions – into universities. The courses provided prestige. There was coverage of Sheffield in the *Times Higher Education Supplement* and the *Guardian* as early as 1954. In 1957 the courses were accorded a *Times* leader. R.A. Butler, the former Minister of Education, congratulated the university, providing a boost internally for the 'marginal' extra-mural department.[96]

Directors were able to demonstrate that their efforts really were bent towards serving *all* sections of the local community. Nottingham saw them as 'a necessary corrective to the *natural tendency* of a university adult education department to find itself mainly serving the grammar school and university educated and to lose touch with two-thirds of the community' (my emphasis, J.McI.).[97] These courses radiated outwards from their initial base in mining. By the mid-1960s Sheffield had developed courses in a similar mould for steelworkers and engineering trade unionists. Nottingham had developed an impressive programme of day release at a variety of private companies often mounted in the workplace. Sheffield looked at the courses very much in trade union terms. Their staff was activist and involved itself in local labour movement and community organisations. They forged particularly close links with the NUM, strengthened as former students rose to positions of responsibility in the union and took up posts in the department.[98] By the early 1960s, eight out of twelve tutorial staff in the department were significantly involved in this work.

Nottingham took a more academic, distanced view of the situation.[99] From the start they theorised a non-conflictual view of serving 'an industrial community'.[100] They saw these courses serving workers, not as trade unionists, but as citizens of a community based on the mine, the factory or the industry. They, therefore, saw benefits accruing to employers from the courses, as

> every contribution of an opening kind that could be made to the knowledge, to the outlook, to the thought, to the intellectual skills of an individual, would be likely to make him a more effective member of the industrial community.[101]

This conception, partaking of the human relations school of pre-sociology, ignored the existence of structured, organised conflicts based upon divisions of interest of such a degree that many of the workers in the pit, factory or industry would reject most of the notions of shared interest often attached to the term 'community'. Just as the extra-mural department claimed to provide a balance of provision for all sections of the larger community, so those that followed Nottingham's path strove for balance *within* industrial provision and ran courses not only for trade unionists but for supervisors, technical staff and administrators and all levels of management.

By the turn of the decade, through the normal process of cross fertilisation and emulation, day-release courses were spreading to other extra-mural departments and WEA Districts. We can trace their initiation: Birmingham 1957-58, Bristol 1961, Oxford 1961, Swansea 1961, Bangor 1961, Southampton 1962. The years are significant. For in a changing industrial relations climate, and with greater interest in its reform, this provision is increasingly shorter and more instrumental, influenced to some degree by the early day release experiments but also by the technical training and Oxford approach. It would be wrong to over-generalise. A department, such as London, which had developed half-day release workplace-based classes in the engineering and printing industries and, in the docks in the late 1950s and, in the next decade, day-release courses for railway workers and transport workers, successfully combined liberal trade union education with some skills training. But, as the 1960s developed, provision in many departments and WEA Districts became increasingly focused on skills and techniques of industrial relations, and increasingly aimed at the shop steward.

The late 1950s had seen the shop steward making the grade as film star and as social problem.[102] The media was beginning to orchestrate a public opinion concern with unofficial 'wild-cat' strikes, the closed shop, wage drift and communist agitators. By 1957, a Court of Inquiry could describe workplace organisation as 'a private union within a union ... in no way officially or constitutionally linked with the union hierarchy'.[103] The comments of the leader of the major union involved were more strident '... subversive elements have been at work at Briggs ... there grew up a shop stewards' committee which is a subversive body ... a sort of Frankenstein's Monster'.[104]

A major influence in the development in the 1960s of the day-release courses is this concern with integrating the steward into the union, and transforming workplace organisation. There was a broad consensus between TUC and employers on the need to use day release for these purposes. In 1958 the Ministry of Labour commended the courses for shop stewards run at Birmingham Extra-Mural Department as a contribution to improved industrial relations in the car industry.[105] This was followed by a joint statement on training by motor industry employers and unions in 1961, specifically set in the context of strikes as a major problem and more civilised shop stewards as a means of minimising them.[106] Further discussion produced a joint statement in the name of the British Employers' Federation, forerunner of the CBI and the TUC General Council.[107]

There was a need, the statement asserted, to increase the amount of training. The syllabus should be agreed with the employers. It would help to define the rules for the shop stewards to help them understand their place in the union, what they could and could not do. 'The aim of training must be to assist stewards to carry out their functions as responsible officers of their unions ... so that more stewards can obtain a broader understanding of their functions and responsibilities.'[108] This would help employers too, for expanded training, 'by bringing about a better understanding of the problems involved ... could lead to a marked improvement in industrial relations'.[109] The positing of such a problematic objective was highly questionable in terms of a liberal credo in which 'improved industrial relations' from the workers' point of view might involve precisely the wage drift and unofficial stoppages that increased day release provision was intended to cure. So, too, of course, was the vetting of syllabus by employers. Education was not mentioned at all. The term 'training' was used throughout this statement. Tutors may be criticised for failing to discuss these issues in any adequately rigorous fashion. It was easy to adopt an 'all classroom activity is education and all education is useful' perspective, eliding the distinct categories of 'training' and 'education', particularly when resources were available for an expansion of the former rather than the latter.

Other factors stimulated the technicisation of day release courses – the increased entry of technical colleges into the field, the establishment of the TUC Regional Education Scheme, the 1964 Industrial Training Act and crucially the 1964 Labour government's economic and industrial policies culminating in the Royal Commission on Trade Unions.

However, until the end of this period, influences mingled. In at least several of the day-release courses it was possible to hold the line for an adaptation of liberal adult education, a marriage between discussion of issues and development of technique. This was particularly true at Sheffield where an attempt to introduce the Oxford approach was taken on and defeated.[110] In other situations 'there seems to have been a tacit understanding on the part of the tutors to explore the areas of agreement rather than of disagreement in industrial relations.'[111] This is, of course, educationally lamentable and certainly in the later 1960s there is evidence of direct management and union pressures, exercised through their control of release, moulding provision.[112]

Recently, there has been speculation on the impact of these courses on mining trade unionism.[113] The development of a left-wing group replacing the existing right-wing leadership in Yorkshire, it is suggested, was influenced by left-wing tutors on the courses at Sheffield and Leeds. It should be pointed out, however, that future leaders of the Union of Democratic Mineworkers in Nottingham, such as Roy Lynk, also attended the courses there. Whilst the left-wing nature of the tutors at Sheffield was in contrast to most other departments, this was far from the position at Leeds.[114] Activists from all parts of the political spectrum attended these courses: their influence would play a small part, together with a wider constellation of factors, in political change within the union. We must await a more detailed scrutiny of the different educational philosophies operating and their relationship to the actions of the protagonists in the industrial arena.

By 1964, the day release experiment had illustrated what could be achieved, albeit in the protected context of a union with a strong tradition and nationalised industries with a community base. However, barriers to significant expansion had already moved into position. A variety of power holders were determined to ensure that future day release would bear the brand of their social purposes. Moreover, if in this period 'the most hopeful development in provision for adults who left school at fourteen or fifteen ... lay in the continued growth of industrial release courses',[115] they made an inadequate and temporary impact on the 'natural tendency' of WEA and university work – growing at around 6 per cent in the 1960s[116] – to cater for the educationally privileged. By 1964, the growth of 'industrial studies' was leading to a rash of new specialist appointments in universities and WEA Districts which expanded, but further professionalised this work, strengthening the tendency to separate it from the mainstream of adult education.[117]

The Triumph of Technical Training?

By the late 1950s strenuous and sustained effort on the part of Congress House had created a distinctive, if small scale provision. The training approach with various emphases had won adherents in both the unions and in the adult education bodies. Yet its architects had to confront a situation in which there was little emphasis on *any* form of educational provision within the unions. This was intimately connected with the empiricism of British trade unionism. Problems of finance added as a barrier to an expansion of training courses that the central leadership of the British unions saw as important.

The TUC had insisted that a training college would only be opened once a firm foundation had been laid.[118] Whilst the take-up – 64 unions nominated students in 1958 – represented a massive increase on the ten or so sending representatives in the early 1950s, 121 eligible unions had still failed to become involved. One view is that the TUC leadership felt that it had been landed by Congress with what it saw as the ramshackle NCLC and WETUC. The prospect of a co-ordinated scheme provided, however, the *potential* for a big expansion, particularly if participation in it by all affiliates was made compulsory. Moreover, what the existing training scheme lacked was a regional organisation. The availability of the NCLC organisers as full-time co-ordinators held a certain attraction. The TUC would also acquire via the NCLC a network of postal courses. Moreover, compared with 1946-48, both the voluntary bodies had moved a distance into the area of technical education and older traditions had weakened. A new scheme, therefore, could both galvanise the unions into greater support for the TUC's provision and create tentacles that could reach deeper into the movement to popularise training as a more organic part of union functions. Such a scheme would, however, have little room for what was still deplored as the NCLC's overly political approach or the eccentricities of its organisers.[119]

In the immediate aftermath of the 1957 resolution, the matter was dealt with by the General Council in terms the resolution's movers had envisaged. What was discussed was an integrated scheme on the model of the aborted proposals of the 1920s covering technical training *and* wider education.[120] In reporting back in 1959 and 1960 on the remitted NUR motion, the General Council leaned strongly towards an integrated scheme based on a TUC takeover of the WETUC and the NCLC. There was a need, they stated, for far more integration and collaboration between the TUC, individual unions and the educational bodies if the education of trade unionists was to be developed. Continuing competition, seen as something healthy in the 1940s, was now viewed as unhelpful. Unions divided on affiliation to the NCLC or WETUC often found it difficult to support both and, as a consequence, sometimes supported neither.[121] When reporting back in 1960, the General Council quoted in detail the broad rubric of the 1922 scheme and specifically aligned the new venture with that philosophy. They continually stressed that they would take over and develop the existing work of the voluntary bodies. The new scheme would supplement the direct efforts of the TUC and the unions in the sphere of technical training, but it would also help to compensate trade unionists for their lack of general education, take particular pains to address their lack of competence in study skills and 'provide specific opportunities for trade unionists to engage in systematic social, economic and political studies relevant to their trade union interests'.[122]

All the speakers in discussion between 1957 and 1964, without exception or reserve, wanted the new provision to cover both technical training and the liberal studies. Beard from the General Council pointed out that

> there seemed to be some danger that the movement might produce increasing numbers of people trained to conduct day to day union business more efficiently but without having the necessary further understanding of the aims and purposes of trade unionism itself.[123]

When, in 1961, the General Council reported in favour of the establishment of a broad, compulsory scheme, financed by all affiliates and based on the takeover of the WETUC and the NCLC, supporters of union education were cheered and reassured. They were particularly pleased by the statement that the scheme would be governed by a Joint Trade Union Education Committee. This would consist of the TUC Education Committee *and* representatives of affiliates who would be elected, representatives of Ruskin and the WEA and other co-opted members.[124] In retrospect one danger signal was that the meeting of all unions promised in 1960 to allow a full discussion of the issues and 'try to find some final agreement' had not been convened.[125]

Celebrations proved short-lived. The 1962 Congress was confronted with a blunt statement that, in view of the fact that the General Council was assuming financial responsibility, it considered that control of the new scheme should rest directly with it 'rather than with a body which would not be accountable to Congress'.[126] ASSET moved an amendment to reinsert the Joint Committee approved in 1961 and now eliminated. The amendment was lost.[127].

The elimination of educationalists from policy making was crucial. The 1962 statement, like its predecessors, committed the new TUC scheme to 'an expansion of suitable facilities for the sustained study of the social and economic subjects relevant to the work of trade unions'.[128] But the exclusion of those likely to act as the custodians of this commitment freed the TUC leadership to create a scheme in their own image. It seems clear that events turned out as they did because the TUC was relating to the changed political situation between 1957 and 1962. By the latter year we were at the beginning, at least, of the era in which

... the TUC's role as general representative of union economic interests has been accompanied by growing centralisation of decision making. The annual Congress proceedings have become increasingly ritualised ... Policy initiatives have come almost universally from the General Council which itself for the most part merely endorses the detailed proposals generated within the TUC Committee structure.[129]

George Woodcock had succeeded Tewson as General Secretary in 1959. Woodcock was an active advocate of tripartite economic planning and industrial relations reform.[130] His philosophy was that the unions had 'left Trafalgar Square a long time ago ... we have to deal with the affairs of the moment in committee rooms with people who have the power ... The whole work of the TUC in my time has been centred on developing this process.'[131] Most of his working life had been spent in Congress House and, as a supporter of incomes policy, he saw the necessity for new powers for the TUC. In the same year that the revised TUC plan for education was accepted, Congress also agreed to authorise a new examination of the structure of the TUC and its relations with affiliates. It also instructed the General Council to prepare its own national wage policy to counter the pressures percolated from the government through the NEDC and prepare for a Labour administration. In this context, and taking into account the discussions at the Ministry of Labour on the joint development of training with employers, it is hardly surprising that the Congress House bureaucracy should seek to concentrate power over the potentially important educational function, particularly given Woodcock's desire to consolidate his own authority and adapt the TUC to the newly emerging environment.[132]

The disaffection of rank-and-file leaders will at all times constitute a general problem for union leaders. But it became an increasingly *specific* problem for an apparatus intent on centralisation of power within the movement. If the TUC could not deliver in the corridors of power, if it could carry with it the leaders of affiliates but they could not deliver their members, then the position of Congress House as a power broker with government was severely limited. If the TUC wished to shift the balance between itself and its member unions in order collectively to negotiate with the state, then to do this efficiently it had to stimulate a shift of balance within the individual unions and the independence of the shop floor.

Shop steward organisation, as we have seen, was increasingly viewed as the nub of a web of recalcitrance to central policies. By the end of the 1950s, the TUC had established an inquiry into shop stewards organisation. Reporting in 1960, the inquiry condemned broad stewards' committees on the grounds that 'their effect is often to challenge established union arrangements'[133] and could 'usurp the policy making functions of unions'.[134] There was a need for more internal policing and control. 'Unions should be more vigilant and if, after a warning, a steward repeats actions which are contrary to the rules or agreements his credentials should be withdrawn.'[135]

In the debates on 'the shop steward problem' at Congress, training had been posed as an alternative means of civilising and domesticating shop stewards.[136] In these years, therefore, the TUC increasingly looked to the training of shop stewards as a means of increasing internal control which in itself was seen as a means of centralising power. The joint initiative of the TUC and BEF, in 1961, was an important formalisation of trends already well developed. One speaker observed, in the ensuing debate at Congress, that this statement, 'seems to be saying pretty conclusively that we could not intimidate the stewards by calling them wild cats so we will train them to become lap dogs'.[137]

These developments gave increasing force to the idea of a centralised TUC scheme and pointed to one that would concern itself almost exclusively with training. Direct TUC control was seen as vital to ensure this. The speaker for the General Council replying to criticisms from the floor on the joint statement on training said that the TUC was

> concerned at the growth of training of shop stewards by organisations which have no relationship with either side of industry in some of the extra-mural departments of universities. I believe that the trade unions can train their shop stewards more effectively than extra-mural departments of universities.[138]

It was important for the TUC, therefore, drastically to limit the role of 'outsiders' who still had some influence with prominent individuals in the movement, as the Congress debates illustrate. They were a quarrelsome lot whose views might often be antagonistic to those of the TUC bureaucracy. The TUC was reminded of this by the debate the evolving scheme engendered, by renewed criticism of the WEA by supporters of independent working-class education, and by the accusation that Millar was proposing 'to file Marxist education in Tillicoultry's waste paper basket.'[139] To invite outsiders into the corridors of power and give them even a semi-formal position in the councils of the TUC could only cause future problems. Far better, from the TUC viewpoint, would be a fresh start, based, Woodcock enunciated, on 'the fundamental principle of responsibility from the top down'.[140] For, 'if education has become a TUC activity, then the TUC must be absolutely in control of it'.[141]

Some had argued from 1960 that, as far as the TUC was concerned, 'socialist education is to be abandoned and replaced with training',[142] and that Millar did not realise what was happening. At this stage Millar's view was that, as the TUC did not take any money from the state, independent working-class education would continue and its traditions would be safeguarded by the involvement of educators in the scheme.[143] NCLC organisers, too, appear to have been satisfied by progress in 1961.[144]

After the 1961 Congress, the official NCLC position was that while the NCLC was to go out of existence 'there is no doubt that its traditions will live on and its activities will not be wiped out'.[145] Millar even went as far as to assert that 'it is difficult to see how the scheme could have been bettered'.[146] Even after the 1962 Congress his view was that the NCLC's whole struggle had been about whether workers would run their own education, or whether universities would do it for them; TUC control would preserve the NCLC's approach.[147]

For the WEA much less was at stake. The Association would

continue in being. On the whole, the loss of payments from unions affiliated to WETUC would be made up by grants from the TUC. Under the new scheme there would not be 'any radical transformation'.[148]

During 1963, the increased and intransigent involvement of George Woodcock in negotiations and the appointment of Ellen McCullough to the TUC Education Department to supervise the initiation of the new scheme – seen as the old enemy delivering the final *coup de grace* – led to increased NCLC opposition to the shape the scheme was taking. Many believed that Dennis Winnard, the TUC Education Secretary and General Council members such as Beard, a supporter of the WEA, were influential in the earlier approach but that its rejection was influenced by Woodcock. Opponents were only willing to take on the General Secretary on issues of importance. This was not one of them.[149] There is other evidence that Winnard supported economic and political education and an independent education committee and that Woodcock, feeling that Winnard had become too educated through contact with the educators, had brought in McCullough to implement his own plans over Winnard's opposition.[150]

There was also opposition in the WEA to the strong stress on centralisation at the expense of local initiative and to the TUC's desire to eliminate WEA trade union advisory committees on the grounds that 'It is undesirable to perpetuate local bodies which duplicate the trade union movement's local organisation.'[151] There was also concern at the TUC's argument that the WETUC and the NCLC had demonstrated that 'educational facilities for trade union members in general cannot be successfully promoted by local voluntary bodies'.[152] Like the NCLC, the WEA was concerned about the limited involvement of educators in the new order of things.

It has been suggested that the NCLC would have been better occupied building bridges to the WEA in order to strengthen opposition to the TUC.[153] However, it was clear from the crucial executive meetings of the NCLC, its special conference in 1964 and the proceedings of the WEA Biennial Conference the same year that there was not a majority in either of the organisations for continued opposition.[154] The NCLC could posit no alternative, and as could be seen from their executive's opposition to the Yorkshire North resolution which called for a revision of the scheme, the WEA felt that, despite its inadequacies, the TUC scheme was something it could live with. Even if there had been stronger and more co-ordinated opposition, the voluntary bodies, in the face of the

TUC, were, like the Papacy, lacking in battalions. The NCLC, which had initiated the venture with an optimism bred of organisational difficulties and a failure to understand the TUC, had overestimated its strength, the functional nature of the TUC's education philosophy, and the amount of time, energy and combativeness that those who took an interest in the field 'were prepared to divert from their own parochial problems to planning trade union education in general'.[155] The final verdict of the man who, more than anybody else, had been its embodiment for four decades, Jim Millar was that the TUC's plans represented 'the complete extinction of everything the NCLC stood for'. He quoted the view of a former leader of the NUM, '... an educational movement under TUC control would be nothing more than a machine for propagating the policy of the General Council ...'[156]

The final scheme provided for direct control by the TUC Education Committee. There was no other body with decision-making powers. The NCLC officials became TUC regional organisers with the brief of developing local programmes. They were to be advised by regional committees with no decision-making powers. The committee would consist largely of the nominees of the TUC Regional Advisory Committees but with the WEA Districts represented. The NCLC's publishing house, *Plebs* and the links with the Labour Party were to find no place in the new order.

The view that educational influence was potentially strong, that

> the educational organisers were no longer outside looking in: they were on the inside ... the NCLC's organisers had been made secretaries of the regional education advisory committee and the representatives of the WEA Districts were given seats. They now occupied key positions in the TUC Regional machinery; they were in the mainstream of authority and influence inside the trade union movement.[157]

was not accepted by keen observers at the time and was not to be borne out by experience.

At the 1964 Congress Woodcock was informing delegates that

> education is not training, it is a very broad activity intended to stimulate the critical faculties. That is perhaps better done by an organisation dedicated exclusively to the task of education and not as a pendant to other activities.[158]

If he was signalling that the TUC scheme was to be about training first and last, his sentiments were those that the educational bodies would have done well to have paid far greater attention to in the years from 1945.

Some Conclusions

The *New Statesman* spoke for many when it commented that, with
the demise of the NCLC, 'we are losing an element in labour life
which wasn't perhaps very efficient in the bureaucratic sense but
which was valuable and unique and an organic part of working class
emancipation'.[159] None the less, as attempts at revival showed, the
tradition of independent working-class education was at least for the
moment exhausted. Its distance from its origins could be gauged by
the fact that the man who was its General Secretary for almost its
entire existence could later list as one of its greatest achievements its
opposition to the left in the unions and Labour Party.[160] This is not to
suggest that much of what the NCLC still stood for in educational
terms was not still important. The assertion that working-class
education should attempt to link industrial activists with political
activists, publish books and pamphlets relevant to workers'
education, produce regular journals of debate – above all, the
argument that the education of trade unionists required an
examination of the economy, the political system and the
organisation of society every bit as much, if not more, than it
required a consideration of meeting procedure and grievance
handling was, and is, of enduring relevance.

If the force of the NCLC's contribution was severely blunted by
post-war conditions and the reaction of its leadership to the demands
for a more practical approach to the education of trade unionists, its
post-war record also raises important doubts as to the efficacy of
attempts to build an alternative working class educational provision
outside and *counterposed to* the orthodox system. The lesson would
appear to be that this is only possible to any degree in a period of
working-class upsurge and social ferment. Normally, we must utilise
the opportunities that exist in the education system *and* experiment in
the labour movement. In periods of social stability, attempts to
construct completely independent *educational* alternatives are
unlikely to receive significant support from trade union leaders
dedicated to collective bargaining routinism. By fragmenting the left
they can derogate from attempts to struggle for working-class
interests within the established educational bodies, attempts which
have a greater chance of (admittedly limited) success because they
relate more sensitively to an unfavourable balance of forces.

Since 1964 the TUC has developed a provision which has limited
itself to training in the techniques of collective bargaining. Morever,
despite the NCLC's identification of the TUC with independent

working-class education, it was, within a decade, receiving not simply a direct subsidy from the state but a subsidy whose disbursement was specifically limited to training courses with the objective of 'improving industrial relations'. The rounded conception of the active trade unionist requiring an education both theoretical and practical, embodied in the rubric of today's scheme, has been ignored by the TUC Education Department.

The general diminution of horizons in this period was not successfully resisted by the universities and the WEA. By 1960 the WEA was catering for a small elite. Established for the working class it had been colonised by the middle class. There was no major entry into the universities by working-class students. The extra-mural departments, where a score or so of tutors were supposed to compensate for the internal bodies' inadequacies by making some contribution to the education of local communities of millions, increasingly replicated the internal bodies' curriculum and social composition. Even within these departments 'industrial studies' covered management as well as unions.

Far from concentrating on the liberal issue-based approach and developing political and economic education to balance the training fostered by the TUC, all too many educators in the responsible bodies joined in. Having clearly demarcated the liberal and technical as pertaining to the educators and the unions respectively, educators were progressively drawn into the technical training. This kind of training *was* required. By involving themselves directly in it, the limited number of WEA and extra-mural tutors ensured that there was *an opportunity cost*. This was the work that was *not* done in developing the equally required political and economic provision. All the evidence shows, moreover, that far from this new emphasis leading to a flood of recruits in liberal WEA and university provision, it simply led to greater involvement in training, a process which accelerated once the anti-liberal TUC scheme found its feet.

Our survey shows that many of the learning methods systematised by the TUC today were, in fact, being explored yesterday. It also shows that a concentration on new learning methods and new approaches was in some cases not a means of overcoming the problem of fusing scholarship with workers' experience. It was a means of escaping from that difficult problem. As educators concentrated far more on skills training and put themselves far more at the service of developing union technical functions; as provision turned far more into the areas of institutional industrial relations and training in procedures, it was these areas which stimulated the development of an active learning approach. New learning methods were not used in union education to make economics or history more accessible. Yet were not economics and history still essential to trade unionists in this period? And are they not still essential today?

These developments were, in this period, not all-pervasive nor fully fledged. The initial day release experiments, for example, illustrated the possibilities of fusing intellectual rigour with workers' experience. But in terms of the future the garden was well seeded. And the changes burgeoning in the 1940s, 50s and 60s all possess a contemporary relevance. In the period we have examined, workers' education gave way to adult education on the one hand, and trade union education on the other. Today, we have seen trade union education evolve into shop steward training, and in the universities a strategy is emerging in response to government pressures which will supersede adult education with continuing education centred on a narrow vocationally related training for professional groups as a contribution to shoring up an ailing economy. Token responses to earlier demands for educational advance such as the extra-mural departments are marked down for extinction. And cuts in expenditure are leading to working-class entrants being squeezed out still further from mainstream higher education.

The irony is that these developments are occurring when the problems which stimulated the growth of working-class education, softened by the post-war boom, are re-emerging in a new sharpened form and when the traditions of educational radicalism have never been more relevant. Today, we are faced with a struggle to open up universities and polytechnics to the working class in the face of the most serious attempts this century to make higher education a commodity and turn it into an illiberal training for social discipline. A small part of that struggle is an attempt to extend the curriculum of trade union education, to democratise its organisation and to relate its concerns more organically to working-class activity.

In pursuing these objectives the main lessons we can draw from the post-war period are simple and age-old ones. Education is not neutral. It is a political battleground in which a variety of interest group seek to impose provision congruent with their own interests. All education is not good education. Training can be antagonistic to education. The provision of adequate education often requires a struggle by the educators. And trade union education is not somehow magically immune from these tendencies: in fact it is an excellent example of them. It is only if we think critically about what we do and say, and reject fudge and compromise with educational principle, that we shall have any chance of success in confronting the threats and challenges of the 1990s.

Notes

[1] P. Gosden, *The Educational System Since 1944* (Oxford 1983), ch.5.

[2] Lord President of the Council, *Scientific Manpower* (London 1946), (The Barlow Report); Parliamentary Scientific Committee, *Memorandum on Higher Technological Education* (London 1954); Committee on Higher Education, op.cit., section on 'Education as an Investment'.

[3] *The Universities in Adult Education: A Statement of Principles* in UCAE: *Report on the Years 1946-7*, p.25.

[4] Ibid.

[5] The following section is based on the *Annual Reports* of the Universities Council For Adult Education 1945-46 – 1963-4.

[6] A.J. Allaway, *Thought and Action in Extra-Mural Work, Leicester 1946-66* (Leicester 1967).

[7] *Adult Education: Adequacy of Provision* (National Institute of Adult Education 1970). See also J. Saunders, 'University Extension Renascent' in S. Raybould, *Trends in English Adult Education* (London 1959), p.78. R. Peers, *Fact and Possibility in English Education* (London 1963), pp.128-32.

[8] Universities Committee on Adult Education, *The Universities and Adult Education* 1961, pp.14-5.

[9] See, for example, S. Raybould, *University Standards in WEA Work* (London 1948); S. Raybould, *The English Universities ... op.cit*; R. Peers, 'The Future of Adult Education', *Adult Education*, Vol. 25, No. 2, 1952; R. Waller, 'The Great Debate', *Adult Education*, Vol. 25, No. 4, 1953; H. Wiltshire, 'The Great Tradition in University Adult Education', *Adult Education*, Vol. 29, No. 2, 1956; P.A.W. Collins,' Mr Wiltshire's Great Tradition: Some Disagreements', *Adult Education*, Vol. 29, No. 3, 1956; T. Kelly, 'The New Approach in University Adult Education', *Adult Education*, Vol. 29, No. 3, 1956.

[10] The following section is based on *The WEA 1946-52 – A Review* (WEA 1952); WEA Annual Reports; *The Future in Adult Education: A Programme* (WEA 1947); *Report of A Working Party on Structure, Organisation, Finance and Staffing* (WEA 1966); J. Harrison, 'The WEA in the Welfare State' in S. Raybould, *Trends in Adult Education*, op.cit.; S. Raybould, *University Extra-Mural Education in England 1945-62, A Study in Finance and Policy* (London 1964); R. Fieldhouse, *The Workers Educational Association: Aims and Achievements 1903-1977* (Syracuse 1977).

[11] *Report of a Working Party ... p.3* (London 1967).

[12] WEA, *Implications of the Ashby Report* (London 1954).

[13] M. Bruce, 'The Universities and Adult Education', *Highway*, November 1952, p.55.

[14] *The Organisation and Finance of Adult Education in England and Wales* (London 1954), (The Ashby Report).

[15] E. Ashby, *The Pathology of Adult Education*, William F. Harvey Lecture (Birmingham 1955), pp.13, 18.

[16] See, for example, J. Campbell, 'Back To The Manual Workers', *Highway*, October 1951; E. Morgan, 'Answering Mr Campbell', *Highway*, November 1951; G. Sedgwick, 'The Manual Workers Question', *Highway*, December 1951; E. Green, *Adult Education: Why This Apathy* (London 1953).

[17] J. Harrison, op.cit., p.12.

[18] R. Lewis, A. Maude, *The English Middle Classes* (Harmondsworth 1953).

[19] Report Of A Working Party ... (WEA 1966).

[20] *Workers Education And The Trade Union Movement – A Post War Policy Report of a Special Sub-Committee of the WETUC* ... (WETUC 1944); A.J. Corfield, *Epoch in Workers Education* (London 1969), Chapter 6; Michael Barratt-Brown, *What has Really Changed in the Educational Needs of Workers, Waves of Activity and Interest*, Lecture to the Society of Industrial Tutors, September 1986.

[21] See P.J. Hills, *A Dictionary of Education* (London 1982), p.275.

[22] See the references in many articles in *Highway* at this period. For example, A. Flanders, 'An American Experiment in Trade Union Education', *op.cit.*, *Highway*, April 1950; H.C. Shearman, 'Trade Unions and Universities in America', *Highway*, April 1952; 'Trade Union Education (WEA 1953), pp.48ff, Appendix IV, 'Trade Union Education in the USA'; S. Raybould, 'Changes in Trade Union Education' in S. Raybould (ed.), *Trends in Adult Education*, op.cit.; R. Dwyer, 'Workers Education, Labor Education, Labor Studies: An Historical Delineation' *Review of Educational Research*, Vol. 47, No. 1, 1977.

[23] *Workers Education and the Trade Union Movement*, ... op.cit., p.9.

[24] Ibid.

[25] Corfield, op.cit., p.98.

[26] For details of specific provision for trade unionists, see the WETUC *Annual Reports*, 1946-50.

[27] H. Nutt, *Education Schemes with the WETUC* (WEA 1951).

[28] Witness the role played by TGWU Education Officer, Ellen McCullough, in fostering these developments within the WEA.

[29] H. Nutt, op.cit.

[30] See A.J. Corfield, op.cit., chapter 8. The resolution was moved by McCullough.

[31] R. Williams, *Politics and Letters* (London 1981), p.78.

[32] J.O.N. Vickers, 'What Becomes of Working Class Education?' *Tutor's Bulletin*, Winter 1948-9; see also J. Harrison, R. Hoggart, R. Shaw, 'What Are We Doing?' *Tutor's Bulletin*, Autumn 1948.

[33] S. Raybould, *The WEA, The Next Phase* (London 1949), pp.50,51.

[34] TUC *Report*, 1948, p.151; TUC *Report*, 1951, p.168; TUC *Report*, 1952, p.160.

[35] F. Pickstock, *Trade Union Education*, paper for Tutorial Classes Committee 1947; F. Pickstock, *Development of Trade Union Education in the Oxford Extra-Mural Area*, 1948, p.6, papers in Archives of Oxford University Department of Extension Studies.

[36] University of Oxford Delegacy For Extra-Mural Studies, *Report*, 1953-54, p.7.

[37] UCAE, *Report on The Year 1951-2*, p.17.

[38] *Results of Enquiry into Trade Union Education Conducted by the North Staffs Branch of the Tutors Association*, n.d. probably 1950-51 in Library, Liverpool University, Department of Continuing Education.

39 University of Leeds Joint Tutorial Class, *Committee Report on Classes 1952-3*, pp.11-13.

40 Ibid., p.13.

41 University of Oxford Delegacy For Extra-Mural Studies, Tutorial Class Committee *Report*, 1948-9, pp.8-9.

42 J. Campbell, op.cit., p.5.

43 Ibid., pp.5-6.

44 A. Bullock, 'The Universities and Adult Education', *Highway*, September 1952.

45 R. Hoggart, 'What Shall the WEA Do?', *Highway*, November 1952.

46 Ibid., p.53.

47 S. Raybould, *The English Universities*, op.cit., p.16.

48 The appointments of Clegg as a Fellow of Nuffield College and Flanders as University Lecturer in Industrial Relations were 'a great stride forward', University of Oxford Delegacy for Extra-Mural Studies *Report*, 1949-50, p.10.

49 University of Oxford Delegacy For Extra-Mural Studies Tutorial Classes Committee *Report*, 1951-2.

50 UCAE *Report on the Year 1951-52*, p.16; UCAE *Report on the Year 1952-3*, p.27.

51 UCAE *1951-2*, op.cit., p.17.

52 Ibid., p.17.

53 Ibid., p.18.

54 R. Fieldhouse, *Adult Education And The Cold War – Liberal Values Under Siege*, op.cit.

55 Ibid., p.22.

56 For example, Communist Party tutors encountered problems in teaching on the TGWU Summer Schools so important to later developments. For the rest of his career Pickstock did his best to stop the employment of Communists and other left wingers as did a number of other extra-mural directors, such as Kelly at Liverpool and Peers at Nottingham. See, for example, Pickstock's letter to N. Marsh re Henry Collins, January 1958 in Oxford Box Files. But there was diversity. Maurice Bruce at Sheffield was surrounded throughout this period by active leftwing tutors of a variety of different hues.

57 UCAE *Report on the Year 1952-3*, p.27.

58 Ibid.

59 Ibid.

60 Ibid., p.28.

61 WEA, *Trade Union Education*, (London 1953)

62 J.A. Mack, 'The Education of Trade Unionists', *Trade Union Education*, No. 2, July, 1955.

63 A.J. Corfield, 'Trade Union Education', *The Highway*, March 1955; A.J. Corfield, 'Reply on Teaching Methods', *Trade Union Education*, No. 5, March, 1957.

64 A.J. Corfield, 'Education in the Transport and General Workers Union' *Rewley House Papers*, Vol III, viii, 1959-60, 9; leaflets on TGWU summer schools, Adult Education Collection, University of Manchester Library; H.A. Clegg, R. Adams, op.cit., pp. 59-60.

65 A. Flanders, 'Introduction', A. Marsh, *Industrial Relations in Engineering* (Oxford 1965). For an excellent dissection of this approach see J.H. Goldthorpe, 'Industrial Relations in Great Britain'; 'A Critique of Reformism' in T. Clarke, L. Clements, *Trade Unions Under Capitalism* (London

1977; and A. Fox, 'Industrial Relations: A Social Critique of Pluralist Ideology' in J. Child (ed.), *Man and Organisation* (London) 1973.

[66] A selection of these documents and a description of the teaching approach can be found in A. Marsh, *A Collection of Teaching Documents and Case Studies* (Oxford) 1966; A.I. Marsh, 'The New Workers Education', *The Tutors Bulletin of Adult Education*, Vol 31, No. 2, 1958; A.I. Marsh, 'Trade Unions and Workers Education' *Rewley House Papers*, Vol III, vi, 1953-8; F.V. Pickstock 'Teaching Trade Unionists', *Adult Education*, Vol 36, No. 2, July 1963.

[67] On this see, G. Mee, *Adult Education and Community Service 1920-1984*, Nottingham, 1984.

[68] A.H. Thornton, F.J. Bayliss, *Adult Education and the Industrial Community* (London) 1965, p.12.

[69] University of Nottingham Department of Adult Education *Annual Report 1949-50*; H.D. Hughes, A.H. Thornton, 'The British Experience and Present Situation', in International Labour Office, *The Role of Universities in Workers Education* (Geneva) 1974.

[70] A.J. Allaway, *Challenge And Response: WEA East Midland District 1919-69*, (Leicester) 1969, p.68.

[71] A.H. Thornton, F.J. Bayliss, op.cit., p.13.

[72] A.H. Thornton, 'Day Release For Liberal Studies', *Adult Education*, Vol. 29, No. 3, Winter 1956.

[73] For the Sheffield courses in this period, see the *Annual Reports* of the Department of Extra-Mural Studies; also M. Bruce, *The University of Sheffield Department of Extra-Mural Studies 1947-68: A Personal Survey* (Sheffield) n.d.; M. Barratt Brown, *Adult Education for Industrial Workers* (London) 1969; D. Hakken, *Workers Education The Reproduction of Working Class Culture in Sheffield, England and Really Useful Knowledge* (unpublished Ph.D. thesis, the American University Washington DC) 1978; J.E. Williams, *The Derbyshire Miners: A Study in Industrial and Social History* (London) 1962. For some of the political activities of staff in this period see P. Kahn, 'Essay in Oral History: Tommy Mullany', *Bulletin of the Society for the Study of Labour History*, 44, Spring 1982. For Leeds see the Annual Reports of the Extra-Mural Department; the reports to the Joint Tutorial Classes Committee; and the comments in S. Raybould, 'Changes in Trade Union Education', op.cit.

[74] On the leading role of extra-mural departments in day release courses see S. Raybould, 'Changes in Trade Union Education', op.cit., S. Raybould, *University Extra-Mural Education in England 1945-62*, op.cit., chapter 3.

[75] Thornton, op.cit., p.203.

[76] *Annual Report 1952-53*, Nottingham University Department of Adult Education, p.6.

[77] Allaway, op.cit., p.68.

[78] Bruce, op.cit., p.13-4.

[79] S. Raybould, 'Changes in Trade Union Education', op.cit., p.43.

[80] Allaway, op.cit., p.68.

[81] R.J. Harrison, 'The Last Five Years' in University of Sheffield Department of Extra-Mural Studies, *Annual Report 1960-61*.

[82] J. Hughes, *Adult Education And Trade Union Research*, unpublished paper, 1974.

[83] University of Leeds, *Reports to Joint Tutorial Classes Committee 1956-57*, p.49.

[84] K.J.W. Alexander, 'A Distant Prospect of Derbyshire' in University of Sheffield Department of Extra-Mural Studies Annual Report 1960-61, pp.15, 16.

[85] University of Leeds *Report to Joint Tutorial Classes Committee* 1954-5, p.32.

[86] J.E. Williams, 'An Experiment in Trade Union Education', *Adult Education*, Vol. XXVII, No. 2, 1954, p.117.

[87] S. Raybould, 'Changes in Trade Union Education', op.cit., p.43.

[88] See M. Barratt Brown, *op.cit.*; J. McFarlane, 'Coalminers at University: A Second Chance in Education', *Adult Education*, Vol. 48, No. 2, 1975; for Nottingham see A.H. Thornton, F.J. Baylis, op.cit., G. Mee, op.cit.

[89] University of Sheffield Department of Extra-Mural Studies, *Annual Report*, 1963-64.

[90] Interview with Royden Harrison, January 1986.

[91] S. Raybould, 'Changes in Trade Union Education', p.44.

[92] Interview with Royden Harrison, op.cit.

[93] A.H. Thornton, F.J. Bayliss, op.cit., p.16.

[94] A. Scargill, *Times*, 28 November 1977; see also Scargill's enthusiastic comments about these courses in A. Scargill, 'The New Unionism', *New Left Review* 92, July-August 1975, '... the best education scheme any trade union in Britain has got', ibid., p.28.

[95] UCAE *Report on the Year 1952-53*, p.28.

[96] University of Sheffield Department of Extra-Mural Studies, *Annual Report 1960-61*.

[97] UCAE *Report on the Year 1962-3*, p.7.

[98] John Mendelsohn and Trevor Park became MP's, but a high proportion of tutors was always active in local politics. Robert Heath was the first student (1956-59) to be appointed to the staff (1966), later followed by Jim McFarlane.

[99] See, for example, A.H. Thornton, *Note of Reservation* to UCAE *Report of Working Party on Industrial Studies*, 1976.

[100] See, for example, Thornton, Bayliss, op.cit., chapter III.

[101] Ibid., p.19.

[102] As in *I'm Alright Jack* and *The Angry Silence*.

[103] *Report of a Court of Inquiry into a Dispute at Briggs Motor Bodies Ltd.* (London 1957).

[104] Bill Carron quoted in *Tribune*, 1 March 1957.

[105] T. Cliff, *Incomes Policy, Legislation and Shop Stewards* (London 1966), p.98.

[106] K. Weller, *What Next For Engineers?* (Solidarity Pamphlet) n.d.

[107] Corfield, op.cit., p.155.

[108] *Industrial Relations in the Motor Industry Statement of Employers and Trade Union Representatives Meeting under the Chair of the Ministry of Labour*, April 1961. Reprinted as Appendix 5 in Training Shop Stewards, TUC, 1968, pp.82-4.

[109] Ibid.

[110] This centred around the appointment of Rex Adams who had produced the 1959 WEA Report with Hugh Clegg and was enthusiastic about testing its ideas – interview with Royden Harrison.

[111] Corfield, op.cit., p.144.

[112] See the comments on Oxford in the eighth essay in this volume.

[113] See, for example, M. Crick, *Scargill and the Miners* (Harmondsworth 1985).

[114] See. J. McIlroy, review of G. Mee, op.cit., *Bulletin of the Society for the Study of Labour History*, Vol. 51, Part I, April 1986. Several of the Sheffield tutors had been CP members but left after 1956.

[115] UCAE *Report of the Year 1968-69*, p.10.

[116] UCAE *Report of the Year 1967-68*, p.6.

[117] On appointments see S. Raybould, *University Extra-Mural Education in England 1945-62*, op.cit., pp.53, 62.

[118] TUC *Report*, 1945, p.90.

[119] TUC *Report*, 1958, p.49; Interview S. Bidwell, February 1987; letter from A. Murie to author, March 1987.

[120] See the speech by Cornes supporting the 1957 NUR resolution: 'there were special jobs that individuals should do for their own members in enlightening them about the work and structure of their own union; a special work that Congress itself should do through its training college ... But for the general approach on the social sciences designed to increase the understanding of the membership as a whole the motion rightly believes that the responsibility is on the shoulders of Congress', TUC *Report*, 1957, p.392.

[121] TUC *Report*, 1959, pp.178-84.

[122] TUC *Report*, 1960, p.169.

[123] TUC *Report*, 1961, p.440.

[124] Ibid., pp.179-80.

[125] TUC *Report*, 1960, p.426.

[126] TUC *Report*, 1962, p.162.

[127] Ibid., p.344.

[128] Ibid., p.162.

[129] R. Hyman, 'Trade Union Structure, Policies and Politics' in G.S. Bain (ed.), *Industrial Relations in Britain* (Oxford p.56).

[130] See, for example, L. Panitch, *Social Democracy and Industrial Militancy*, op.cit., Chapter 2; H. Pelling, *A History* ... op.cit., chapter 12.

[131] TUC *Report* 1963, p.390.

[132] H. Pelling, op.cit., p.255.

[133] TUC *Report*, 1960, p.126.

[134] Ibid.

[135] Ibid., p.130.

[136] Ibid., p.350.

[137] TUC *Report* 1963, p.430-432.

[138] Ibid., p.432

[139] W. Kendall, letter to *Tribune*, 6 July 1960.

[140] TUC *Report*, 1964, p.483.

[141] Ibid.

[142] W. Kendall, letter to *Tribune*, 19 August 1960.

[143] J.P.M. Millar, letter to *Tribune*, 29 July 1960.

[144] See letters from S. Bidwell, *Tribune*, 17 March 1961; 16 June 1961. Cf Millar's view in early 1962 that the scheme was 'quite certain to be on the lines wanted' and that it represented 'a great step forward'. 'Trade Union Education – Some Vital Issues', *Plebs*, April 1962.

[145] J.P.M. Millar, 'A New Chapter in Trade Union Education', *Plebs*, October 1961.

[146] Ibid.

147 J.P.M. Millar, letter to *Tribune*, 30 November 1962.

148 Corfield, op.cit., p.152.

149 See Millar, *The Labour College Movement*, pp.162ff; J.P.M. Millar, correspondence in *Bulletin of the Society for the Study of Labour History*, Vol. 51, Part I, April 1986. Millar's growing opposition to the scheme was related to developments in the postal courses takeover, public statements by Ellen McCullough and his experiences with the TUC Education Committee. See, for example, correspondence with McCullough in EC Minutes 1963; GSR to EC, 25 November 1963; Proposals from NEC of NCLC to General Council of the TUC, December 1963; GSR to EC, 14 December 1963, J.P.M. Millar, letter to EC, 9 January 1964. They were apparently shared by other prominent NCLC'ers such as Cornes and Lowthian, c.f. Jack Martin of the NUR, 'The NCLC was not a fascist organisation to be hounded out of existence,' EC Minutes 21 March 1964. Gradually opposition crystallised around the TUC's conception of the structure of the new scheme. However, the organisers motivated by a desire for greater security and stability supported the takeover, S. Bidwell to Millar, 21 April 1964.

150 F.V. Pickstock, *Notes on Private Discussion with D. Winnard*, 18 October 1962 (Oxford University Department of External Studies (Box Files).

151 D. Winnard, *Factors Affecting the Question of Regional Organisation* (TUC 1963); see also *WEA Comments on Proposals for Regional Machinery of a TUC Education Scheme*, n.d.

152 Winnard, op.cit.

153 Corfield, op.cit., p.153. See Millar *The Labour College Movement*, p.164ff; A.J. Corfield, pp.154ff.

154 See Corfield, op.cit., pp.154ff.

155 J.P.M. Millar, *The Labour College Movement*, p.167. The important point to stress is that there was insufficient support within the NCLC for breaking off with the TUC. As far as the Executive was concerned it was too late to turn back. The organisers were becoming rebellious at Millar's approach, see Millar to B. Preuss, 9 April 1964. When a special working party consisting of the inner cabinet recommended continuing negotiations this was overruled at the executive, EC Minutes, 20 June 1964. The final conference, faced with an executive recommendation to accept the takeover, excited opposition largely from lay delegates, Minutes of National Conference, 22 August 1964. Woodburn seems to have played an important role by distancing himself from Millar, letter from J. Connell, op.cit.

156 'NCLC Out Like a Lamb', *Tribune*, 20 August 1964, quoting Millar, quoting Ebby Edwards, ex-NUM General Secretary.

157 A.J. Corfield, op.cit., pp.155-6.

158 TUC *Report*, 1964, p.484.

159 Diary, *New Statesman*, 30 October 1964.

160 J.P.M. Millar, correspondence, *Bulletin of the Society for the Study of Labour History*, loc.cit.

John McIlroy
8 Trade Union Education for a Change

The Development of the TUC Scheme

The early years of the new TUC scheme were years of internal conflict. The former NCLC organisers alleged witch-hunts, threatened industrial action and in several cases voted with their feet.[1] There was constant emphasis on the need to concentrate on technical bargaining skills. As far as the TUC was concerned, the work of many in the NCLC had 'reflected an essentially political attitude and approach'.[2] This had to change. Courses on socialism and economics were eliminated.[3] Day-release courses – there were only 21 involving 269 students in 1965-66 – were seen as the major format for expansion. Because of the numbers requiring training, courses of ten to twelve days' duration were favoured rather than the longer provision organised by the universities and WEA.

It was 'axiomatic', the TUC stated, that it should not become the recipient of public funds, as this could compromise its independence. It should support increases in funds for the educational bodies. TUC control of course content was viewed as vital, and this could be best achieved by the education bodies appointing tutors who would spend most of their time on TUC courses.[4]

The defenders of independent working-class education carried on a rearguard struggle. Socialist critics analysed the growth of shop steward training as a development of past attempts to 'educate our masters',[5] weaken workplace organisation,[6] and subject stewards to 'brain washing'.[7] There was a short-lived attempt to keep existing labour colleges in being and extend them as Centres for Socialist Education.[8]

At the 1966 Congress an NUM speaker pointed out that the delegates had spent their time discussing a wage freeze, inflation, the

Gnomes of Zurich, Ghana, Rhodesia and Vietnam. The TUC curriculum reflected few of these concerns and was limited to how to bargain effectively. An NCLC veteran condemned ' ... the almost complete irrelevance of the education being provided by the General Council. These courses are ideological bankruptcy and betrayal.'[9] A motion calling for the establishment of a National Advisory Council involving lay trade unionists, educators and local committees to supplement the Regional Education Advisory Committees was carried.[10] This success received a stony response. The 1967 Congress was treated to a tortuous and unconvincing justification for inaction. The failure to move reference back showed that the opposition had been worn down. The scheme was now completely in the hands of Congress House and for the next two decades there would be no initiatives taken that did not originate there.[11]

Developments continued to be conditioned by the reaction of the TUC to state pressures. The TUC was closely involved in the formulation and policing of the 1964 Labour government's incomes policy.[12] Woodcock believed that

> in order that the wages problem be grasped the central authority and influence of the TUC would need to be increased at the expense of the jealously preserved sovereignty of individual unions ... the structure of the movement must be reformed ... their procedures, particularly their relationship with shop floor organisations were inadequate for the modern tasks.[13]

He put his influence behind the proposal for an inquiry into trade unions.[14]

The increasing identification of shop-floor organisation with the failure of incomes policy was a powerful impetus in the appointment of the Royal Commission on Trade Unions and a major theme in its product, the Donovan Report.[15] The core of the commission's analysis was that unofficial strikes, wage drift, restrictive practices and the other ills which made industrial relations, and crucially wage costs, unamenable to planning, were the consequence of powerful, relatively autonomous workplace organisation. This had undermined the regulative power of national agreements and disputes procedures. There was a need to build new codified rules and institutions and to transform the quasi-independent shop-floor leaders into agents of a new industrial legality operating a reformed network of rules constitutionally. Employers and unions must 'recognise, define and control the part played by shop stewards in our collective bargaining system'.[16]

The report's ethos was one of rational enlightenment. Once the industrial relations actors had overcome their ignorance, matters would be swiftly set to rights: 'the task to be performed, therefore, was essentially educational'.[17] In this context 'the need for shop steward training is immense'. There was a need

> to develop competent teachers and adequate syllabuses with a view to using training of shop stewards as part of a planned move to more orderly industrial relations based on comprehensive and formal factory or company agreements ... to prepare union officers at all levels for the reconstruction of industrial relations ... .[18]

Woodcock was a member of the commission and influential in its prescriptions.[19] The report went to some pains to emphasise that it did not favour 'indiscriminate expansion of courses for trade unionists' but 'training in the formal procedures of collective bargaining and trade unionism'.[20] This was at one with TUC thinking, as was the view that the required expansion should flow through the TUC, not through individual unions, and be financed via the industrial training boards.[21] In 1968 the TUC's own consultative group on training reported. Whilst in the Donovan mould this report, not surprisingly, emphasised training as an instrument of union control. It argued that ' ... it is the responsibility of those charged with the government of a union to maintain discipline and unity, yet there are practically no sanctions for bringing dissidents into line'.[22] A strategy of integration was, therefore, 'morally legitimate' and training, as a component, could help to 'win co-operation of key representatives in pursuing constitutionally agreed objectives'.[23]

Management and unions had a common interest in promoting such training. Employers, too, were 'concerned that [the steward] should act within the constitutional procedures of his union and industry and observe agreements reached. Training cannot guarantee this but it does give the opportunity for the purpose and nature of these rules to be examined.'[24] The TUC had a clear view of the distinction between training and education:

> ... training means systematic instruction, study and practice that will help to equip union members to be competent as representatives of their union in the workplace. Obviously this excludes consideration of their wider educational needs as citizens or even potential general secretaries or cabinet ministers.[25]

The divorce from the older traditions of education for social understanding and action was apparently complete. A danger was that 'too much of the syllabus tends to be devoted to extensive general information on economics and industrial relations to the neglect of subjects specifically related to the duties in which the representative is actively engaged'.[26]

The temporary turn by Labour to legal regulation of industrial relations did not affect strategies for trade union education. The White Paper *In Place of Strife* can be seen, in retrospect, as introducing the theme of direct state support, which was to become increasingly important in the next decade.[27]

The advent of the Heath regime, by contrast, *did* represent a new challenge. By the turn of the decade a small programme of courses at Congress House, largely for full-time officials, had stabilised. The postal courses were in decline. The programme of weekend and linked schools which provided an outlet for those who wished to study wider issues had diminished, while the TUC was pleased with the response to its television series, *Representing The Union*. Despite the attention devoted to the day-release provision there were only 331 ten-day courses involving a little over 5,000 students. There was satisfaction that the criterion of 'direct relevance' to the representatives' job was reflected in the pattern of programmes 'in which shop steward training and industrial relations and collective bargaining subjects now overwhelmingly predominate'.[28] None the less, greater standardisation was required 'especially by means of more extensive preparation and distribution of teaching materials by the TUC Education Department'.[29]

This echoed TUC experience of the campaign against the Industrial Relations Act. The teaching kits produced represented the TUC's most sophisticated experiment yet. The problem of ensuring that teaching met pre-determined objectives was diplomatically articulated: 'One dilemma was the need to explain the Act but not to be drawn into such complications on the legal side that members became fascinated by it and drifted into the use of parts of it which were contrary to TUC policy.'[30] In this context the materials were the message. The lesson that programmed documentation *could* standardise, structure and influence the direction of what happened in the classroom was later to be extensively utilised.

A line was also drawn with the philosophy of the universities and WEA where the majority of TUC courses were still being mounted. Trade union education, it was stated, was 'designed to serve the needs of trade unions as organised entities or of the trade union movement as a whole rather than those of individual union members'. It was therefore education planned by 'trade union organisations' 'rather than education predominantly shaped by the spontaneous demands of individual students or student groups'.[31]

Further development was set in train by the 1972 report of the Commission on Industrial Relations (CIR), the body established by Labour to stimulate and monitor the industrial relations reforms recommended by Donovan.[32] As far as the TUC was concerned, the consensus with state and employers had depended on the guarantee of its own specific role as the final recipient of the shop steward's loyalty.

Now the CIR report split the shop stewards straight down the middle: they had workplace industrial relations responsibilities and they had wider union responsibilities. Training for the first set of functions was prioritised. It should take place in the workplace with an enhanced role for management and increased funding from the Industrial Training Boards. The TUC saw themselves excluded from involvement in the key public policy area of workplace industrial relations training and driven back into the marginal trade union training of the 1950s.

In response to this threat to its institutional interests Congress House asserted the indivisibility of the shop steward's role as workplace bargainer *and* union officer. The former stemmed from the latter. Given its primacy the unions should have primary control over *all* shop steward training. The importance of education in the training experience was now invoked to keep courses in the universities and colleges where they were more amenable to TUC control than if mounted in the workplace by employers. It was now, the TUC argued, absolutely vital to ensure that training included 'an essential education element' and contributed to the personal development of the individual. They now stated, with a presumption bred of expediency, 'For trade unionists industrial relations training is synonymous with trade union education.'[33]

The CIR report was never implemented but the shock it delivered to the TUC influenced the change of approach apparent in 1974.

The Response from Adult Education

By 1964 the expansion of day release courses was accelerating.[34] Technical colleges were now involved but were still mounting only a small part of the total programme.

In Sheffield the university and the WEA had moved from mining into steel and engineering and the railways, using their long-course model. The majority of Nottingham's provision was now in the private sector but the courses were shorter – 24 days or half-days was usual. In Leeds the extra-mural department was reporting that by

1965 most of the courses that they had developed in private industry extended over two years. In Manchester, two-year courses were run in the mid-1960s with the Lancashire miners but the thrust was towards shorter courses increasingly under TUC aegis. The same could be said for Liverpool.

By 1968 full day release courses for railway workers on a three-year basis had been launched in London. Hull followed the long day-release approach while in Oxford courses were based on half-day release although by the end of the decade a large programme of block full-day-block week and two-week courses based on British Leyland was flourishing.

The thrust was away from the group of industrial workers studying social studies subjects towards the group of shop stewards studying 'applied industrial relations', more employer sponsorship and involvement and shorter provision.[35]

The objectives of those who *allowed* release at a time when this was purely discretionary if in 'the national interest' was bound to inform content and approach. It was clear, for example, that management expected provision to reflect their 'concern that shop stewards should observe the rules ... [and] ... that bargaining should be conducted in a reasoned fashion'.[36] Most managers would place 'a relatively high premium on the inculcation of notions of "constitutionalism" '.[37] The end product should be the shop steward as 'a custodian of collective agreements, a keeper of social order and a realistic bargainer'.[38] Union officers also perceived the objective as 'to increase the activist's awareness of union services and policies to cement loyalties and create involvement'.[39]

The universities and the WEA, however, were dedicated not to training but to liberal adult education, an approach which focuses on issues and arguments and attempts to explore specific issues and problems through an open and critical examination of competing viewpoints. Liberal adult education for trade unionists in the tradition of Tawney and Cole had emphasised student choice of subject and control of syllabus. Few of those allegedly committed to this tradition offered any clear critique of training or any counter position.

The educators themselves often justified expansion in the language of economic instrumentalism. Many of the tutors constituted a tiny fourth estate to the tripartite consensus, working for the Prices and Incomes Board and the CIR and in management training.[40] This produced the use of the term 'industrial studies' rather than the more partisan 'trade union studies'. A few were prepared to state forthrightly that the purpose of shop steward training was to mobilise support for contentious policies such as wage restraint and productivity bargaining:

> ... it is the business of adult education to make sure that people do understand it [government policy] because if they understand it they'll be in favour of it ... the lack of understanding is now so abysmal that it is bound to be true that if more people were to understand there would be better support for certain policies.[41]

This kind of thinking lay behind an attempt, in 1967, to engineer a large scale expansion of academic resources for day release. Industrial Studies tutors, acting through the Universities' Council for Adult Education, approached the Department of Economic Affairs suggesting the creation of 40 new posts to be shared between the universities and the WEA. For a variety of reasons, the initiative failed. There was conservative resistance from within extra mural departments. Those who wanted shorter more practical training courses with quick results were chary of putting all their eggs in the university basket. They looked in the direction of the technical colleges for an expansion of short steward training. This rebuff and criticism of the UCAE as too unimaginative, cumbersome and slow moving, led a number of tutors in extra-mural work to plan the creation of their own organisation. By the end of the 1960s the Society of Industrial Tutors, a mixture of a communication network, a learned society and a pressure group, had several hundred members. It ran a range of conferences annually and orchestrated an innovative publishing venture in trade union studies in collaboration with a major publishing house.

The society aimed 'to advance the general education of men and women in industry and commerce through day release and similar provision in the spirit of the adult education liberal tradition'.[42] It recruited tutors not only in the universities and WEA but in technical colleges, training boards, companies and trade unions. In the early years of the society, there were useful discussions about educational values and philosophy; but its first decade was characterised, on the whole, by a toleration of different traditions and approaches, rather than by any rigorous attempt to clarify them. Members of the society often tended to follow the prevailing current running so strongly in favour of training, rather than fight it. However, as the TUC moved decisively in an interventionist and anti-educational direction, the SIT took up the cudgels in defence of broader education, and the value of an independent organisation open to all involved in trade union education became ever more apparent.

In the early 1960s, the day release work was still largely justified as 'liberal'. But statements that 'these day release courses are in no sense vocational courses or courses of training, they are courses of liberal study'[43] gradually gave way to the view that this provision, 'while basically liberal in character, has an important element of professional training in it'.[44]

There was a tendency to consider the day-release programme as a unified and essentially liberal corpus of work. Little analysis was applied to the diversity and to the contradictory approaches embodied within it. More acute observers noted the real distinctions. 'Some such as London and Nottingham devote themselves to broader educational work. Whilst others such as Oxford run training courses on topics specific to stewards' vocational needs.'[45]

Sheffield, discussed in the previous essay, and Oxford, may be taken as polar cases. Sheffield maintained its original emphasis: 'any narrow approach to trade union studies restricted to the examination of union rulebooks, conciliation procedures and national agreements has been eschewed'.[46] Its tutors were often active in the Labour Party and unions as well as in the Society of Industrial Tutors and the Institute of Workers Control. Their writings consisted of both analysis of industrial and political developments and more practical work.[47] The majority saw themselves as left-wing socialists operating within the liberal tradition. As one who styled himself 'a socialist educator' stated, 'This related not to the conclusions at which we thought the student should arrive but to the issues we thought that they should be addressing. It is an agenda question not a conclusion question.'[48]

Oxford was just as committed, but in a right-wing Labourist mould. Its tutors were heavily involved with the Royal Commission, with management education and consultancy, and with a variety of state agencies.[49] One eminent critic of the Oxford school, which he characterised as 'enlightened managerialism', pointed out that

nowhere in the Donovan Report or in the entire tradition of academic industrial relations writing on which it drew so heavily is there to be found any systematic consideration of how the functioning of the economic system as a whole and of its constituent units of production is founded upon and sustains vast differences in social power and advantage. Nor of how there are then generated, on the one hand, objective oppositions of interest and, on the other, subjective responses of frustration, resentment and antagonism and also, in some degree, aspiration and movements towards an alternative disposition.[50]

This could apply equally to much of the work done at Oxford. A follow-on course on the economics of the motor industry provided some scope for a consideration of wider issues. But from the early 1960s the core provision dealt with four main areas: the background of engineering management; the background of engineering unions; the framework of national agreements and case studies in the working of procedures. Later a greater emphasis was placed on the role of the shop steward and on company and plant. The horizons of these courses were sharply circumscribed.

Wider issues, tutors were told, should only be introduced

> ... when some engineering issue needs to be put into wider perspective. The argument in justification of this is one of immediate relevance. Shop stewards are practical people faced by immediate problems. They very rarely have any ready interest in education for its own sake.

The heavy documentation was to provide a 'programmed discussion' of engineering institutions. The flavour of the courses can be gauged from the teaching materials.

> The aim of this document is twofold. It is intended to make the student familiar with the layout of the 'Handbook of National Agreements' so that he will be able readily to turn up any agreement which may be relevant to a problem ... [The materials] are designed in the main to illustrate the practical problems which arise particularly in the application of national agreements. Few cases are included which have no reference at all to such agreements ... they are planned in order to give students some practical experience in how to arrange material for presentation in procedure.[51]

There were criticisms. One tutor pointed out that 'if industrial relations academics devote themselves to the service of management they will reduce themselves to mere technicians'.[52] The Oxford courses were, in their turn, defended against charges that 'they seek to keep stewards on the lines of agreed procedure and reduce unofficial strikes'. The framework of 'rational procedures and restraints' in industry, it was claimed, was surely 'one of the most civilised social achievements open to man'. It was 'as much an expression of fundamental social values as our system of political democracy'; there was a need for training in its operation 'informed by liberal values'.[53]

The problems with this argument are numerous. Parallels with political democracy are specious. The British Leyland car-workers could not vote out their managers. What 'rights' they did have depended on the degree of power they could mobilise through collective bargaining. And that in its turn might depend on treating a procedure or agreement as a tactical truce, not constitutional law. Given the essential background of economic and social inequalities and consequent conflicts, which the Oxford approach suppressed, there was nothing particularly irrational about this. The national engineering procedure, far from being the product of rational reflection, had been imposed on the workforce after a lock-out.[54] Education based on liberal values would examine and discuss these and other alternative views. The Oxford courses on the whole did not.

None the less, in the cut and thrust of classroom discussion wider issues will intrude. This may entail policing from those interested in direct benefits to the employer in 'profitable' rather than 'unprofitable' day release.[55] From the start, BMC management were clear as to what benefits they required: the courses were to be 'in the spirit' of the 1961 joint statement aimed at curtailing stoppages and encouraging adherence to procedure. Whilst this appeared to place an immediate constraint on the spirit of critical inquiry, the university was to be given 'entire responsibility for the teaching and educational content of the courses'.[56]

This prerogative seems to have been sparingly exercised. From the start the company drew a link between the courses and plant strike rates. The Delegacy was congratulated on a decline in stoppages,[57] and management was re-asserting that 'the value of these courses will obviously be judged on whether they help to improve industrial relations within the plant'.[58] There was a successful campaign by management, who had full rights to sit in on the courses, to exclude ordinary members, 'unless we *get through* to the shop stewards, I think there is far less likelihood of our succeeding.' (My emphasis, J.McI.)[59]

There does not appear to have been any riposte from the university, any assertion of the fact that they were supposed to be *educators* who saw 'improved industrial relations' as problematic, whose job was to critically examine the issues, not to do management's job for them.

By 1967 management was expressing dissatisfaction. The facts of life were laid crudely on the line.

Industrial relations training should have one major objective, that is, the creation of industrial peace between the workers and the company. To attain this major objective two major topics appear necessary – one that presents the economic necessities of life in a viable manufacturing industry – and one that describes the rules within which both sides of this industry have to work.[60]

The courses, they argued, should be restructured to achieve these ends and make clear

> ... the need for the acceptance of change in the way that things are manufactured ... That increases in pay should be linked with increases in output and that length of service or simply having lived another year does not automatically indicate that more money is deserved ...

Within this context there was a crying need to establish 'whether subjects are being learned'.[61]

This manifesto drew no counter conception. These classes were a prestigious investment. Far from challenging this view of courses as a conveyor belt for management objectives, Pickstock tried to ensure the courses were changed and adapted. The pattern was management initiatives and Delegacy accommodation.[62] Only after university management meetings were the unions selectively involved. This required some nimble footwork as the formal position of at least one of the unions was that 'the only facility we seek from management is paid leave of absence to attend the courses. The subject matter and the conduct of the courses is a matter between the unions and the delegacy.'[63] The records disclose a state of affairs far distant from the student choice and freedom to pursue the argument wherever it may lead of the liberal model. Of course attention to what Pickstock referred to as 'this peripheral bothersome thing' when management had 'great issues on your hands' varied.[64] Several of the tutors had minds of their own and there was no guarantee as to what would happen in the classroom. After 1970 there appears to have been less company scrutiny and greater freedom for the university.

If other universities and WEA districts reflected to different degrees the Sheffield and Oxford polarities, all were affected by the development of the TUC Scheme. What follows analyses the main thrust of TUC policy as developed at Congress House. But mediated, as it was, through regional officers with different backgrounds, views and degrees of autonomy, its impact was different in different regions. It would, moreover, be wrong to review events too simply in terms of a hostile utilitarian TUC polluting for its own purposes the pure milk of liberalism. Contamination was already in the air.

None the less, the responsible bodies were soon arguing that

> the new policies of the TUC have cut across traditional adult education practices and susceptibilities in three ways by insisting on (i) the priority of 'training' over 'education', (ii) syllabuses being approved by the TUC and

not by the democratic choice of the prospective students, (iii) a measure of standardisation in syllabus content and on length of courses.[65]

The present general secretary reflected that:

> The WEA would propose subjects for study such as unemployment problems, developments in the economy, the role of the media and so on. The Regional Education Advisory Committee would usually endorse these proposals; and Congress House would regularly refuse financial support, usually with no reason given.[66]

A tutor doubted the wisdom of 'an educational scheme which seems to have no room for the discussion of ideas and the development of a critical faculty'.[67]

It was asked whether 'if the fate of industry is too important to be left to the managers, can we afford to leave the fate of trade union education exclusively in the hands of trade union officials ...?'[68]

Some educators were simply prepared to meet TUC imperatives. Others, where the regional education officers were sympathetic or abstentionist, could achieve a large measure of liberalisation.

The problems that existed can be seen from the case of Sheffield.[69] The TUC REO wanted shorter training courses and saw the technical colleges as the natural vessel for their expansion. There were conflicts of philosophy with the university. The REO's view was, for example, that ' ... trade union education is conducive to greater harmony in industry and hence greater efficiency'.[70] The university was refused representation on the Regional Education Advisory Committee (REAC) although a member of staff sat in another capacity.

In 1966-67 the university and the WEA were negotiating for courses of 72 days' duration for union representatives in engineering and local government. The TUC became involved and the resultant courses were assigned by the REO to local technical colleges to be taught there as short courses using the TUC standard syllabus. The university was assured that it had a specific role in advanced courses. This never materialised.

One of the unions, BISAKTA, suggested that the TUC should pay the fees for the department's courses for steelworkers. Consequently, the university syllabus had to be sent to the TUC Education Department for approval. In 1971 the TUC REO agreed with BISAKTA to transfer the first year of one of the courses for the Stocksbridge and Tinsley Park Steel groups to Stocksbridge Technical College not previously involved in courses for trade unionists. It was clear that the intention was to run a self-contained 24-week course largely taught by works management and by trade union officers. Moreover, the classes were to be held jointly with supervisors.

The university was assured that the second and third years of the courses would go ahead. In March 1972, however, with no consultation, the university was informed that once current students had completed their three-year course in the department no further courses would be required for the two steel groups.

Two months later the department was informed that the new 36-week technical college course would apply throughout BSC. The three-year courses the university provided for the Rotherham and Scunthorpe steel groups would be phased out once students had completed their courses. BISAKTA had requested that their members be removed from university courses

a) because the courses in the second and third year were too concerned with education and too little with the technical training that their members needed, and b) because certain books and arguments were used on these courses which were openly critical of the union and its arrangements.[71]

In September BSC and the TUC decided that students in mid-course would now be sent to Rotherham Technical College where they would pursue the Stocksbridge syllabus. The issues was raised at that month's REAC meeting attended by Dennis Winnard. The BISAKTA divisional officer repeated the earlier statements specifying 'that the tutor should not teach with any books or on any matters which the union did not approve'.[72] The TUC REO's decision to close the courses was supported by the committee and by Dennis Winnard and later confirmed in writing. It was stated that 'The TUC Education Department could not approve courses which are in essence devoted to liberal adult education and the affiliated unions believe that the first and most fundamental priority is the training of shop stewards.'[73] The TUC had made its position very clear. The Sheffield tutor on the Education Advisory Committee resigned in protest at 'the restrictive attitude of the TUC to what for three-quarters of a century at least has been recognised as working-class education'.[74]

The Social Contract, Thatcherism and Trade Union Education

TUC identification with the policies of the 1974-79 Labour governments was almost complete. Labour's industrial relations legislation, with its stimulation of an extended formalised collective bargaining staffed by more professional stewards, represented a development of the Donovan strategy. Both this and the wider social contract required a return to the expansion of steward training predicted in 1968. Greater union control was, for the TUC, an important concession.[75]

Expansion was to be underpinned by legal rights for union representatives to paid time off to attend training courses, approved by their trade union or by the TUC, in aspects of industrial relations relevant to the representatives' industrial relations duties. Time off must be 'reasonable' and related to the 'operational requirements' of the employers. The legal objective of provision was now to be 'the improvement of industrial relations'.[76] In a further reversal of established policy this system was to be fuelled by an annual memorandum of agreement between the TUC, the Department of Employment and the Department of Education and Science. This provided for a public grant to the TUC to mount an agreed range of courses. A proportion would be passed on by the TUC to affiliated unions for their own use.[77]

This new system institutionalised the shop steward training developed over the two previous decades; it enshrined its functional basis as 'profitable paid educational leave'; it skewed control over the system to the unions and specifically to the TUC; but it did give the courts important influence on the content and organisation of trade union provision. Trade union education was now legally determined as having one major end: the reproduction of 'responsible' collective bargaining agents in the interests of industrial peace, greater efficiency, greater profitability. The new system was explicitly justified in terms of cementing support for government policies.

> The success of any government's industrial and economic strategies will inevitably involve the co-operation of trade unions. Their willingness to co-operate will not only depend on the extent to which they are in agreement with the policies ... but also to the extent that union activists have a wide and comprehensive understanding of the policy issues and improve their competence in those areas where new responsibilities arise for them.[78]

From 1975 the TUC weekend schools were scrapped. The postal courses were in severe decline. The courses at Congress House and the summer schools continued as small components in the programme. A further television series was mounted. But it was now overwhelmingly the ten-day release courses which were central.

TUC Day-Release Course Provision, 1975-86

Year	Total Number of Courses	Students	Number of Health and Safety Courses
1975-76	1,147	16,264	361
1976-77	1,560	21,372	578
1977-78	2,008	27,479	741
1978-79	3,100	43,856	1,744
1979-80	3,032	38,981	1,441
1980-81	2,473	33,917	879
1981-82	2,397	30,085	714
1982-83	2,332	30,968	526
1983-84	2,409	29,207	631
1984-85	1,667	20,537	587
1985-86	1,542	18,752	599

Source: *TUC Annual Reports*

The table illustrates the dramatic surge in these courses. The state subsidy also increased from its initial £400,000 to more than £1.4 million by 1979. This expansion required, from the TUC's viewpoint, careful monitoring if they were to realise Len Murray's 1975 statement 'We claim the right to determine the training of trade union representatives on the achievement of trade union objectives. This is a principle from which we will not deviate.'[79]

If the TUC saw liberalism and politics as a problem in the responsible body sector, they were concerned about managerialism, arcane time-tabling and lecture-based teaching methods in the technical colleges. The majority of shop stewards naturally started from their immediate situation. In the past tutors had struggled to widen horizons. The tendency now was to develop the orientations stewards brought to the classroom in the most limited fashion.

A formal control of syllabus was in this context insufficient. The TUC wished to 'standardise courses throughout the country because it is no good having a different course in London to that given in Scotland'.[80] A Curriculum Development Unit (CDU) was established. The TUC staff saw themselves as the educational cadre training the trainers. 'We tell the voluntary institutions that we are going to have a program about stewards but we are the experts on their training and what they need.'[81] The package approach in which the centre controls knowledge and its production and consequently 'the nature of the teaching that takes place. In addition, the pace of work and form in which knowledge is presented is all carefully controlled from the centre' had proved its efficacy at the time of the Industrial Relations Act.[82] By 1977 the CDU had developed a detailed 200-page package for the basic TUC courses. This was followed by detailed documentation for other courses.

The ambit of this approach can be seen from the various sections of the basic course: 'The Job of a Shop Steward', 'Trade Union Organisation', 'Terms and Conditions of Employment', 'Disputes and Grievances', 'Discipline at Work', 'Job Security', 'Rights at Work', 'Organising for Safer Work', 'Industrial Democracy', 'Skills for Shop Stewards'. The basic method used discussion with programmed questionnaires and answers. The approach was a narrow one, based on a limited conception of a shop steward as a custodian of workplace agreements. The course notes stated, 'Most of the stress has got to be on strengthening and extending collective bargaining.' Even the section on industrial democracy began:

> We do not attempt to discuss in detail here the wider ranging issues of how industrial democracy links with political democracy. We concentrate instead on the practicalities of everyday life on the shop floor or in the office.

The familiar headings then follow: 'Strengthening Trade Union Organisation', 'Improving your Collective Agreements' and 'Negotiating New Agreements'.[83]

The materials were informed throughout by Donovanite collective bargaining. Problems not susceptible to a written agreement found little place. Tutors who inquired as to the absence of materials on organising industrial action or links between the Labour Party and the unions, or on the burning issue of the period, wage restraint, were told that they would have to produce their own. There was no way that materials which eschewed the narrow workplace bargaining approach could find their way into the national packs.[84]

At first the TUC explicitly demanded conformity. The packages were accompanied by a set of timings for each exercise. One Congress House functionary declared that he wanted to be able to know what every course in the country was doing at 11.00 on any morning.[85] A modified approach characterised the materials as 'a resource bank'. Nonetheless, the very existence of the documentation was a means of discipline.

> There was sometimes a conflict on the tutor's part between covering the full range of material in the TUC package and taking advantage of learning opportunities which might arise during the process of well informed discussions.[86]

Many tutors were new to the field and tended to rely largely on the TUC materials. Obviously others attempted to take full advantage of the educational dynamic that can be unleashed through open discussion.[87] Many perceived the TUC insistence on standardisation, and the limitations on the autonomy of the class, as a problem.

> The second ranked obstacle, that of TUC policy, may well have been largely identified as perceived insistence on syllabus uniformity ... a situation where the TUC would expect tutors to adopt their teaching packages and to use them fairly rigorously ...[88]

This approach was supplemented by tutor briefings. These were in no sense round-the-table seminars but one-way transmission mechanisms in which Congress House staff inducted the tutors into their materials, philosophy and values. A 'no briefing, no course' rule was developed by the TUC as a means to influence selection of tutors.[89]

The power situation was an essential background. If a TUC regional education office was dissatisfied with the approach of the WEA, then some courses could be placed in one technical college, some in another local technical college. The opportunities for divide and rule were maximised by the lack of any formal links between the responsible bodies and the FE sector. If the TUC threatened to withdraw courses there appeared to be little the educational institution could do. HMI's did not wish to intervene. In practice more sophisticated methods of steering students between institutions could be used: all applications for courses went direct to the TUC. Links between tutors and educational bodies to discuss courses outside the TUC's framework were actively discouraged. TUC officers also cultivated a direct army of part-time tutors, some dependent on these courses. Patronage was extended by the fact that TUC regional education officers sat on appointment panels.[90]

In substance, direct funding incarnated the TUC as a responsible body. Unlike other responsible bodies it refused to employ its own tutors or trust the tutors at hand. It was, therefore, forced to develop strategies of power building and colonisation in order to control the classroom.

However, educators in this period could see fruit being borne particularly in the follow-on courses on financial information, new technology and rights at work, and in provision for black workers and women trade unionists. A lot of effort was put into developing both a system of bridging courses for women members who might be interested in becoming shop stewards and in attracting more women into the mainstream provision. Of particular value was the development at both Ruskin and the Northern College of four-week advanced courses. And tutors reported the development of voluntary groups on the study of work hazards or local labour history and useful links between workplaces and unions influenced by the burgeoning of TUC courses. Some attention was devoted to the question of membership education, but by 1980 the system was still almost totally dominated by shop stewards.[91]

In the harsh climate of the 1980s the number of students and the number of courses declined. The previous structure by which all students attended a basic general course followed by a specialist subject-based course was amended and the latter removed from the programme. The new structure involved two ten-day courses, Stage I and Stage II.

> Stage I is particularly concerned to help representatives develop the basic skills they need to represent their members. Developing skills include making notes, giving reports, interviewing members, participating in meetings and negotiating with management. The Stage II courses are intended to offer the opportunity of in-depth exploration of the issues raised in Stage I.[92]

The problem was that, at the very time when the limitations of British trade unionism's attachment to sectional workplace bargaining were being unmasked by unemployment and political offensive, the TUC was placing an even greater emphasis on workplace organisation and workplace bargaining.

This was accompanied by a shift in official methodology, a new stress on student self-direction. The earlier emphasis on activism in the classroom had seen an essential role for curriculum, and for tutorial guidance.

> The tutor's job is to see that the theme is kept to, structure the discovery and to give it shape and order by asking leading provocative challenging questions ... He should bring about a pause for summary at key points; suggest lines of approach ... ensure that at the end everybody is clear about what has been achieved.[93]

Now the TUC was urging that *all* the course work should be done by the students alone in small self-directed groups handling self-selected problems related to their workplace, utilising TUC documents as learning aids 'with a stress on moving away from a classroom with a front reserved for a teacher ... do not keep a special place for yourself; as course tutor you are a course member like everybody else'.[94] It was argued that 'The more tutored a course is, it is likely that the less self-reliance and self-activity are produced in the students.'[95] In 1979 the tutor's role was seen as 'controlling' and 'disciplining' student activity. By 1982 this kind of approach was denounced in demagogic terms: 'it represents a common deviation: it's called the prima donna style ... '[96] The job of the tutor was simply, through the provision of documents and visual aids, 'to arrange the learning situation'. Discipline-based expertise was redundant.

> The student-centred method grounds classroom teaching activities upon the experience of the steward; the experiences of the tutor being of no more and no less value than anybody else's on the course. In so far as the tutor's views differ from others in the class then, as an equal, these can be put.

Not only did this approach mean 'starting with the problems shop stewards bring into the class', it meant *finishing* there.

> We must at all times avoid the tutor-centred approach to the identification of problems ... there is a danger that prepared case studies can mask the stewards' identification of problems; the case study being *at least one step removed* from particular workplace experience.

However, for the purposes of securing day release, 'some apparently structured timetable must be printed to convince employers that the course is valid'.[97]

This approach was never argued, merely asserted. Parallels with child-centred learning were drawn. Yet the experience of trade union activists, whilst an immensely valuable resource, is in the end no more adequate in itself for educational fulfilment than that of children. Real learning requires both hard work and rigorous engagement, not only with wider experience but with established knowledge. Yet, during this period, all booklists were removed from the TUC basic course materials. Self-direction is simply one useful learning method along with the punctuated lecture, the question-and-answer seminar, the small group-programmed discussion. Yet these methods were rejected with horror as involving tutor imposition. The essential weaknesses of this kind of 'progressivism' have been ably analysed in other fields of education and require little elaboration here.[98] Moreover, the choices offered to students were, in practice, severely limited: the curriculum prescriptions of workplace industrial relations inherent in the legislation could not be ignored. The materials students had available to utilise in their self-directed groups heavily reflected this and the emphasis was policed by TUC Regional Education Officers.

For whilst the new approach undoubtedly possessed some democratic impulse, the overall framework, with its insistence on collective bargaining, stimulated the production of a real curriculum focused on skills training, a system acceptable to external scrutiny. One danger facing the TUC from 1979 was that prescriptive materials on such subjects as trade union law could have threatened the annual grant, a subsidy that the TUC was not prepared to lose. A broader political approach could have attracted government attention in the same way as have materials produced by the Open University. This was made explicit in a series of speeches through 1982 by the then Employment Minister, Norman Tebbit. The following year, the TUC accepted that a proportion of the state grant would be used for courses which required specific employer endorsement as to content. In 1984 the DES and the TUC held talks on the introduction of sections on 'economic literacy' into the courses. If the government was to continue directly financing union education it was going to utilise finance to influence what was learnt. The TUC was apparently willing to comply.[99]

Perhaps more encouragement could be taken, by 1986, in educational development within individual unions. The mid-1970s witnessed an upturn in individual union schemes. ASTMS, the General and Municipal Workers, the NUR and the National Union of Teachers were amongst the unions taking advantage of the new climate to open residential colleges. A union like the National Graphical Association developed from an almost negligible presence in this field in the early 1970s into a strongly staffed department integrally linked with research by the end of the decade. At first much of this provision was basic steward training but, as the decade advanced, individual unions sought to redress the narrowness of the TUC provision by providing a broader range of courses. The TGWU, NALGO, NUPE and the GMWU, addressing themselves to the new political challenges confronting the unions, mounted imaginative forays from industrial relations training into the field of economic and social issues. Even with recession and membership loss many unions strove energetically at least to maintain expansion. A good example is the TGWU. It was spending £46,000 on education in 1974. By 1982 the figure was £548,000. Courses on political action and alternative economic strategies were mounted, as was provision for women and black members unknown in earlier years. The union had, by 1986, started its own advanced distance learning scheme in collaboration with several universities. And it was expressing dissatisfaction at the limitations of the central TUC system.

An important achievement has been the appointment of local trade union education officers aimed at rooting education within normal membership activities. Several unions were placing an emphasis on branch education and urging that new appointments should be seen as a stimulus for educational self-activity by members, not a substitute for it. The uncelebrated and still small-scale development of lay tutors, induction courses for members, lunchtime meetings and weekend schools justify careful nurturing. A major problem, however, remains the degree to which the TUC duplicates much of the basic training which unions devote to their new representatives. Moreover, educational retrenchment, as part of wider economies by unions such as the engineers and the mineworkers, underlined the fact that there could be little cause for complacency.[100]

The Demise of Workers' Education?

By the mid-1970s the question was being posed as to whether the WEA had 'forsaken all credibility as a promoter of liberal education for trade unionists by accommodating too readily the TUC's demands for training courses'.[101] Since 1964 'WEA provision very much reflected the conceived objectives and lines of development of the TUC scheme', and, by 1978 'trade union studies' – almost completely TUC provision – constituted a quarter of all WEA class meetings.[102] The WEA was mounting over 25 per cent of TUC day-release courses. The Russell Report on Adult Education, published in 1973, had urged the WEA to expand in four directions: education for the deprived in the inner city; educational work in an industrial context; political and social education; and courses of liberal and academic study below the level of university work. The surge in this *one* area, institutionally closed off from branch life, staffed by professional tutors and administered directly by the district office, caused tensions within the WEA. The provision was criticised for its narrowness and the TUC for its cut-price cannibalisation of WEA resources.

The strategy adopted was two-fold. By maintaining a central role within the TUC provision, it was argued, the WEA could act to civilise it and broaden its concerns. Moreover, the reservoir of students generated by the TUC courses could, if the correct connections were built, be conducted into the mainstream activities of the WEA. The mechanism for a rehabilitation of workers' education was the industrial branch consisting wholly of trade unionists. Several of these branches had been formed in the early 1970s and there were soon almost twenty.[103]

This strategy failed to stave off problems. The North Staffs District moved to limit courses. North Yorkshire voted to withdraw from the TUC scheme, a decision only later modified. In 1979, after patient negotiations with the DES produced an offer of new appointments, the WEA districts baulked at the final hurdle: seventeen posts were lost.[104] Viewing the WEA as an unstable and volatile satellite, the TUC turned even more towards the more amenable and predictable technical colleges. By 1983 the WEA was providing less than 15 per cent of TUC provision and 80 per cent of TUC courses were mounted in the further education sector.[105] Nor had the industrial branch experiment achieved any great success. In one or two areas branches had taken off. One ran, over a year and a half, 39 courses, eleven teach-ins and seven day school.[106] The majority, however, oscillated between periods of activity and inactivity, and relied on one or two dedicated volunteers or on service from the professionals. Most ran small annual programmes. No sizeable workers' education was produced as a result of involvement in the TUC courses. Nor did the WEA presence qualitatively broaden these courses.

By 1986, the WEA was mounting only half the number of ten-day release courses for the TUC it had provided in 1979. Moreover, the WEA was suffering the impact of financial cutbacks and a new funding formula. An attempt to extend the work with unemployed groups under the MSC's Voluntary Projects Programme came to grief on the tutors' opposition to the illiberality of the MSC's philosophy.[107] The WEA was being propelled into a search for short-term funding which militated against any long-term educational strategy, and placed a premium on money making and against provision for the underprivileged – certainly against provision free from external constraints. The new cold climate led to a tendency for districts involved in TUC work to attempt to hang on to what they had. Tutors who, in recent years, have raised criticisms of the TUC scheme, have found themselves facing not only hostility from the TUC but from their district secretaries.[108]

In the universities there was a tendency for some of the longer day-release courses 'to become narrower – though never as narrow as those sponsored by the TUC'.[109] The longer courses, with their synthesis of theory and practice, were in many areas still in a healthy state. One tutor reported that a current class dealt with basic skills,

> but it also deals with the aims and organisation of British trade unionism, trades councils, the TUC, the Labour Party, trade union history, industrial democracy, government pay policy, socialism, unemployment and inflation, the multi-nationals ...[110]

However, within a few years these three year courses for railworkers had become ten-week TUC courses.[111]

Concern at the intensifying encroachment of the TUC produced a UCAE Working Party. A conference of representatives of nineteen universities in October 1975 clearly illustrated divisions in attitude. The most coherent argument asserted that 'The policy pursued still by some universities of offering more and more basic day release courses ... serves to discredit the concept of a unique role for the universities.'[112] Effort should be concentrated on the longer sustained work, research and tutor training.

A major problem was TUC refusal to recognise the contours of the educational system. An attempt should be made to persuade the TUC of the need for a tiered system of basic work in the colleges, leading to advanced courses in universities. There was, it was argued, a need for unity. Private deals done by individual departments looking only to immediate needs were quickly quoted as precedents by the TUC 'to other universities that feel they cannot accept and the university is threatened with the loss of its work'.[113]

Supporters of the view that 'only a national approach to the TUC to establish a common framework for university provision can prevent further deterioration in the situation' pointed to the problems of recent TUC pronouncements in relation to academic freedom: ' ... the movement must have a decisive voice regarding the syllabuses and programmes of courses, the employment of tutors, teaching methods and teaching materials'. A newly appointed regional education officer had stated quite unambiguously that 'A syllabus approved by the TUC should not be altered, there should be no academic deviation.'[114]

Others were chary of a national approach. The perennial arguments that short courses led to recruitment for longer courses, that the TUC position was changing and that Congress House was beginning to see a specialised role for the universities were put.[115]

The final UCAE Report called for an expansion of university resources, a mix of courses, greater co-ordination and a distinctive role for the universities in research and teacher training. There was no forceful detailed reformulation of a philosophy based on the social purpose strand of liberal adult education. Many felt that the real drift of the report was that departments should be allowed to get on with whatever they wanted with greater funding.[116] An approach to the DES was unproductive, whilst a hesitant and unconvincing delegation encountered a blank wall at the TUC.[117]

The drift continued, but it became a drift out of trade union work.

In the five years from 1977 the proportion of TUC day-release courses mounted by extra-mural departments was halved. Having failed to hang together, several departments hung separately. When the TUC courses were withdrawn from Southampton, and there were attempts by the TUC officer to interfere in courses at Liverpool and Manchester, many of the fundamental questions and criticisms which arose from the TUC link were raised by universities whose voice had been muted in the earlier discussion. As the decade neared its end one authority commented:

> One by one, depending upon the extent of local TUC pressure, universities have cut down their commitment to this work ... universities remain in this field only where they work with individual unions or where the local TUC education officers ignore the rigidities of their own organisation's training requirements.[118]

However, a survey conducted in 1982-83 showed fourteen universities still mounting TUC provision.[119] But the financial position of universities and the attempts at restructuring adult education bode ill for the future. In 1984 Oxford, the progenitor of the famous 1908 Report, was recording the virtual extinction of its day release courses for trade unionists 'which a decade ago were numerous enough to occupy four industrial relations staff tutors'.[120]

Tutors began to argue that it was time to change direction

> ... a reappraisal of the content of workers' education is needed ... The widespread illiteracy of our students concerning alternative forms of political and economic organisation must be recognised by the educational arm of the movement.[121]

The TUC had initially promised both industrial *and* political education but 'whilst it has shown great skill, energy and some ruthlessness in fulfilling the first task it has ignored the second one completely'.[122]

Counter arguments were raised. Despite the rooting of this critique in contemporary trade unionism its proponents were accused of subscribing to erroneous conceptions of a past golden age.[123] Attempts to encourage discussion about education in the wider labour movement met with only limited success. But some groups of trade unionists did begin to express their concern.[124] It would be wrong to see any spontaneous growndswell of opposition to prevailing trends in trade union education. But has not the *stimulation* of workers always been what distinguished the intellectual from the technician?

Conclusions

Lack of space precludes a detailed programme for reform; but the direction of change is surely clear. In the context of two decades of crude or refined attempts at thought control by the TUC, a recent careful study concludes that the core of today's trade union education has

> not attempted to assist students in tracing the pattern of 'cause and effect' spreading from their own actions at the workplace and then throughout the whole economic and political structure. In failing to provide the student with a sense of perspective necessary to understand society in its 'concrete interrelated totality' these courses have been unsuccessful in safeguarding the traditions of workers' education ... The TUC courses attempt to assist trade unionists to tackle their immediate employment problems and little else – by being so narrowly conceived the courses do not provide for the broader educational needs of workers.[125]

The declaration that 'trade union education is synonymous with industrial relations training' has been largely implemented. The bulk of provision is given over to technical training in technical colleges. The residential sector, where broad and rigorous study is undertaken, is tiny. It provides, for example, at Ruskin and Northern College, the two bodies most identified with the trade unions, some 250 student places. The TUC's own four-week scheme comprised in 1986 only six courses involving 54 students. In the same year a grand total of 150 students were studying the history of the British working class and social and industrial history on the shrunken postal course provision.

Any system which concentrates to this degree on training as against education; on industrial relations skills as against political understanding; on representatives at the expense of members and on white men at the expense of women and black workers is not doing its job. Trade unionists *do* need industrial relations skills. They also need, *as trade unionists*, history and politics and economics. The present imbalance can only reinforce rather than redeem the weaknesses of the labour movement.

This point needs underlining. 'The control of industry in the interests of the community' (AUEW); ' ... the securing of a real measure of control in industry ... in the interest of labour' (TGWU); 'to co-operate with other organised workers in the transference of industry from private ownership for the common welfare of the people' (TASS); 'to work for the supercession of the capitalist system by a socialist order of society' (NUR). These are all extracts from the aspirations of TUC-affiliated unions spelt out in the rules of these unions. They relate to issues discussed daily ad infinitum in the universities, polytechnics and colleges up and down the country. Is it really asking too much to require that trade union education should give explicit, thorough and critical examination to them?

Notes

[1] S. Bidwell, MP. Interview, February 1987; 'TUC Education Officers Protest to General Council', *Tribune*, 25 July 1965; 'George Woodcock: A Shocking Letter', *Plebs*, July 1965.
[2] *Considerations Affecting Regional Facilities and Regional Organisation* TUC Education Committee (London 1966); Bidwell interview.
[3] Bidwell interview, c.f. J.P.M. Millar, *The Labour College Movement* (London) n.d. pp.168-9. 'What Future For Movement Education?', *Tribune*, 1 September 1965. c.f. 'It was also expected that the confinement of the curriculum to technical training would protect members from some of the more disruptive influences of the more radical political ideas which crept into some liberal studies syllabuses,' R. Fieldhouse, *The WEA Aims and Achievements 1903-1977* (Syracuse 1977), pp.38-9.
[4] *Considerations Affecting Regional Facilities ...* op.cit.; R. Jackson, 'Training Shop Stewards', *Plebs*, July 1966.
[5] R. Palme Dutt, 'Notes of the Month', *Labour Monthly*, September 1963.
[6] T. Cliff, *The Employers' Offensive* (London 1970), p.218:
[7] Quoted in E. and R. Frow, *Engineering Struggles* (Manchester 1982), p.470.
[8] 'Socialist Education A Draft Proposal', *Plebs*, November 1964. 'The Future of Socialist Education', *Plebs*, May 1965.
[9] TUC *Report* 1966, pp.516-7.
[10] Ibid.
[11] TUC *Report* 1967, pp.214-5; 519-2.
[12] TUC, *Trade Unionism: Evidence to the Royal Commission on Trade Unions* (London 1966), pp.79-82.
[13] P. Jenkins, *The Battle of Downing Street* (London 1970), p.13.
[14] Ibid., p.12
[15] *Report of the Royal Commission on Trade Unions and Employers Associations*, (London 1968).
[16] Ibid., p.120.
[17] H.A. Clegg, *The Changing System of Industrial Relations in Great Britain* (Oxford 1979), p.317.
[18] *Report of the Royal Commission*, p.190-1.
[19] 'Under the strong influence of George Woodcock and Hugh Clegg as commissioners the commission itself tried to find a political formula which would be as acceptable to the unions as to the employers and government.' L. Panitch, *Social Democracy and Industrial Militancy, The Labour Party, the Trade Unions and Income Policy 1945-1974* (Cambridge 1976), p.166.

c.f. 'the report reflected [Woodcock's] outlook as well as that of Hugh Clegg', E. Silver, *Victor Feather: TUC: A Biography* (London 1973), p.131.

[20] *Report of the Royal Commission*, p.191.

[21] J. Hughes, *Trade Union Structure and Government*, Royal Commission on Trade Unions Research Paper 5, (London 1967), p.50; TUC *Report*, 1967, p.215.

[22] TUC *Training Shop Stewards*, p.11.

[23] Ibid.

[24] Ibid., p.12.

[25] Ibid., p.9.

[26] Ibid., p.21.

[27] *In Place of Strife: A Policy For Industrial Relations*, (London 1969).

[28] TUC *Report*, 1970, pp.288-91.

[29] TUC *Report*, 1971, pp.143-5.

[30] Report of speech by R. Jackson, *The Industrial Tutor*, March 1972.

[31] TUC *Evidence to Russell Committee on Adult Education: Supplementary Note on Trade Union Education*, p.12.

[32] Commission for Industrial Relations Report No.33, *Industrial Relations Training* (London 1972).

[33] 'Shop Steward Education and Training: statement of TUC Education Committee Chair at meeting with Parliamentary Under Secretary, DES May 1973', reprinted in *Industrial Tutor*, September 1973; TUC Education Committee, *Training Workplace Representatives: A Statement of Policy*, February 1973.

[34] F. Pickstock, *Survey of Day Release Courses for Industrial Workers* (Oxford 1966).

[35] Based on Annual Reports of the various departments; For the WEA specifically see F. Bayliss, *In Factory and Mine*, (London 1964). I. Jordan, *Shop Steward Training: The Case For Day Release* (Edinburgh 1969).

[36] J. Lovet, 'Shop Steward Training: Conflicting Objectives and Needs', *Industrial Relations Journal*, Spring 1976.

[37] W. McCarthy, *The Role of Shop Stewards in British Industrial Relations*, Royal Commission on Trade Union Research, Paper I, (London 1966), p.77.

[38] Lovet, op.cit., p.29.

[39] McCarthy, op.cit., p.76.

[40] This was even more true of internal university staff, c.f. 'virtually all leading British academics in the field of industrial relations have worked for the Prices and Incomes Board, the Commission on Industrial Relations or the Department of Employment, the policies of which tend towards the consolidation of managerial control over wages and the use of labour at the level of the individual enterprise and the economy as a whole', R. Hyman, *Strikes* (London 1972), p.158.

[41] F. Bayliss, 'Education and Economic Policy', *Adult Education*, November 1967.

[42] Society of Industrial Tutors, *The Aims of the Society 1969*. For the approach to the DEA see UCAE and WEA, *Proposals for the Development of Education for Social Responsibility in Industry* (Leicester 1967), UCAE and WEA; *Proposals for the Expansion of Provision for the Liberal Adult Education of the Industrial Community* paper circulated by A.J. Allaway (Leicester 1967); information from G. Stuttard. For the approach and activities of the SIT see the issues of the Society's journal *Industrial Tutor* 1969

and the 'Trade Union Industrial Studies' series published jointly with Arrow Books between 1975 and 1980. For the tendency in the later 1960s and early 1970s for tutors to react somewhat indiscriminately to 'demand' – which was increasingly demand for training courses, see B. Houlton 'Supply and Demand Relationships in Industrial Adult Education', *Industrial Tutor*, September 1971. For an early comment on the formation of the Society see M. Barratt Brown 'Adult Education and the Liberal Tradition' in K. Coates (ed.), *Essays in Socialist Humanism* (Nottingham 1973).

[43] R. Peers, *Adult Education: A Comparative Survey* (London 1958), p.167.

[44] University of Southampton, Department of Adult Education, *Annual Report*, 1967-68, p.10.

[45] J. Goodman, T. Whittingham, *Shop Stewards in British Industry* (London 1969), p.236.

[46] University of Sheffield, Department of Extra-Mural Studies, *Annual Report*, 1964-5, p.11; M. Barratt Brown, *Adult Education For Industrial Workers* (Leicester 1969), National Institute of Adult Education and Society of Industrial Tutors.

[47] Harrison and Barratt Brown maintained close links with Alexander and Hughes from the earlier period and contributed regularly and collaboratively for *Tribune*, see for example, Panitch, op.cit., p.94, 287. Barratt Brown wrote four pamphlets for the Institute of Workers' Control, see G. Foote, *The Labour Party's Political Thought* (London 1986), pp.202-4 for an assessment of his ideas. Heath, McFarlane, Smith and Park contributed to the IWC related *Trade Union Register*. This was not at the expense of academic work: Alexander, Harrison, and McCormack and Hampton went on to chairs. Hughes and Barratt Brown became principals of Ruskin and the Northern College respectively.

[48] Interview with Royden Harrison, January 1986.

[49] Hugh Clegg was a commissioner; McCarthy, Director of Research; Fox and Marsh wrote research papers; and Flanders was seen as a strong intellectual influence on the final report. He was connected with the Socialist Vanguard group which coalesced around *Socialist Commentary*, by the mid-1950s, 'an identifiable revisionist periodical', closely supporting right-wing Labour, to which McCarthy, Marsh and Pickstock contributed. Pickstock was a moving force in the Gaitskellite Campaign for Democratic Socialism and in this period was Lord Mayor of Oxford. McCarthy was an adviser to Barbara Castle and identified closely with Tony Crosland; see S. Haseler, *The Gaitskellites* (London 1969), p.210; Foote, op.cit., pp.202-4; S. Crosland, *Tony Crosland* (London 1982).

[50] J. Goldthorpe, 'Industrial Relations in Great Britain: A Critique of Reformism' in T. Clarke, L. Clements, *Trade Unions Under Capitalism* (London 1977), pp.212.3.

[51] A. Marsh, *A Collection of Teaching Documents and Case Studies* (Oxford 1966), pp.1-3, 49, 53.

[52] R. Jones, 'Industrial Relations', *Adult Education*, Vol. XXXVIII, No. 2, 1965, pp.213-15.

[53] A. Fox, 'Adult Education Values', *New Society*, 30 September 1965.

[54] ' ... its basic features remain those devised by the federated employers in 1898 ... it has commonly been charged with excessive delay, with a bias towards management, and with failing to resolve positively enough the questions referred to it.' R. Hyman, *Disputes Procedure in Action* (London

1972), pp.1, 6, 7.

[55] The distinction is made in J. Killeen, M. Bird, *Education and Work* (London 1980).

[56] Foreword to *Brochure of Courses for Motor Industry Workers*, 1961, in Oxford University, Department for External Studies Box Files.

[57] R. Chapman, Group Personnel Director to F. Pickstock, 7 August 1963, OUDES., Box Files.

[58] K. Edwards Group Staff and Training Manager to F. Pickstock, October 1964, OUDES.

[59] Edwards to Pickstock, 14 August 1964, OUDES.

[60] BMC, *Report on Shop Steward Training Courses*, 1967, OUDES, c.f. 'No manager attempted to place any limitation upon the kind of subject taught or the manner in which the classes were conducted,' A.J. Corfield, *Epoch in Workers' Education* (London 1969), p.142.

[61] Ibid.

[62] Pickstock appears to have had few firm views on course content and approach. For example, he wrote to a tutor in the Bristol Department 'I am meeting some resistance to our DR classes at Pressed Steel from their own Personnel Manager. He is holding up what you are doing as a model. From his description it would be a better and more favourable arrangement for us and I am willing to learn from you'. The reply saw few differences in content between the two courses but pointed out that the Bristol courses had the advantage of being residential with excellent accommodation and food. 'This treatment seemed to influence the stewards not a little. This new environment has probably more effect on them than the course itself'. Correspondence between Pickstock and J.T. Thomas, September 1966. This is an interesting example of the utility of day release as a welfare benefit or perk for the workers and as PR for management. It would be wrong to overlook this aspect: many workers were only too pleased to receive a day off and were not likely to wax too critical on its content. Marsh, who was teaching in a private capacity at the company's staff college, advised that the courses must be reviewed to ensure that they were 'primarily on procedures'. F. Pickstock, Notes on meeting with A. Marsh, OUDES.

[63] M. Young (AUEW) to F. Pickstock, 19 February 1968, OUDES.

[64] Pickstock to Edwards, 19 June 1967, OUDES.

[65] F. Pickstock, *Courses for Trade Unionists*, UCAE, 1974.

[66] R. Lochrie, 'The Service from the WEA' in T. Schuller ed., *Is Knowledge Power? Problems and Practice in Trade Union Education* (Aberdeen 1980), p.93.

[67] R. Fieldhouse, letter in *WEA News*, September 1971; R. Fieldhouse, 'Workers in the Field', *WEA News*, January 1972.

[68] T. Park, 'Trade Union Education' in K. Coates, T. Topham, M. Barratt Brown (eds), *Trade Union Register* (London 1969), pp.96-100.

[69] This section is based upon Sheffield University Department of Extra-Mural Studies, *Closure of Trade Union Courses conducted by Sheffield University Extra-Mural Department and the Workers Education Association, Yorkshire District South*, n.d.; see also the comments in J. Halstead, 'Workers Education in a British University', *Labor Studies Journal*, Winter 1980, p.220.

[70] P. Simpson, *Liberal Adult Education For Industrial Workers Theory and Practice*, unpublished M.Sc Thesis (Edinburgh University 1970), p.88; A.

Kitts, 'Sheffield Leads the Quiet Revolution', *Sheffield Forward*, January 1968.

[71] *Closure* ..., p.2.

[72] Ibid., p.3.

[73] *Scunthorpe Evening Telegraph*, 21 April 1972, quoted in D. Moir, *Industrial Day Release courses B.S.C. Scunthorpe*, Ruskin College Thesis, Oxford, 1976. A specific irritant was an article by a WEA tutor connected with the work, critical of some aspects of the steel unions, in a volume partly edited by a member of the department. See. G. Chadwick, 'Steel Workers: Control and Redundancy' in K. Coates, T. Topham, M. Barratt Brown (eds), *Trade Union Register*, (London 1969).

[74] University of Sheffield Department of Extra-Mural Studies, *Annual Report*, 1970-71, p.3.

[75] For surveys of this period see D. Coates, *Labour in Power? A Study of The Labour Government, 1974-79* (London 1980); M. Holmes, *The Labour Government 1974-79: Political Aims and Economic Reality* (London and Basingstoke 1985); K. Coates (ed.), *What Went Wrong?* (Nottingham 1979); P. Whitehead, *The Writing on the Wall: Britain in the Seventies* (London 1985); M. Jacques, F. Mulhern (eds), *The Forward March of Labour Halted?* (London 1981).

[76] See J. McMullen, *Rights At Work* (London 1983), pp.318ff; L. Wedderburn, *The Worker and the Law* (London 1986), pp.310ff.

[77] TUC *Report* 1976, pp.184ff.

[78] TUC *Report* 1975, pp.197-8.

[79] Ibid., p.443.

[80] Quoted in A. Nash, 'British And American Labour Educators', *Labor Studies Journal*, Winter 1980.

[81] Ibid.

[82] S. Westwood, 'Adult Education and the Sociology of Education' in J. Thompson (ed.), *Adult Education For A Change* (London 1980), p.38.

[83] TUC *Introductory Course* 1977; TUC *Tutors Notes to Introductory Course* 1977. See. J. McIlroy, 'Adult Education And The Role of the Client – The TUC Education Scheme 1929-80', *Studies in the Education of Adults*, April 1985.

[84] C. Edwards *et al.*, 'Student Centred Learning and Trade Union Education: A Preliminary Examination', *Industrial Tutor*, Autumn 1983; J. Brown *et al.*, *The TUC Stage II Core Course and its Implications for Wider TUC Education*, unpublished paper n.d.

[85] c.f. 'The new course will ensure a standard syllabus for introductory courses throughout the country', TUC *Report*, 1977, p.126.

[86] *Report by HM Inspectors on a Survey of Shop Stewards Courses in England and Wales 1979-80*, Department of Education and Science (London 1982).

[87] 'Tutors were prepared to reduce the time on those sections considered less immediately relevant and introduce other topics supported by college developed notes.' *Report of HM Inspectors*, op.cit.

[88] D. Bright, T. McDermott, *Survey of Trade Union Studies Tutors: Report to Social Science Research Council*, 1980, p.48; c.f. 'TUC determination of syllabuses presented an obvious problem within institutions whose members have a strong commitment to the notion of academic freedom.' J. Halstead, 'Workers Education, the Universities and the Funding Crisis: A View from Sheffield', *Industrial Tutor*, Spring 1984. p.26.

274	*The Search for Enlightenment*

[89] J. Brown *op.cit*; G. Powell, P. Stanton, *The TUC Stage II Core Course: A discussion document* mimeo circulated by TUC n.d.; *The TUC Education Scheme in the North West* mimeo circulated by 14 trade union studies tutors.

[90] McIlroy, *The TUC Education Scheme ... op.cit.*

[91] See for example, J. McIlroy, 'Fighting Racism in the Classroom', *Industrial Tutor*, September 1981; R. Elliott, 'Something Stirring: Women and TUC Education', *Industrial Tutor*, Spring 1982; R. Moore, 'Political Education In Practice', *Industrial Tutor*, September 1981.

[92] TUC *Report*, 1982, pp.236, 237; J. McIlroy, 'Trade Union Education in Recession', *Adult Education*, Autumn 1983.

[93] 'Teaching Hints and Aids' in E. Coker, G. Stuttard (eds), *Industrial Studies I: The Key Skills* (London 1975), p.135.

[94] TUC, *Methods in Trade Union Education*, 1983, pp.10,11.

[95] D. Gowan, 'Student Centred Approaches Revisited', *Trade Union Studies Journal*, Winter 1982.

[96] A.J. Topham, *Teaching Trade Unionists* (Hull 1979); Gowan, op.cit.

[97] All quotations from G. Powell, P. Stanton, op.cit.

[98] For a general critique see B. Simon, 'Problems in Contemporary Educational Theory: A Marxist Approach' in *Journal of Philosophy of Education*, Vol. 12, 1978; for a recent comment see B. Schwarz, 'Cultural Studies: The Case For the Humanities' in J. Finch, M. Rustin (eds), *A Degree of Choice* (Harmondsworth 1986); for trade union education see J. McIlroy, 'Goodbye Mr Chips?' *Industrial Tutor*, Autumn 1985.

[99] J. McIlroy, 'Lessons in Conformity', *New Statesman*, 23 September 1983.

[100] On this see for example S. Williams, R. Nicola, 'Education in NUPE', *Trade Union Studies Journal*, Winter 1982; F. Cosgrove, 'Re-shaping Trade Union Education, TGWU Proposals for Government Support', *Industrial Tutor*, Autumn 1983; G. Hayward, 'Education in the NGA', *Trade Union Studies Journal*, Summer 1983; R. Kibel, 'Education in NALGO', *Industrial Tutor*, Spring 1984.

[101] R. Fieldhouse, op.cit., 1977, p.57.

[102] M. Doyle, 'Reform and Reaction – The Workers Educational Association Post Russell' in J. Thompson, op.cit., p.137.

[103] See. M. Doyle op.cit; R. Fieldhouse, K. Forrester, 'The WEA and Trade Union Education', *Industrial Tutor*, Spring 1984.

[104] J. Roberts, *Trade Union and Industrial Work* (North Staffs 1979); T. Topham, *An Open Letter* (Hull 1980).

[105] A. Campbell, J. McIlroy, 'Trade Union Studies in British Universities, Changing Patterns, Changing Problems', *International Journal of Lifelong Education*, July-September 1986.

[106] P. Fryer, 'Education From Below', *Trade Union Studies Journal*, Summer 1983.

[107] See the contributions in *Trade Union Studies Journal*, Summer, 1983.

[108] M. Turnbull, 'WEA Tutors', *Times Higher Education Supplement*, 5 July 1985, ' ... in Liverpool two experienced tutors have recently resigned arguing undue interference by the TUC in course provision and the District Secretary's acquiescence in this ... the background to all this is the TUC's attempt to safeguard its government grant by controlling course curricula.'

[109] G. Brown, 'Working Class Adult Education' in A. Thornton, M. Stephens, *The University in its Region* (Nottingham 1977), p.55.

[110] J. Fyrth, 'Trade Union Education', *Labour Monthly*, February 1975.

[111] J. Fyrth, 'Industrial Studies and the Labour Movement' in E. Coker, G. Stuttard (eds), *Industrial Studies, 3, Understanding Industrial Society*, p.154.

[112] R. Dyson, *The Role of the University*, UCAE paper, 1975, p.2.

[113] Ibid.

[114] Quoted in E. Jenkins, *Universities and Trade Union Education: Shop Steward Courses*, UCAE, 1975, p.1.

[115] M. Barratt Brown, *The Options Open: Priorities and Resources* (UCAE 1975); *Record of UCAE Conference on Industrial Studies*, October 1975 in files of Manchester University Department of Extra-Mural Studies.

[116] UCAE *Report on Industrial Studies*, Leicester, 1976.

[117] Minutes UCAE Council Meeting, 9 December 1977.

[118] R. Dyson, *Determining Priorities For University Extra-Mural Education*, Inaugural Lecture (Keele 1978).

[119] Campbell and McIlroy, op.cit.

[120] UCAE, *Annual Report*, 1983-84, p.6.

[121] T. Topham, 'The Need For Political Education', *Industrial Tutor*, September 1981.

[122] F. Pickstock, *Trade Unions and Political Education*, unpublished paper, 1981, p.23, see also C. Gravell, 'Trade Union Education; Will State Funding Lead to State Control?', *Trade Union Studies Journal*, Winter 1986; A. Campbell, *et al.*, 'Beyond Industrial Relations Training', *Trade Union Studies Journal*, Summer 1986.

[123] T. Nesbit, S. Henderson, 'Methods and Politics in Trade Union Education', *Trade Union Studies Journal*, Winter 1983.

[124] J. McIlroy, 'Beyond the Workplace', *Tribune*, 16 December 1983 and the correspondence in ensuing weeks; also of interest are the comments of a recent TUC-WEA class in Liverpool, ' ... criticisms were made of the course methods, some of them being lack of organisation and structure, loss of course aims, lack of direction, failings of group work ... political criticisms of methods linking them to the new realism approach. Crucial necessity for steward to be politically aware ... more leadership needed from tutor. Desire for a more traditional education approach.'

[125] T. Smith, 'Trade Union Education: Its Past and Future', *Industrial Relations Journal*, Summer 1984. For proposals for change see Society of Industrial Tutors, *The Future of Paid Educational Leave* (London 1987); Labour Party, *Education Throughout Life* (London 1986); A. Campbell, *et al.*, op.cit. The necessity for rights to release to *any* course of the student's choice should, in the light of the experience recounted here, require little emphasis.

Bob Fryer

9 The Challenge to Working-Class Adult Education

Imagine the honest, sober, reflecting portion of every town and village in the kingdom linked together as a band of brothers, honestly resolved to investigate all subjects connected with their interests, and to prepare their minds to combat with the errors and enemies of society ... Think you a corrupt government could perpetuate its exclusive and demoralising influence amid a people thus united and instructed? **William Lovett**

The purpose of an adult education worthy of its name is not merely to impart reliable information, important though that is. It is still more to foster the intellectual vitality to master and use it, so that knowledge becomes, not a burden to be borne or a possession to be prized, but a stimulus to constructive thought and an inspiration to action. **R.H. Tawney**

Almost forty years ago, Thomas Hodgkin set out to 'raise certain questions about the relations between adult education and our society'. In particular, Hodgkin was concerned to examine the impact of social change and the extent to which the established arrangements for adult education in Britain themselves required modification. Whilst his concerns were straightforward, they were of profound importance. As he argued, a 'failure to work out the correlation between adult education and the broader processes of social change has serious practical disadvantages. It makes it more difficult for us to know where we are going today – or where we ought to go'[1] In this essay the aim is to make a contribution to the analysis begun by Hodgkin.

Over the past forty years, there have been enormous changes in the social, economic, political and cultural maps of Britain. Most of these changes have had an impact upon working-class life, either directly or indirectly. Some commentators have seen fit to discern in this the *de*composition of the British working class, resulting especially from industrial and economic change.[2] Against this others have asserted that nothing essential or of any great import has changed about class in Britain and that a premature 'retreat from class' has been declared.[3] Whilst this is not the place to elaborate this key and complex debate, the position adopted in this chapter is that rather than declining or decomposing, the British working class has been undergoing a profound *re*composition over the past forty years. It manifests itself in numerous ways, from occupation to ideology and from gender to political orientation. This aspect of social and political change at large alone calls for a reconstitution of the agenda for adult education. The task is to develop a comprehensive political economy capable of unravelling social complexities and imparting a technical competence that can contribute to working-class initiatives. Some steps are already being taken in this direction, but the extent of the opportunity to open up new fields and adopt fresh approaches has yet to be recognised. The focus of vigorous adult study today should be not only on education *for* and *by* working-class people, but also *about* the working class as a topic of study, a range of experiences and as an *agency* for social change.[4] In character it should be both analytical and practical, in method it should combine variety with democracy and embody an involvement of students which enables them to make intellectual tools their own, in the manner R.H. Tawney so admirably advocated, as a means to individual and social emancipation. But to work out an agenda incorporating these principles and aims today takes discussion further afield than has traditionally been the case and involves consideration of some contentious issues.

The Labour Market

Past failings are, perhaps, the strongest stimulus to rethinking. In this context, a striking feature of social change in Britain since the Second World War has been the enormous shift that has taken place in its industrial structure. Over the past forty years, but especially during the last decade, Britain has witnessed a dramatic movement from extractive and manufacturing industry to services and process work and from heavy manual labour to lighter assembly operations, routine clerical work and low-skilled service employment.[5] In retrospect, it was little short of a disaster that there was a virtual absence of a coherent and vigorous adult education designed to address both the decline of established employment and the growth of new areas of work lacking a tradition of associated adult education.

The background to industrial change was redundancy, unemployment and early retirement. If full employment had been part of the so-called post-war settlement with labour (and the extent of the commitment was always exaggerated), the contract was progressively abandoned from the mid-1960s onwards. When the Labour Party came to power in 1964, unemployment nationally stood at 1.7 per cent and advocates of higher levels of unemployment to combat inflation and workers' power were regarded as rather cranky. Organised labour, it was asserted, would never again tolerate the levels and duration of unemployment witnessed between the wars. Yet, twenty years later a Conservative government was re-elected in 1983 with unemployment standing at 13 per cent, and re-elected in 1987 again after a period of office in which the number out of work had rocketed from 1.4 million to over 3 millions.

Where unemployment was concerned, some aspects of adult education moved into action with greater speed, aided on occasion by government funding redirected from other adult education work towards the MSC on the one hand and the Department of Education and Science's REPLAN programme (originally the Adult Unemployed Programme) for work with the long-term adult unemployed on the other. From 1981 onwards, the TUC took the initiative in establishing Unemployed Workers' Centres and by 1984 over 200 of those had been established with a threefold role of giving counselling and advice on opportunities and assistance for training, providing a focal point for contact in the community for unemployed people and representing the interests of the unemployed in the development of MSC schemes and in the provision of local services. In addition, many UWCs took on a campaigning role, not only on their own behalf but in support of other groups and organised programmes of adult education, sometimes in conjunction with the WEA or adult education divisions of the LEA. Adult education tutors from the University of Leeds were especially active in promoting both detailed research and extensive educational work in UWCs and in bringing them together for periodic exchanges of experience at Ruskin College, Oxford. Between 1982 and 1986 these courses attracted more than 3,000 unemployed people in Leeds and Bradford alone, with the tutors employing four different approaches in their adult education work. These they called the 'community approach' (working with active community groups, such as tenants' associations and neighbourhood groups), the 'institutional approach' (working in close collaboration with LEA's and other agencies), the 'organisational approach' (working directly with Centres) and the 'trade union approach'.[6]

Similarly, the Northern College ran residential and outreach courses for both full-time workers and rank and file members from centres throughout Yorkshire, North Derbyshire and in special projects funded by REPLAN and local authorities. Courses for unemployed people were also provided in return to study, community organisation and writers' workshops. Together with the WEA, the College was the base for one of the most successful of the REPLAN projects with the long-term adult unemployed.[7]

In addition to such localised initiatives, the WEA produced its own manifesto, *Working with the Unemployed*, and the Further Education Unit of the DES published a detailed project report on *Adult Unemployment and the Curriculum* based on several case studies of existing practice. Throughout the country adult educators gathered in seminars, discussion groups and conferences to share ideas and experiences of educational work with the adult unemployed, so much so that one writer spoke of an 'unemployment bandwagon'.[8] Others discerned a shift away from an earlier concern with sharpening campaign skills amongst courses for unemployed people, towards an increased desire 'to reflect on, and communicate with, the quality of life on the dole', arising partly out of a recognition of the difficulty of easily identifying clear and achievable objectives where education work with unemployed adults was being undertaken.[9]

Turning to demographic trends, we find a striking picture of the changing relative participation rates of men and women. Between 1971 and 1985 economic activity rates for men fell from 81 to 74 per cent and for women increased from 44 to 48.7 per cent. Behind these broad changes there were even more dramatic shifts. Over the same fourteen-year period, the economic activity rate for men aged between 60 and 64 fell from 83 to 54 per cent; meanwhile, women aged between 25 and 34 increased their economic activity rate from 45 in 1971 to 62 per cent.[10] As older men in the labour force were made redundant, they faced effective early retirement (often without adequate financial provision and mostly with no proper educational preparation). At the same time more and more younger women were staying in or returning to paid employment, often in low-paid jobs and in response to employers' demands for a flexible labour force. They presented new educational needs in terms of the content, organisation and methods appropriate for them.

The expansion of women's participation in the labour force,

especially in areas of work not hitherto characterised by strong trade unionism and well established collective bargaining, presents an enormous challenge to union organisation and trade union education alike. There are implications, too, which extend far beyond the workplace and which touch upon sexual divisions and changing patterns of behaviour in the wider society which will be referred to again below. So far, there is little sign of any significant narrowing of the earnings gap between men and women: in 1985 women's pay stood at 74 per cent of the average hourly pay of men, and women's average earnings were only two-thirds of those of men.[11] Occupational segregation of the labour market by gender is still striking, with women concentrated in routine and clerical and secretarial work, in hotels and catering, in cleaning, in retail and the caring occupations. Women still constitute only 10 per cent of management and 20 per cent of senior professional occupations outside health, education and welfare. This issue of women's subordinate position in the labour market should constitute a key topic not only for trade union education for women, but for adult education in general, and be related closely to wider considerations of women's position in society, in unpaid labour, in the family, as represented in the media and culture, in creative work and in sexual identity. Each of these is linked to women's economic position and place in paid employment and provides a challenging arena for innovative analysis, study and debate in adult education. At present, published information indicates that, as far as current involvement in adult education is concerned, although women outnumber men, the latter are far more likely to enjoy time off with pay to take part in courses, including those which lead to occupational and other qualifications.[12]

Redundancy, early retirement and greater longevity have all presented adult educators with a challenge and an opportunity. While much attention has understandably focused upon the need for adult education and training for the young unemployed and school leavers, to date insufficient thought has been given to devising absorbing and valuable programmes for older people. Some colleges, like the Northern College, have worked closely with Pensioners' Action Groups in providing residential courses for their members and other retired people locally. Since 1981, an organisation known as the University of the Third Age has been active in Britain, inspiring more than 6,000 people in over 80 local branches to become involved in adult educational activity, in many cases for the first time in their lives. One of the movement's key polemicists has argued that activists in the University of the Third Age begin from a recognition of the failure of higher education to meet their needs and of the remoteness and unresponsiveness of most LEA and other adult education provision. Self-activity, autonomy and independence for the older students has provided them with the slogan that 'an Englishman's [*sic*] home is, or could be, his college'.[13]

Finally, as far as this brief review of the changing labour market is concerned, it is imperative that organised labour and working-class adult education should give concerted attention to the changing nature of work itself. First, there is the continuing (and in some quarters, increasing) evidence of managerial strategies for de-skilling labour and for substituting new technology for workers. In many respects, the impact of so-called new technology, utilising micro-electronics and bio-technological processes, has scarcely been felt on anything like the scale that can be expected over the next decade or so. Courses in information technology and computerisation are rightly much in demand, particularly for women so often excluded from these areas of study elsewhere in the educational system.[14] Here, as elsewhere, adult education has the dual responsibility not only to repair earlier damage and meet the express needs of adult students, but also to do this in a manner and through an educational process which is designed to combat their powerlessness and subordination. In the study of, and familiarisation with, new technology, as in other fields, adult education must uphold democracy as both a process and an objective at the same time as facilitating access to essential technical skills and demystifying technology through the debunking of established barriers to skill acquisition.

Alongside changes in technology, management are also seeking wholesale restructuring of their workforces. Their aim is to narrow down the core labour force to a small number of flexible workers, available for deployment across a wide range of tasks.[15] Such workers will enjoy relative security of employment and continuity of work. Around this core it is intended to create a periphery of short-term, temporary, sub-contract and state-subsidised 'trainee' labour, with few rights and even fewer prospects of job security. Allied to the widespread demise of systematic industrial training in this country, the prospects for self-development and realisation of human potential amongst these workers is bleak. Even where so-called training schemes exist, all too often they amount to a combination of the inculcation of work discipline (punctuality, following of routines, rule observance) and narrow job-specific techniques rather than the training of genuine skills and the sponsoring of judgement and critical independence. Once more, the challenge for working-class adult education is self-evident, although several doughty alternatives have been to hand with a very different perspective to promote, including the MSC and its successors, private training agencies and various in-house schemes. However, it is not against the successes of the latter that our criticisms should principally be levelled, but at the failure of a convincing, robust and popular alternative to such shallow approaches to have been developed from the world of adult education. The expansion of the MSC was, in this respect, not so much a testimony to its strength as to the failure of traditional adult education and training programmes.[16]

Behind the turbulence of changes in the labour market outlined above have stood equally momentous changes in Britain's economic organisation since the Second World War. These include especially the century-long decline of Britain from a position of economic pre-eminence in the world. As late as 1899 Britain still enjoyed a third of the value of the world's export of all manufactured goods, and, even up to the Second World War British manufactures accounted for more than a fifth of world manufactured exports. Although the immediate aftermath of the Second World War gave a temporary respite to Britain's growing difficulties on the global market, her share of world manufactured exports fell from 26 per cent in 1950 to under 10 per cent by the end of the 1970s. A new landmark was reached in 1983 when, for the first time since systematic and reliable records had been kept, Britain became a *net* importer of manufactured goods. After entry of the UK into the EEC, these trends markedly accelerated. By 1984 the EEC accounted for 39 per cent of all British exports and 50 per cent of imports, and by 1984 the deficit in the value of British manufacturing trade with the EEC had reached £8.38 billion annually. Whilst manufactured exports to the EEC had risen by 66 per cent between 1973 and 1984, imports from the EEC had increased by 300 per cent. In 1984, 60 per cent of the overall EEC trading deficit was with West Germany and 44 per cent of the £5 billion deficit in manufacturing trade was in motor vehicles alone.[17] Yet, in these circumstances, in which British workers often shared the same or linked employers with workers in Europe, familiarity with other languages and cultures was shamefully low and almost universally absent from the working-class adult education curriculum. That challenge is now even more urgent with the approach of the European 'single market' in 1992. Enhancing workers' chances of understanding and controlling their own working lives must entail working-class education increasingly embracing the study of foreign languages and the social and political structures of other countries.[18]

Explanation and debate about Britain's declining relative economic competitiveness and strength abound. As Gamble puts it, 'a great ocean of writing appeared in the 1960s and 1970s' attempting to explain it, although very little of the analysis has percolated down to adult education.[19] Of course, there were available several orthodox and largely anti-working class explanations for Britain's economic decline. What organised labour lacked was its own account and its own educational and political programme for dealing with the issue in a manner that would benefit rather than further disadvantage workers. Here slogans and demands from the labour movement for 'more investment' cannot alone constitute a sophisticated and satisfactory alternative workers' strategy, in which the full implications have been worked through, a process which requires analysis, reflection and debate. Thus, economic problems were handled, when they were recognised at all, by conventional Keynesian demand management, public sector investment and deflation. Successive government strategies of the 1960s and 70s were characterised by their critics as 'stop-go', as periods of buoyancy, expansion and (often) inflationary growth were followed by credit squeezes, cuts and the imposition of wages policies. In all of this, the working class stood by as observer, victim and occasional beneficiary! Where analysis, education and mobilisation would have promoted the essentially *activist* notion of the class as agency, Keynesian economic policy, punctuated by externally imposed restraint, prescribed *passivity* and impotence. The failure to construct a convincing and easily understood critique of orthodox Keynesianism from within working-class adult education (or at least for it), represented an enormous weakness for the class itself and the development of its own economic strategy.

Political choices, strategic decisions and practical economics are not matters of moment only in company boardrooms and government offices, but of direct concern to working-class citizens and their families. It is the task of working-class education to provide the information and concepts enabling men and women to engage effectively in current debates about the British economy and the future of society, rather than figuring as no more than a problematic element to be handled as government chooses. It should be seen as the key task to combat what has been a pervasive fatalism in some quarters, or at the least an assumption that there is no alternative to the liberation of 'market forces' while also imposing an authoritarian state machinery. In short, adult education needs to provide men and women with the confidence and understanding to offer their own version of what is and what might be.

Successful Interventions

To turn now to positive steps, it may be suggested that the launching in 1968 of the TUC Annual *Economic Review* was of signal importance. Although a publication employed for debate with politicians, in the mass media, or at union conferences, this has broached the task of improving the economic literacy and critical outlook of both trade unionists and the public at large. The standards of analysis have been high, the breadth impressive and presentation increasingly attractive. This has made an obvious contribution to education even if there has been limited success on the political front; this is also the case of a raft of similar, if more selective, publications by individual unions covering the economic and employment problems of their own members.

But what about elsewhere in working-class adult education? If economics can fairly be dubbed the 'dismal science', it has to be admitted that the kind of thorough-going educational political economy required to focus critical study on the issues only touched upon here, is virtually absent from the wider working-class adult education map. Political economy is underdeveloped in our educational system anyway, including the learned universities and schools of research. Ironically, it has been much more the organisations and institutions of the avowed political right, such as the Institute of Economic Affairs and the Adam Smith Institute, who have returned to a vigorous analysis of political economy during the last fifteen to twenty years.

Again, it would be wrong to assume that nothing at all has occurred to point working class adult education in the desired direction. To take but one example, in the early 1980s the GMBATU in the North-East of England co-operated with two academic researchers in their enquiry into the impact of big business in that part of the country in the wake of the huge run-down of the Northumberland and Durham coalfields. Their report, a discussion document presented to the union's region and entitled *Global Outpost*, is an outstanding example of well-researched, clearly written and challenging analysis.[20] In a limpid and extremely accessible style, the two researchers report the experiences of men and, especially, women in the recently transformed economy of the North East of England. Through the words and language of trade union members and officials, a vivid picture is presented of insecurity, uncertainty and increased exploitation. As the two authors point out, their findings underline the need for a searching review of regional policy, economic planning and trade union strategy. A notable feature of this example is that the researchers do not put themselves forward as substitutes for those individuals and groups they interview, nor do they set out to blur the distinction between their own intellectual and educational work on the one hand and political or trade union action on the other. Their contribution is to provide information, open up analysis and help to delineate the arena for debate. In this they provide both a first-class example of, and a huge challenge to, a working-class adult education which is seeking to provide a basis for understanding and responding to the changing social structure and class relations of late twentieth-century Britain.

Other initiatives have also sought to pursue a similar path. Thus, for example, the establishment of a new publication, *International Labour Reports* (ILR), in 1984 was concerned with providing documentation to trade union subscribers in several countries about comparative economic, political and labour conditions around the world. The latest development of this small but energetic group is to venture into the field of conference organisation and the preparation of teaching and study materials, thanks to a small grant from the EEC. In this work, the ILR staff are continuing the tradition of the valuable and informative Labour Research Department (LRD) which, for well over half a century, has provided detailed information on government policy and employment conditions to British trade unionists and other working-class organisations. Again, what is required is the systematic and widespread development of purpose-designed study materials and well organised arrangements for disciplined educational activity in connection with such useful publications.

Adult education courses are also well able to handle the difficult and complex issues of social and economic inequality about which information is regularly provided by the TUC, LRD, the Low Pay Unit and bodies like the Counter Information Services and Child Poverty Action Group. These are plainly of pressing concern to working-class men and women at the bottom end of the current distribution of income and wealth, to whose needs adult education must pay more attention. One successful instance was the class run by Coates and Silburn in Nottingham in the 1960s.[21] The students' work and publication of their findings made a vital contribution towards the 'rediscovery' of poverty in a Britain in which it was assumed that the combined effects of full employment, economic growth and wage increases had virtually eliminated the scourge that had wrecked working-class life in earlier times.

One somewhat unexpected consequence of industrial and economic change in contemporary Britain has been a growing public concern with the effects of science, the application of technology and the vulnerability of the environment. Traditionally, and perhaps understandably, working-class adult education has emphasised study of the humanities and, later, the social sciences. Natural science was avoided, and even thought inappropriate, with its apparent dependence upon cumulative technical knowledge and skills and its self-proclaimed adherence to absolutist canons of objectivity and law-governed processes. The reasons for this neglect need not detain us here, but include the adoption by working-class adult education of the intellectual programme of the academy as it came to be established in the late nineteenth and early twentieth centuries. The consequences, however, have been severely limiting for working class people and their industries, occupations and communities. Despite the fact that many men and women, by virtue of their jobs and vocational training, achieved high levels of technical competence and scientific application, this did not lead to an inclusion of science and technology on the agenda of adult education and debate. Working-class people were thus virtually appropriated into a science and technology that were both given as established facts and developing apparently according to their own logic, without the benefit of critical and reflective human intervention.

Fortunately, such passivity has been halted by a criticism launched from both within and without. From within the scientific community, distinguished individuals and groups of like-minded colleagues have questioned the methods, purpose and application of science. The traditions of individuals such as J.B.S. Haldane (who wrote a popular science column in the old *Daily Worker* until it was suppressed during the Second World War) have been continued by radical scientists in such organisations as the British Society for Social Responsibility in Science and the Radical Statistics Group. Public concern about issues as varied as acid rain, damage to the ozone layer, de-forestation and nuclear power has also called in question the remorseless march of science and technology. More recently, feminist analysis has suggested that many of the preoccupations of traditional science not only emphasise sexual violence in their metaphors of conquest and exploitation, but also subordinate themselves to the goals of profit and militarism, hidden behind the twin cloaks of questionable objectivity and selective focus.[22]

A science and technology *for* working people urgently requires not simply that more working-class men and, especially, women gain access to science courses and careers, but that science and technology become essential topics of study on the adult education agenda. Nor will this entail only being able to engage in informed philosophical discussion about the *consequences* of scientific application. It involves also the development of technical skills and knowhow in an array of disciplines which range from, for example, 'hands-on' ability with computers to the technology of fertility. The implications of a drive to establish science and technology firmly within the working-class adult education curriculum should be plain enough. If understanding and control are in part mediated through education, scientific knowledge and control over technology must lie increasingly at the centre of working-class adult education and this will require developing teaching skills, study materials and an appropriate methodology as well as drawing up stimulating and challenging curricula.

Changes have been charted in employment and economic organisation which have had their most immediate effect on domestic relations. The changing pattern of women's paid employment, higher levels of unemployment and early retirement, new consumer goods, the persistence of economic inequality and poverty have all contributed to changes in the family and household. But there has also been change as a consequence of technical and political developments and emerging from the heart of domestic relations themselves. A frequent common feature has been the position of women in the household – as daughters, sisters, wives and mothers, as well as the link between their domestic situation and their experiences at school, in the labour market, in sexual relations, and in their representation in the press, popular culture and advertising.

Mention has already been made of the changing position of women in employment, including the growth of jobs in white-collar work, in services and, especially, in part-time jobs. It is estimated that, by 1990 the ratio of part-time to full-time jobs in the economy as a whole will have increased from 1:5 in 1971 to 1:3.[23] Whilst women's pay still lags far behind that for men, part-time workers are especially vulnerable to low pay and poor working conditions. Women continue to experience discrimination in respect of training and promotion, are refused entry to 'male-only' careers (by a combination of socialisation and hostility) and are at risk from sexual harassment at work.[24] Trade union and adult education has begun to tackle some of these issues, both in women-only courses (where a main aim has been to raise the confidence and consciousness of women away from the potentially inhibiting presence of men), in mixed courses and, more rarely, in courses directed primarily at men.[25] Although beginning with a primary focus upon women and work and their position in trade unions, such educational activity has been obliged to extend the purview of its studies into a consideration of the wider situation of women in British society. The reciprocal influence of these wider social relations and the particular experience of work and the labour market are especially important with regard to women in the domestic sphere. Here, too, there have been important variations requiring careful analysis. The position of black women, from African, Caribbean and Asian backgrounds, cannot be assumed to be exactly the same as those from a white European background, even though their common gender produces aspects of similar experience and treatment.[26]

One immediately obvious link between employment and the domestic sphere is the contribution of low pay to the poverty of women and their households. Contrary to much received opinion, low pay remains a major element of dire poverty in our society and so it is more than mere coincidence that women (and their dependants) figure largely in statistics of both.[27] Thus, for example, one recent official estimate suggests that, out of just over 6 million workers earning low wages (two-thirds of mean manual earnings or *below* the supplementary benefit level) 4.5 million were women, half of them working on a part-time basis. Academic analysis has argued that these figures are probably underestimates of the problem and they are plainly proper topics for study and debate not only by adults but by all pupils and students in our educational system. It needs to be asked *how* and *why* such gross disparities of income come about, *whether* or not they require changing, *how* best that might be done and *what* would be the likely consequences of such an intervention. Similarly, information published by Peter Townsend and by the campaigning Child Poverty Action Group, underlines both the number of women (and their children) reliant upon social security and the sexist assumptions of their economic dependence upon men prevalent in social security legislation and administrative practice.[28] Here, too, there is much that adult education must make its subject matter.

Even where women are in paid work, there is little evidence of any diminution in the assumption by other household members that their unpaid domestic workload should continue. In their provision of food, cleaning, washing and ironing, care and comfort and sexual pleasure, women are most immediately involved in the reproduction of the population in general and of labour power in particular. One consequence of renewed feminist enquiry has been to reopen discussion about the experience, value and character of housework and domestic labour and, whilst some of this debate has been conducted in the more inaccessible tones of academic and Marxist scholarship, the issue figures with increasing prominence in adult education. In many respects, such topics have all the promise of good adult education practice. In particular, they provide ample opportunity for women (many of whom may not have engaged in such discussion before) to reflect upon and value their own experience as an important component of study. Exchange of different views and varying interpretations (as well as shared experiences) also enables the study to embrace new ideas and concepts, including an attempt to reach beyond the orthodox everyday explanations available in order to examine alternative theories and perspectives which seek to provide a systematic analysis of women's position in society. Of course, in such an educational journey, controversy and contention are bound to prosper and the impressively growing literature of empirical information, first-hand experience and theoretical enquiry is of invaluable use to adult students and their tutors in curriculum development and the organisation of course work.

The richness of this extending literature can hardly be exaggerated and feminist publishing initiatives have helped popularise ideas, information and topics of study that even two decades ago were largely hidden from view. One topic opened up for discussion has been the position of women and girls in the family, a primary locale of early socialisation and one in which female subordination is first reproduced and then continued into adulthood. The crude characterisation of 'typical' families and households beloved of advertisers and politicians alike, has been increasingly subject to scrutiny. Closer study reveals a plurality of family patterns in our society brought about by individual choices, a liberalisation of divorce laws and the usual toll of accident, ill health and misfortune. Recent statistics published by the Equal Opportunities Commission (EOC) indicate that there are now just short of 1 million one-parent families in Britain and that the number has been slowly increasing over recent years; of these, 89 per cent are headed by women.[29]

For women (as indeed for all adult students) with dependent

children part of the opportunity to engage in study depends not only upon available and accessible courses, but also some kind of provision for children, including creches and child care, which are still the exception rather than the rule. Good quality child care is expensive and difficult to organise and, whilst such arrangements are growing, they are often of a very limited nature and depend heavily upon voluntary support. Nor is the experience automatically edifying for parent and child, and more imagination and finance needs to be given to the provision of enjoyable facilities to the children of adult-education students.[30]

The expansion of women's studies in adult education has paralleled the increasing number of studies of women in the published literature.[31] Biographical accounts, historical recovery and reinterpretation and comparative analyses abound. This has also been reflected in institutional developments. Thus, in the WEA, a new twice-yearly journal has been established, entitled the *Women's Studies Newsletter*, giving publicity to courses, conferences and events. It acts as a point of contact for women students and tutors, provides a lively arena for debate on the principles, content and methods of women's education and includes both reviews and short articles on relevant new developments. The WEA has also launched a series of pamphlets, *Breaking our Silence*, in which women's adult education practices are examined. Special training packs for tutors have been prepared and an active Women's Educational Advisory Committee oversees the Association's work in women's education.

Similar initiatives are evident in part of the LEA system and, especially in the buoyant voluntary sector where women's organisations make up the majority of the recently formed Voluntary Adult Education Forum (VAEF). VAEF's own first educational venture was a conference on One Parent Families, reflecting the importance of this topic for specialist large-scale women's organisations such as the Women's Institute, Townswomen's Guild, the Co-operative Women's Guild, as well as for others, including the Pre-School Playgroups Association, churches and community groups. Independent initiatives by groups of women in a wide range of locations, for example in resource and information centres and in libraries, in rape crisis groups and in counselling services, have also provided the space, opportunity and facilities for women to meet, discuss, research and study. These activities continue a vital tradition, begun by working-class autodidactics, of informal and non-institutional learning and enquiry. Some groups, of course, may additionally draw upon the adult education provision of the LEAs or WEA; rape crisis groups have used the Northern College's residential facilities to undertake systematic study of the history of sexuality and state policy in respect of women. In addition, some individual women, first given the support and inspiration for reflection and debate in such groups, go on to enrol in one or another parts of the adult education system.

It is impossible in a limited space to do justice to the impressive diversity of courses for and about women which have been established over the past fifteen years, but as well as including the widespread and pioneering programmes of New Opportunities for Women, they also extend to specialist studies of images of women, drawing on developments in media and cultural analysis of sexual stereotyping, linguistic construction and encoding, the technology and ideology of mass communications and the representation of women in literature and films.[32] Courses also address themselves to matters of health and illness, the food industry and diet and women's position in the labour market, including the provision of purposely-designed courses offering women the chance to study technology, computerisation and science.[33] In addition, women also figure in large numbers in the enormous proliferation of 'open access' courses providing preparatory study and familiarisation with study methods for those adults seeking admission to further and higher education without conventional academic qualifications. Open College federations and networks have taken this initiative further and, as part of their work, have sought to introduce systematic recognition of experiential learning into course and individual assessment procedures.[34]

Indirectly, the women's movement has also made its contribution to educational method. Although discussion-based learning has long featured in good adult education practice, the women's movement's emphasis upon the value of relatively instructured groups, free from the constraint of hierarchy and excessive formality have been important. This has provided a further impetus to the importance of building up confidence, engaging students in the development of the curriculum and expanding adults' capacity for both autonomy and participation in democracy. All of this, of course, presents a huge challenge to adult education tutors and underlines the relative absence of a rigorous adult education pedagogy (or androgy, as specialists call it) or even, more modestly, adequate staff development opportunities.

Not, of course, that all adult-education initiatives emerge from the world of the professionals, nor are all necessarily expressed through the formal panoply of courses, tutors and official curricula; far from it. One of the most exciting areas of growth in recent adult education for working-class women has arisen directly from their involvement in the 1984-85 miners' strike. The activities of women in mining communities and in support groups, women against pit closures and miners' wives' groups, has continued in some localities, sometimes with the support of the men, sometimes in the face of their indifference or opposition. Such groups have been supported by LEA's, by the WEA and, in South Yorkshire, by the Northern College. Amongst the wide range of studies these women have selected, one of the most innovative and prolific has been the writers' workshop. Meeting over a period of weeks and months, occasionally going into a short period of residential study, groups of women have produced collections of short stories, individual autobiographies, anthologies of poetry and accounts of their own communities. Many of these have taken the strike and the women's involvement in it as their focus, others have sketched a broader picture of the history, organisation and character of their particular community.[35] Creative writing provides for these women a tangible opportunity for self-expression and emancipation. Through the activities of the writers' workshops, experiences can be shared and explored and a self-awareness heightened by the discipline of literary composition and the careful choice of words. As a practical example of restoring confidence and recognising the pleasure and enthusiasm to be obtained from systematic adult education, the writers' workshop can scarcely be bettered.

This brief review of some of the shifts and changes occurring in women's lives and on the domestic front cannot be concluded until some reference has been made to other developments. Amongst its many useful tasks, adult education has always provided a valuable opportunity for working-class men and women to understand better the experiences of their children. Notions of childhood and adolescence change as much as other social relations, none more so than in the world of education where children and young people spend so much of their early life. Changes in organisation, teaching methods, topics of study and systems of assessment, have been legion in education since the Second World War. Unless adult education takes it upon itself to provide understanding of those changes and the confidence to question and challenge those developments, working-class parents will be as powerless to influence their children's educational experience as their parents were to affect their own schooling. Puzzlement and confusion, to say nothing of a frequent deference to the teacher, remains a common working-class response to the educational system. Providing a corrective to this unsatisfactory state of affairs remains one of the many virtually uncharted challenges for contemporary working-class adult education. Here and there, admittedly, a start has been made, not only with specialist courses provided for parents but also, in some places, an opportunity to go into schools and colleges to see at first-hand their children's education in practice. Such isolated examples stand in stark contrast to the ritual of parental nail-biting and queuing to hear cursory teachers' reports and reviews of children's work that remain the stock-in-trade of open evenings and school visits.

Finally, in this section, a further short note needs to be added about the changing age profile of our population. Each year, the number of people of pensionable age in Britain is increasing: over the next fifty years alone, the projection is that the ratio of those of pensionable age to each 1,000 working will increase from 296.3 to 419.7.[36] Here is a reserve of talent, time and opportunity which adult education must avail itself of. Reference has already been made to the University of the Third Age and the provision that residential colleges such as the Northern College can make. Adult education is not something which terminates with retirement from paid work or the diminution of responsibilities for children. Enjoyment, under-standing and (perhaps, above all) the knowledge to maintain healthy independence and self-respect, can all be gained from a substantial expansion of adult education provision for older men and women in our society.

Competing Approaches

There have been a number of milestones in the analysis of the related spheres of culture and ideology which have an immediate bearing on working-class education, some erected by those directly concerned themselves with working-class education. A review of these leads on to the whole question of community structure and varied approaches to community education which deserve careful consideration.

Of particular importance here was the publication of Richard Hoggart's *The Uses of Literacy* and the two seminal books by Raymond Williams, *Culture and Society* and *The Long Revolution*.[37] Hoggart's book was especially concerned to examine the extent of cultural change amongst the 'working classes' in the urban north of England, born and brought up from the 1920s and 30s onwards and coming to adulthood in Britain after the Second World War. Its approach was to examine language and manners of speaking, changes in dress and the 'thousands of other items from daily experience [which] help to distinguish this recognisably working-class life', including, of course, division of rank, status, attitude and behaviour within the class.[38] Although later critics were to reject some of Hoggart's categories and to impugn the alleged romanticism of his perspective, this innovatory account opened up a whole new field of study, with its broad approach to the diversity of working-class oral traditions, the impact of the mass media, changing leisure pursuits and sport, responses to advertising and consumption, attitudes to religion and fatalism and the contemporary culture of youth.

Of particular interest for this review, was Hoggart's concern throughout his book in what he called the 'earnest minority' of working-class people who, through trade unionism and working-class adult education, occupied positions of influence within the class. Through disciplined study and rigorous enquiry, they would be able critically to comprehend the palliatives of new mass art and consumption of post-war Britain and the lives of the 'candy-floss world' proffered enticingly to British workers and their families. Whilst it is plainly vital for this earnest minority to be at least maintained, the real challenge for working-class adult education (and for other working-class institutions) is systematically and relentlessly to widen the circle of men and women so involved. Simultaneously, this should strengthen their collective chances of changing the aims, focus, analysis and programmes for action in and through that education.

More explicitly concerned to counteract the conservatism and exclusiveness of the traditions of Arnold, Leavis and Eliot, the impressive scholarship of Williams also envisaged a key part of its project as understanding the role of culture and communication in the making and transformation of British society. Begun in this involvement in the radical journal *Politics and Letters* and brought to fruition in *Culture and Society*, this demanding task was carried forward most clearly in *The Long Revolution* and given a more restricted focus in subsequent work on communications, television and in his influential and imaginative *Key Words*.[39] Again, it should not escape notice that Williams's own background was in adult education and the concerns and topics of the two early path-breaking publications arose directly out of his adult-education courses.

The same was true of that other monumental example of intellectual and historical recovery of the time, Edward Thompson's unsurpassed *Making of the English Working Class*.[40] Indeed

Thompson pays a special tribute to the members of his tutorial class from whom, he says, he 'learned a great deal' and with whom (as he writes in his introduction) he discussed 'many of the themes treated' in his path-making book. The close interest of Williams and Thompson in the components of culture and in its complex historical relationship with class arose principally out of their own theoretical and political predispositions. But no doubt it was influenced and perhaps even formulated in the process of teaching (and learning from) working-class students, with their own specific experiences of working-class life. If such students were to grasp the changing character of British society in its creative and dynamic essentials, a sound understanding of the part played by culture in all its forms was inescapable. Moreover such an approach to the study of class – as evidenced by both these authors – was a key premiss in rescuing the concept from a threatening rigidity and barreness, at that time dominant, in which historical relationships, experiences and concepts were mechanically subordinated to overwhelmingly determinate structures and crude categorisation. It may be that it was the actual experience of working-class education which itself led to a new and welcome flexibility in interpretation and understanding.

British culture or, more accurately, cultures were themselves changing rapidly in the period under review and these changes are providing important topics of study amongst adult educators and working class adult students. Changing leisure habits, especially the decline in popularity of mass spectator pursuits, such as going to football or the cinema, and the rise of television, are obvious features of our period. The arrival of migrant workers from the West Indies, Asia and Africa, drew attention not only to their own cultural traditions and behaviour, but also to entrenched racism and assumptions of white supremacy in British, including some working-class, cultural forms. For black working-class students, a 'recovery' of their own history and analysis of the global relations of colonialism and migration, have been an important part of strengthening their own sense of position and their continuing struggle against oppression.

Technological innovation, cheapened production and the impact of new marketing techniques and fashion, were also important aspects of the changes in post-war British society. Following the influential work of Hoggart, Williams and Thompson, there developed the almost wholly new intellectual terrain of cultural analysis, including the founding and opening of the Birmingham Centre for Contemporary Cultural Studies. Unfortunately, some of the authors writing about this aspect of social life have presented their ideas in an obscure and mystifying language absent from the founding texts. This unhelpful complexity acts as a barrier to adult students seeking an understanding of significant areas of contemporary experience. This is all the more regrettable in that the alternatives available to such students appear to be either an unreflective absorption into (even celebration of) those experiences or else a crude characterisation of them as nothing other than the distortions of 'bourgeois' ideology. It is precisely this latter perspective which hinders thorough and thoughtful adult education practice and to which the approach being advocated here is opposed.

Fortunately, again there are exceptions to these difficulties. In the important area of popular culture, for example, Frith's exploration of the phenomena of pop and rock music is especially rewarding.[41] Nobody can doubt the significance of contemporary popular music in our society: it relates closely to the tape and record industry, to aspects of radio and television, to notions of dress and sexuality and to the character of enjoyment and experience. Here again, it is seductive simply to assimilate popular music as creativity or experience into music as product and commodity in the capitalist market. Even self-consciously non-commercial movements, such as 'punk' music in the mid-1970s, are rapidly absorbed and exploited by the popular music industry. But, as Frith eloquently indicates, such processes by no means exhaust the significance of popular music. Its meanings and experiences cannot simply be deducted from its immediate commodity form. The same is true for other aspects of popular culture and valuable work has been undertaken on such diverse topics as television 'soap operas', Hollywood film stars, popular magazines, television news production and voluntary groups, such as the Scouts and mass women's organisations.[42]

The value of this work should be self-evident for working-class education: the people have been, and continue to be, involved with precisely these cultural forms in their everyday life. Critical reflection upon these experiences, including both their pleasures and their frustrations, is not only an essential part of their studies but also a valuable educational starting point. The approach is not without its pitfalls, especially given the twin dangers of a dismissive denial of any merit in serious study on the one hand and the trite characterisation of culture as 'capitalism pure and simple' on the other. Nowhere is this more evident than in the key area of media studies. In common with all other areas of adult education, it requires serious application, sustained hard work and the development of particular study skills if it is not to fall into the traps outlined above. Through the study of the media of television, radio, film and newspapers, students are able to grasp the complex inter-relationship of technology, composition, technique, organisation, ideology, market, form, content and meaning. What appears on the screen or in the newspaper and the manner in which it is viewed or read requires sophisticated analysis and systematic study. Moreover, these media of communication also offer exciting opportunities for creativity and innovation, especially as technical change and lower costs bring them more within the reach of working-class men and women and their organisations.[43]

An important component of working-class adult education in the media is the opportunity for demystification opened up by systematic study. Thus, seeing at first-hand how video programmes are constructed can have great educational value, from initial idea through the preparation of scripts and the arrangements of shooting up to final editing and presentation. The aim here is not to *substitute* video production in an adult education setting for that carried out in the institutions of public broadcasting or in professional studios. 'Hands on' experience, together with analytical and conceptual critique, is oriented towards generating understanding and the ability of students to comprehend and criticise the programmes heard and viewed by British people each day of their lives. In this connection, the TUC and a number of individual trade unions (notably those in television), have produced extremely valuable publications and educational materials for use in trade union education.[44] It is in this particular way that a sense of independence and autonomy can be fostered probably more so than in the somewhat romantic idea that everybody can be their own director and producer.

Of course, as with many other elements of culture, video, newspapers, photography and radio can be used as method and resource in adult education as well as topic for study. The Open University has pioneered work of this kind in Britain and, although difficulties of isolation and excessive academicism are sometimes associated with the educational initiatives of the Open University, it provides many examples of imaginative practice that may be drawn on by adult education. Sadly, of course, recruitment to Open University courses has not demonstrated the anticipated expansion of working-class students. But, as far as can be ascertained, this appears to be less to do with the use of television as such than with wider questions of class experience and responses to education.[45]

If the concept of culture is an essentially elusive and contested one, then that of 'community' is positively treacherous. However, like so many dangerous and forbidden areas of life, it has proved an extremely attractive and useful notion for intellectuals, activists and politicians alike and figures prominently in approaches to adult education. Very often, of course, the idea of community integrated with the other dimensions of society already touched upon, such as the labour market, or aspects of the economy, in connection with family and household and in relation to culture. As an ideal, 'community' has served as a rallying cry for conservatives as well as socialists, for radicals as much as traditionalists. At its best, the term implies all that is most positive in the idea of the social mutuality, reciprocity, solidarity, understanding and common interests. At its worst, it may represent prejudice, hostility to outsiders, reaction, insularity and suffocation of individual initiative and change.

It is with such contradictions clearly in the mind that the notion of community is valuable to a working-class adult education committed to exploring changes in British society and class relations. It is particularly in the representations of themselves and others that British and non-British people have deployed by reference to talk of community. Thus, one of the most pernicious but revealing uses of the notion has been in the expression of white hostility to black migrants and their offspring. Egged on by certain politicians and confirmed in their racist prejudices by so many cultural trappings in our society, some white people have ensured that black people have suffered verbal and physical attacks because of their supposed threat to the integrity and essentialness of the white community. At its most extreme, of course, such opposition finds its legitimacy and opportunities for mobilisation in political groups such as the National Front or British Movement, who also seek recruits from amongst the working class, especially young people. More insidiously, it is expressed in a myriad of everyday experiences for black men and women and their children. From housing and employment to jokes and sexual imagery, from educational experience to portrayal in the media, racism and racial hostility daily manifest themselves to black and ethnic minorities in our society and often go quite unnoticed by whites. This narrow and exclusive notion of community is plainly a challenge to any broader notions of citizenship or a genuinely plural society. As such, it is a critical topic for all adult students, not simply for those black people who make an explicit concern with the history and practice of racism a feature of their studies.

Drawing on the notion of community from a different angle, men and women of Caribbean, African, Asian and southern European origin have also deployed the concept of community, as both description of their situation in British society or as a line of defence and identity. Thus, for example, Sivanandan makes use of the concept of the black community in his review of Asian and Afro-Caribbean struggles in Britain.[46] Attracted and often directly recruited to this country in response to either labour shortage or the now much diluted notion of Commonwealth citizenship, black migrants were disproportionately represented in a limited number of occupations: general labouring, textiles, clothing manufacture, engineering and professional work (particularly medicine). Lack of choice, white hostility and an understandable desire to live with friends and relatives, brought many black workers together into particular localities and areas of housing.[47] These became communities not simply by virtue of propinquity but also because of the richness and diversity of the cultural, social and economic life created by black people themselves. One aspect of that cultural innovation has been the establishment of black study and community centres, providing opportunities for black men and women to engage in adult education work. Part of that work has entailed a recovery and celebration of history akin to that undertaken by adult students in social and labour history classes over the past eighty years. One aspect of the exploration has entailed an examination of the consequences of imperialism and colonisation for the black experience. Not that this means that the analysis of race and racism can be simply reduced to another dimension of class structure, but neither can their intimate connection to capital accumulation and the politics of the capitalist state be ignored either.[48] As in so many areas of the changing composition of British society, it is precisely in the need to explore competing theories and perspectives that the challenge to working-class adult education resides, for white students as well as for black.

Change in the community and its implications for working-class men and women has also figured in relation to the employment, economic, domestic and cultural shifts already outlined above. For example, the pit closure programme in the British coal industry has brought enormous changes in many of the coalfields and, during the miners' strike of 1984-85, the defence of mining communities and their own ways of life became an important feature of the fight against the policies of the (then) National Coal Board and the Conservative government. Coal mining has often been portrayed as one of the archetypal proletarian communities in Britain, as in other countries. Along with fishing, dock work, shipbuilding, railways and the printing industries, such geographical and occupational communities are said to manifest a common cluster of identifiable characteristics in which working life spills over into family, leisure, sexuality and politics. These concern not simply the dominance of heavy, manual labour, but virility, awkward independence, heavy drinking, strong trade union organisation, militancy and a sense of solidarity and mutuality. Needless to say, such crude characterisation requires careful modification according to the individual circumstances of the life and organisation of particular communities. Even so, in so far as certain traditions of working-class community have been associated with particular identities, sexual divisions and character formation, their decline and persistence provide a poignant terrain for exploration, self-discovery, challenge and potential liberation. The link with women's experience in the miners' strike is just one example.

Even if the circumstances in which people exist cannot be said to be entirely subject to their own wills and influence, it remains true that the particular manner in which they make their own history requires respectful investigation. In this process, working-class education, especially perhaps that devoted to the recovery and exploration of people's own history, can provide a powerful sense of place and an evocative vocabulary of identity. Working-class autobiography, oral history and the history workshop tradition are all aspects of this work. The Ruskin College inspired *History Workshop* seminars and publications lie in this impressive tradition, as do WEA local history courses and especially also independent, community-based publishing ventures, based on working-class writers groups, and involving women, gays, blacks and others normally denied access to publishing facilities.

Such groups have mushroomed over the last ten years and more, many being linked together in the Federation of Worker Writers and Community Publishers. Organisations such as Centerprise in London, Gatehouse and Common Word in Manchester, the Yorkshire Arts Circus and many others provide a base and a committed group of full-timers who have been extraordinarily effective in promoting such activities and in facilitating eventual publication of many books and magazines, both on a local and a national basis. Financed often by local authorities (or groups of authorities), sometimes gaining support from the Urban Aid Programme and regional Arts organisations (Greater London Arts, North West Arts, Yorkshire Arts, etc.), these provide premises, facilities and above all a base from which self-organised writers groups can gain assistance, encouragement and support. Some of these, like Gatehouse in Manchester, are concerned primarily with adult basic education – their workshops and publications derive from assistance towards literacy through publication. Others focus on local history, poetry, short stories and reminiscences. Much has been published. The extent to which such groups now exist across the country is not known; but that there has been a great expansion in this area is certain.

Such activities are a central aspect of adult education and the raising of consciousness, and hold considerable hope for the future. There can be no doubt that the destiny of life in our inner cities presents one of the greatest challenges to adult education. The apparent despoilment, vandalism, violence and drug abuse endemic in certain areas of our country require both satisfactory analysis and a positive response. In the best traditions of working-class education it is undesirable that enquiry and solutions are imposed from the outside by experts or those in authority. Unfortunately, the track record of working-class adult education in this feature of contemporary society is limited. Why this should be the case may be far easier to explain than the problems themselves; lack of resources, an absence of systematic information and the dominant preoccupations of adult education all contribute to the relative absence of study in this area. Where exceptions do occur, as in the imaginative and energetic alternative plans for London's docklands, or in the painstaking work of tenants' associations and community groups, the results can be impressive.[49]

Community education often sets out to include such topics within its purview, especially where collaborative activity is established alongside specialist organisations such as NACRO, the NSPCC, Age Concern, Shelter and the Child Poverty Action Group. All of these bodies produce information packs and educational materials, principally for their own members and campaigns. Here and there these are used as resources for adult education and, on occasion, joint ventures have been undertaken with the WEA, LEA adult education classes and even individual trade unions. Thus the National Union of Public Employees has launched a Community Education project in Scotland, to add to its expansion of educational work not only in more conventional areas of trade unionism but in respect of peace and disarmament and anti-racism.

In this country, as in the United States of America, there was an enormous expansion of community organisation and of so-called 'community activists' during the 1960s and early 1970s. In part, this was a response to the failure of statutory authorities to respond to the growing crisis of exploitation and decay which was gripping older inner cities. In part, it grew out of government- and local authority-sponsored community development projects in areas of economic change and social deprivation.[50] In some areas, not surprisingly, new forms of community action by both paid workers and local people extended to embrace adult educational activity and attempts were made to articulate a distinctive adult-education philosophy, or rather perspective, reflecting the assumptions, methods and preoccupations of this development.[51] Rejecting traditional liberal formulations of the tasks of education (allegedly trapped in its own 'opinionated moral exhortation') the radical approach advocated drew parallels with the work of the Antigonish Movement in Canada in the 1920s and the Highlander Folk School established in Tennessee in the 1930s. The development of this radical approach to adult education was closely related to new forms of community work and local intervention, often under the umbrella of local and national state finance and organisation. In adult education as in social work and political analysis, the ideas of the radicals provoked intense debate, not least amongst professionals. Thus in Liverpool and Northern Ireland, practices and philosophies were elaborated hand in hand.[52]

From the point of view of adult education, an additional impetus was given by the then contemporary popularity of the ideas of Illich on 'deschooling' and, especially, Freire, on the relationship between education and liberation. Drawing on these radical philosophies of knowledge and pedagogy on the one hand and a robust conception of exploitation and oppression on the other, this new and engaged practice of community adult education represented one of the most stimulating developments in working class adult education for a generation. But, like all movements and burning enthusiasms, the new perspective also abounded in hyperbole and excess. There was a tendency in some quarters to give more emphasis to the importance of collectivity, group and community than had been customary in conventional adult education's tradition of individual achievement and an inclination to dismiss the virtues of individual educational attainment and preoccupation (sometimes, it has to be said, advocated by those who were themselves precisely the product of individual activity). These new prophets of collective advance were also initially sceptical of the possibilities of reform and amelioration within the present system, although this view was modified subsequently by more considered and sophisticated analysis, especially in respect of the contradictory locations of those who were both 'in' and 'against' the state.[53]

Amongst the wide range of new approaches to working-class community education which emerged (and which are still to be found in practice), four deserve particular comment. Each has its own limitations as a way forward for working class adult education. Firstly there were those who, drawing enthusiastically and often uncritically upon the literature and policy initiatives of the United States, saw in community development and its associated educational practice an opportunity for the poor, the 'deprived' and the dispossessed to begin to reclaim their territory and reverse the drive towards local impoverishment and state centralisation. These developments, it was suggested, owed little to capitalist social relations, still less the consequences of class strategy by employers and state institutions, and were to be seen widely in Western society.[54] Changing relations within communities, improving links between the home and the school and local initiatives, it was felt, all offered some hope for the future. It was easy to criticise and even pillory this approach, to condemn its reformism and naïvety and this was undertaken with some vigour from the outset.

The second approach to community education was based upon a sustained critique of the first, and went on to elaborate a distinctive project for working class adult education. Beginning with a view that the first perspective on community development outlined above 'should not, in fact, be taken seriously' the task in hand was to evaluate how adult education might gain through an association with what were termed programmes of 'local social action'.

This would entail a threefold change of direction:

> internal institutional and professional reform; the establishment of new types of relations with working class activists; [and] the development of means by which social consciousness and awareness can become an explicit feature of an adult education programme.[55]

Just as this second approach held out interesting, and even exciting possibilities, so it was also, from a strictly, educational and intellectual point of view, unexceptional and unobjectionable. This was to be no easy alternative to the commitment to, and demands of, thorough study and rigorous analysis. Some of the dangers of the second approach to community education were signalled by the advocates early on, especially the dilution of educational objectives by calling any community activity 'education' or the insidious 'encapsulation' by adult education of independent social, recreational or political activity by terming these 'informal adult education' or 'learning by doing'.

The approach did not necessarily even entail any 'explicit intention to engage in local social action' by adult educators themselves. But, even so, therein lay potentially the severest threat and the most alluring danger. In its concern with the development of social consciousness and the process of 'conscientisation' (horrible word!), an unwitting trap was laid for the incautious, the undiscerning and the enthusiastic disciples of the new creed. Where skilled and highly professional adult educators could continue to draw the line between education and political action, between understanding and intervention, between class analysis and involvement in class struggle, others simply overlooked the distinctions or denied their validity. Of course, adult educators in common with other members of society have every right, as citizens and political persons, to emphasise the second aspect of each of these couplets and even to do so on the basis of their insights gained from adult educational work. But that is not the same as merging the two into one, and even worse, effectively submerging the discipline and outlook of education in the expressions of political ideology and the preoccupations of political practice.

This last characterised and gave rise to the third approach to working-class community adult education, in which the respective responsibilities and contributions of the adult educator and political activist were to be understood as merely a kind of explicitly political division of labour. A minority approach, it was both a snare and an illusion. It snared both educator and 'student' (despite the valuable criticism of the inappropriateness of the latter term, laden with misleading assumptions and conventions, no satisfactory substitute has yet been agreed upon in adult education). It was an illusion in supposing that education could equate with, let alone substitute for, wider class activity, in which the organisations of the working class alone could undertake the kind of political activity envisaged. It was an error to blur so crudely the distinction between politics and education and it was deceptive to give credence to the view that working class men and women could take critical decisions about themselves, their families and communities simply on the basis of educational enthusiasm and insight alone.[56]

This third, over-politicised approach, also purported to give the adult tutor the grounds for legitimate intervention in an area in which that person had no particular political competence, at the same time as denying the value of a distinction between 'tutor' and 'student'. Thus the virtue of a genuine discussion and negotiation of the curriculum could be simply subordinated to the demands of the participants, irrespective of the difficulties involved, including the unavailability of satisfactory educational materials and methods to deal with the topic in hand, or the unreadiness of the participants immediately to tackle the issues. My objection to such an approach is certainly *not* a matter of suggesting that adult educators 'know better' than others what is important in society or even what should be studied or that working class adult education should preach some phoney neutrality. However, it is an affirmation of the skills, professionalism and responsibilities of adult educators which are still clearly recognised in the second approach, even if the ambiguities and nuances of some it advocates' analyses always opened up the possibility of such an unfortunate distortion. What supporters and theoreticians of the second approach were calling for required poise, control and considerable restraint. In the event, while some held tenaciously to the high wire, others toppled off, jumped with enthusiasm or simply preferred the deceptively solid ground of unadulterated community intervention.

The fourth approach also grew out of, and eventually distorted, an admirable and well established feature of good adult education practice. This rightly shows that adult education cannot be an imposition upon men and women entering tentatively into the daunting world of study and learning. Still less can it be a quantum leap into otherwise defendable and quite properly more refined and sophisticated areas of knowledge and enquiry. Good and successful practice begins 'where students are'; it validates and takes seriously their own lives, perspectives and experiences and builds upon their preoccupations and concerns. But it does not stop there: it is not the validity of empirical fact or truth that adult education legitimates, but the authenticity of experience as real, diversity as valuable and everyday life as worthy of debate. Taken to absurdity, the perspective that effectively accepts that experience is all, not only implies what may be termed an excessively *idealist* perspective upon the world, in which images, definitions and experiences are everything, but must also be prepared to tolerate the silly assertion that a ball is square or that black is white. One is reminded not only of Polonius imagining he is humouring the fevered young Hamlet in describing a cloud variously as a camel, weasel or whale, but also of Orwellian double-speak. In any case, exactly *whose* images, definitions and experiences are to count? As the great American sociologist C. Wright Mills memorably remarked, is it not surprising that 'the expectations of some men seem a little more urgent than those of anyone else?' He answered his own irony directly: it is because they have more power, and it is this relationship exactly that adult education needs rigorously to explore. As both Schwartz and Hall have convincingly argued, naïve libertarianism in which student experience alone predominates runs the risk merely of reproducing a subordinate and corporate culture: 'We have to work with but also work *as* experience. We need to bring something to bear on experience. We need to be able to deal with it critically.'[57]

Some advocates of this fourth, purely experiential, approach attempt to move beyond this initial position by sleight of hand and on the basis of assumption. Beginning with experience, they believe that sooner or later (or sooner *better* than later?) any rational human being will reach the awareness and consciousness of their position which has already been revealed to the educator! In this approach the job of education as revelation is not so much a journey of exploration and discovery but more an organised trip to the truth! Nothing could be more damaging to the promise of adult education: no perspective could more clearly sell the pass of the challenge it faces in contemporary Britain.

This analysis of tendencies within community education in the recent past is intended to clarify, by an evaluation of different developments and standpoints, what is to be avoided and what to be supported in the years ahead. One lesson may be that the greatest rewards may be derived from the encouragement of deep-seated tendencies already existing which build on the sharpening aspirations of ordinary people, perhaps especially of those largely excluded, by virtue of poverty, race, gender, from access to the essential means to self-expression, and so to a heightened consciousness. The work of the community publishing projects such as Centerprise, Gatehouse and others gives an idea as to how development from the bottom up may have immense value. One objective must be the strengthening of the whole complex of networks comprising adult education in its widest sense; recognition of its scope and potential, and a clear perspective for the future.

Changes in the 1980s

The conflicts of the past forty years, particularly those of the last decade, reflect each of the aspects of changing class relations referred to in this discussion and which arise in the course of educational activity. The changing pattern of industrial conflict since the Second World War is related to modifications in industrial organisation, the structure of the labour market and economic organisation.

Conflicts of attrition are more common today in industry than a decade ago, despair and bitterness more evident, divisions more obvious and state power more readily deployed against workers and their supporters. The combined use of police, the courts, social security provision and political condemnation of the striking miners and the NUM is simply the most obvious and widely commented upon aspect of what Gamble calls the 'strong state' in evidence in contemporary Britain. Similarly, it was precisely in the miners' dispute that the complex relationship between industrial conflict and political confrontation, between work and community, men and women, notions of action and support were revealed. This is not simply a fascinating topic for adult-education enquiry and debate as *object*, but more poignantly, involves people who as *subject* constitute an energetic and valuable element of working-class education and history. Their oral testimony is not simply a rather quaint and colourful resource to enliven historical accounts, *through* adult education it can become a powerful testimony of meaning and an expression of human agency in the processes of social change.

If industrial conflict in the 1980s in some senses represents what has been called the 'downturn', then both the 1960s and 70s amounted broadly to the vigorous manifestation of workers' opposition and demands in certain key industries. First was the unofficial, rank-and-file, fragmented and informal militancy at shopfloor and factory levels in the 1960s and early 1970s, so often studied and commented upon by academic researchers and official enquiries alike. Secondly, came the national, official and often innovatory disputes of the public sector, especially the public services. Beginning in the very early 1970s before shopfloor militancy in engineering, docks and mining had significantly reduced (although even here the pace varied), these disputes often turned on the imposition of incomes policy upon public sector workers. The conflicts embraced a clearly political dimension in that limited regard at least, as well as spilling over into the more self-evidently political arenas of private health care, energy policy, the so-called social wage, public expenditure, privatisation and offensive against state and public employment as such which increasingly became a feature of disputes throughout the 1970s. At the very least, working-class adult education has the task here of exploring whether these experiences were false leads or lost opportunities. They are not simply academic or empirical accounts.

Whilst it would be a nonsense to deny the sectional interests and practical concerns expressed by the workers immediately involved in these conflicts, from an analytical and educational point of view it would be equally short-sighted to overlook their wider implications. Sometimes these were more manifest, as in the defence of the National Health Service, attempts to resist privatisation in telecommunications or in the struggles of the miners to resist pit closures and to restore coal to its key role in both energy policy and the economy. Elsewhere, the wider issues were more latent, but none the less significant, in the critique mounted from left and right alike (in different ways and with contrasting objectives) against nationalisation, public bureaucracy, 'statism' corporatism and rigid insensitivity. Whether manifest or latent, these matters contained within them more or less well worked out conceptions of what should constitute a desirable moral as well as political economy in our society and should be the very stuff of searching and critically informed adult education study and critical public discussion. This is, in part, precisely the promise of an education for emancipation alluded to at the beginning of this chapter.

Responses from those in authority to industrial conflict also carry clear views of society. On the one hand there came in the 1970s the growing cries of chaos and disorder from those who discerned a seamless web of social breakdown running from strikes and sit-ins to street crime and international terrorism in Britain.[58] For some, this required moral regeneration; for others it called for the planning of quasi-militaristic, low intensity operations, the strengthening of the hands of the police and the introduction of draconian laws and tough custodial sentencing. On the other hand, of course, there has been the view, expressed in no less urgent tones, that the levels and diversity of conflict in our society, distressing though they may be to individuals and groups directly involved, signal the passing of an old order and the creation of new ways. Not surprisingly, the nature of such a supposed emergent society is again in dispute. For example, some see in the epic miners' strike a tragic confrontation of Grecian dimensions that was the death-knell of a peculiar tradition of heroic proletarian struggle.[59] Others perceive a threatening shadow of neo-fascism and a widening and embattled state of siege in society, as state force, private security and a virtual war of all against all offers the frightened individual cold comfort in isolation. Yet again, some see in the conflicts and confrontations recognition of deep-rooted social problems and the opportunity for their resolution in the creation of a more progressive, humane and genuinely open society. The roads open, then, might be just as much to freedom as to serfdom, to a new dawn of enlightenment as much as to darkness and despair. Of course, precisely which, if any, of the possible routes actually becomes the way forward for the British working class, is not just a matter of Hobson's choice, nor should the march to date necessarily be assumed to have been either uniformly forward or prematurely halted.[60] The point of all of this is that industrial conflict presents working-class adult students with a key opportunity for study and reflection rather than (otherwise somewhat craven) celebration. Evaluation of the origins, meaning and responses to these disputes provides insights into not only the working of contemporary society but also the possibility of alternatives.

If the study of these often perplexing shifts and balances in Britain is precisely the proper arena for rational debate and enquiring review in adult education, then research, education and reflection are plainly to be preferred to assumption, propaganda and prejudice. As one of the earlier sections on culture and ideology briefly implied, the public representation and interpretation of these shifts is itself a key component of them, and also requires rigorous review. Nowhere is this truer than in two of the more explosive and seemingly threatening arenas of social conflict – Northern Ireland and what have been dubbed the 'riots' of inner-city protest and violent confrontation.

Responses to the Irish question in English culture are deeply overlaid with a history of plantation, occupation, religious bigotry, lampooning and ridicule. Despite conditions, on occasion, of near civil war, visible and strong army occupation, changes in judicial processes in the province, tragic levels of apparently sectarian murder and the segregation of some areas of housing and employment along religious lines, adult education's neglect contributes to English ignorance of, and even contempt for, the intricacies, suffering and possible futures for the people of Ulster. Yet, from a working-class adult-education point of view, much is to be learned for it has been in circumstances of oppression and suffering that expansion and remarkable versatility of community groups in Ulster have given rise to innovative approaches to community adult education.[61]

The riots of Brixton, Toxteth in Liverpool, St Paul's in Bristol, Broadwater Farm and Birmingham also constitute major instances of social conflict in the recent history of Britain. It cannot be assumed that, in their provenance and major focus, each of the instances bear entirely common features or were interpreted in a homogeneous fashion by those immediately and subsequently involved. Where black people were concerned, the particular representations of the conflicts and the reactions and behaviour of whites, especially those in authority, is of crucial importance. Caricature of, and racial hostility to blacks and a refusal to examine deep-seated causes and issues, requires a thorough critique and a wide airing. Assumptions of an easily attainable (or even actually existing) racial and cultural pluralism, or of a smooth transitional path to peaceful co-existence and genuine equality, will appear to many blacks (perhaps especially the dispossessed black youths born in Britain) as not merely naïve but perverse and even dangerous. The language and imagery of an existence within 'Babylon', with its corresponding need for resistance and struggle, cannot be brushed aside as a rhetorical flourish, unrelated to the lived experience of police harassment, racist attacks, economic exploitation and severe alienation from white society. At the same time, of course, we need to know more about, understand and explore ways of transcending the fears, aggression and bitterness inherent in the racism of whites and its embeddedness in social institutions and everyday practices.[62] Regarding attacks upon black people as either only to be expected (or, to put it another way, 'natural') or the action simply of an extremist minority (or, 'pathological') each merely attempt to explain the issue away. This is clearly difficult terrain, but its very difficulty alone is not sufficient grounds for working class adult education to avoid it or rush to early and easy judgement. Reaching out for sophistication and rationality by way of humanity and equity is a challenging act of faith in the teeth of such conflicts and in circumstances of the damage and danger of ethnic minorities in British society.

Not that it is being suggested here that adult education alone can resolve these matters. Its contribution is likely to be modest and far less important than the exercise of power both from within and from beyond the boundaries of our society. What is being said, however, is that in its expansion of information and understanding and its advocacy of skills of reasoning and independently minded study, contentious issues of conflict and change at least stand the chance to be addressed in a manner which might enable working people to depend upon their own critical judgement and autonomy somewhat more and be somewhat less at the mercy at the manipulations and distortions which might otherwise be imposed upon or dangled before them.

Conclusion

If the analysis and suggestions in this brief survey of changes in British society have any merit, they amount to not only a challenge for working-class adult education but also an agenda. In conclusion, it is worth underlining some of the principles and key features which should inform the construction of such an agenda. First, as to *purpose*. That can, in my view, be no better expressed than it was by R.H. Tawney in a stimulating lecture about the WEA delivered in 1953 and reproduced at the head of this essay. To reiterate his main point here, adult education has not merely the purpose of imparting information. Its main function is to foster intellectual vitality to master and use it. So knowledge becomes neither a burden to be born, nor simply a possession to be prized, 'but a stimulus to constructive thought and an inspiration to action'.

Second, the *character* of working-class adult education would be both analytical and practical. It would draw creatively upon experience, including the experiences of oppression and exploitation, but would seek to synthesise such reflection with conceptual and theoretical insights so as to transcend the otherwise obvious threat of a mere reproduction of the language and conditions of subordination. Third, the *focus*, would be a critical and creative analysis of social, political, economic and technological life in contemporary Britain and in her relations with the rest of the world. In this sense, working-class adult education cannot concern itself only with the important question of dramatically widening access for working-class adult students to existing further and higher education provision, (what Bill Schwartz has rather unkindly labelled the 'labourist reflex'[63]). It must also promise, partly through an increase in working-class students in education at all levels, a widening and deepening of the topics for study and debate and a critical expansion of the analytical frameworks and programmes of action open to discussion. In this, of course, the plurality of institutions of working-class adult education, from the residential colleges and WEA on the one hand to the community groups and trade unions on the other, has a key role to play.[64]

Fourth, the *method* of such a working-class adult education would represent a combination of variety with professionalism and democracy. Hence, it would be a process involving active education, in which student involvement in curriculum negotiation and study should be promoted, in which listening and contributing each found an honourable place and in which the role of the tutor exhibited the highest professional standards as well as the expectation also to learn from the exchange of experiences and the critical evaluation of competing explanations and programmes.[65] Certainly, such an education would not make a fetish of any one particular method nor seek to replace the content of adult education merely by the process or medium. Critical adult education cannot be allowed to degenerate into, at worst, the mere sharing of ignorance or, at best, a compilation of undiluted experience.

Fifth, the *intellectual tools* of such an education would be a huge increase in working-class capacity for understanding, analysis, explanation, communication, debate and listening and dissemination. Clarity of expression and the development of lucid writing thus become powerful and legitimate forms of intellectual intervention. Adult education as a craft to prize and to emulate would thus seek to make its contribution to eliminating the instances of anti-intellectualism which so damagingly hobble working-class advance in our society and would help to uncouple education from its suffocating association with class domination and snobbery.

Sixth, the *location* of such an adult education would also be diverse. Of course, a bridgehead should be forged into the established institutions of further and higher education. Most certainly more support must be given (not least by the labour movement) to the residential colleges, to trade union and political education and to the WEA. But, the approach advocated in this essay would also suggest the further stimulation of, and support for, educational initiatives in the plethora of voluntary and community groups, campaigns and pressure organisations so vibrant in our society. It would be part-time as well as full-time, combine home-based and local study with periods of residence. Distance learning, use of radio and television and independent study circles would also be expected to expand and link up with other locales of study.

Seventh, of course, will be the necessary *allocation of resources*. The present Conservative government, triumphant in a third successive general election, can scarcely be expected to accept the analysis begun in this essay. Wedded to a view that the workings of the market and, within that, industry and commerce should provide the major social frame of reference for public and personal decisions alike, the Conservative government will not be inclined to shift resources to working-class education. But this means that a continuous battle needs to be fought precisely to extend and enhance the provision of public resources into this field – just as a continuous battle is being waged for the defence and extension of The National Health Service, for education generally and for other areas essential to social welfare. The potential fund of public support for such a policy should not be underestimated. The need is there and widely felt. More and more resources may have to be found from working class people themselves, and from the institutions of the working class itself. But at the same time a consistent struggle needs to be carried through for a fair share of publicly available resources to provide opportunities for the extension of adult education in its widest sense; so that men and women can study the extent, causes and possible alternatives to unemployment and de-skilling, inequalities of income, wealth and life chances, the subordination of women and their continued economic restriction, and all the other crucial issues now surfacing in contemporary Britain.

Eighth, as to its contribution to *social aims and values*, an adult education seeking to explore the themes and issues outlined above would hope to contribute to the goals outlined in the International Charter of Workers' Education. Meeting in Norway in 1980, the International Federation of Workers' Educational Associations adopted a statement of principles, policies and programmes of action which sought to recognise that education is inseparable from the human struggle for freedom and dignity, equality and justice.

> Education is of great importance to people in their struggle to overcome deprivation, exploitation and oppression. In leading to a better understanding of human problems, and assisting the search for possible solutions, education can be a liberating factor.[66]

Finally, there can be little doubt that an adult education which sets out to provide opportunities to tackle this agenda and more faces a formidable challenge. Moreover, whilst it will require far-reaching, imaginative and democratically committed *political support*, such an adult education must not make the mistake of seeking to substitute itself for politics or political action. On the contrary, even the politics which seeks genuinely to support the kind of educational programme suggested by the analysis outlined in this chapter, must itself be a topic for study, debate and review. The tasks of the adult educator in this view of the challenge now to be faced, are to help pose and sharpen the questions, to foster the self-confidence and technical skills needed to tackle the problems and to encourage the critical creativeness necessary to work out the range of individual and collective initiatives required to meet the challenges to working class life entailed in the changes discussed in this chapter. As Tom Lovett has appropriately put it, this

> does not mean getting students to define all the questions and conferring validity on the proferred answers. It is neither an epistemological relativism nor an abdication of the responsibility to teach. What it is is a meeting of the ways between the practicalities of the working class life and the contribution of disciplined inquiry.[67]

Nor is this an assumption that education is a neutral or value-free process. As has already been made clear, values and commitment have their legitimate (and, in some degree, inescapable) place in working class adult education, but they too must be open to scrutiny and critical evaluation.

To be sure, the chances of adult education embarking upon this exciting journey will be greatly enhanced where political support provides the financial resources, educational climate and social conditions in which a truly independent working-class education can thrive. But the initial drive, continued application and unwillingness to be satisfied by cliches and fashionable formulae are what will give such an adult education its independent character. State funding and the enactment of a supportive legal framework need not, of themselves, imply incorporation and subordination to the perspectives of the state or its agents. On the other hand, resources and greater opportunities cannot alone guarantee the maintenance of a vigorous and independent programme of education and innovation. To that extent, whilst the proposals in the Labour Party's policy statement, *Education After 18: Expansion with Change* are to be welcomed, with their emphasis on additional resources, a universal entitlement to adult education and educational leave and reformed admission and administrative arrangements, there is still a need to work through the implications for thorough-going political support of the issues touched upon in the main body of this chapter. That task has now been started by Labour's most recent policy, *Education Throughout Life*, especially in the recognition of the contribution adult education can make to the stimulation of an informed, critical, skilled and participative democracy.

If that commitment is now to be worked out in detail and developed into a convincing political programme, the challenge to Labour party orthodoxy will be at least as great as it is to working-class adult education. The temptation will clearly be to play down the importance of class analysis, especially in some of its profounder structural aspects, with a view to emphasising the undoubted importance of goodwill and democratic ideals. What is required, of course, is not the rhetorical commitment to democracy that even some of its bitterest enemies sometimes find it expedient to mouth, but the combination of a genuinely democratic practice with determination and purpose. In such a way it might prove possible that 'the idea of education as the means of developing the competences, cultures and powers of individuals and communities should be restored to a central place in a socialist vision of the future.'[68]

Despite the perplexing extent of change in contemporary Britain and the challenge that it represents for working class adult education, the message of this analysis should not be one of despair. Jonathan Rée concludes his elegant account of the role of proletarian philosophy in socialist culture in Britain from 1900 to 1940 on a note of pessimism, or at least regret. The quest of proletarian philosophers to think 'connectedly' having been annihilated, he doubts any search can now succeed,

> for the cultivation of unconfined and unrelenting reflection, for an opportunity to try to sort out your most fundamental values and beliefs, your sense of how your own initiatives and intentions fit in with the larger rhythms of life, human society, and the universe as a whole.[69]

Similarly, Alisdair MacIntyre doubts the possibility of re-creating the idea of an 'educated public', which first found expression in the climate created by eighteenth-century Scottish universities. 'It is a ghost haunting our educational system,' he declares. Three conditions must be met to establish such a public. First, it requires the creation of 'tolerably large body of individuals, educated both into the habit and opportunity of active rational debate'. Second, there must exist shared and rational standards against which argument is to be judged and, third, there must be a 'large degree of shared background beliefs and attitudes, informed by the widespread reading of a common body of texts'.[70] Unless these conditions thrive, then modern education systems cannot simultaneously serve their twin aims of fitting people for their social roles and occupations on the one hand and the promotion of their ability to think independently on the other. The challenge for working-class adult education is how to contribute to the re-establishment of that 'educated public', the better to transcend the current contradiction between education's twin obligations. A working-class adult education worthy of the name cannot afford to neglect either.

It may be that the case argued here for a renewal of working-class education for emancipation will seem too restrained, imprecise and cautious to qualify as a worked out philosophy. I am inclined to agree, but it is offered as a step in the right direction. Whether or not it proves to be decisive and lasting, hesitant or forgettable, will depend upon later elaborations, criticism from others, alternative formulations and, by no means last, the degree of expansion of opportunity to explore different approaches.

Notes

[1] T.L. Hodgkin, 'Adult Education and Social Change', *Adult Education*, Vol. XXIII. No. 1, 1950.

[2] See, for example, Z. Baunman, *Memories of Class* (London 1982).

[3] Ellen Meiksins Wood, *The Retreat from Class: A New 'True' Socialism* (London 1986), and B. Fine, L. Harris, M. Mayo, A. Weir and E. Wilson, *Class Politics: an answer to its critics* (London) n.d.

[4] For an excellent discussion of the working class as agency, see P. Anderson, *Arguments within English Marxism* (London 1980).

[5] See I. Linn and R.H. Fryer, *Change at Work* (Barnsley 1987); A. Callinicos and C. Harman, *The Changing Working Class* (London 1987); B. Roberts, R. Finnegan and D. Gallie (eds), *New Approaches to Economic Life* (Manchester 1985).

[6] K. Forrester and K. Ward, 'Organising the Unemployed? The TUC and Unemployed Workers' Centres', *Industrial Relations Journal*, Vol. 17, No. 1, 1986; see also B. Spencer (ed.), *Adult Education with the Unemployed* (Leeds 1986).

[7] FEU/REPLAN, *Adult Unemployment and the Curriculum: A Manual for Practitioners* (London 1985); FEU, *Opening Doors: creating further education opportunities for the Unemployed* (London 1986); J. Groombridge, *Learning for a Change* (Leicester 1987).

[8] K. Ward, 'The Unemployment Bandwaggon' in Spencer (ed.), op. cit.

[9] J. Field, (1985) 'From Trade Union Education to Work with the Unemployed', *Trade Union Studies Journal*, 11; see also J. Field, 'Residential Adult Education in the Workless State', *Adult Education* Vol. 58, No. 1, 1985.

[10] DE, 'The Labour Force in 1985', D.E. *Gazette*, August 1986.

[11] EOC, *Women and Men in Britain: A Statistical Profile* (London 1986).

[12] B. Jennings, *The Education of Adults in Britain: A Study of Organisation, Finance and Policy* (Hull 1985).

[13] E. Midwinter, *Age is Opportunity: Education and Older People* (London 1982); see also C. Morris, 'Universities of the Third Age', *Adult Education*, Vol. 57, No. 2, 1984.

[14] J. Pillinger and M. Zukas, *New Technology and Adult Education: Targetting Specific Groups* (Leeds 1988); see also C. Cockburn, *Machinery of Dominance: Women, Men and Technical Know-How* (London 1985).

[15] J. Atkinson and D. Gregory, 'A Flexible Future: Britain's Dual Labour Force', *Marxism Today*, April 1986; see also Incomes Data Services, *Flexibility at Work* (London 1986). For a powerful critique of the flexibility thesis, see A. Pollert, 'The Flexible Firm: Fixation or Fact?', *Work, Employment and Society*, Vol. 2, No. 3, 1988.

[16] Northern College/SCPS, *Work for the Future: a new strategy for training and employment* (London 1986); Unemployment Unit, 'Square Pegs in round holes: Employment Training: Quality or Workfare' (London 1988).

[17] S. Dearden, 'EEC Membership and the United Kingdom's Trade in Manufactured Goods', *National Westminster Bank Quarterly Review*, February, 1986. For other easily accessible data on the British economy, see J.D. Hey, *Britain in Context* (Oxford 1979), and S. Fothergill and J. Vincent, *The State of the Nation* (London 1985).

[18] The recently merged trade union Manufacturing, Science, Finance has recently published (1988) a challenging ten-point plan in its booklet *Europe 1992: What about the Workers?* See also J. Trubshaw, 'Teaching Languages to Adults', *Adult Education*, Vol. 57, No. 2, 1984.

[19] A. Gamble, *Britain in Decline* (London 1981) and 1988. For a stimulating collection of articles see especially D. Coates and J. Hillard (eds), *The Economic Decline of Modern Britain: the Debate Between Left and Right* (Brighton 1986). Channel Four television ran a critical history on British history and produced an excellent book to accompany the series L.M. Smith (ed.), *The Making of Britain: Echoes of Greatness* (London 1988).

[20] H. Beynon and T. Austrin, *Global Outpost: The Working Class Experience of Big Business in the North-East of England 1964-1979* (Durham) n.d.

[21] K. Coates and R. Silburn, *Poverty: The Forgotten Englishmen* (Harmondsworth 1970).

[22] H. Rose, 'Nothing Less than Half the Labs!' in J. Finch and M. Rustin (eds), *A Degree of Choice: Higher Education and the Right to Learn* (Harmondsworth 1986).

[23] V. Beechey, 'The Shape of the Workforce to Come', *Marxism Today* August, 1985. For excellent analysis of women's paid employment and the issues concerned, see also V. Beechey, *Unequal Work* (London 1987); A Hunt (ed.), *Women and Paid Work* (London 1988); S. Dex, *The Sexual Division of Work* (Brighton 1985); J. Martin and C. Roberts, *Women and Employment: A Lifetime Perspective* (London 1984).

[24] N. Hadjifotiou, *Women and Harassment at Work* (London 1983); see also TUC, *Sexual Harassment at Work* (London 1983).

[25] See, for example, J. Beale, *Getting it Together: Women as Trade Unionists* (London 1982); R. Elliot, 'Something is Stirring: Women and TUC Education', *Industrial Tutor*, Vol. 5, 1982; J. Brown, E. Kelly, J. Owen and S. Webb, 'Education for Equality: Enabling Women to Take Their Place in the Trade Union Movement', *Industrial Tutor*, Vol. 3, 1980; WEA, *Working Towards Change* (London 1986).

[26] H.V. Carby, 'White woman listen! Black Feminism and the Boundaries of Sisterhood' in Centre for Contemporary Cultural Studies, *The Empire Strikes Back* (London 1982).

[27] See A.B. Atkinson, (1974) *Unequal Shares*, (Harmondsworth 1974) and LRD, *The Widening Gap: Rich and Poor Today* (London 1987).

[28] P. Townsend, *Poverty in Britain* (Harmondsworth 1979).

[29] EOC, op. cit.

[30] M. Hughes *et al.*, *Nurseries Now!* (Harmondsworth 1980).

[31] See, for example, J.L. Thompson, *Learning Liberation: Women's Response to Men's Education* (London 1983); J.L. Thompson, 'Adult Education and the Women's Movement' in T. Lovett (ed.), *Radical Approaches to Adult Education* (London 1988), S. Walker and L. Barton (eds.), *Gender, Class and Education* (Sussex 1983).

[32] See, for example, J. King and M. Stott (eds.), *Is This Your Life? Images of Women in the Media* (London 1977). For a critical and lively review, see J. Williamson, (1981) 'How Does Girl No. 20 Understand ideology', *Screen Education* No. 40, 1981.

[33] See Jane L. Thompson (1983) *op. cit.* and the guides to courses given regularly in the Feminist Library Newsletter, obtainable from Hungerford House, Victoria Embankment, London, WC2.

[34] Open College Federations now exist in many parts of the UK, including Manchester, South Yorkshire, Lancashire and Inner London.

[35] There is a huge, and still growing, literature here. See, as examples only, Worsborough Community Group, *The Heart and Soul of It* (Huddersfield 1986); North Yorkshire Women Against Pit Closures, *Strike 1984-85* (Leeds 1986); Barnsley Women Against Pit Closures, *Women Against Pit Closures* (Barnsley 1985).

[36] Central Statistical Office *Annual Abstract of Statistics* (London 1985). For an excellent review of the issues, see P. Johnson, 'Old Age Creeps Up', *Marxism Today*, January 1989.

[37] R. Hoggart, *The Uses of Literacy* (Harmondsworth 1957); R. Williams, *Culture and Society* (Harmondsworth 1961) and *The Long Revolution* (Harmondsworth 1963).

[38] Hoggart, op. cit., p. 21.

[39] R. Williams, *Key Words* (London 1976).

[40] E.P. Thompson, *The Making of the English Working Class* (Harmondsworth 1963).

[41] S. Frith, *Sound effects: Youth, Leisure and the Politics of Rock and Roll* (London 1983) and *Music for Pleasure: Essays in the Sociology of Pop* (Oxford 1988).

[42] J. Williamson, *Consuming Passions: The Dynamics of Popular Culture* (London 1986).

[43] See, for example, R. Williams, *Television: Technology and Cultural Form* (London 1974); J. Downing, *The Media Machine* (London 1980); A. Goodwin and J. Field, 'Teaching Media Studies to Trade Unionists: Developments at Northern College', *Industrial Tutor*, Vol. 4. No. 2, 1985 and A. Goodwin, 'Striking Contrasts – Media Studies at Northern College', *Screen*, Vol. 26, No. 5, 1985.

[44] TUC, *Behind the Headlines* (London 1980) and *The Other Side of the Story* (London 1983). See also D. McShane, *Using the Media* (London 1979) and P. Behrrel and G. Philo (eds.), *Trade Unions and the Media* (London 1977).

[45] M. Tight, *Part-time Degree-level study in the UK* (Leicester 1982) and E.G. Edwards, *Higher Education for Everyone* (Nottingham 1982).

[46] A. Sivanandan, *Race, Class and the State* (London 1976) and 'RAT and the degradation of the Black Struggle', *Race and Class*, Vol. XXVI.No. 4, 1985.

[47] Notably J. Rex and R. Moore, *Race, Community and Conflict* (London 1967) and J. Rex, *Race, Colonialism and the City* (London 1973).

[48] Centre for Contemporary Cultural Studies, *The Empire Strikes Back: Race and Racism in 70's Britain* (London 1982); A. Sivanandan, 'From Resistance to Rebellion: Asian and Afro-Caribbean Struggles in Britain', *Race and Class*, Vol. 23, 2/3, 1982.

[49] See, for example, Newham Docklands Forum and GLC, *The People's Plan for the Royal Docks* (London 1983).

[50] The CDPs (so-called) produced a large number of reports based upon local projects and analyses. Increasingly, they focussed upon the local impact of deindustrialisation and the collapse of traditional manufacturing industry. See, for example, Birmingham Community Development Project, *Workers on the Scrapheap*, (London 1977); Canning Town CDP *Canning Town to North Woolwich: The Aims of Industry* (London 1977); CDP Inter-project Editorial Collective, *The Costs of Industrial Change* (London 1977).

[51] See, especially, Tom Lovett, *Adult Education, Community Development*

and the Working Class (London 1975) and C. Clarke and A. Kilmurray, *Adult Education and Community Action*, (London 1983).

52 Lovett, op. cit.

53 London Edinburgh Weekend Return Group, *In and Against the State* (London 1980).

54 The most emphatic of the post-industrial and anti-class analysts were Seymour Martin Lipset, see *Political Man* (London 1960) and Daniel Bell, see *The End of Ideology* (London 1960).

55 Keith Jackson, 'The Marginality of Community Development: Implications for Adult Education', *International Review of Community Development* 29/30, 1973.

56 It might, with some justification, be argued that this was not the *intention* of this perspective. But it *was* a clear *implication*.

57 A.M. Wolpe, *Is there Anyone here from Education?* (London 1983).

58 R. Clutterbuck, *Britain in Agony* (Harmondsworth 1980).

59 See, for example, Martin Adeney and John Lloyd, *The Miners' Strike: Loss without Limit* (London 1986).

60 E. Hobsbawm, 'The Forward March of Labour Halted?', *Marxism Today*, September 1978.

61 See, Lovett, op. cit. and Lovett, Clarke and Kilmurray, op. cit.

62 See, for example, R. Bhavnani *et al.*, *A Different Reality: An Account of Black People's Experiences and their Grievances before and after the Handsworth Rebellion of September 1985* (Birmingham 1986); Bethnal Green and Stepney Trades Councils, *Blood on the Streets*, (London 1978); London Strategic Policy Unit, *Racism Awareness Training: a Critique* (London 1987).

63 In Finch and Rustin (eds.), op. cit., 'Cultural Studies: The Case for the Humanities', p. 169.

64 See the excellent review of current provision in Jennings, op. cit.

65 See Lovett, Clarke and Kilmurray op. cit., for an excellent discussion of this, especially p. 144.

66 International Federation of Workers' Educational Associations *International Charter of Workers' Education* (London 1980).

67 Lovett *et al.*, op. cit.

68 M. Rustin, *Comprehensive Education After 18: A Socialist Strategy* (London) n.d.

69 J. Rée, *Proletarian Philosophers* (Oxford 1984).

70 A. MacIntyre, 'The Idea of an Educated Public' in G. Haydon (ed.), *Education and Values: the Richard Peters Lectures* (London 1987).

The Contributors

Margaret Cohen After leaving school at 16, Margaret Cohen worked as a shorthand-typist before taking a degree at Leeds University. She works in adult education in the Manchester area. She undertook research into Independent Working Class Education in the North West whilst studying part-time for a higher degree at Manchester University.

Roger Fieldhouse Now Professor of Adult Education and Director of Continuing Education at the University of Exeter, Roger Fieldhouse worked for six years as WEA Tutor Organiser in North Yorkshire before appointment as lecturer (later senior lecturer and director of extramural studies) in the Adult Education Department at Leeds University. His books include, *The Workers' Educational Association: Aims and Achievements, 1903-1977* (1977), *University Adult Education in England and the U.S.A.* (1985, with R. Taylor and Kathleen Rockhill) and *Adult Education and the Cold War: Liberal Values under Siege, 1946-1951* (1985). He has also recently edited *The Political Education of Servants of the State* (1988). He has written several articles on the history of adult education as also on local history, particularly in the Yorkshire area.

Edmund and Ruth Frow Joint founders of the Working Class Movement Library now officially housed at Salford, Edmund (Manchester District Secretary of the Amalgamated Engineering Union, 1961-1971) and Ruth (retired teacher) have written several books, for instance, *1868 Year of the Unions* (1968, with Michael Katanka), and *To Make that Future – Now!: a History of the Manchester and Salford Trades Council* (1976). They have also written and published many pamphlets on working class history and contributed articles to *History Workshop Journal*, *Marxism Today* and other journals.

Bob Fryer Principal of Northern College at Wentworth Castle, Barnsley, South Yorkshire since 1983, Bob Fryer was previously Senior Lecturer in Sociology at the University of Warwick, where he retained a close connection with adult education. He has written extensively on trade union organisation and employment, his books including *Redundancy and Paternalist Capitalism* (with Roderick Martin), *Organisation and Change in the National Union of Public Employees*, and *Law, State and Society* (joint editor). Among many articles contributed on trade union issues is 'Trade Unionism in Crisis' in Huw Beynon (ed.), *Digging Deeper*.

John McIlroy Staff Tutor in Industrial Relations in the Department of Extra-Mural Studies, University of Manchester, John McIlroy was previously a tutor in the University of Oxford Department of External Studies. He has also worked for the WEA and taught in comprehensive schools in Liverpool and London. He has been involved in trade union education since 1970. He is the author of *Going to Law* (1980), *Getting Organised* (1981), *Industrial Tribunals* (1983), and *Strike!* (1984). He has recently contributed to several books on adult education and other issues, for instance *Opportunities for Adult Education* (M. Tight, ed., 1984), *Policing the Miners' Strike* (B. Fine and R. Millar, eds., 1985), *Political Issues in Britain Today* (B. Jones, ed., 1987) and, with Bruce Spencer, *University Adult Education in Crisis* (1987).

Brian Simon Emeritus Professor of Education, University of Leicester, Brian Simon is an educational historian and author of a three volume series of studies in English education: *The Two Nations and the Educational Structure, 1780-1870* (first published as *Studies in the History of Education, 1780-1870*, (1960)), *Education and the Labour Movement, 1870-1920*, (1965) and *The Politics of Educational Reform, 1920-1940* (1974), a fourth volume is in preparation. He has also written on contemporary educational issues, for instance *Intelligence Testing and the Comprehensive School* (1953), *New Trends in English Education* (1964), and more recently *Does Education Matter?* (1986) and *Bending the Rules, the Baker 'Reform' of Education* (1988).

Index

Aberystwyth, University College of, 54

Adam Smith Institute, 284

Administration, teaching of, 191–2

Adult Education Reconstruction Committee, 51

Adult School Union, 45

Age Concern, 301

Agricultural Workers' Union, 33

Antigonish Movement (Canada), 302

Amalgamated Engineering, Shipbuilding and Draughtsmen's Union (AESD), 40

Amalgamated Engineering Union (AEU), 32–3, 40, 82, 93, 96, 109, 192, 268

Amalgamated Society of Carpenters and Joiners (ASCJ), 71

Amalgamated Society of Engineers (ASE), 71, 73, 82

Amalgamated Society of Locomotive Engineers and Firemen (ASLEF), 96

Amalgamated Society of Railway Servants, 20; see also National Union of Railwaymen

Amalgamated Society of Scientists, Engineers and Technicians (ASSET), 229

Association of Scientific, Technical and Managerial Staffs (ASTMS), 263

Amalgamated Society of Woodworkers (ASW), 92–3

Amalgamated Union of Building Trade Workers (AUBTW), 31–2,

40, 41, 46–7, 82, 89, 90–1, 92–3, 96, 101, 106, 112, 134

Anti-Communism, 170, 188

Apprentices' strike, 132

Army Bureau of Current Affairs (ABCA), 210

Army School of Education, 210

Ashby Committee, 209

Ashton-in-Makerfield, 75

Ashton-under-Lyne, 78

Association of Education Committees (AEC), 155

Bacup, 93

Birkenhead, 75, 82, 95

Birmingham, 87, 126; riots, 309

Black study and community centres, 299

Black workers, 260, 263, 268; (women) 288, 295, 298–9, 309–10

Board of Education, 20, 22, 27, 38–9, 40, 42, 44, 46, 51, 56, 57, 68, 153, 156–7, 158ff.; see also Department of Education and Science and Ministry of Education

Bolton, 81; (WEA branch) 157

Bradford, 28, 87

Bristol, 25

British Employers' Federation, 225, 230; see also Confederation of British Industry

British Institute of Adult Education, 163

British Motor Corporation (BMC), 252–3

BISATKA, 255–6

British Movement, 298

322

Name Index